PROFITABLE MENU PLANNING

Second Edition

John A. Drysdale

PRENTICE HALL
Upper Saddle River, New Jersey 07458

Library of Congress Cataloging-in-Publication Data

Drysdale, John A.
   Profitable menu planning / John A. Drysdale. — 2nd ed.
     p.   cm.
   Includes index.
   ISBN 0–13–646944-2
   1. Menus.   I. Title.
TX911.3.M45D79   1998
642'.5—dc21   97-26733
                                    CIP

Acquisition Editor: Neil Marquardt
Director of Production and Manufacturing: Bruce Johnson
Managing Editor: Mary Carnis
Marketing Manager: Frank Mortimer, Jr.
Editorial/production supervision and
   interior design: Inkwell Publishing Services
Cover design: Marianne Frasco
Manufacturing Buyer: Edward O'Dougherty

© 1998, 1994 by Prentice Hall, Inc
Simon & Schuster / A Viacom Company
Upper Saddle River, New Jersey 07458

Printed in the United States of America
10 9 8 7 6

ISBN 0-13-646944-2

Prentice-Hall International (UK) Limited, *London*
Prentice-Hall of Australia Pty. Limited, *Sydney*
Prentice-Hall Canada Inc., *Toronto*
Prentice-Hall Hispanoamericana, S.A., *Mexico*
Prentice-Hall of India Private Limited, *New Delhi*
Prentice-Hall of Japan, Inc., *Tokyo*
Simon & Schuster Asia Pte. Ltd., *Singapore*
Editora Prentice-Hall do Brasil, Ltda., *Rio de Janeiro*

In memory of my father,
F. Clark Drysdale

Contents

5
Menu Analysis *97*

6
Nutrition *113*

7
Menu Content   *141*

8
Truth in Menu   *171*

9
Menu Layout and Printing   *181*

10
Quick Service Menus   *219*

13
Banquet/Show Menus *287*

14
Buffets *323*

15
Cafeteria and Cycle Menus *337*

16
The Menu as a Management Tool   *351*

Preface

The old adage that everything starts with the menu is as true today as it was a hundred years ago. In today's complex makeup of food service management, the menu is involved in nearly every facet of the operation. Add to this the diversity of restaurants from quick service to fine dining as well as the nonprofit food service segment and the subject of menu planning suddenly becomes quite intricate. It is for this reason that *Profitable Menu Planning* was written. While there are some excellent textbooks on the market dealing with the various aspects of menus, few, if any, cover all the points necessary for a complete dialogue on the subject.

This second edition has some major changes, both in content and in layout of the chapters. It is divided into four areas beginning with planning the menu. In the first section, market segmentation, demographics, and food preferences of the customer are discussed, along with updated material and illustrations. The capabilities of the staff and equipment to produce the menu are also included in this section. The second part deals with menu profitability. Creating cost cards, menu selling price (markups), and menu analysis are covered to assure a profitable operation. The software included with the book plays an integral part of this section. The third section deals with writing the menu and covers nutrition, which is a new chapter as well as menu content, descriptive terminology, and "truth in menus," concluding with menu layout and printing. The fourth section delves into the many types of menus from quick service to fine dining and everything in between. The software contains questions along with the correct answers for every chapter in the text.

Proper menu planning and writing is vital in today's society with consumer advocate groups demanding fresh and healthful listings, corporate boardrooms demanding more sales and profits, and government bureaucracy demanding accurate menu terminology. This text attempts to help the student, manager, or owner answer these demands with clear, easy-to-read, solutions to the problems.

ACKNOWLEDGMENTS

While the author's name appears on the cover, producing a textbook is definitely a team effort. Walt Klarner, an English Instructor at Johnson County Community College, as well as an author and editor in his own right, was the first to convince me that I could write a book, and he encouraged and advised me throughout the entire process. Without his help, this project never would have happened.

I am also indebted to the following people who took time out from their busy schedules to review and critique the manuscript page by page and make valuable comments that vastly improved the quality of the book.

Jennifer Aldrich, Johnson & Wales University

Tom Connolly, Norwalk Community College

James Bardi, Penn State University—Berks Campus

Brother Herman Zaccarelli, California Culinary Academy

Michael Piccinino, Shasta College

Maureen P. Cooper, Alfred State College

Terence McDonough, Erie Community College

Jared Mauri, The State University of New York at Buffalo

William Jacobi, Grand Rapids Community College

Paul Mach, Pennsylvania College of Technology

Steven E. Carlomusto, Johnson and Wales University

To my colleagues and students at Johnson County Community College, a special thank you. First, the head of the department Jerry Vincent, CEC, AAC for his patience for the many times I requested "Can I give you the report later—I've got a deadline." To Judy Boley, who dropped everything to get letters and permission slips out for illustrations that were needed yesterday and also tested the software. To Patrick Sweeney, CEC, AAC for his review and help with the manuscript. To Lindy Robinson, who not only reviewed the rough draft, but who taught several classes from it and gave me very valuable, thought-provoking feedback. And finally to the students who endured taking their menu planning class with an incomplete text and who put up with my office door being closed because I was "on a roll" writing.

To the industry professionals who gave of their time to read and critique various chapters, I thank you. To those who supplied me with menus, illustrations, and charts and who guided my requests through their legal departments, I am indebted to you. To those who tried and couldn't get it done, I thank you also for trying.

To the people at Prentice Hall who advised me and helped make sense of all of the in's and out's of publishing, particularly Fred Dahl and Rose Mary Florio. To Robin Baliszewski, Director of

Marketing, who encouraged, counseled, and guided, but never pushed. And last, but not least, to Neil Marquardt, who pushed the whole project through the publication process.

And finally to my family, Judy, Jeanne, Jackie, and my mother who put up with my stress attacks when things were not going right or deadlines were creeping near. Your patience and understanding were very much appreciated.

John A. Drysdale
Overland, Kansas

About the Software

The program accompanying the *Profitable Menu Planning* textbook is based on the chapters covering Costs, Pricing, and Menu Analysis. In addition, there is a module that will quiz you on 10 questions from each chapter. It is capable of operating from the diskette without being installed on the computer's hard drive.

SYSTEM REQUIREMENTS

The Profitable Menu Planning program requires an IBM PC compatible system.

The program may be used with computers that have Excel 5.0 for Windows or Excel 7.0 for Windows 95. This program does not operate with Excel 97 at this time. To begin using this program, make a backup copy of the diskette and use it with a computer that has a printer configured to work with Excel software.

Upon inspecting the contents of the diskette, you will notice that there are several Excel spreadsheets on them. You must start your work with the "Menuplan.xls" spreadsheet.

INSTALLATION

The program may be used directly from the diskette or copied to your computer's hard drive using standard diskette copying techniques.

STARTING THE PROGRAM

Double click on the menuplan.xls file in Windows File Manager or Windows 95 Explorer. If the machine is misconfigured, double-clicking on menuplan.xls might not work properly. In that case:

Start Excel.

Select Open from the File menu.

Change the drive to A: if you are using the diskette.

Double-click on Menuplan.xls when it appears in the file list.

COST CARD

Enter the Header Information

1. Click on the Enter Header Toolbar button.
2. Click on each of the text boxes and enter the information. The Cost Card will reflect your responses.

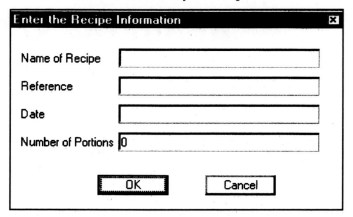

For each ingredient that will be added:

1. Double-click on the ingredient's light blue cells and respond to the following dialog boxes:

Ingredient Quantity Column (1st Column)

1. Double-Click on the Quantity column.
2. Click on the text box and type the amount into the edit box or click on the arrows to select the quantity.

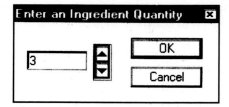

Ingredient Unit Column (2nd Column)

1. Double-Click on the Ingredient Unit column to select the unit of measure.
2. Click on a unit of measure, then click on OK.

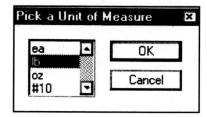

Ingredient Name (3rd Column)

1. Double-Click on the Ingredient column.
2. Click on a Food Category, then click OK.

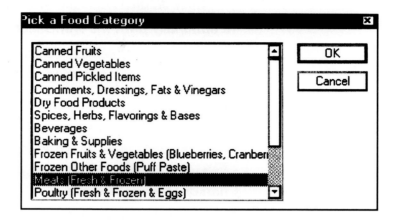

3. Click on an ingredient, then click OK.

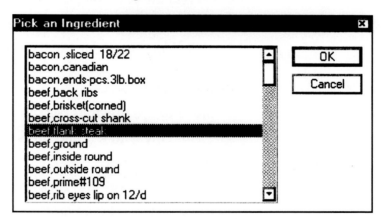

When you pick items using this method, the nonblue cells will be calculated automatically. This includes the invoice, recipe, and extension information. Automatic conversions are done between "oz" and "lb" unit entries. Otherwise, you must perform the "recipe unit to invoice unit" conversion prior to entering the unit in the Recipe Unit column. Invoice units for items on file include "lb," "oz," "ea," and "#10."

For ingredients not presented

Enter the recipe ingredient and invoice columns one at a time. After entering these columns, the recipe cost, recipe unit, and extension columns will be calculated automatically.

1. Click on the cell.
2. Type the information.
3. Press the Enter key.

If you enter the same unit for the recipe and the invoice columns, the extension will be automatically calculated.

To return to the main menu

1. Click on the File menu, then click on Exit.

To optionally print the worksheet

1. Click on the File menu, then click on Print Preview.
2. Click on the Print button near the top of the screen.

PRICING THE MENU

Select the worksheet to work with

1. Click on the File Menu. Then click on Income Statement and Chart or Markup Methods.

Enter the information in the blue cells

1. Type the information without dollar signs or commas.
2. Press the Enter or Tab key to enter the next cell.

To return to the main menu

1. Click on the File menu, then click on Exit.

Additional Information

To move to the previous cell

1. Hold the Shift key and press the Enter or Tab key.

To move to any cell

1. Point to the cell and click on the left mouse button.

To optionally print the worksheet

1. Click on the File menu. Then click on Print Preview.
2. Click on the Print button near the top of the screen.

MENU ANALYSIS

Select the worksheet to work with

1. Click on the File Menu. Then click on Stars, Plow Horses, Puzzles, and Dogs or Scoring.

Create as many item rows as you need

1. Immediately add as many rows as you need by continuously clicking on the Add Item toolbar button.

2. Enter the information in the blue cells.
3. Type the information without dollar signs or commas.
4. Press the Enter or Tab key to enter the next cell.

To return to the main menu

1. Click on the File menu, then click on Exit.

Additional Information

To move the previous cell

Hold the Shift key and press the Enter or Tab key.

To move to any cell

Point to the cell and click on the left mouse button.

To delete a row item

Click on any row item except the first or last row item, then click on the Delete Item toolbar button.

To print the worksheet

1. Click on the File menu, then click on Print Preview.
2. Click on the Print button near the top of the screen.

QUESTIONS

Select the chapter

1. Click on the Chapter select toolbar button.
2. Click on the Chapter you wish to work with.
3. Click on OK.

Answer the questions

1. Double click on the answer choice (a, b, c, or d) that best answers the question.
2. You will be prompted as to the correctness of your response beneath the answer choices.
3. Click on the Next Question toolbar button to proceed to the next question.

To return to the main menu

1. Click on the File menu. Then click on Exit

Additional Information

To display the previous question

1.   Click on the previous question toolbar button.

To print the question

1.   Click on the File menu, then click on Print Preview.
2.   Click on the Print button near the top of the screen.

CHAPTER ONE

Know Your Customer

OBJECTIVES By the completion of this chapter, the reader should be able to:

- Explain the difference between demographic surveys and feasibility studies.
- Describe how competition can influence a restaurant's menu listings.
- Differentiate between the popularity of certain foods among age groups, ethnic origins, education, occupation, and income.
- Explain the difference between fads and trends and how to use them to an advantage.

IMPORTANT TERMS

Demographics	Trends
Fads	Market saturation
Competition	Disposable income
Feasibility studies	

INTRODUCTION

One of the most important aspects of menu planning is determining and defining the customer. The location of a restaurant, more than anything else, determines who will patronize it. For a restaurant to be successful, its menu must cater to this person. Statistics show that, for the most part, people stay close to their homes or places of work when dining out. *Close* is defined as within a three-mile radius. Therefore, it is important for the restaurant to know who resides or works within this radius. In other words, a restaurant is successful, not simply because of its location per se, but rather because its menu caters to the customer in that particular location. Prior to writing a menu, the location, the customers and their desires, and the relationship between these factors must be explored.

Statler, the hotel magnate, once stated that three criteria were necessary for success: location, location, and location. Of course Mr. Statler was referring to the hotel business. In the case of the restaurant business, there are relatively few areas in this vast country where a restaurant could not be successful *if* (and that's a big if) the menu caters to the restaurant's customers.

All too often, people confuse good locations with busy intersections, shopping malls, or heavily populated residential neighborhoods. Locations with traffic obviously are important to certain types of restaurants such as fast food operations. But the location rule has exceptions. People who celebrate a special occasion with dinner out will travel farther than the aforementioned three miles. Others may take a day trip, with a little country inn located in the middle of nowhere as a destination.

Consider this case in point. While vacationing in the backwoods of northern Minnesota's Voyager Country, a relative suggested having lunch at the Kettle Falls Hotel. We rode in a boat for 35 miles, viewing beautiful scenery along the way, docked the boat, hiked two miles, and finally arrived at the hotel. Imagine my surprise when we had to wait for a table because the place was packed! There were no roads. The only access to this hotel was by boat and by hiking the last two miles. Why was this place successful? Three reasons: One, it has been in business since the 1800s (word gets around after a while); two, the menu catered to the clientele with fresh walleye as the feature; and three, the competition was very limited (nonexistent). No frills or surprises. The menu was right, the preparation was right, and the service was right. The point is that, while location is important to some facets of the restaurant industry, it is by no means the crucial factor. Indeed, the menu must cater to the customer no matter what the location.

Seth Hays, who was Kit Carson's cousin and Daniel Boone's great grandson, came to Council Grove in 1848. He was sent by the U.S. Government as the official agent to the Kaw Indians.

In 1857 Hays built this building straight on the Santa Fe Trail - the street now askew with the Hays House. On this site he traded and served food.

In the mid to late 1800's this building was also the site of many activities to serve the needs of the local citizens. Mail was distributed here; the government rented space and held court here; bottles were covered Saturday nights and church held here Sundays; the first local newspaper was printed here on the press Hays brought to Council Grove.

Theatricals were held on the second floor in early years when the roof was peaked. Then, probably after a roof fire, the east and west walls were raised to make the roof flat and ten hotel rooms were constructed on the second floor. General Custer and Jesse James probably stayed here.

In addition to the Hays House, Council Grove is home to many other National Registered Historic Landmarks and is eager to show them. Please ask us for further information to guide you to the many points of historical significance preserved from the days of our pioneers!

We now welcome you to our table as the Hays House continues the tradition of the trail where no person is a stranger. Our aim is to share good food, then send you on your way refilled and refreshed.

Rick and Alisa Paul

FIGURE 1.1. This restaurant is located 100 miles from the nearest metropolitan area, yet draws much of its business from that area. (*Menu courtesy of the Hays House, Council Grove, Kansas*)

Hays House Specialties

Beulah's Ham

We bake thick slices from bone-in hams in fruit juices, wine & spices for a delightful flavor. $9.95

Skillet Fried Chicken

Fresh chicken dipped in egg & milk, then in our crunchy mix and fried in cast iron skillets. $9.25
You may request all white meat. $9.95
(Please allow 30 minutes to prepare)

Brisket

Beef marinated in seven seasonings, then baked slowly until very tender & flavorful. $9.50

Chicken Fried Steak

Fresh beef we bread to order & grill in real chicken fat until golden brown. $8.50

Chicken Livers and/or Gizzards

Freshly dipped by hand & sauteed in chicken fat. $7.95

Pork Chops

Two center cut chops charbroiled to enhance their naturally good flavor. $10.95

ALL DINNERS INCLUDE ...
Our garden fresh salad bar featuring several house dressings.
Choice of the fresh vegetable of the evening, homemade curly fries,
fresh hash browns, baked potato or steak fries.
Our special recipe Hays House bread, hot from the oven, with real butter.

For the Lighter Appetite

Lite Beef Supper

Marinated steak pieces beside an interesting salad of crisp lettuce,
orange segments, sliced ripe olive and topped with our tarragon dressing.
Served with fresh vegetable of the evening and a homemade muffin. $8.25

Charbroiled Chicken Breast

A boneless, skinless breast served with a garden salad, fresh vegetable
and a homemade muffin. $7.95
You may add Blackened Seasoning for $.50 or Herb Butter for $1.00.

Vegetarian Platter

Three fresh vegetables (seasonal) served with a choice of potato or rice. $7.95
If you would also like a salad bar. $9.95

Small Servings of some favorites ...

SS Fried Chicken Thigh $5.50   SS Pork Chop $6.75   SS Beulah's Ham $6.25
SS Fried Chicken Breast $6.50   SS Brisket $5.95   SS Hot Spiced Shrimp $8.95

Small Servings include homemade bread and a choice of two of the following...
garden salad (salad bar is $2 extra), fresh vegetable of the evening or choice of potato.

FIGURE 1.1.   *(Continued)*

Beef Bill of Fare

Hays House
Eleven ounces of well marbled rib-eye.
Fine enough to carry our name. $13.95

Little Steak
A smaller cut of 6 ounces from
the same choice rib-eye. $9.95

KC Strip
A thick 13 ounce steak
flavorful and hearty. $14.50

Filet
Six ounces of the leanest tenderloin
wrapped in bluestem bacon. $13.25

You may add Blackened Seasoning for $.50 or add Garlic Cream Sauce for $2.00.

Friday & Saturday Nights Only
Hays House Prime Rib
We roast the finest prime ribs and cut them for your enjoyment.
Regular Cut (11 oz.) $13.95   Extra Thick Cut (16 oz.) $18.25

Fish & Seafood

Orange Roughy
A premium white filet. Your server will tell you how it is prepared this evening.
Price varies with each preparation.

Charbroiled Fish
A thick and tender 8 oz. fish steak.   Salmon $11.25   Halibut $12.25
You may add Blackened Seasoning for $.50 or Herb Butter for $1.00

Catfish
We fry a meaty whole fish, so big it takes 30 minutes. $9.75

Hot Spiced Shrimp
A crock of steaming jumbos boiled
and ready to peel. $13.95

Scallops
Large morsels in a light and
crispy coating. $12.50

Breaded Shrimp
Big and delicious
in a crispy coating. $12.50

Shrimp stuffed with Crab
Large shrimp, stuffed
and lightly breaded. $12.95

Fresh vegetables are a hallmark of our dinners.

A 15% gratuity will be added to parties of 10 or more.

FIGURE 1.1. (*Continued*)

~•~ Hays House Pies ~•~

Cranberry-Strawberry Pie
Our famous sweet-tart creation piled high into a graham cracker crust. $3.25

Godiva Chocolate Pie
Incredibly rich chocolate flavor and silky texture make this pie irresistable. $3.25

Grasshopper Pie
A rich, minty filling is heaped into a chocolate crumb crust. $3.25

Kahlua Pie
Creamy, smooth and coffee flavored; set into a chocolate cookie crust. $3.25

~•~•~•~

Homemade Ice Cream

When was the last time you tasted real homemade ice cream ?
We use fresh cream and whip it into an array of delightful flavors.
Please ask about today's selection because our flavors change daily. $2.25

~•~•~•~

Also Available...

Fresh Fruit Platter small $3.25 medium $4.50

Ice Cream vanilla $1.50 **Sherbert** lime or raspberry $1.50

Beverages

Coffee rich & flavorful $.85 **Tea** fresh brewed, hot or iced $.85

Hand Squeezed Lemonade honest to goodness ! $1.75

Apple Cider steaming hot or in a frosty cold mug $1.25

Milk white or chocolate $1.25 **Soft Drinks** includes one refill $1.25

FIGURE 1.1. *(Continued)*

DEMOGRAPHICS

The study of location and the potential customer is known as *demographics*. More specifically, according to *Webster's New Collegiate Dictionary, demographics* is "the statistical study of populations with reference to size, density, distribution, and vital statistics and the ability (of the market) to expand or decline."

In order to use demographics properly in menu planning, two factors must be evaluated.

1. The demographic study itself. In other words, who exactly is the customer in our market?
2. The matching of these customers, along with their needs and preferences, to the proper menu.

First, look at the demographic study itself. How does it develop? There are basically three sources for this information:

1. Feasibility studies
2. Demographic surveys
3. Personal knowledge

FEASIBILITY STUDIES

A feasibility study is a creative, objective, and rational process whereby marketing and financial data are collected and analyzed. It is an in-depth study that attempts to predict with reasonable accuracy whether or not a potential business will succeed or fail. Feasibility studies are quite large, sometimes running several hundred pages in length. Needless to say, they are very complete documents which explore every variable that would indicate whether or not a business has the potential to make a profit. Normally these studies are performed by accounting firms or consultants who are members of the Foodservice Consultants Society International (FCSI). You could perform this task yourself, but it is very time consuming and the professionals have the knowledge of where to obtain the data. Make sure that the person or firm conducting the study has a good track record and is reliable. Two parts of the feasibility study that are of particular importance to the menu planner are the sections dealing with demographics and competition.

DEMOGRAPHIC SURVEYS

For those restaurants or food service firms that do not need a complete feasibility study, demographic surveys are available from a number of companies for a reasonable fee. The larger firms have the demographics for the entire United States on computers. These studies can be broken down to any size quadrant for any area that the customer desires. They list the general population by age group, median age, ethnic origins, household type, marital status, occupation, education, housing, income, number of vehicles, and other related data. Specialized data can also be obtained which detail consumer restaurant expenditures for the area and can further refine this statistic by giving a breakdown by category such as fast food, coffee shop, fine dining, etc.

Those not wishing to purchase a demographic study could opt to do the project themselves. While it would be somewhat time consuming to do this, a demographic survey is far less extensive and, therefore, takes less time to complete than a feasibility study. Data are available from the Census Bureau, the local Chamber of Commerce, City Hall, or other governmental and private sources.

PERSONAL KNOWLEDGE

The third source for demographic information is a person's own knowledge, even a feeling, for an area. While this approach is certainly unscientific, it can be valid if it is not used haphazardly. Too often persons going into the restaurant business pick what they feel is an excellent location, only to open the business and go broke. Odds are, they failed to sell what their customers wanted. They didn't have the right menu listings or selling prices to fit their clientele. Of course, other factors could have contributed to their loss such as lack of working capital, unknowledgeable management, poor service, poor quality, or a dirty operation. The restaurant business comprises many details, each one affecting overall performance. But it all starts with the menu. List the wrong items at the wrong price and the project is done before it starts.

On the other hand, a personal feel for the market is an important tool if used properly. Demographic studies look at an area with cold, hard facts. Knowledge of situations behind these facts is quite important. For example, if an area demographic study indicated that the average income was in the upper middle range and that a large share of the market owned their own homes, this would indicate at the outset a good restaurant location. However, if the majority of people in the target area had their homes heavily mortgaged, their disposable income would be low and their propensity to dine out would be less.

SOCIO-ECONOMIC PROFILE: 1990
Cleveland, OH: Brookpark Rd & Pearl Rd
3 Mile Ring

Claritas Data Services
4/28/97

POPULATION	146,346	
POPULATION IN......		%
Households	145,379	99.3%
Group Quarters	966	0.7%
College	0	0.0%
Institutions	895	0.6%
Other	71	0.0%
OCCUPATION	66,643	%
Prof/Tech	9,630	14.5%
Mgr/Prop	6,898	10.4%
Clerical	13,744	20.6%
Sales	7,495	11.2%
White Collar	37,767	56.7%
Crafts	8,501	12.8%
Operatives	8,507	12.8%
Service	8,675	13.0%
Laborer	2,885	4.3%
Farm Worker	309	0.5%
Blue Collar	28,876	43.3%

LABOR FORCE			UNEMPL	PARTIC
Male	38,475	57.7%	6.6%	70.4%
Female	32,490	48.8%	5.1%	51.5%
In Armed Forces		0.2%		

WORKERS PER FAMILY		Avg. Income
0	18.1%	$20,568
1	28.8%	$30,431
2	40.8%	$43,113
3	12.3%	$57,895

SCHOOL ENROLLMENT		%Private
Nursery school	2,308	51.1%
Elementary/High	19,850	33.3%
College/Univ	8,188	21.3%

HOUSING UNITS	63,745	
Owner Occupied		65.0%
Renter Occupied		30.9%
Vacant Year Round		3.9%
Seasonally Vacant		0.1%

DWELLINGS	**Period of Construction**		**Year Moved In**	
	Owner	Renter	Owner	Renter
1985-90	0.7%	0.9%	16.4%	22.6%
1980-84	0.4%	0.7%	6.9%	4.5%
1970-79	3.0%	6.0%	15.0%	3.6%
1960-69	9.1%	6.1%	13.2%	1.0%
<--1959	54.6%	18.4%	16.2%	0.6%

INCOME	**HOUSEHOLD INCOME**		**FAMILY INCOME**	
Total	61,175	%	39,942	%
Under $5,000	3,068	5.0%	1,333	3.3%
$5,000-$9,999	6,034	9.9%	1,425	3.6%
$10,000-$14,999	6,073	9.9%	2,823	7.1%
$15,000-$19,999	6,242	10.2%	3,301	8.3%
$20,000-$24,999	6,007	9.8%	3,641	9.1%
$25,000-$29,999	5,627	9.2%	3,932	9.8%
$30,000-$34,999	6,042	9.9%	4,581	11.5%
$35,000-$39,999	4,853	7.9%	3,860	9.7%
$40,000-$49,999	7,342	12.0%	6,281	15.7%
$50,000-$74,999	7,602	12.4%	6,735	16.9%
$75,000-$99,999	1,629	2.7%	1,469	3.7%
$100,000-$124,999	364	0.6%	331	0.8%
$125,000-$149,999	137	0.2%	123	0.3%
Over $150,000	111	0.2%	100	0.3%
Median Income	$27,622		$33,672	
Average Income	$31,043		$37,209	

Vehicles Per Household		%
0	7,840	12.8%
1	24,837	40.6%
2	21,120	34.5%
3	7,366	12.0%

Non-English Speaking Households	
Spanish	0.43%
Asian/PI	0.11%
Other	3.10%

UNITS/STRUCTURE		%
1	43,958	69.0%
2	6,506	10.2%
3-4	1,114	1.7%
5+	11,005	17.3%

SCHOOL YEARS COMPLETED	
Pop Age 25+	101,652
Less than 9th	8.3%
Some high school	20.4%
High School Dipl.	38.0%
College 1-3 years	22.1%
Bachelor's degree	8.2%
Grad/Prof Degree	2.9%

ANCESTRY	139,553
(Number Reporting)	
	%
Arab	1.1%
Austria/Swiss	0.6%
Belgian/Dutch	0.6%
Canadian	0.3%
Central European	20.1%
English	4.5%
French	1.0%
German	24.2%
Greek	1.0%
Irish	9.8%
Italian	9.1%
Polish	13.0%
Portuguese	0.0%
Russian	1.0%
Scandinavian	0.7%
Scottish	1.6%
Sub-Saharan Afric	0.0%
United States	2.8%
West Indian	0.0%
FOREIGN BORN	6.9%

Source: 1990 Census, STF3

Claritas Data Services / 4676 Admiralty Way Ste 624 / Marina del Rey, CA 90292 / (800) 633-9568

(CS)
800222

FIGURE 1.2. An example of a demographic study for a three-mile radius of the intersection of Pearl and Brookpark in Cleveland, Ohio. (*Courtesy of Claritas Data Services, Marina Del Rey, California*)

INCOME: 1990-1996-2001
Cleveland, OH: Brookpark Rd & Pearl Rd
3 Mile Ring

Claritas Data Services
04/28/97

	1990 Census	%	1996 Estimate	%	2001 Projection	%
POPULATION	146,346		144,376		141,343	
In Group Quarters	966		973		1,017	
PER CAPITA INCOME	$12,977		$14,541		$16,872	
Aggregate Income ($Mil)	1,899.1		2,099.4		2,384.7	
HOUSEHOLDS	61,175	%	62,159	%	61,238	%
By Income						
Less than $ 5,000	3,068	5.0%	3,154	5.1%	2,400	3.9%
$ 5,000 - $ 9,999	6,034	9.9%	5,422	8.7%	3,865	6.3%
$ 10,000 - $ 14,999	6,073	9.9%	5,626	9.1%	5,059	8.3%
$ 15,000 - $ 19,999	6,242	10.2%	5,122	8.2%	4,627	7.6%
$ 20,000 - $ 24,999	6,007	9.8%	5,674	9.1%	4,156	6.8%
$ 25,000 - $ 29,999	5,627	9.2%	4,526	7.3%	4,425	7.2%
$ 30,000 - $ 34,999	6,042	9.9%	5,530	8.9%	4,161	6.8%
$ 35,000 - $ 39,999	4,853	7.9%	5,372	8.6%	4,079	6.7%
$ 40,000 - $ 49,999	7,342	12.0%	6,738	10.8%	8,701	14.2%
$ 50,000 - $ 59,999	4,529	7.4%	5,864	9.4%	5,471	8.9%
$ 60,000 - $ 74,999	3,074	5.0%	4,490	7.2%	6,607	10.8%
$ 75,000 - $ 99,999	1,629	2.7%	2,807	4.5%	4,247	6.9%
$100,000 - $ 124,999	364	0.6%	1,123	1.8%	2,014	3.3%
$125,000 - $ 149,000	137	0.2%	300	0.5%	852	1.4%
$150,000 +	111	0.2%	410	0.7%	575	0.9%
Median Household Income	$27,622		$31,405		$37,362	
Average Household Income	$31,043		$33,659		$38,811	
FAMILIES	39,942	%	37,591	%	34,750	%
By Income						
Less than $ 5,000	1,333	3.3%	1,170	3.1%	818	2.4%
$ 5,000 - $ 9,999	1,425	3.6%	1,563	4.2%	1,009	2.9%
$ 10,000 - $ 14,999	2,823	7.1%	1,853	4.9%	1,731	5.0%
$ 15,000 - $ 19,999	3,301	8.3%	2,477	6.6%	1,529	4.4%
$ 20,000 - $ 24,999	3,641	9.1%	2,910	7.7%	1,865	5.4%
$ 25,000 - $ 29,999	3,932	9.8%	2,614	7.0%	2,109	6.1%
$ 30,000 - $ 34,999	4,581	11.5%	3,395	9.0%	2,300	6.6%
$ 35,000 - $ 39,999	3,860	9.7%	3,792	10.1%	2,294	6.6%
$ 40,000 - $ 49,999	6,281	15.7%	5,163	13.7%	5,456	15.7%
$ 50,000 - $ 59,999	3,930	9.8%	4,694	12.5%	4,081	11.7%
$ 60,000 - $ 74,999	2,804	7.0%	3,875	10.3%	5,021	14.4%
$ 75,000 - $ 99,999	1,469	3.7%	2,450	6.5%	3,613	10.4%
$100,000 - $ 124,999	331	0.8%	981	2.6%	1,691	4.9%
$125,000 - $ 149,000	123	0.3%	275	0.7%	749	2.2%
$150,000 +	100	0.3%	380	1.0%	483	1.4%
Median Family Income	$33,672		$38,711		$46,817	
Average Family Income	$37,209		$41,676		$49,288	

Source: 1990 Census, March 15, 1996 UDS Estimates.   (INP)
Claritas Data Services / 4676 Admiralty Way Ste 624 / Marina del Rey, CA 90292 / (800) 633-9568   800222

FIGURE 1.2. *(Continued)*

DEMOGRAPHIC TRENDS: 1990-1996-2001
Cleveland, OH: Brookpark Rd & Pearl Rd
3 Mile Ring

Claritas Data Services
4/28/97

	1990 Census		1996 Estimate		2001 Projected	
POPULATION	146,346		144,376		141,343	
In Group Quarters	966		973		1,017	
HOUSEHOLDS	61,175	%	62,159	%	61,238	%
1 Person	18,879	30.9%	20,453	32.9%	21,068	34.4%
2 Person	20,000	32.7%	20,027	32.2%	19,522	31.9%
3-4 Person	17,416	28.5%	17,265	27.8%	16,689	27.3%
5+ Person	4,880	8.0%	4,414	7.1%	3,959	6.5%
Average Hhld Size	2.38		2.31		2.29	
FAMILIES	39,942		37,591		34,750	
RACE						
White	139,573	95.4%	131,157	90.8%	124,048	87.8%
Black	3,111	2.1%	9,069	6.3%	12,780	9.0%
Asian/Pacific Islander	1,554	1.1%	2,073	1.4%	2,467	1.7%
American Indian	270	0.2%	290	0.2%	309	0.2%
Other	1,838	1.3%	1,788	1.2%	1,740	1.2%
HISPANIC ORIGIN	4,212	2.9%	6,081	4.2%	7,694	5.4%
AGE		%		%		%
0 - 5	12,079	8.3%	10,092	7.0%	9,306	6.6%
6 - 13	13,547	9.3%	15,928	11.0%	15,822	11.2%
14 - 17	6,101	4.2%	6,551	4.5%	6,813	4.8%
18 - 20	4,952	3.4%	4,262	3.0%	4,383	3.1%
21 - 24	8,014	5.5%	6,842	4.7%	6,906	4.9%
25 - 34	27,124	18.5%	23,332	16.2%	19,655	13.9%
35 - 44	19,079	13.0%	20,624	14.3%	20,128	14.2%
45 - 54	13,163	9.0%	15,867	11.0%	18,134	12.8%
55 - 64	14,431	9.9%	13,499	9.4%	14,530	10.3%
65 - 74	16,953	11.6%	15,882	11.0%	13,961	9.9%
75 - 84	8,893	6.1%	9,191	6.4%	9,120	6.5%
85 +	2,011	1.4%	2,307	1.6%	2,587	1.8%
Median Age	35.6		37.3		38.8	
MALES	69,279	%	68,328	%	66,737	%
0 - 20	18,730	27.0%	18,785	27.5%	18,503	27.7%
21 - 44	27,167	39.2%	25,278	37.0%	22,960	34.4%
45 - 64	12,561	18.1%	13,439	19.7%	14,983	22.5%
65 - 84	10,284	14.8%	10,204	14.9%	9,561	14.3%
85 +	537	0.8%	622	0.9%	730	1.1%
FEMALES	77,067	%	76,048	%	74,605	%
0 - 20	17,949	23.3%	18,048	23.7%	17,820	23.9%
21 - 44	27,050	35.1%	25,520	33.6%	23,729	31.8%
45 - 64	15,033	19.5%	15,927	20.9%	17,680	23.7%
65 - 84	15,562	20.2%	14,868	19.6%	13,519	18.1%
85 +	1,474	1.9%	1,685	2.2%	1,857	2.5%
Owner-Occupied Hhlds	41,450		41,458		40,428	
Renter-Occupied Hhlds	19,726		20,701		20,810	

FIGURE 1.2. *(Continued)*

RETAIL POTENTIAL: RESTAURANTS
Cleveland, OH: Brookpark Rd & Pearl Rd
3 Mile Ring

Claritas Data Services
04/28/97

1996 ESTIMATE		Population 1995	Households 1995	Median Hhd Income, 1996	
AREA	**3 Mile Ring**	144,376	62,159	$31,405	
BASE	**United States**	265,253,151	100,066,882	$34,497	
		Area Sales ($ Mill)	Area Per Capita	Base Per Capita	Index
FOOD IN	**TOTAL**	$95.30	$660.05	$584.91	113
RESTAURANTS	Fast Food/Take Outs	$39.21	$271.59	$245.73	111
1996	Family/Coffee Shops	$31.15	$215.79	$193.65	111
	Cafeterias	$3.82	$26.46	$23.38	113
	Atmosphere/Specialty	$21.11	$146.22	$122.15	120
ALCOHOLIC	**TOTAL**	$14.40	$99.74	$87.27	114
BEVERAGES	Beer & Ale	$5.20	$36.01	$31.52	114
1996	Wine	$3.43	$23.73	$20.56	115
	Other Alcoholic Beverages	$5.77	$39.99	$35.19	114

2001 PROJECTED		Population 2001	Households 2001	Median Hhd Income, 2001	
AREA	**3 Mile Ring**	141,343	61,238	$37,362	
BASE	**United States**	276,918,306	104,497,652	$41,779	
		Area Sales ($ Mill)	Area Per Capita	Base Per Capita	Index
FOOD IN	**TOTAL**	$106.77	$755.43	$666.30	113
RESTAURANTS	Fast Food/Take Outs	$43.93	$310.83	$279.92	111
2001	Family/Coffee Shops	$34.91	$246.97	$220.59	112
	Cafeterias	$4.28	$30.28	$26.63	114
	Atmosphere/Specialty	$23.65	$167.35	$139.15	120
ALCOHOLIC	**TOTAL**	$16.11	$114.01	$99.31	115
BEVERAGES	Beer & Ale	$5.81	$41.12	$35.83	115
2001	Wine	$3.84	$27.20	$23.45	116
	Other Alcoholic Beverages	$6.46	$45.69	$40.03	114

FIGURE 1.2. *(Continued)*

Population+Graphics (National Base)
Cleveland, OH: Brookpark Rd & Pearl Rd
3 Mile Ring

Claritas Data Services
04/28/97

		Population	Households	Families	Median Age
3 Mile Ring		144,376	62,159	37,591	37.3
United States		265,253,151	100,066,882	67,724,960	34.6

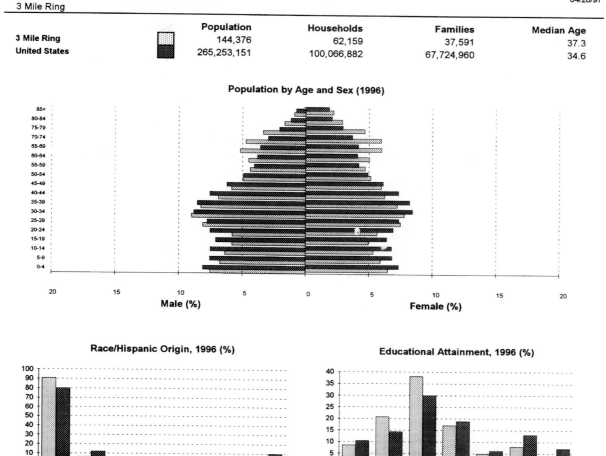

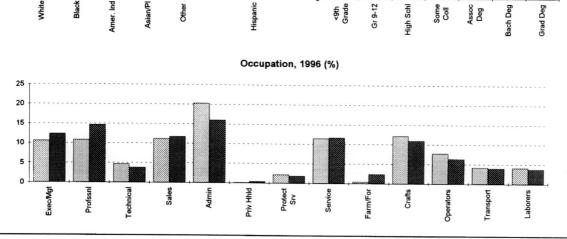

Source: March 15, 1996 UDS Estimates
Claritas Data Services / 4676 Admiralty Way Ste 624 / Marina del Rey, CA 90292 / (800) 633-9568

(CPNX)
800222

FIGURE 1.2. *(Continued)*

EXECUTIVE SUMMARY
Cleveland, OH: Brookpark Rd & Pearl Rd
3 Mile Ring

Claritas Data Services
04/28/1997

POPULATION
* the population is expected to decline slightly during the 1990's
* the population declined during the 1980-1990 period
* population density is low
* the median age is very near the national average
* there is an above average population of Polish ancestry
* a well-above average percentage of the adult population did not complete high school

HOUSEHOLDS
* household size is smaller than the national average
* an above average share of households are single person

INCOME
* average income is below national levels
* an above average share of income is derived from Social Security
* an above average share of the income is derived from retirement sources

EMPLOYMENT
* unemployment rates are at average levels

HOUSING
* a majority of housing units are owner occupied
* low residential turnover
* a majority of the houses were built before 1950

NOTE: This report is intended as a brief snapshot of the selected area. Only those key characteristics which are considerably different from national average values are reported. There may be other unique features of this area that are not reported. Use this report only in conjunction with a thorough review of the actual report figures.

FIGURE 1.2. (*Continued*)

FIGURE 1.2. *(Continued)*

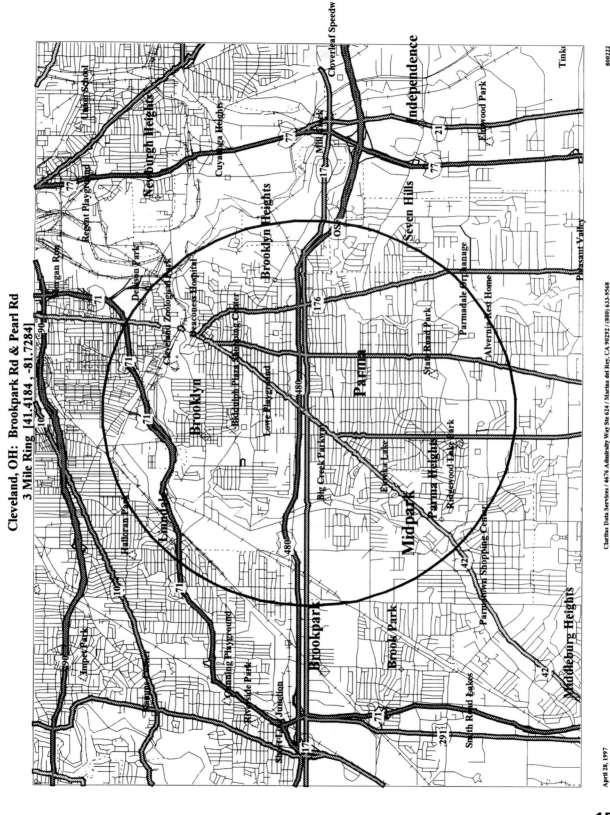

Cleveland, OH: Brookpark Rd & Pearl Rd
3 Mile Ring [41.4184 , -81.7284]

Claritas Data Services / 4676 Admiralty Way Ste 624 / Marina del Rey, CA 90292 / (800) 633-9568

April 28, 1997

COMPETITION

Another factor that personal knowledge can contribute to is competition. Although feasibility studies include a section on competition, demographic studies do not. Just exactly what is competition? In a broad sense of the word, it is any business that sells food. Thus, a grocery store or supermarket could be considered competition for a restaurant. In a strict sense of the word, *competition* includes any food service that sells a similar product at a price similar to your operation's. Care must be exercised when planning a menu, since a market will support only a given number of similar operations. When this maximum number of competing businesses are operating in a market, the situation is known as *market saturation.*

Many people and companies are afraid of competition, but competition is healthy. It promotes a good price-value relationship, excellent service, and a quality product. In a competitive market, businesses are forced to excel in order to succeed. Market saturation, on the other hand, is not a healthy situation to get into, as the number of available customers can be spread only so thin. Personal knowledge of this condition is important to the person responsible for writing the menu. Rather than copy the competition, attack it via menu listings, thus turning a problem into an opportunity. For example, an area that has an overabundance of deli-style operations would probably welcome a restaurant that features excellent soups and salads and downplays sandwiches.

Analysis of the demographic study is necessary for matching the customers with their needs. Although some research has been conducted on this subject, it is also necessary to rely on generalizations based on observation and experience.

AGE GROUPS

Knowledge of customer age groups is vital to proper menu selection. For purposes of this discussion, the age groups are bracketed as follows: children, teens, young adults, middle-aged adults, and older adults.

Why in the world would children be included? Children, more than anyone, influence and oftentimes dictate, the decision as to where a family will dine out. Remember also that children are heavily influenced by television, both in advertising and programming.

In an area that is family-oriented with children (as opposed to families with teenagers) certain considerations must be made in menu selection. The choices are not easy as the menu writer is torn between two sets of criteria: one, the parents want their children to have a well-balanced meal; and two, the children, being bombarded with slick ads, tend to opt for high-fat, high-sugar, high-calorie food. Since the children usually influence the decision as to where to eat out, they must be satisfied. Since the parents are paying for the experience, they too must be satisfied. The chapter on nutrition delves into ways to offer children their favorite menu items while making them nutritious. In addition to the regular menu, the restaurant can cater to the children in other ways, with special menus, prizes, and clean plate clubs. The experience must be enjoyable for both the children and the parents.

Teenagers pose special problems of their own. On the one hand they still cling to their childhood eating habits, and on the other hand they are beginning to mature into adulthood. Consequently, many are refining their tastes and requiring a nutritionally balanced diet (many, but not all!). They also need to be considered as two separate markets: one, as part of the family unit that is dining out; and, two, as a market of their own.

When dining out with the family, teens are more nutritionally oriented, probably more as a result of parental coercion than independent choice. They disdain children's menus and will order from the regular menu, frequently consuming more than their parents. When eating out with their peers, they often revert to the junk food syndrome. Theirs is a large market, with more disposable income than many restaurateurs realize.

The young adult market needs to be further broken down into three divisions: singles, couples with no children, and families. Although the type and style of food for this market are similar, menu considerations must be made for each division. Overall, this group is becoming more health conscious. They are concerned about physical fitness and, consequently, about lighter, healthier, and more natural foods. They are beginning to avoid junk foods and fried foods. They particularly enjoy fresh fruits and vegetables. The person responsible for menus in this market should consider salads; fresh fruits (both as a menu offering and as a garnish); natural breads such as bran or fruit muffins, wheat and stone ground breads; more broiled entrees (chicken, fish, seafood) and fewer fried entrees. This group is also particularly trendy. According to the National Restaurant Association, pizza, bakery items, barbecue, and pasta are particularly popular with those in the 25-to-34 age group. Apparently, this group is more willing to try new foods. It is imperative that one stay on top and ahead of trends.

As far as the market breakdown of this group is concerned, special considerations for menu planning need to be mentioned. Singles, as a group, have more disposable income and are less inclined to take the trouble to cook for one person. Consequently, they tend to eat out more and are not as concerned with price as are others in their market. The restaurant needs to be trendy with appropriate decor and, most of all, fun. The menu should offer a variety of foods that reflect the theme and decor of the establishment.

FIGURE 1-3. Distribution of restaurant traffic.

	Percent of Eater Occasions**	
Where Eaten:	Households with Children under 13	Households with no Children under 13
Total quickservice	**79%**	**61%**
Hamburger	29	22
Pizza	18	10
Chicken	5	5
Ice cream	5	3
Other sandwich	4	4
Mexican	4	2
Donut	2	1
Fish/Seafood	1	1
Oriental	1	1
Other quickservice	10	12
Total midscale	**16**	**28**
Family style	3	4
Family steak	2	2
Hotel dining	1	1
Cafeteria	1	3
Mexican	1	1
Oriental	1	1
Italian	1	1
Sandwich	1	1
Other midscale	5	14
Total moderate-check upscale	**4**	**8**
Fish/seafood	1	1
Oriental	1	1
Mexican	1	1
Other moderate-check upscale	1	5
Total higher-check upscale	**1**	**3**
Hotel dining	1	1
Other higher-check upscale	*	2
Total restaurants	**100%**	**100%**

*Less than one-half of one percent.

**An eater occasion is one meal eaten by one person.

Young married couples, if they are renting, tend to follow the same menu criteria as singles, particularly if both partners are working. They have a high disposable income and tend to spend a large portion of this eating out. On the other hand, young couples who are purchasing a home have an entirely different set of standards. Mortgage payments, yard and lawn care, decorating, and furniture purchases tend to consume a large portion of their disposable income, leaving a smaller amount for eating out. Although the diet demands of this group do not differ from those of renters, price becomes a more dominant criterion in selecting a restaurant. When a young couple starts raising a family, two changes take place: one, price becomes more important; and two, restaurants catering to children and families become very attractive.

Taking all these factors into consideration, it becomes increasingly clear that the menu writer in a market consisting of young adults needs to investigate further the specific factors of that market. Referring to the demographic studies done for the restaurant makes this an easier chore.

The middle-aged market tends to be more traditional in its menu selection. Basically, they cling to the older standards. Larger portions and fried foods are more popular, as well as value for their dollar. Patrons from 35 to 49 show a preference for chicken and pasta entree items, as well as baked goods. Middle-of-the-road, family-style restaurants are the norm with an occasional experience in fine dining for special occasions with the children being tended by a baby-sitter. When the family dines out, price is a factor. On special occasions price is less of a factor.

Patrons aged 18 to 49 are heavy consumers of hamburgers. After age 49, this item drops drastically in overall sales. Sandwiches are popular with those 18 to 49 who make up a large portion of the work force and are more likely to eat out for lunch.

The older segment of the population is probably the most predictable of all the age groups. Smaller portions and balanced meals become the norm. Those 55 to 75, representing 24 percent of the population, prefer roast beef, steak, fish or seafood, and veal entrees, which should be considered by restaurateurs wanting to attract older customers. After the family has grown and prior to retirement, price is less of a factor because during this time span income is at its greatest and financial responsibilities at their lowest. As this group retires and relies on fixed incomes, price becomes more important. Cafeterias and coffee shops are predominant in this group.

ETHNIC ORIGINS

Another factor to be taken into consideration when selecting items for the menu is the ethnic makeup of the restaurant trade area. Certain ethnic groups prefer particular foods over others. Caution should be key here, as many members of ethnic groups do not partake exclusively of the basic foods of their native land. It is fascinating how people enjoy trying foods of countries other than their own native land or the land of their ancestors. As a matter of fact, even the cuisine that is known as American borrows heavily from other countries in its own "melting pot" fashion.

When discussing ethnic foods, two areas should be covered: one is North American consumers purchasing ethnic foods of other cultures; the other is persons purchasing food from their own native cultures. The former is dealt with in a subsequent chapter. The discussion here focuses on ethnic likes and dislikes. Stereotyping is a dangerous thing when it comes to groups of people; however, it works quite well when dealing with menu planning. For example,

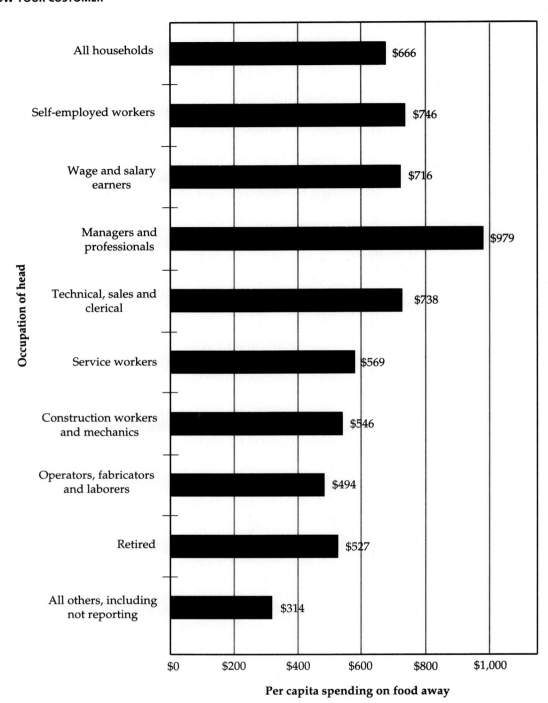

Source: Bureau of Labor Statistics, *Consumer Expenditure Survey, 1993*; National Restaurant Association.

FIGURE 1.4a.   Per capita expenditures on food away from home by occupation of household head.

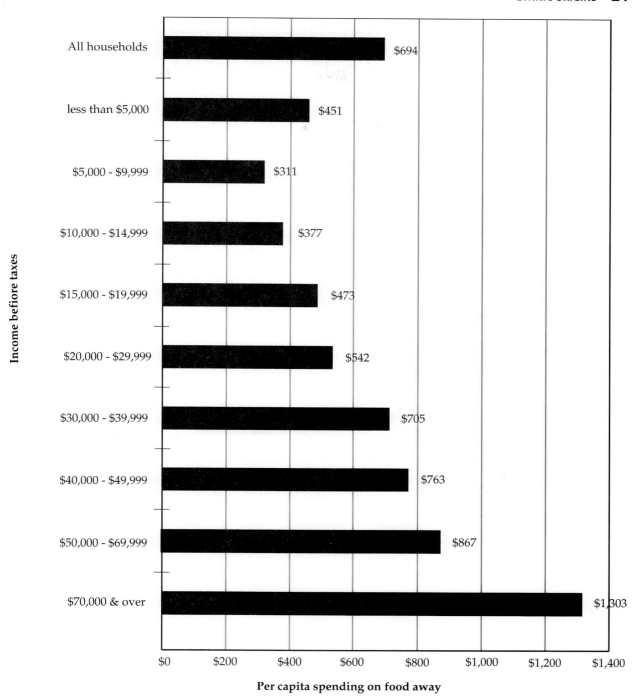

*Complete income reporters only; see glossary.

Source: Bureau of Labor Statistics, *Consumer Expenditure Survey, 1993*; National Restaurant Association.

FIGURE 1.4b. Per capita expenditures on food away from home by household income before taxes.*

FIGURE 1-5a.   Customer profile: On-premise dinner at fast food restaurants—lifestage/income.

(n=)	Fast Food Dinners (722)	All On-Premise Dinners (2926)	Index
Lifestage			
Young parent (under 45, all children under 6)	18%	13%	138
Middle parent (under 45, any child over 6)	20	17	118
Older parent (45+, child living at home)	26	25	104
Young couple (under 45)	10	11	91
Working older couple (45+)	11	14	78
Retired couple (45+)	6	7	86
Young singles (under 35)	2	2	100
Middle singles (35-65)	4	6	67
Older singles (65+)	1	1	100
Roommates (same sex, 18 and over)	4	4	100
Household Income			
Under $35,000	43%	38%	113
$35,000+	57	61	93

Source: National Restaurant Association, *Dinner Decision Making—1995.*

FIGURE 1-5b.   Customer profile: On-premise dinner at self-service cafeteria, buffet restaurants—lifestage/income.

(n=)	Cafeteria/ Buffet Dinners (425)	All On-Premise Dinners (2926)	Index
Lifestage			
Young parent (under 45, all children under 6)	9%	13%	69
Middle parent (under 45, any child over 6)	20	17	118
Older parent (45+, child living at home)	28	25	112
Young couple (under 45)	8	11	73
Working older couple (45+)	16	14	114
Retired couple (45+)	8	7	114
Young singles (under 35)	2	2	100
Middle singles (35-65)	6	6	67
Older singles (65+)	0	1	0
Roommates (same sex, 18 and over)	3	4	75
Household Income			
Under $35,000	43%	38%	113
$35,000+	57	61	93

Source: National Restaurant Association, *Dinner Decision Making—1995.*

FIGURE 1-5c. Customer profile: On-premise dinner at sit-down restaurants ($10-$20)—lifestage/income.

(n=)	Sit-Down ($10-$20) Dinners (722)	All On-Premise Dinners (2926)	Index
Lifestage			
Young parent (under 45, all children under 6)	11%	13%	85
Middle parent (under 45, any child over 6)	13	17	76
Older parent (45+, child living at home)	24	25	96
Young couple (under 45)	13	11	118
Working older couple (45+)	15	14	107
Retired couple (45+)	8	7	114
Young singles (under 35)	2	2	100
Middle singles (35-65)	6	6	100
Older singles (65+)	1	1	100
Roommates (same sex, 18 and over)	5	4	125
Household Income			
Under $35,000	31%	38%	82
$35,000+	69	61	113

Source: National Restaurant Association, *Dinner Decision Making—1995.*

FIGURE 1-5d. Customer profile: On-premise dinner at sit-down restaurants ($20 or more)—lifestage/income.

(n=)	Sit-Down ($20+) Dinners (425)	All On-Premise Dinners (2926)	Index
Lifestage			
Young parent (under 45, all children under 6)	10%	13%	77
Middle parent (under 45, any child over 6)	10	17	59
Older parent (45+, child living at home)	27	25	108
Young couple (under 45)	14	11	127
Working older couple (45+)	15	14	107
Retired couple (45+)	5	7	71
Young singles (under 35)	3	2	150
Middle singles (35-65)	10	6	167
Older singles (65+)	0	1	0
Roommates (same sex, 18 and over)	6	4	150
Household Income			
Under $35,000	26%	38%	68
$35,000+	74	61	121

Source: National Restaurant Association, *Dinner Decision Making—1995.*

Jewish people for the most part do not partake of pork or shellfish and do not mix dairy with meat. Mexican people eat more pork and chicken than they do beef. Persons from the Pacific Rim eat more vegetables and little meat. Remember that, although the majority of an ethnic group might like certain foods, seasonings, or cooking methods, not everyone in the group agrees. The menu writer needs to take into account the fact that particular foods appeal to certain ethnic groups most of the time. This is not to suggest that this holds true all of the time.

EDUCATION, OCCUPATION, AND INCOME

These three factors are tied together as they normally tend to influence each other. For example, a person with a high school education or less would tend to have a blue collar occupation, while a person with a postsecondary education would tend to have a white collar position. Generally, a person in a white collar position earns more than a person in a blue collar job. There would be, however, no noticeable income difference on the upper blue collar scale and the lower white collar scale.

As far as menu planning is concerned, education and occupation play a minor role in contrast to income. With income the primary factor, the key determination for the menu writer becomes affordability for the market. Another key factor is not necessarily the income in a particular demographic area, but the disposable income in that market. Disposable income is that part of earnings and investment income that is left over after the basic needs of food, shelter, clothing, and other necessities have been met. It can generally be stated that the higher the person's income, the greater the available disposable income. When more disposable income becomes available, two things happen: people tend to eat out more often and they tend to trade up.

Income analysis shows that people in the under–$5,000 level surprisingly spend more per capita income eating out than do people in the $5,000-to-$15,000 range. After that, as income rises, per capita expenditures for food away from home also increase.

POPULARITY POLLS

Several popularity polls are available to assist the menu writer with listings that are popular with the restaurant-going population as a whole. However, a generic menu that lists only popular items is, for the most part, dull. Therefore the menu writer also needs to be concerned with trends within a demographic area. Take, for example, fish that has good to moderate acceptance across the spectrum. In the past, deep fried cod would have been an acceptable menu listing. However, studies have shown that there is a trend away from fried foods. This does not mean that this item must be removed from the menu, but rather it needs to be altered to gain customer acceptance. Changing the entree to broiled cod with a lemon sauce would fit this criterion. Next, is it priced right? Does it fit the criteria for family/singles, ethnic groups, age, and so on? In a high-income area, broiled cod might be changed to broiled filet of Dover sole at a higher selling price.

A word of caution should be given here. Although it is important to be aware (and even on the cutting edge) of trends, do not overreact. Avoid embracing the trend completely. For example, when light, broiled, lean meats along with fresh fruits and vegetables became the trend, less than a third of the population ordered these items when dining out. The media would lead one to believe that everyone was, or should be, eating this way. Certainly one-third of our customer base is important, but don't forget the two-thirds who do not wish to participate.

Recognize also the difference between fads and trends. A *fad* is an idea that comes and goes quickly, while *trends* stay around for a while and many times become the norm. If you react to fads, the ink will barely be dry on the new menu, the storeroom will be full of new ingredients, and no one will be purchasing them. Following fads costs money; following trends can make money. Many successful independent restaurateurs, as well as chains, have made careers developing trends. They have already started the next trend as soon as the rest of the industry is following their lead.

CONCLUSION

Know your trade area and your customers: their lifestyles, income, ethnic origins, occupations—all about them. Fit the menu selections and price specifically to your customers. Ride the trends. Successful restaurateurs do this all the time. You should, too. It's just that simple.

QUESTIONS

1. In your own words, define the term *demographics* and relate it to proper menu planning.
2. Discuss the difference between a *demographic study* and a *feasibility study*. Tell what information from each would be useful in developing a menu.
3. Using the demographic study in Figure 1.2, tell what type of restaurant would most likely be successful in that area and write a menu for that restaurant.

4. Research one square mile in your area. List the number and type of restaurants. Describe the type of restaurant you feel would be successful with the competition you have plotted. Determine who will be your customer and develop a menu to meet your customer's preferences.

5. Using a typical coffee shop menu in your area, create a children's menu that is nutritious and yet at the same time will appeal to children.

6. Discuss the difference between *fads* and *trends*. What new concepts, themes, or specific menu items have been developed in your area? Are they fads or trends? Defend your answer.

7. Which is more important to the menu planner, income or disposable income? Why?

CHAPTER TWO

Know Your Restaurant

OBJECTIVES
By the completion of this chapter, the reader should be able to:

- Recognize what considerations need to be made when changing the menu in an existing operation.
- Explain the importance of product availability, selling price, equipment availability, station capacities, flow, skill level, and theme when making menu changes.
- Describe how the new operation interrelates with and is totally dependent on the menu.

IMPORTANT TERMS

Product availability	Cross utilization
Equipment availability	Theme
Station capabilities	Staff skill level
Product flow	Traffic flow

INTRODUCTION

Before attempting to write a new menu or add new items to the present menu, the menu writer must fully understand the capabilities and limits of the restaurant involved. The same holds true for writing a menu for a new operation in the planning stage. Everything starts with the menu. The layout, design, decor, theme, equipment, and staffing all depend on the menu and specifically on the items selected for that menu. As previously discussed, the menu should reflect the needs of the potential customers as outlined by the demographics portion of the feasibility study. To discuss restaurant capabilities further, it is necessary to approach the issue from two different points of view:

1. That of the existing restaurant needing a menu change
2. That of the new restaurant in the planning stage

THE EXISTING OPERATION

Several factors need to be taken into consideration when contemplating menu changes in an existing operation. These are product availability, cross utilization of products, selling price, equipment availability, physical capabilities of the station, traffic and product flow, staff skills, and the theme of the restaurant.

Product Availability

The first factor, product availability, is often overlooked by menu planners. How many times have you seen "available in season only" printed after a menu listing? All of the ingredients necessary to produce the new menu item should be available on a year-round basis from a local source. If the proposed listing has seasonal ingredients, it should be listed only if the restaurant's menu is printed using an in-house computer. If the menus are printed by a commercial printer, a seasonal listing should be merchandised via table tents or clip-ons, and/or verbally by the wait staff rather than printed on the permanent menu.

If the new listing has an anticipated sales volume that could be considered extraordinary, assurances should be sought from the purveyors that they will be able to supply the demand. Nothing is more embarrassing than to roll out a new menu listing with marketing and advertising only to tell the customer, "I'm sorry, we're out of it."

Cross Utilization of Products

When deciding on new menu listings, the optimum situation is to use ingredients already on hand. Whenever possible, avoid increases in the number of items carried in inventory since this decreases cash flow and increases the chance for theft and waste. Additional use of existing products also increases the purchases of that item and possibly decreases the cost per unit.

Unfortunately, cross utilizing products is not always possible when adding new menu listings. You need to make a decision regarding how well the new item will sell in relation to the added cost of an expanded inventory.

Selling Price

As discussed in a subsequent chapter, the food cost of a menu item is a key factor in determining the selling price of that item. When checking the availability of the ingredients from the purveyor, the menu planner should also determine their cost. The cost of labor must be investigated in addition to the food cost. The new menu item should not be more involved or more labor-intensive than the current menu listings. If it is, and if the menu writer still feels strongly about the new item, then the selling price must include a factor to reflect the additional labor cost. At this point, care must be exercised that the listing can be sold at a price compatible with the price range of the present menu. The price should also be within the range that the restaurant's demographically identified customers would be willing to pay.

Equipment Availability

The third factor, equipment availability, requires the menu writer to ascertain that the necessary equipment is on hand to produce the proposed item. This encompasses the whole kitchen. The storage area—including refrigerator, freezer, and dry storage—needs to be checked to see whether capacity is sufficient to handle the ingredients that the new menu item will require. The production area must be evaluated in terms of the particular piece or pieces of equipment needed to produce the new listing. If this task is not carried out thoroughly and accurately, the results could be disastrous.

A Case in Point. In a particular trade area, Mexican and southwestern fare became quite popular, with several new chain operations opening up. A popular local tavern decided to add some of these entrees to its menu to capture a share of this up-and-coming market and to stem the flow of its regular customers to these trendy new spots. The tavern in question was basically a bar and short order/appetizer operation, its revenue coming mostly from drinks. Two pieces of equipment were lacking to produce the new items: a steam table to hold the burrito and taco fillings and a cheese melter or back-shelf broiler to finish off the products. To solve the problem, burritos, tacos, and enchiladas were put into a microwave. As a result, the fillings came out hot and bubbly but

MENU CHANGE FORMAT
EXISTING RESTAURANT

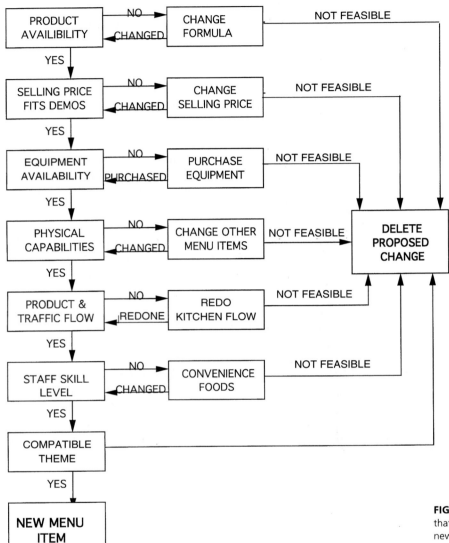

FIGURE 2.1.   A model showing the steps that should be taken in determining whether a new item should be placed on an existing menu.

the tortilla shells were dry and tough; the product was unacceptable and inferior to the competition's. Consequently, this previously popular watering hole lost additional sales, as well as product credibility and customer confidence.

Too often, menus are indiscriminately changed with consideration given only to sales. Certainly sales are important, but if the product cannot be presented properly, the theory reverses itself and sales are the ultimate loser.

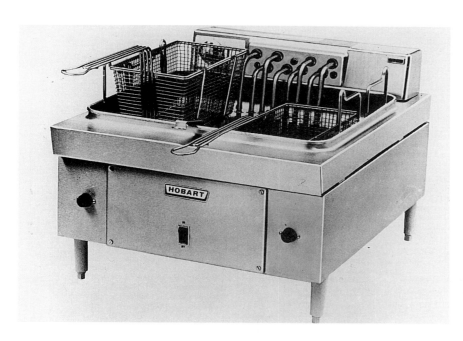

FIGURE 2.2. The capacities for this particular fryer are listed in the accompanying illustration. (*Photograph courtesy of the Hobart Corp., Troy, Ohio*)

Physical Capabilities

The next factor to consider, physical capability, is closely related to equipment availability. However, in this case, we assume that the proper equipment is in place and now consider whether the equipment has the capacity to produce the proposed new listing.

Two factors must be considered: first, whether the equipment itself can handle the increased demand and, second, whether the station can handle the increased volume. First, consider that every piece of equipment in the kitchen has its maximum production capacities. This maximum is stated in the manufacturer's product specification books. Most often these capacities are stated under optimum conditions. (To expect more from the equipment is foolhardy.) To ascertain whether a particular piece of equipment can handle an increase in production, take its usage during peak hours in the operation and subtract this from the manufacturer's maximum production capacity. Compare this difference with the anticipated sales of the new menu item to see whether the item can be prepared in a timely manner. For example, assume that the manufacturer's stated capacity for a griddle is 1,200 six-inch pancakes per hour; the peak sales for this item at breakfast are 300; and the proposed new menu listing is French toast with estimated sales of 150 pieces per hour. When the math is completed, it becomes obvious that the griddle could adequately handle the additional production. Investing the time and research early in the planning process ensures the successful introduction of the new menu item. Proper planning prevents the long wait by dissatisfied customers that would result from a new menu item being added haphazardly.

CK20-CK201
ELECTRIC FRYER

SPECIFICATIONS: Listed by Underwriters Laboratories Inc and by National Sanitation Foundation.

GENERAL: Freestanding electric fryer holds up to 28 lbs. of shortening.

CONSTRUCTION: Stainless steel cabinet and support head. Mounts on 4″ plastic legs (furnished). Optional 4″ stainless steel legs are available. Accommodates accessory shortening removal and straining device; furnished with two standard fry baskets. Enclosed tubular stainless steel heating elements which swing up and burn clean in the raised position. Shortening container is equipped with easy-grip, lift-out handles; scored to indicate level of fat-fill.

CONTROLS: "Power On" switch ties in with signal light on heating unit support head. A separate signal light adjacent to the "Power On" signal light, cycles with the thermostat, indicates when fryer is heating and when preset temperature is reached. Preheats to 350°F in 6-7 minutes. Temperature range: 200-400°F. QUAD-GUARD control protection features two contactors and two thermostats to provide reliable interruption of power to heating elements to prevent overheating. Extra fuses protect thermostat circuit. Temperature-limiting thermostat is reset manually by raising heating units and pressing exposed reset lever. Stan-

dard internal POWER TURNOFF (optional on **CK201**) connect fryer (via terminal block located behind ⁷/₈″ diameter knockout) to hood fire-extinguishing system circuit.

ELECTRICAL TIMERS: CK201 has two integral push button timers with automatic reset and adjustments from 0-15 minutes. Each timer activates one basket lowering and lifting mechanism for automatic, simultaneous frying of identical or different products requiring the same or different processing times.

CAPACITY: 28 lbs. of shortening in a removable container (one furnished). Produces up to 61 lbs. or 313 two-ounce servings of raw-to-done French fried potatoes or 600 two-ounce servings of blanched potatoes per hour.

ELECTRICAL: 12KW (3 phase models); 9.8 KW (1-phase CK20). See "Electrical Data" block for phase loading.

ACCESSORIES:

BASKETS
Full size fry basket, standard mesh **(CK20).**
Extra pair standard twin size fry baskets.
Twin fry baskets, fine mesh.
Triple fry basket, fine mesh **(CK20).**

(Left) One twin basket, standard mesh.
(Right) One twin basket, standard mesh.

LEGS
Set of four 4″ adust. stainless steel.
Set of four 4″ adjust. plastic.

OTHER
Miraclean siphon w/filter bag.
Miraclean w/extra long arm f/use w/cutting board.
Extra filter bags (set of 6).
Extra fat container.
Cover **(CK20).**

For fryers **without** TOUCHTIME® basket lifts:
Step-down transformer from a 480-volt, 240-volt or 208-volt supply source to 120-volt power for the control circuit of fryers **without** TOUCHTIME® lifts where a four-wire supply source or separate 120-volt power are not available.

WEIGHT: (Approximate)

	Shipping	Net
CK20	75 lbs.	60 lbs.
CK201	108 lbs.	88 lbs.

As continued product improvement is a policy of Hobart, specifications are subject to change without notice.

FRYING GUIDE

FOOD	TEMP. SETTING °F	TIME (IN MIN.)	CAPACITY/LOAD	
			1-PHASE	3-PHASE
French-Fried Potatoes ³/₈″ strips one-temperature method	375	6-9	5.4 lbs.	6.1 lbs.
Two-temperature method blanch	325	4-6	4.62 lbs.	5.25 lbs.
brown	375	2-3	7.94 lbs.	9.02 lbs.
Potato chips, thin slices	350	3-4	1.70 lbs.	1.94 lbs.
Fish Fillets, 5″ x ½″	365	3-4	7.7 lbs.	8.8 lbs.
Shrimp	375	2-3	4.9 lbs.	5.58 lbs.
Oysters and Clams	395	2-3	3.3 lbs.	3.7 lbs.
Chicken, 2-lbs. size quartered (8-oz. serving)	325	12-13	6 portions*	7 portions*
halved (1-lb. serving)	325	12-16	6 portions*	7 portions*
Croquettes	365	3-4	7.7 lbs.	8.8 lbs.
Fritters, fruit, vegetable or meat 2½″ dia.	375	4-5	26*	30*
Doughnuts, 2½″ dia.	375	2-3	26*	30*
French Toast, 4″ x 4″ slices	325	2-3	10*	12*
Turnovers, fruit, vegetable or meat 4″ x 2½″	375	3-4	16*	18*

*Capacities given are limited by energy available to maintain continuous frying temperature, except those marked with an asterisk(*) in which case capacity is limited by surface of the item in preparation.

FIGURE 2.3. A typical equipment specification cut sheet showing the capacities of a Hobart CK 20 Fryer. (*Courtesy of the Hobart Corp., Troy, Ohio*)

The second factor to consider under physical capabilities is the station's capacity to handle a new menu item. A *station* in a kitchen is the same thing as a work center. It is an area where a group of closely related tasks are performed. These are normally performed by one person, but, in rare instances of extremely high volume, the tasks could be performed by more than one person. Examples of stations on a production line could include a sauté, fry, broil, and/or grill station. Two circumstances should be considered when evaluating a station to see whether a new listing can be added to the menu. One factor is the station's capacity, a consideration similar to that in the previous discussion on equipment, only here several pieces of equipment need to be considered. The question to be answered is whether the station, as a collective whole, can handle the increased demand.

The second consideration is the ability of the person working the station to keep up with the extra requirements necessitated by the additional listings. All people have physical limitations beyond which they cannot perform more duties. To require them to do so causes delays in orders being produced. This does not refer to their skill level, which will be discussed later, but rather to their ability physically to handle the volume of the station. Anyone who has ever worked at a restaurant, in either service or production, has probably observed a station being swamped at peak hours. This problem is caused by the improper selection of employees, poor training, or an improperly written menu. More often than not, it is the latter. Why this condition exists is puzzling since the solution is so simple: Change the menu to reflect the production capabilities of the physical plant.

A Case in Point. An Italian restaurant that served a downtown location for over 50 years decided to open a second operation in suburbia. The new restaurant used the same menu as the original, but, due to demographic differences, the new restaurant saw a substantial increase in orders for sauté items. The sauté station, consisting of one 8-burner range and one sauté cook, could not adequately handle the orders during peak periods; the result was as much as a 45-minute delay for the customer. For the servers, this further complicated the logistics of trying to obtain orders from other stations.

This scenario is identical to that of adding new items in an existing restaurant with no forethought given to overloading a station. The solution to the problem was simple: Eliminate several sauté items and replace them with broiled and roasted items, thus giving the production area a smoother flow. This change resulted in excellent timing and well-served, satisfied customers. The physical capability of stations is the principle most often overlooked and violated when new listings are added to the menu. Unfortunately, when this happens the intent of the menu change is reversed: Instead of increasing sales, sales are lost.

Product and Traffic Flow

The third factor to be considered, product and traffic flow, involves consideration of new menu items in relation to existing flows within the restaurant. A well-designed restaurant has both people and products moving in such a way that cross-traffic and backtracking are avoided: People don't bump into each other. The menu writer needs to analyze each potential new menu item to see whether such an addition will result in a flow change.

For example, in order to increase sales, a fast food restaurant decided to add lemonade and limeade to its beverage selection and use a Jet Spray® to merchandise these drinks properly. The only available counter space was at the end of the line, some 8 feet away from the current beverage station. The beverage attendant had to cross two direct traffic lines twice, both going and returning, to obtain these drinks. The result was staff traffic congestion in the serving area and undue delays to the customer. Foresight on the part of the menu writer could have prevented this disorder.

Conversely, if a restaurant had poor traffic and product flow, an astute person could quite possibly correct this problem with one or several menu changes.

Staff Skill Level

The skill of the staff, both the kitchen and service personnel, is another factor to consider when contemplating new menu items. Most often this problem arises when the restaurant is attempting to upgrade itself. However, prior to an evaluation of skill levels, consideration must be given to the demographics of the area and a determination made as to whether customers will accept such upgrading. Only after confirming that this alternative is viable should an analysis of the current staff's abilities be carried out.

Production staff skills can be expressed in four levels. The first level is that of a line cook who has the ability to cook an item to order and plate it according to the restaurant's specifications and standards. The second level is the prep cook, who has the ability to follow structured and tested quantity recipes. The third level is a chef who can carry out more complicated recipes. The fourth level is a chef with the genius to create cutting-edge recipes. The menu planner must carefully evaluate the complexity of the new menu addition in order to avoid exceeding the skill level of the kitchen staff.

Likewise, the abilities of the service personnel must be taken into consideration. Four basic styles of service are used in this country: self-service, American, Russian, and French styles. Each of these styles has different characteristics and requires a different level of expertise. *Self-service*, predominant in fast food operations, requires customers to place and pick up the orders themselves. In *American* or *table service*, an order is prepared and plated in the kitchen and delivered to the customer. This style of service is more predominant in coffee shops and theme restaurants. Self-service and American service are sometimes combined, as in the case of buffets, where the customers serve themselves and the servers bring the beverages and clear the table. With *Russian service*, the order is prepared in the kitchen and plated at the table by the server. *French service* carries the process one step further. The order is partly prepared in the kitchen, but finished and plated at the table. The last two styles are normally reserved for fine dining establishments; however, many Oriental restaurants use a variation of Russian service.

In adding new items to a menu, the safest rule to follow is to stay within the bounds of the style presently in use. If it is deemed necessary to upgrade an operation in terms of menu offerings, then the decision must be made as to whether the production and service staff can be trained to handle the upgrade.

Theme

The last factor to consider before putting a menu change into effect in an existing operation is the theme of the restaurant. The menu writer must take care that the new items are compatible with the theme as well as with the decor. All too often, restaurants destroy their image by veering slowly but surely away from their original theme when they introduce incompatible items. Quite often the intention is to create a new market, but the effort to be all things to all people destroys the originality that made the restaurant unique in the first place.

In retrospect, all these factors—product availability, selling price, equipment, physical capabilities, flow, staff, and theme—need to be considered before a new item is added to the menu. For example, a seafood restaurant would be wise to analyze fully the addition of beef to the menu. First, is there product availability? Probably. Second, would the selling price be compatible with the seafood menu? Probably. Third, since beef is an entirely new product, is the equipment the right type to handle beef properly? Maybe. This area would require analysis. Could the station chosen to handle this item prepare a product of a different nature? Maybe. Is the staff skilled enough or could they be trained to prepare a beef item? Probably. Would beef fit into the decor and theme of the restaurant without destroying its ambience? Probably not.

An excellent way to answer these questions is to do a *walk through,* that is, "walk" the item through purchasing, storage, production, and service. Will the item fit into the already established parameters of the restaurant? Finally, will the market expand because of this item or will the existing customers resent the addition, feeling that this is no longer a specialty restaurant? Is the quality of seafood lowered because of the new listing? Only after these questions are satisfactorily answered can the addition be made.

THE NEW RESTAURANT

To create a menu for an entirely new restaurant is quite different from revising an existing menu. In the new operation, the menu becomes a planning tool. The old adage "everything starts with the menu"

FIGURE 2.4. This menu and accompanying photographs illustrate how theme, decor, and menu go hand in hand. (*Menu and photographs courtesy of The Colonial Williamsburg Foundation, Williamsburg, Virginia*)

FIGURE 2.4. (*Continued*)

Chowning's TAVERN

Inn keep-er

APPETIZERS	Sliced Fresh MELON with *Smithfield* HAM 2.95	Crock of *Cheddar* CHEESE with SIPPETS 4.50	Potato and Leek SOUP 1.75

Josiah Chowning's Brunswick STEW DINNER

Potato and Leek SOUP, *Josiah Chowning's Brunswick* STEW (made from Young FOWL and Garden VEGETABLES, seasoned to Taste and served up Hot), Garden GREENS with Choice of DRESS-ING, *Chowning's* Good BREAD, BEVERAGE, and a Pecan TART with Vanilla ICE CREAM
17.25

Suggested wine: Bin No. 40 or No. 91

Hen

Chowning's Chesapeake DINNER

Potato and Leek SOUP, Garden GREENS with Chutney DRESSING, Sautéed Backfin CRAB-MEAT and HAM (a Slice of *Smithfield* HAM com-plemented with *Chesapeake* Backfin CRABMEAT, topped with BUTTER, and laced with SHERRY), VEGETABLE of the Day, Baked POTATO, *Chowning's* Good BREAD, BEVERAGE, and Buttered Apple PIE with *Cheddar* CHEESE
23.95

Suggested wine: Bin No. 93 or No. 71

Josiah Chowning's SPECIALTIES

PRIME RIB

Roast PRIME RIB of BEEF (cut to your Liking Rare, Medium, Well Done), HORSERADISH, Baked POTATO, and VEGETABLE of the Day
20.75

Served with *Smithfield* HAM 21.75
Suggested wine: Bin No. 84 or No. 42

Cow

Barbecued RIBS

Broiled Pork Back RIBS braised in a Barbecue SAUCE served with a Baked POTATO and Garden VEGETABLE
18.25

Suggested wine: Bin No. 197

Pig

Chowning's SPECIAL of the Day
Market Price

Duck

Mr. *Chowning's* Favorite DISH

Fillet of Chicken BREAST stuffed with Fresh CRABMEAT and CHEESE. This Delicious BIRD is topped with a White Wine SAUCE and served with a Baked POTATO and Garden VEGETABLE
19.95

Suggested wine: Bin No. 194

Roast DUCK with Orange SAUCE

Served over Blended Wild RICE with a Garden VEGETABLE
17.95

Suggested wine: Bin No. 40 or No. 88

All selections are served with *Chowning's* Garden GREENS and Good BREAD.

DESSERTS

Please ask your Server for our Complete MENU of Homemade DESSERTS.

BEVERAGES

Cup and Saucer.

Sparkling APPLE CIDER	1.50	Iced TEA	.95
APPLE CIDER	.95	ORANGEADE	.95
Hot COFFEE or Hot TEA	1.25	MILK	.95
MINERAL WATER	1.50	Carbonated BEVERAGES	.95
LEMONADE	.95	Root BEER	1.50

Please, NO SMOKING inside the Tavern.

Several popular tavern foods are available at M. DuBois Grocer's Shop on Duke of Gloucester Street and at EVERYTHING *Williamsburg* on Prince George Street. A complete selection of tavern china and other accessories can be found at Craft House adjacent to the Williamsburg Inn and at Craft House at Merchants Square. Recipes for many tavern foods can be found in *The Williamsburg Cookbook* and *Favorite Meals from Williamsburg*. These cookbooks may be purchased at M. DuBois Grocer's Shop, Craft House, EVERYTHING *Williamsburg*, and other Colonial Williamsburg stores.

3/93

FIGURE 2.4. *(Continued)*

Williamsburg, *October* 10, 1766

"I HEREBY acquaint the publick that I have opened tavern . . . where all who please to favour me with their custom may depend upon the best of entertainment for themselves, servants, and horses, and good pasturage.

JOSIAH CHOWNING"

THE "publick" that frequented Chowning's Tavern on Market Square were mostly local residents—farmers who sold produce at the market, those with business at the Courthouse, and idle bystanders with time to kill. Some were shoppers at the market or in the uptown stores, craftsmen who repaired weapons or delivered supplies to the Powder Magazine, and militiamen who mustered on Market Square green. Occasionally a traveler dropped in.

In size, clientele, and services Chowning's bore more resemblance to rural Virginia taverns located at ferries, crossroads, and courthouses or to small English alehouses than to the larger taverns nearer the Capitol. Despite Chowning's boast of the "best of entertainment," the selection of food and drink at his tavern was limited. Most customers drank rum, local beer, or cider, although Josiah also stocked a little wine and brandy and provided bowls of punch on demand. His customers were content with the plain fare that he set before them. The few travelers who patronized this establishment probably lodged together in one room upstairs.

Little is known about Josiah Chowning and his family. In many modest Virginia taverns like Chowning's the tavern keeper and his wife and children lived on the premises so they could help with the work of waiting on customers, cooking, cleaning, and laundering.

Tavern keeping was often a precarious trade for small operators like Chowning who rented a tavern; Chowning's business here lasted only two years. After his death in 1772, some land that Chowning owned and one of his slaves were sold at an auction held in front of the Courthouse—within sight of his former tavern.

Modern-day travelers and locals alike gather informally at Chowning's Tavern for hearty food and drink just as their counterparts did two hundred years ago.

Chairs, benches, and tables represent the sturdy, country-made furniture found in colonial taverns catering to the middling sort. Excavated fragments show that the yellow rooster on the dinnerware was one of several colorful bird motifs that appeared on the tablewares used by eighteenth-century Williamsburg residents. Iron candlesticks, called "hogscrapers" because some early Americans used the base to scrape hair from hogs, are listed in inventories of several colonial Virginia taverns. Other accessories—utilitarian salt and pepper shakers and sugar casters made of stoneware, plain tin sconces, simply framed maps and prints—further accentuate the informality of Josiah Chowning's Tavern.

All income from Chowning's Tavern is used for the purposes of The Colonial Williamsburg Foundation, which operates the Historic Area of Williamsburg, and to carry forward its educational programs.

Colonial Williamsburg also welcomes tax-deductible contributions. Friends interested in discussing gifts to the Foundation are asked to write the President, The Colonial Williamsburg Foundation, Williamsburg, Virginia 23187.

The print reproduced on the cover, "DOCTOR SYNTAX in the Middle of a smoking hot Political squabble, wishes to Whet his Whistle," was drawn by Thomas Rowlandson and was published in London by Thomas Tegg sometime between 1807 to 1821. Courtesy, Library of Congress.

The illustrations used inside the menu are reproduced from catchpenny prints, popular eighteenth-century English engravings.

FIGURE 2.4. (*Continued*)

FIGURE 2.4. (*Continued*)

holds true here, for the most part. However, one important process takes place before the menu is planned—the feasibility study. The demographics section of the feasibility study dictates to a large degree the type of menu written and, consequently, the type of restaurant to be opened. Opening a fine French restaurant in a blue collar factory neighborhood, for example, would be a mistake.

Once the style of restaurant is determined, the menu can be planned. From the menu, the theme and decor can be determined, the equipment selected, and the staff hired.

Theme and Decor

Theme, decor, and menu go hand in hand. When planning the menu, the items selected should match the chosen theme. The descriptive terminology should reinforce and elaborate the theme and decor. For example, a restaurant that sports an Old English Tudor style of architecture with dark, heavy wood and stucco interior would support a menu of beef, lamb, and North Atlantic fish. Descriptive terminology would contain key and familiar English phrases. The menu would probably be on parchment-style paper with an Old English style of type. All these factors are discussed in detail in subsequent chapters; at this stage it is enough to recognize the relationship between the menu and the restaurant's theme.

Equipment

When building a new restaurant or food service operation, one of the major expenses is the purchase of equipment. Therefore, it is important to determine exactly which pieces are needed and to buy only what is necessary. To do this, the menu must be reviewed on an item-by-item basis and the equipment needed to produce each item must be listed. For example, to produce a hamburger, the following pieces of equipment are needed:

Schedule for Equipment in Use

Equipment	6:00	7:00	8:00	9:00	10:00	11:00	12:00	1:00	2:00	3:00	4:00
Deck Oven 1		XXXX	XXXX	XXXX	XXXX		XXXX	XXXX	XXXX	XXXX	
Deck Oven 2			XXXX	XXXX	XXXX	XXXX					
Range—O.B.	XXXX	XXXX	XXXX	XXXX	XXXX				XXXX	XXXX	XXXX
Flattop	XXXX	XXXX	XXXX	XXXX	XXXX	XXXX	XXXX	XXXX	XXXX		
30 Gal Steam Kettle	XXXX	XXXX	XXXX	XXXX			XXXX		XXXX	XXXX	XXXX
10 Gal Steam Kettle					XXXX	XXXX	XXXX	XXXX			
Tiltskillet		XXXX	XXXX	XXXX	XXXX				XXXX	XXXX	XXXX
Oven—Steamer		XXX			XXXX	XXXX	XXXX	XXXX			XXXX
Steamer						XXXX	XXXX				XXXX

FIGURE 2.5. A chart showing the schedule of equipment used during various parts of the day. Any additional menu items would have to fit in with this schedule.

Refrigeration—to store the hamburger patties, garnishes, and condiments

Dry storage

Griddle or broiler—to cook the hamburger (Note: A decision must be made here as to the style of cookery.)

Plate lowerator or plate shelf

Refrigerated make-up table

Pick-up station with heat lamp

Wait station

Dishwasher

Each item on the menu should be reviewed in this manner until a complete list is developed for the entire menu. The second step is to determine the sizes and numbers of pieces needed to produce the menu. Three factors are considered:

1. The number of different menu items produced on each piece of equipment. A broiler, for example, might be used to produce several items on the menu.

TYPICAL KITCHEN PRODUCT/TRAFFIC FLOW

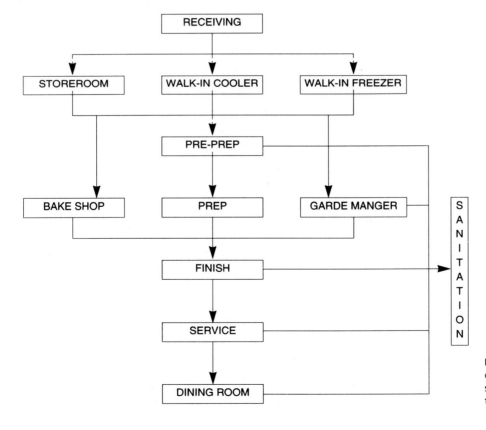

FIGURE 2.6. A chart showing the movement of product through a kitchen from receiving to service. Notice how crisscrossing and back-tracking are virtually eliminated.

2. The capacity of the dining room in terms of number of seats and the anticipated turnover of those seats.

3. The projected sales mix of the proposed menu.

When this information is assembled, an estimate can be developed for the number of each item sold. This can then be compared to the manufacturer's stated capacity for each piece of equipment. From these data, the size and number of pieces to be purchased can be determined.

The third step involves planning the layout of the necessary equipment. The two most important factors affecting layout are product flow and traffic flow. *Product flow* encompasses all foodstuffs necessary to produce the menu from raw state to finished product and the paths they take through the restaurant. *Traffic flow* concerns itself with people and their patterns of movement with the product. The key goals in managing product and traffic flow are to have no backtracking and no crossovers. To develop good flows in a restaurant, start with the receiving function, the raw products, and trace them through the entire operation to the point of customer service and then on to the warewashing function. Next, consider the employee functions and trace those movements through the restaurant. Chances are, if product flow is smooth, traffic flow will be smooth as well. Although this holds true for the most part, there are exceptions; so check both flows to make sure. Mistakes made at this point of the planning stage could last over the life of the restaurant. Several hours of careful planning will help to prevent years of problems.

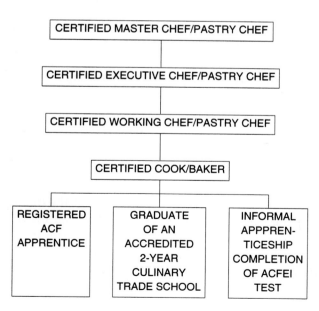

**CAREER LADDER
ACFEI CERTIFICATION**

CERTIFIED MASTER CHEF/PASTRY CHEF

CERTIFIED EXECUTIVE CHEF/PASTRY CHEF

CERTIFIED WORKING CHEF/PASTRY CHEF

CERTIFIED COOK/BAKER

REGISTERED ACF APPRENTICE

GRADUATE OF AN ACCREDITED 2-YEAR CULINARY TRADE SCHOOL

INFORMAL APPPRENTICESHIP COMPLETION OF ACFEI TEST

FIGURE 2.7.   A chart depicting the ACFEI certification process. (*Courtesy of the American Culinary Federation, St. Augustine, Florida*)

The type and amount of equipment as well as the proposed layout should all be done on scratch paper because numerous changes, additions, and deletions will be necessary prior to the final plan. As stated earlier, this is only an overview of what goes into the planning of a new restaurant. Well-qualified consultants, many of whom are members of the Foodservice Consultants Society International (FCSI), can assist in this stage of development.

One final word on equipment selection and layout: All decisions to this point have been based on the proposed menu. As the Scottish poet Robert Burns so aptly put it, "The best laid plans of mice and men oft times go astray." Check the plans to make sure that some flexibility is built in. No matter how much research goes into planning a new restaurant, there is no assurance that the proposed menu will sell. Changes will probably have to be made on at least a part of it. Allowances made on equipment selection for flexibility will offer the menu writer a wide latitude for changes. As previously discussed, any menu additions must be within the scope of equipment availability.

Staffing

The last factor to be considered is the staffing of the new operation. Prior to hiring new employees, it is important to develop job descriptions, and the menu should be an integral part of this procedure. Review the proposed menu to determine the skill levels needed to produce the items desired. These skill levels should then become an integral part of the job description. All too often a new restaurant hires overqualified (and overpaid) people to produce a menu when a person with less skill could do the job. Conversely, a worse scenario involves hiring unqualified employees to produce a menu for which they are totally untrained. The result? Dissatisfied customers, lost sales, and bankruptcy. For example, when the proposed skill level of a chef has been determined, use the various achievement levels of the American Culinary Federation to select an individual with the proper training to do a proficient job at the appropriate salary level. With careful hiring practices, employees are skillful at performing their jobs and more trainable; thus turnover is minimized.

CONCLUSION

Proper preparation is an integral part of menu planning. As the menu writer's knowledge of the operation increases, the potential for rewards to the business grow. Take all these factors into consideration: equipment, physical capabilities, traffic flow, staff skills, and theme. They all play an important role in producing a menu. By all means don't forget the discussion in Chapter 1—the customer, for whom all of this is done. If you do all this, the menu will reflect a smooth-running, profitable operation. It's just that simple.

QUESTIONS

1. Define and explain the importance of the following terms in relation to writing a menu:
   a) product availability
   b) cross utilization of existing products
   c) equipment capabilities
   d) station capabilities
   e) skill level
   f) product flow

2. Using the menu in Figure 2.8, list three new items you could add and:
   a) List all the ingredients necessary to produce the new items and determine whether they are available in your locale.
   b) List all the pieces of equipment necessary to produce these three items.
   c) Determine the skill level of production and service staff necessary to produce the items.
   d) Defend how those items fit the theme of the operation.

3. Assuming the attached menu is a proposal for a new restaurant:
   a) Describe demographically what type of customer you could expect.
   b) Describe the decor of the establishment.
   c) List the major equipment needed to produce the menu.

4. Investigate several food service operations in your area. Are some stations "swamped" during peak times? Determine whether the problem lies with the menu or with the personnel. As the manager of that unit, what would you do to correct the situation?

5. Look through the local yellow pages and generate a list of theme restaurants. Pick one restaurant and go look at the menu. Does it meet your expectations by variety and the demographics of the people dining at the establishment? What would you change and why?

6. List staff and skill issues you believe are unique to your region of the country. What concerns will this create in your menu design for a local operation?

FIRST COURSES

GOAT CHEESE TERRINE
spiced pepper sauce & balsamic glaze ... seven

CHILLED SELECT OYSTERS
smoked red pepper mignonette ... market price

SOUP
saffron, sweet onion and penn cove mussels ... seven

COLD SMOKED AHI TUNA
cucumber wasabi vinaigrette & daikon sprouts ... nine

5-SPICED OYSTERS
banana curry & roasted apple ... eight

THE ULTIMATE SEAFOOD SAMPLER
a trio of hot oysters, gravlax & smoked tuna ... fourteen

COFFEE & ORANGE-DUSTED QUAIL
bittersweet chocolate sauce & bok choy ... ten

TEQUILA-CURED GRAVLAX
chickpea fritter, marinated cukes & tomato ... nine

PAN-SEARED HUDSON VALLEY FOIE GRAS
spiced pear puree & fresh mango ... fourteen

SEARED SCALLOPS
tomato, grilled fennel & citrus broth ... eleven

SALADS

CARAMELIZED PEAR & HAZELNUTS
field greens & cider vinaigrette ... six

ROASTED BEET & SHALLOT VINAIGRETTE
tossed with field lettuces ... six

MEDITERRANEAN CAESAR
smoked mussels & clams ... eight

FRESH SPINACH
warm brown butter & goat cheese vinaigrette ... seven

DUNGENESS CRAB & FENNEL
with citrus & tarragon ... nine

A gratuity of 17% will be added to parties of 6 or more

Monique Andrée Barbeau - Executive Chef
William Belickis - Chef de Cuisine

FIGURE 2.8.   *(Menu courtesy of Fuller's Restaurant, Seattle Sheraton Hotel and Towers, Seattle, Washington)*

ENTRÉES

SAFFRON & SUMAC-DUSTED DEMI RACK OF LAMB
barley & black-eyed peas, port & mango
twenty-eight

PAN-SEARED SALMON
black olive basil jus & potato fennel casserole
nineteen

SEASONAL FISH
artichoke chervil broth, fingerling potatoes & asparagus
twenty-one

GRILLED OREGON RABBIT
herb spaetzle, roasted carrots & madeira
eighteen

GRILLED RARE AHI TUNA
kimchee salad & pickled vegetables
twenty-two

FULLERS' SIGNATURE VEGETARIAN ENTREE
eighteen

CERVENA VENISON
sage gnocchi & red onion jam
twenty-three

EAST COAST SCALLOPS
english pea jus & ginger risotto
twenty-two

STILTON & GRILLED ENDIVE STUFFED BEEF TENDERLOIN
mushrooms & truffle oil
thirty

ROASTED SONOMA SQUAB
truffled israeli cous cous, pearl onions & wild mushrooms
twenty-four

SIDES

Truffled Israeli Cous Cous
Ginger Risotto
Potato Fennel Casserole
Honey-glazed Carrots
Grilled Fennel
three

The chef will prepare a tasting menu for your table for forty-eight dollars
per person
Please ask your server for this evening's courses

It is our pleasure to meet your special requirements

FIGURE 2.8. *(Continued)*

CHAPTER THREE

Costs

OBJECTIVES   By the completion of this chapter, the reader should be able to:

- Develop a cost card from a standardized recipe, including a conversion of invoice costs into recipe costs.
- Describe the difference between AP (as purchased) and EP (edible portion).
- Cost a complete meal.
- Calculate the cost of a salad bar or an "all you can eat" buffet.

IMPORTANT TERMS

Standardized recipe	EP (edible portion)
AP (as purchased)	Q factor
Conversions	Premix
Cost card	Postmix

INTRODUCTION

One of the most important functions of menu planning is charging the correct amount of money for items listed on the menu. Failure to do so results in a selling price that is too high or too low. Both of these situations are bad for the restaurant. In order to determine the correct selling price, it is imperative that the exact costs be known because selling prices are figured, to a large extent, on food cost. This chapter explores how to figure costs for standardized recipes, meats and shrinkage, beverages, sandwiches, complete meals, buffets, and salad bars. A word of caution is in order here. Ingredient costs vary from area to area and, in many cases, can change from day to day. Do not be concerned about the costs used in the examples as many of them will be obsolete by the time you read this. Rather, master the concepts. They do not change: costs do.

STANDARDIZED RECIPES AND COST CARDS

To place into effect a solid control system in any restaurant, standardized recipes are a necessity. They control the quantity and quality of ingredients used to prepare a particular dish, as well as control the portions that are to be served. They are also a necessary tool in figuring the costs. Simply having standardized recipes in an operation is not enough; it is imperative that everyone follow them. Any deviation from the standardized recipe results not only in poor quality, but in inaccurate costs being figured for that item and, consequently, an incorrect selling price.

AP and EP

There are two methods used to write standardized recipes. They are the *AP* method, which means "as purchased" and the *EP* method, which stands for "edible portion." There is a large difference between the two methods which affects both the quality of the recipe and the costs.

In the AP method, all ingredient quantities are listed on the standardized recipes in the form in which they are purchased. For example, if a recipe were to call for "10 pounds of onions, diced," the cook would weigh the 10 pounds of onions with their skins on (as purchased), then peel the onions, dice them, and add them to the recipe. In costing the recipe, the invoice cost of 10 pounds of onions would be used.

In the EP method, all ingredient quantities are listed using the edible portion only of that particular ingredient. For example, "10 pounds of diced onions." In this case the onions would be peeled, diced, then weighed, and added to the recipe. To obtain a cost in this instance, the original weight of the product would have to be used. Thus, if we started with 11 pounds of onions, to obtain 10 pounds EP of diced, we would use the 11-pound figure to determine our costs.

Unfortunately, most recipes do not come with the headings AP or EP. It is up to management to decide how to cost them appropriately. Normally there are clues in the directions of the recipes themselves. For example, the onion illustration (10 pounds of onions diced vs. 10 pounds of diced onions) gives a clue. Take 20 pounds of ground chuck and then brown would be AP; 20 pounds of browned ground chuck would be EP. To further confuse the issue, quite often one recipe has both AP and EP directions mixed within it; one ingredient is listed AP and the next ingredient, EP.

FIGURE 3.1. AP-EP conversion chart. Weight of edible portion from one pound as purchased.

	lb		lb
Apples	0.78	Lettuce, head	0.76
Asparagus	0.53	Lettuce, leaf	0.66
Avocado	0.67	Lettuce, romaine	0.64
Bananas	0.65	Mangoes	0.69
Beans, green or wax	0.88	Mushrooms	0.98
Beans, lima	0.44	Nectarines	0.91
Beets	0.77	Okra	0.87
Blueberries	0.96	Onions, mature	0.88
Broccoli	0.81	Orange, sections	0.40
Brussels sprouts	0.76	Parsnips	0.83
Cabbage, green	0.87	Peaches	0.76
Cabbage, red	0.64	Pears, served pared	0.78
Cantaloupe, served		Peas, green	0.38
without rind	0.52	Peppers, green	0.80
Carrots	0.70	Pineapple	0.54
Cauliflower	0.62	Plums	0.94
Celery	0.83	Potatoes, sweet	0.80
Chard, Swiss	0.92	Potatoes, white	0.81
Cherries, pitted	0.87	Radishes, without tops	0.94
Chicory,	0.89	Rhubarb, without leaves	0.86
Collards, leaves	0.57	Rutabagas	0.85
Collards, leaves		Spinach, partly trimmed	0.88
and stems	0.74	Squash, acorn	0.87
Cranberries	0.95	Squash, butternut	0.84
Cucumber, pared	0.84	Squash, Hubbard	0.64
Eggplant	0.81	Squash, summer	0.95
Endive, escarole	0.78	Squash, zucchini	0.94
Grapefruit, sections	0.52	Strawberries	0.88
Grapes, seedless	0.97	Tomatoes	0.99
Honeydew melon,		Turnips, without tops	0.79
served without rind	0.46	Watermelon	0.57
Kale	0.67		

Source: Adapted from Food Buying, Guide for School Food Service, U.S. Dept. Agriculture, Washington, D.C., 1980.

Divide the weight of EP in the recipe by the factor given above. For example: if the recipe calls for 15 pounds EP of head lettuce, 15 pounds EP ÷ .76 = 19.7 or 20 pounds to purchase.

The EP method, in spite of being more time consuming for figuring costs, is the preferred method because it is more exact. If you gave several cooks an onion to peel, some would remove the skin only and some would remove the skin along with one or two layers of the onion. Thus while everyone started out with the same amount, the yield in each case would be different.

To simplify matters, for those operations using the EP method, conversion charts are available to assist in determining costs. These charts work well in most cases. However, if a restaurant uses an inordinate amount of a certain ingredient, yield tests should be conducted periodically to ascertain whether the correct costs are being maintained.

Cost Cards

To figure costs based on a standardized recipe, it is advisable that a cost card be used. To make the entire cost control system effective, there should be a cost card for every multiple-ingredient item listed on the menu. The object of cost cards is to get an accurate cost per portion so that the proper selling price can be determined.

To properly fill out a cost card and figure standardized costs, follow these steps:

1. Copy the ingredients used for a particular dish from the standardized recipe to the cost card.
2. List the amount and unit used for each ingredient in the appropriate column.
3. From the invoice(s), list the cost of each ingredient as well as the unit listed on the invoice. (Notice that the unit called for in the recipe is quite often different from the unit listed on the invoice. For example, a recipe unit could be in pints, although that particular item was purchased in gallons.)
4. Break the invoice unit down to the same unit for the recipe in the recipe column and figure the cost per recipe unit. If the recipe is AP, use the invoice cost. If the recipe is written EP, use the cost after trim.
5. In the last column, figure the extended cost by multiplying the number of units needed for the recipe times the recipe cost per unit.
6. Add together the cost of all ingredients in the extension column.
7. Divide the total cost by the number of portions the recipe will produce to get the cost per portion.

Although this may seem complicated and confusing at first glance, in reality it is quite simple. For example, developing a cost card for Salad Del Monte would be as shown in Figures 3.3 and 3.4.

FIGURE 3.2. Portion cost card.

NAME OF RECIPE_____ REFERENCE_____

DATE_____ NUMBER OF PORTIONS_____ COST PER PORTION_____

RECIPE		INGREDIENTS	INVOICE		RECIPE		EXTENSION	
AMT	UNIT		COST	UNIT	COST	UNIT		
						TOTAL		

After listing the ingredients, amounts of ingredients, and invoice costs and units, the next step is to break the costs down into the base unit used in the recipe. The first ingredient, frozen asparagus, costs $86.91 for a case of 12 2½-pound boxes. Therefore, we need to determine the cost of asparagus per pound. To do this, multiply the 12 boxes times 2½ pounds per box to get 30 pounds per case. Next, divide the cost per case ($86.91) by the 30 pounds to get the cost per pound ($2.897). The cost per pound, $2.897, is then multiplied by the amount of asparagus called for in the

Salad Del Monte

YIELD: 50 portions	EACH PORTION: 3 oz. asparagus	
Ingredients	*Quantity*	*Method*
Asparagus, cooked, drained, chilled	10 lb.	1. Arrange asparagus on crisp lettuce or lettuce cups.
Lettuce, washed and trimmed	4 heads	2. Decorate with thin strips of pimento placed diagonally across asparagus.
Pimentoes	7 oz.	
Hard-cooked eggs, chopped	14	3. Sprinkle with chopped, hard-cooked eggs mixed with fresh chopped parsley.
Parsley, chopped	1 oz.	4. Serve with French dressing.
French dressing	1¼ qt.	

FIGURE 3.3. Recipe for Salad del Monte from *The Professional Chef* by Folsom, Copyright 1974 by CBI, reprinted by permission of Van Nostrand Reinhold.

recipe (10 pounds) to get the total cost of that ingredient, $28.97. This figure is then put in the extension column.

This process is repeated for each ingredient on the cost card. For example:

Lettuce—24 heads to the case at a cost of $19.25 per case. Base unit—head. $19.25 divided by 24 equals $.80 per head. Four heads of lettuce are needed. $.80 times 4 equals $3.20 which represents the total cost of lettuce for this recipe. $1.44 goes in the extension column.

Pimento—24 14-ounce cans to the case. Base unit—ounce. Twenty-four cans times 14 ounces equals 336 ounces per case. Cost per case equals $32.89 divided by 336 ounces equals $.098 per ounce times 7 ounces called for in the recipe equals a total cost of $.686 for pimento.

Eggs—$.84 per dozen. Base unit—each. Cost per dozen, $.84, divided by 12 equals $.07 per egg times 14 eggs called for in the recipe equals $.98 total cost of eggs.

Parsley—1 ounce. This is a negligible cost and will be assigned a total cost of $.10. This method is employed to avoid the time-consuming task of breaking down a price when the result of that price would not substantially affect the total cost of that recipe. This method can also be utilized when the recipe refers to such items as salt and pepper to taste.

French dressing—4 one-gallon jars to the case. Base unit—quart. Four quarts to the gallon times four gallons equals $33.90 divided by 16 quarts equals $2.118 cost per quart times 1.25 (1¼ quarts called for in the recipe) equals $2.64 total cost for the French dressing. Another approach to use on the French dressing would be to break the cost into ounces. To do this, first get the cost per gallon, $33.90, divided by 4 (4 gallons to the case) which equals $8.475. Next, divide $8.475 by 128 (number of ounces in a gallon) which equals $.066 per ounce. There are 32 ounces in a quart, so multiply

FIGURE 3.4. Portion cost card.

NAME OF RECIPE _Salad Del Monte_   REFERENCE _Pro Chef Pg. 233_

DATE _Jan 1, 1998_   NUMBER OF PORTIONS _50_   COST PER PORTION _$0.732_

RECIPE		INGREDIENTS	INVOICE		RECIPE		EXTENSION	
AMT	UNIT		COST	UNIT	COST	UNIT		
10	Lb.	Frozen Asparagus	$86.91	12/2.5 Lb.	$2.897	Lb.	$28	970
4	Heads	Lettuce	19.25	24 Heads	0.80	Head	3	200
7	Oz.	Pimento	32.89	24/14 oz.	0.98	Oz.		686
14	Ea.	Eggs	.84	Dozen	0.07	Egg		980
1	Oz.	Parsley	.10	Recipe				100
1.25	Qt.	French Dressing	33.90	4 Gal.	0.66	Oz.	2	650
							TOTAL	$36 586

32 times 1.25 (1¼ quarts called for in the recipe) which equals 40 ounces needed for the recipe. Then multiply 40 times $.066 (cost per ounce) to get the total cost of French dressing of $2.650.

When the costs for each ingredient are placed in the extension column, the next step is to add these costs which gives us a total cost to produce this recipe of $36.586. Finally, the total cost of $36.586 is divided by the number of portions (50) that the recipe will produce, which gives us a cost of $0.732 per portion. For most

FIGURE 3.5. Equivalent measurement chart.

Fluid

3 teaspoons	= 1 tablespoon	= 1/2 ounce	
4 tablespoons	= 1/4 cup	= 2 ounces	
5 1/3 tablespoons	= 1/3 cup	= 2.8 ounces	
8 tablespoons	= 1/2 cup	= 4 ounces	
11 tablespoons	= 2/3 cups	= 5.4 ounces	
16 tablespoons	= 1 cup	= 8 ounces	
2 cups	= 1 pint	= 16 ounces	
2 pints	= 4 cups	= 1 quart	= 32 ounces
4 pints	= 2 quarts	= 1/2 gallon	= 64 ounces
4 quarts	= 16 cups	= 1 gallon	= 128 ounces

Dry

8 oz.	= 1/2 lb.	
16 oz.	= 1 lb.	
8 quarts	= 32 cups	= 1 peck
4 pecks	= 1 bushel	

Note: A general rule of thumb in commercial cooking is that solid ingredients are weighed where applicable while liquid ingredients are measured by volume.

Source: Food Buying, Guide for School Foodservice, U.S. Dept. of Agriculture, Washington, D.C. 1980

students the most complicated part of figuring recipe cost cards is the conversion of units from the invoice to the base recipe unit.

This is a necessary skill in the food service industry, not only in costing, but in converting recipes into smaller or larger quantities. The more one works with conversion, the easier it becomes. Eventually, the conversions are committed to memory and become second nature to the astute manager or executive chef.

COSTING MEAT ITEMS

Some items on the menu do not require cost cards. Listings such as roasts, steaks, or chops—in other words, single items listed—are figured individually. In the case of meats, in particular, the shrinkage and trim must be taken into account.

A Case in Point. Imagine my surprise on a recent consulting job, when confronting a restaurant owner who was losing money. "You're not getting enough for your prime rib," I stated. "Oh, yes," was the reply. "It costs me $3.45 per pound, which is $.22 per ounce, with a 10-ounce portion costing $2.20. I sell it for $6.95. That's a 31-percent food cost." What he neglected to take into account was the fact that part of the fat cover was trimmed off after roasting, that the rib bones were removed, and that the menu shrinks when it is roasted. After taking these facts into consideration, I pointed out that the prime rib was costing him $4.93 a pound, $.31 an ounce, and $3.10 a portion, resulting in a food cost of 44 percent. In other words, he was costing out the prime rib on AP (as purchased) price rather than on an EP (edible portion) price. A very critical mistake!

To figure the cost to serve on a roast follow these steps:

1. Determine the total cost of the roast as purchased (price per pound times the number of pounds equals the total cost AP).

FIGURE 3.6.   Cooked yields of meat.

Type of Meat	Net Servable Cooked Yield
Beef	
Roast sirloin (boneless)	70%
Pot roast	60%
Chopped beef	75%
Short ribs (bone in)	60%
Corned beef (brisket)	60%
Beef liver	75–90%
Stew (boneless)	75%
Swiss steak	70%
Tenderloin steak	90%
Sirloin steak (boneless strip)	75%
Sirloin steak (bone in strip)	80%
Minute steak (boneless butt)	80%
Boneless top and bottom round roast	70%
Knuckle butt roast	65%
Shoulder clod roast	70%
Oven-prepared beef rib	50%
Chef's delight beef rib	60%
Boneless round	60%
Fresh bone in beef brisket	45%
Hotel special rib steak roll	75%
Beef round, rump and shank off	50%
Lamb	
Roast leg	45%
Roast loin	40%
Lamb stew (boneless)	75%
Veal	
Veal cutlet (boneless)	80%
Calf's liver	75%
Roast leg	50%
Roast loin	50%
Veal loin chop (bone in)	75%
Veal rib chop (bone in)	75%
Pork	
Breaded tenderloin	100%
Sausage patties	55%
Breaded pork chop (boneless)	90%
Pork chops (bone in)	80%
Spareribs	65%
Roast pork loin	50%
Ham steak (bone in)	80%
Baked ham (bone in)	65%
Roast fresh ham	50%
Poultry	
Fried chicken, 2 lbs.	100%
Turkey, 18 lbs./up	40%

All yields are general averages based on many hundreds of tests. They allow for waste in trimming the meat, cooking, shrinkage, and small-end waste. Determination of exact shrinkage for each meat item cooked is advisable.

Source: Food Buying Guide for School Foodservice, U.S. Dept. of Agriculture, Washington, D.C. 1980.

2. After roasting and trimming (bones, fat, silverskin, etc.), weigh the roast. The result is the saleable weight or EP (edible portion).

3. Divide the total cost as purchased by the saleable weight. The result is the cost per pound to serve.

4. Divide the cost per pound to serve by 16 (number of ounces in a pound). The result is the cost per ounce to serve.

5. Multiply the cost per ounce to serve times the standard portion size. The result is the cost per serving.

To illustrate this further, take an example of a barbecue restaurant that serves brisket. Assume they paid $1.80 a pound and received 75 pounds. The total cost as purchased of these briskets would be $135 (step 1). The briskets were then smoked in the pit and removed when done, and the excess fat trimmed from them. At this point assume they weighed 38 pounds (step 2). The cost to serve the briskets would then be $3.55 a pound (step 3) or $.22 an ounce (step 4). Assuming a 4-ounce standard portion is served, the cost per serving would be $.88 (step 5). As shown in the example, this formula can work for several roasts of the same kind. It is just as effective on one.

Although many charts are available for calculating cooking loss and trim, each restaurant should conduct their own tests, particularly on items that have a high volume in their operation. The charts are fine for rule-of-thumb planning, but oven temperature, personnel, and even the same cuts of meat vary, giving a cost different from that in the charts. The results could be disastrous when the primary income is dependent on the accurate cost of an item.

The shrink and loss test would not be used on all meat items on the menu. Items such as steaks and chops are all listed on the menu as precooked weight. Thus, if you were to purchase a pre-portioned 14-ounce strip steak, the cost would be the same as the invoiced cost. Assume that the strip steak costs $3.50 a pound; it would be $3.50 divided by 16 or $.22 an ounce times 14 ounces, for a cost of $3.08 for that steak.

On the other hand, if an operation were to cut its own steaks, then the trim loss would have to be taken into account. For example, a beef tenderloin is purchased for the purpose of serving filet mignon. Assume the tenderloin weighs 7 pounds at a cost of $4.50 per pound for a total cost of $31.50. The person cutting the steaks would first trim off all the fat and the connective tissue (silver), then weigh the tenderloin again. The result is the saleable weight. Assume the saleable weight is 5 pounds. The cost to serve would then be $6.30 a pound or $.394 an ounce (total cost divided by saleable weight). The cost per oz. would then be multiplied by the standard portion size for filet mignon. Assuming a 10-ounce portion, the cost would be $3.94.

Since filet mignon comes only from the center portion of the tenderloin, the ends (tips) would have to be used on another menu item such as a beef brochette. That item would have the same cost of $6.30 per pound. Some industry people use a different method to determine the cost of tips based on percentage of value of the entire carcass. This system can get quite complicated. The point is that some dollar value needs to be assigned to the ends. Do not make the mistake that many restaurants make when they say, "The scraps do not cost anything. I'm making 100 percent profit on them." Wrong!

COFFEE COST

In addition to knowing how to determine the cost of recipes and meats, it is also important to know the methods of costing out beverages, as they have the highest markup of any item on the menu. Start with coffee, which accounts for the highest percentage of beverage sales in most restaurants.

1. Multiply the number of gallons of water (usually 2½ gallons per pound of coffee) times 128 (number of ounces per gallon) to get total ounces.
2. Multiply total ounces by 10% (water absorbed by the coffee grounds).
3. Subtract the loss from total ounces to get the net yield per urn of coffee.
4. Divide the net yield by the number of ounces served per cup to get the number of cups per pound. NOTE: If the brewing ratio and cup size do not change, then this number stays the same and you can start the formula with step 5.
5. Divide the cost per pound by the number of cups per pound. The result is the cost of coffee per cup.
6. Take the cost of cream and sugar per serving and divide by 2 (assuming 50 percent of the customers use cream and sugar).
7. Add the cream and sugar cost to the cost of the coffee per cup. The result is the net cost per cup to serve.
8. Multiply the net cost per cup times the average number of refills per customer plus the original cup. (If you charge per cup with no refill, then ignore this step.)

Different sections of the country brew coffee in varying strengths so the brew ratio (step 1) can change. If the brewing ratio is different in your area, then substitute the correct ratio. Assuming that the brewing ratio is 3 to 1, that is 3 gallons of water to 1 pound of coffee, that the coffee costs $2.25 per pound, and that a 6-ounce cup is served, the cost per cup is shown in Figure 3.7.

FIGURE 3.7.   Coffee cost problem.

Brew ratio—3:1		Cream $1.80/qt. (1 oz. serving)
Coffee cost—$2.25/lb.		Sugar .35/lb. (1/2 oz. serving)
Serving size—6 oz.		Refills—one

Step 1
$$
\begin{array}{rl}
128 & \text{(oz. in gal.)}\\
\times\ \ 3 & \text{(brew ratio)}\\
\hline
384 & \text{(total oz.)}
\end{array}
$$

Step 2
$$
\begin{array}{rl}
384 & \text{(total oz.)}\\
\times\ .10 & \text{(absorption loss)}\\
\hline
38.4 & \text{(loss)}
\end{array}
$$

Step 3
$$
\begin{array}{rl}
384.0 & \text{(step 1)}\\
-\ 38.4 & \text{(step 2)}\\
\hline
345.6 & \text{(net volume)}
\end{array}
$$

Step 4

$$57.6 \text{ (cups per 1 lb.)}$$
$$6 \text{ (oz. serving)} \overline{)\,345.6}\ \text{(net volume)}$$

Step 5

$$\$\ .039 \text{ (cost per cup)}$$
$$57.6 \text{ (cups per lb.)} \overline{)\,\$2.25}\ \text{(cost per lb.)}$$

Step 6

$$.056 \text{ cream}$$
$$32 \text{ oz./qt.} \overline{)\,\$1.80/qt. \text{ cream}}$$

$$.011 \text{ sugar}$$
$$32 \text{ (1/2 oz./lb.)} \overline{)\,0.35/lb. \text{ sugar}}$$

$$
\begin{array}{l}
.056 \text{ cream}\\
\underline{.011} \text{ sugar}\\
.067 \text{ total}
\end{array}
$$

$$.034 \text{ cost}$$
$$(50\% \text{ usage}) \ 2 \overline{)\,.067}$$

Step 7
$$
\begin{array}{l}
\$.039 \text{ coffee}\\
\underline{.034} \text{ c/s}\\
\$.073
\end{array}
$$

Step 8
$$
\begin{array}{rl}
\text{original cup} & 1\\
\text{refill} & \underline{+\ 1}\\
& 2
\end{array}
$$

$$
\begin{array}{l}
\$.073\\
\underline{\times\ \ 2}\\
\$.146 \text{ net cost}
\end{array}
$$

CARBONATED BEVERAGES

In investigating carbonated beverages, there are two types to consider—premix and postmix. *Premix* is that type in which the syrup and carbonated water are mixed at the factory in 5-gallon cans or cartons. *Postmix* is that type for which the syrup and carbonated water are mixed on location. The syrup is delivered in 5-gallon tanks or cartons. This is mixed with water that has passed through the carbonator to give it its effervescence, and is then mixed in the mixing chamber at the point of service. Postmix is less expensive than premix and thus has a lower cost and a higher gross profit. However, postmix needs water, electricity, and a drain running to the unit and requires a larger investment in equipment. For these reasons some operations opt for the premix even though the profit margin is lower.

In addition to the aforementioned differences, the costs of premix and postmix are also figured differently. Premix is relatively simple to figure since the product is ready to serve as purchased. When costing cold beverages, if the restaurant has an ice machine, the cost of ice is normally not figured in, as it is usually so negligible that it does not have an impact. If, however, an operation is purchasing ice from a vendor, then its cost would be great enough to be added to the beverage cost. Paper supplies, such as cups or straws, are, in most operations, considered a supply cost and therefore are not figured in food cost. Some operations, however, consider these items to be a part of the product cost and in these instances their cost would be added in. Check with your company's operations manual to ascertain whether these costs should be included. Since the majority of firms do not consider ice and paper supplies a cost of goods, we do not include them in the examples. If a garnish such as a lemon or lime wedge is used, it is by all means added to the cost.

Premix Carbonated Beverages

1. Multiply 128 (the number of ounces in a gallon) times 5 (the number of gallons in a premix tank/box) to get 640 ounces (in a 5-gallon tank/box).

2. Divide the cost of the tank/box by 640 to get the cost per ounce.

3. Subtract the amount of ice displacement from the total ounces of the serving container to get net ounces of product served.

4. Multiply net ounces of product served by the cost per ounce to get net cost.

FIGURE 3.8. Premix cost example.

Cost per 5 gal. tank—$20.00
Serving size—16 oz.
Ice displacement—8 oz.
Ice cost—N/A

Step 1

$$\begin{array}{r} 128 \quad \text{oz. in gal.} \\ \times \quad 5 \quad \text{gal. tank} \\ \hline 640 \quad \text{oz. in tank} \end{array}$$

Step 2

$$640 \text{ oz. in tank } \overline{\smash{)}\,\$20.00} \quad \begin{array}{l} .031 \text{ cost per oz.} \\ \text{cost per tank} \end{array}$$

Step 3

$$\begin{array}{r} 16 \quad \text{oz. serving size} \\ - \quad 8 \quad \text{oz. ice displacement} \\ \hline 8 \quad \text{oz. of product served} \end{array}$$

Step 4

$$\begin{array}{r} .031 \quad \text{cost per oz.} \\ \times \quad 8 \quad \text{oz. of product served} \\ \hline .248 \quad \text{net cost} \end{array}$$

Postmix Carbonated Beverages

To figure the cost of postmix, utilize the following formula. This formula assumes mixing the water and syrup at a 5-to-1 ratio, that is, 5 parts water to 1 part syrup. If a different ratio is used, the formula should be changed accordingly.

1. Multiply 5 gallons of water by 5 gallons of syrup to get 25 gallons of water (5-to-1 ratio).
2. Add the 5 gallons of syrup to the 25 gallons of water to get a 30-gallon yield per 5-gallon tank/box of syrup.
3. Multiply 30 gallons of product by 128 (number of ounces per gallon) to get total ounces of product per syrup tank/box (3,840). NOTE: If the ratio does not change, then this number does not change and you can start the formula with step 4.
4. Divide the cost per tank/box of syrup by 3,840 to get the cost per ounce of product.
5. Subtract the amount of ice displacement from the size of the serving container to get the amount of product served.

FIGURE 3.9.   Postmix cost example.

Cost per 5 gal. tank syrup $18.75
Serving size—16 oz.
Ice displacement—8 oz.
Ice cost—N/A
Water cost—N/A
Water-to-syrup ratio   5:1
Step 1

$$
\begin{array}{rl}
5 & \text{gal. water} \\
\times\ 5 & \text{gal. syrup} \\
\hline
25 & \text{gal. water}
\end{array}
$$

Step 2

$$
\begin{array}{rl}
25 & \text{gal. water} \\
+\ 5 & \text{gal. syrup} \\
\hline
30 & \text{gal. product}
\end{array}
$$

Step 3

$$
\begin{array}{rl}
30 & \text{gal. product} \\
\times\ 128 & \text{oz. per gal.} \\
\hline
3,840 & \text{oz. of product}
\end{array}
$$

Step 4

$$
\overset{\$0.005 \text{ cost per oz.}}{3{,}840 \text{ oz. of product} \,\big)\, \underline{18.75 \text{ cost of 5 gal. syrup}}}
$$

Step 5

$$
\begin{array}{rl}
16 & \text{oz. serving container} \\
-\ 8 & \text{oz. ice displacement} \\
\hline
8 & \text{oz. of product served}
\end{array}
$$

Step 6

$$
\begin{array}{rl}
.005 & \text{cost per oz. of product} \\
\times\ 8 & \text{oz. of product served} \\
\hline
\$0.040 & \text{net cost}
\end{array}
$$

6. Multiply the amount of product served by the cost per ounce of product to get total cost.

To figure the cost of other beverages which require the addition of water, such as frozen orange juice concentrate, lemonade, or powdered punches, simply follow the formula for postmix carbonated beverages. Be careful in step 1 as these products all have varying water-to-syrup (or base) ratios.

Ready-to-serve beverages, such as milk or canned juices, are relatively easy to figure. Simply divide the cost per container by the number of ounces per container and multiply this figure (cost per ounce) by the number of ounces served. Don't forget to subtract ice displacement (if applicable) from the size of the serving container.

SINGLE SERVICE ITEMS

The next area of costing to consider is single service items. Previous discussion concerning cost cards centered around batch-cooked items that have multiple yields such as 25, 50, or more portions. Single service items yield one portion and have multiple ingredients in their makeup. These include such items as sandwiches or appetizers. One of the more important considerations in this segment is remembering to include low-cost items such as condiments. For example, when a hamburger is costed out, all too often the mustard, ketchup, and pickle are overlooked because of their low cost. Consider, for a moment, the consequences of this omission. Assume the condiments cost $.02 and the restaurant is working on a 30-percent food cost. The omission of $.02 cost would result in a selling price $.06 lower than what it should be. (Mark-up concepts are explained in the next chapter.) If this restaurant were to sell 100 hamburgers a day, the lost income would come to $6.00; if it were open 350 days a year, lost income of $2,100 could be expected. All over a lousy $.02 omission! Is it any wonder that knowing the *exact* cost is imperative in running a successful restaurant?

To illustrate the cost of a sandwich, take the example of a bacon, lettuce, and tomato (BLT).

Bacon—The 18/22 refers to 18 to 22 slices per pound. Where a range is given on an invoice price, it is advisable to use a worst case scenario. This gives the restaurant some protection and allows for a margin of error. Therefore, figure only 18 slices per pound for cost even though the yield will probably be more like 20. In case it is 18, the house is covered. Divide the cost per pound by 18 to get the cost per slice.

FIGURE 3.10.   Portion cost card.

NAME OF RECIPE   Bacon, Lettuce, & Tomato   REFERENCE   House File #3-72

DATE   7/28/97   NUMBER OF PORTIONS   1   COST PER PORTION $0.542

RECIPE		INGREDIENTS	INVOICE		RECIPE		EXTENSION
AMT	UNIT		COST	UNIT	COST	UNIT	
3	Slices	Bacon (18/22)	$16.35	15 Lb.	.061	Slice	183
2	Leaves	Lettuce	6.00	12 Heads	.025	Leaf	050
3	Slices	Tomato	18.00	5×6 Lug	.030	Slice	090
2	Oz.	Mayonnaise	20.00	4/1 Gal.	.039	Oz.	078
2	Slices	Bread	.95	Loaf	.048	Slice	096
1	Spear	Pickle (85–105 Count)	23.00	6/10	.045	Spear	045
						TOTAL	542

Lettuce—A wide variation in cost can be experienced in produce like lettuce. Heads can either be tight and heavy or loose and light. Price per case also varies greatly depending on the season. Again, use a worst case scenario with the highest price expected at the lowest yield.

Tomato—Another highly seasonal item, tomatoes, must be costed for a period when supplies are low and prices high. Tight purchasing specifications help to determine yield. Always purchase the same size (e.g., 6 by 6 or 5 by 6, etc.). The numbers refer to the number of tomatoes in a layer. Thus, 5 by 6 would yield 30 tomatoes and 6 by 6 would yield 36 tomatoes. The smaller the numbers are, the larger the tomatoes will be. On the accompanying cost card, a 5-by-6 size tomato was used with a yield of 10 slices per tomato. Therefore, the pricing would be 5 times 6, which equals 30 tomatoes to the layer times 2 layers to the lug, which gives 60 tomatoes times 10 slices per tomato, or 600 slices to the lug. Divide the cost per lug by 600 to obtain the cost per slice.

Mayonnaise—Take the cost per gallon divided by 128 (ounces per gallon) to get cost per ounce times the 2 ounces needed.

Toast—Slices per loaf vary by the weight of the loaf and the thickness of the slice. In the example, 20 slices per loaf were used, divided by the cost per loaf to obtain the cost per slice which is multiplied by the two slices needed.

Garnish (Pickle spear)—The count for this item is given in a range and is usually listed on the can. In this example, the count is 85–105. Again, using the worst case scenario, simply divide the count (85) by the cost per can.

Speaking of garnish, I recently saw a large sign in a kitchen admonishing the wait staff, "Don't forget the garnish." While reviewing the cost structure of this particular restaurant, I questioned the owner as to how much he had allowed for garnish cost. "I don't include it," he replied. (Yes, the same one who messed up on the prime rib.) Don't forget the garnish!

COMPLETE MEALS

The next area of planning is finding the cost of a complete meal. There are four steps to this process. The first step is to get a total cost of accompanying items that would be the same on all meals served. Let's assume that above the entrees, the following listing occurred. "All entrees served with a crisp garden salad with your choice of dressing; baked potato or fresh vegetable, and warm cinnamon rolls with butter." The first step, therefore, is to get a total cost of all these items. To do this, cost cards need to be developed for all of the accompanying items.

As was previously illustrated, the worst case scenario should be used. In the case of the garden salad, the highest-cost dressing (bleu cheese) would be used. Do not list on the menu "Bleu cheese dressing 25¢ extra"—tacky! tacky! Rather include it in the cost and ultimately the selling price. If the customer orders French dressing more profit will be made. If bleu cheese dressing is ordered, profit will be maintained. The same principle applies to the vegetable: use baked potato with butter and sour cream for cost. Once the cost

FIGURE 3.11. Portion cost card.

NAME OF RECIPE Dinner Salad   REFERENCE House File #8-3

DATE 7/28/97   NUMBER OF PORTIONS 50   COST PER PORTION $0.355

RECIPE		INGREDIENTS	INVOICE		RECIPE		EXTENSION	
AMT	UNIT		COST	UNIT	COST	UNIT		
5	Heads	Iceburg Lettuce	$11.75	Cs.-24 Hds.	.490	Head	2	450
6	Ea. AP	Leaf Lettuce	9.50	Cs.-12 Ea.	.791	Ea.	4	746
1	Lb. AP	Cucumbers	24.00	50 Lb.	.480	Lb.		480
1	Lb. AP	Radishes	4.00	5 Lb.	1.25	Lb.	1	250
1	Lb. AP	Carrots	9.85	25 Lb.	.394	Lb.		394
5	Ea.	Tomatoes	18.00	5×6 Lug	.300	Ea.	1	500
		Total Salad Cost					10	820
		Cost Per Portion (50 Portions)						216
		Bleu Cheese Dressing (2 oz. Portions)						139
						TOTAL		355

cards are figured, the cost of the accompanying items, using the most expensive, are totaled and this number is used in figuring the total cost of the accompanying items.

The second step in the process is to figure the cost of the entree itself. In the case of multiple-ingredient single service listings or batch-cooked items, cost cards are used. For single-ingredient listings such as steaks or chops, the cost per item is used.

The third step is to figure any additional costs for each listing, such as an accompanying side dish or special garnish. For example,

FIGURE 3.12. Portion cost card.

NAME OF RECIPE Baked Potato _____ REFERENCE House File #10-22 _____

DATE 7/28/97 _____ NUMBER OF PORTIONS 50 _____ COST PER PORTION $0.516 _____

RECIPE		INGREDIENTS	INVOICE		RECIPE		EXTENSION	
AMT	UNIT		COST	UNIT	COST	UNIT		
50	Ea.	Baking Potatoes	$15.00	90 Ct.	.167	Ea.	8	350
4	Oz.	Shortening	39.64	50 Lb.	.050	Oz.		200
6.5	Lb.	Sour Cream	3.65	5 Lb.	.730	Lb.	4	745
6.5	Lb.	Butter	2.00	Lb.	2.000	Lb.	12	500
							TOTAL	$25	795

rice pilaf with a beef brochette, spiced whole crabapple with a stuffed pork chop, or sautéed button mushrooms with a strip sirloin steak.

Finally, the Q factor is added. This covers all the incidentals that have not been accounted for in the cost cards and includes such items as the salt and pepper on the table, crackers, steak sauces, and possibly butter. The dollar amount that is assigned to the Q factor varies from restaurant to restaurant depending on circumstances surrounding the "extras" that are provided the customer.

FIGURE 3.13. Portion cost card.

NAME OF RECIPE   Cinnamon Rolls   REFERENCE   House File #4-43

DATE   10/21/97   NUMBER OF PORTIONS   48 (2 Rolls Ea.)   COST PER PORTION $0.153

RECIPE		INGREDIENTS	INVOICE		RECIPE		EXTENSION	
AMT	UNIT		COST	UNIT	COST	UNIT		
2	Oz.	Dry Yeast	$18.40	10 Lb.	.115	Oz.		230
1.5	Cups	Water, Warm	No	Cost	—	—		—
3	Cups	Water, Hot	No	Cost	—	—		—
3	Oz.	Dry Milk	73.00	50 Lb.	.091	Oz.		273
1	Lb.	Sugar	15.75	50 Lb.	.315	Lb.		315
1	Lb.	Shortening	27.00	50 Lb.	.540	Lb.		540
2	Oz.	Salt	Per	Recipe	—	—		100
9	Ea.	Eggs	.90	Dozen	.075	Ea.		675
5.5	Lb.	Flour	7.50	50 Lb.	.150	Lb.		825
12	Oz.	Butter	2.00	Lb.	.125	Oz.	1	500
2	Lb.	Sugar	15.75	50 Lb.	.315	Lb.		630
1	Oz.	Cinnamon	18.25	5 Lb.	.228	Oz.		228
		Total Cost Per Recipe - Yield 96 Rolls					$5	316
		Cinnamon Roll Cost Per Portion (2 Ea.)						111
		Butter (2 Ea. Pats)						042
						TOTAL		153

FIGURE 3.14. Total cost of accompanying items.

Dinner salad with bleu cheese	$ .355
Baked potato with sour cream and butter	.516
Cinnamon rolls with butter (2 ea.)	.153
Total	$1.204

FIGURE 3.15. Total meal cost chart.

Entree	Cost	Garnish	Acc. Items	Q Factor	Total
Broiled chicken half	$1.225	.300	1.024	.150	$2.699
Poached salmon	$2.965	.355	1.024	.150	$4.494
Strip sirloin steak	$3.080	.420	1.024	.150	$4.674
Rack of lamb	$3.745	.195	1.024	.150	$5.114

BUFFETS AND SALAD BARS

The last area of recipe costing to be investigated is the one pertaining to all-you-can-eat buffets and salad bars. The object is to get an average cost per customer. Several theories express the quickest and simplest way to achieve this. They are useless. The only way to get an accurate cost is via the inventory method.

	Starting inventory (number of units)
Plus	Additions to the table (number of units)
Minus	Ending inventory (number of units)
Equals	Number of units of product sold
Times	Unit cost of product
Equals	Total cost of product used

The formula should be used for each product on the buffet table or salad bar. Inventory what is placed on the table at the start of service. Add replacements. Subtract reusable leftovers at the end of service. It is important to remember that only that product which is reusable should be subtracted. If it is not reusable and is thrown away, it is not subtracted and becomes part of cost. After subtracting, take the number of units used for each item and multiply this by the cost per unit. Add together the costs of each item. Divide this total by the number of customers partaking of the buffet or salad bar to get a net cost per customer.

FIGURE 3.16. Salad bar cost analysis.

Item	Unit	Start (+)	Additions (+)	(+)	(+)	(+)	Total =	End (−)	Total =	Unit Cost (x)	Total Cost =
Tossed greens	lb.	3	3	3	2	2	13	2	11	.50	$5.50
French dressing	qt.	1	1				2	1/2	1½	1.32	1.98
Italian dressing	qt.	1	1	1			3	1/2	2½	1.56	3.90
Tomato wedges	lb.	1	1	1	1		4	1	3	.65	1.95
Green onions	lb.	1/2	1/2				1	1/4	3/4	.30	.23
Shred. carrots	lb.	1/2	1/2	1/2			1½	1/2	1	.25	.25
Sliced cukes	lb.	1/2	1/2	1/2			1½	—	1½	.50	.75
Sliced radishes	lb.	1/2					1/2	1/4	1/4	.80	.20

Cost per customer

Customer count | Total cost

Total cost	$14.76
Customer count	48
Cost per customer	.308

KEEP CURRENT

Now that the costs for the menu have been determined, there is one more consideration to keep in mind. Keep current. Every menu item should have a cost card filed in a book and these cards should be kept up to date. This is not to say that every time an item in inventory increases or decreases in price, the cost card should be refigured. This would quickly develop into a full-time job. Rather, key ingredients should be monitored and when their prices pass a certain level, cost cards containing these ingredients should be changed accordingly and a determination should be made regarding a price increase or decrease. For example, in recipes using 80/20 ground beef, if a cost of $1.50 a pound were used and it eventually crept up to $1.65 a pound, then all recipes utilizing this ingredient would be refigured.

COMPUTER APPLICATIONS

There are many computer programs on the market that can and will do everything discussed in this chapter. The user enters the data concerning the recipe and the invoice costs. The program does the rest by completing the math and figuring the cost per portion on the cost cards. Some of the more sophisticated programs that have a complete accounting package change cost cards as invoices are posted to the accounts payable ledger. Thus, as costs increase or decrease, the cost cards are automatically adjusted. As a result, cost per portion is monitored and the user alerted when costs have increased to a predetermined level.

CONCLUSION

The science of keeping accurate costs and figuring the proper selling price is an exacting one. However, as seen in the next chapter, the astute chef, manager, or owner who has the knowledge and takes the time to accomplish these tasks greatly increases the odds for survival. Exact knowledge of costs leads to charging the correct amount for a product, which leads to profitability. It's just that simple.

QUESTIONS

1. In your own words, define and explain the importance of the following terms:
   a) standardized recipes
   b) cost cards

Portion cost card.

NAME OF RECIPE_____ REFERENCE_____

DATE_____ NUMBER OF PORTIONS_____ COST PER PORTION_____

RECIPE		INGREDIENTS	INVOICE		RECIPE		EXTENSION	
AMT	UNIT		COST	UNIT	COST	UNIT		
						TOTAL		

   c) AP vs. EP

   d) Q factor

2. Figure the cost of a 5-ounce cup of coffee using a brew ratio of 3-to-1. Assume the coffee costs $3.25 a pound, cream $.02 per serving, and sugar $.02 per serving. No refills are given.

3. Explain to a new manager the method used to figure the cost per person of an all-you-can-eat buffet.

4. Using the following data and recipe, complete the blank cost card provided here including the cost per portion.

Egg Foo Young
Yield: 50 portions

1 lb. fresh mushrooms	mushrooms $1.89 per lb.
1 No. 10 can bean sprouts	bean sprouts $15.80—6 No. 10 cans
2 lb. onions AP	onions $11.60 per 50 lbs.
3/4 cup cooking oil	oil $33.00 per six 1-gal. cans
40 eggs	eggs $23.50 per 36 doz.
1 lb. cooked chicken	chicken $24.90 per 10 lb.
2 qt. sauce	sauce $3.50 per gal.

5. What part of the standardized cost cards could be computerized? What systems in the operation would you evaluate from the back of the house systems?

Software Applications

This exercise is intended to show how computers can be used to speed the process of creating cost cards as well as to keep them updated. While many programs on the market perform this function, this one was designed as a cross-representation, so that, by learning it, you can readily adapt to most of the others. While most commercial programs are quite complex, this program has been modified to fit on one disk and therefore has some limitations.

All of the recipes for this exercise have come from the textbook *On Cooking* by Sarah R. Labensky and Alan M. Hause (© 1995 by Prentice Hall). The page numbers refer to the pages in the first edition.

Prior to starting this exercise, read the complete directions printed in the front of this book.

Recipe #1. Carolina Barbecued Ribs, p. 358:

Carolina Barbecued Ribs ...

Yield: 6 Servings, approx. 4 ribs each		Method: Baking
Salt and pepper	TT	TT
Crushed red pepper flakes	1 Tbsp.	30 ml
Pork backribs, 3–4 lb. (1.3–1.8 kg) slab	2	2
White vinegar	1 pt.	450 ml
Sauce:		
Onion, chopped coarse	5 oz.	150 g
Garlic cloves	3	3
Green bell pepper, chopped coarse	4 oz.	120 g
Plum tomatoes, canned	1 pt.	450 ml
Tabasco hot sauce	8 oz.	225 g
Brown sugar	10 oz.	300 g
Lemon juice	2 oz.	60 g

- Double click on the "Menuplan.xls" file. When the page appears on the screen, double click on "COSTS" and a cost card will appear.

- Click on the enter header toolbar button.

- Enter the information from the recipe onto the recipe information box.

- Scroll down to the cost card and in the blue box put the cursor on the first line of the quantity column. On the first line of the recipe is salt and pepper to taste. Put "TT" in the quantity column.

- Move the cursor over to the ingredient column (skip the unit column) and type in "salt/pepper."

- Move the cursor all the way over to the extension column and type in ".10."
- Since salt and pepper is to taste and is a negligible amount, what we have just done is assign it an arbitrary cost of $0.10.
- Move the cursor to the next line under the ingredient column and type in "red pepper flakes."
- Move the cursor all the way over to the extension column and type in ".10."
- Again we have assigned an arbitrary cost of $0.10.
- Move the cursor to the next line under the quantity column and put in "8."
- Move over to the unit column, double click, and choose "lb."
- Move over to the ingredient column and double click. You will see a group of categories. Select "meat fresh, frozen." Double click and scroll until you find "pork, spare ribs 2.5."
- Double click and the cost breakdown, as well as the extension for pork spare ribs, will appear. (Notice that we used a worst case scenario for the ribs as the recipe called for 2 each 3–4 pound ribs.)
- Move the cursor to the next line under quantity and type in "16" under "unit oz." You will notice that the recipe calls for 1 pint. In this program only ounces, pounds, each, or #10 can will be accepted. All volume measures will have to be converted to ounces. This should help you in learning conversions.
- Next double click on the ingredient column and select "Condiments, Dressings, Fats and Vinegars." Scroll down to "vinegar, white" and double click. The cost and extension have been figured for you.
- Continue in this fashion with the rest of the ingredients. In the case of garlic, convert the three cloves to 0.5 (1/2) ounce and the 1 pint of tomatoes to .16 of a #10 (use canned tomatoes from the inventory list). Where conversions of this type are necessary, use one of the many conversion charts available in cooking or purchasing textbooks.

When completed, the recipe's total cost should be $17.29 and the portion cost $2.88.

Print the recipe, because you will need the hard copy for an exercise in the next chapter. There is only one cost card template due to limited disk space.

Recipe #2. Shrimp with Olive Oil and Garlic, p. 506:

Shrimp with Olive Oil and Garlic

Yield: 4 Servings		Method: Sautéing
Garlic, chopped	4 Tbsp.	60 ml
Extra virgin olive oil	4 oz.	120 g
Shrimp, 26–30 count, in shell	2 lb. 8 oz.	1 kg
Coarse sea salt	1 Tbsp.	15 ml
Lemon juice	2 Tbsp.	30 ml

1. Sauté the garlic in the olive oil until translucent.
2. Add the shrimp and salt. Toss to coat the shrimp with the oil and cook just until the shrimp are pink, approximately 5 minutes. Add the lemon juice.
3. Arrange the shrimp on warm serving plates: top with the oil, garlic and lemon juice left in the pan. Serve immediately.

- Remove the old recipe by deleting each cell in the information box as well as the cost card. **Make sure that you have printed the prior recipe for future use.**

- Select the information box by double clicking on the header toolbar and type in the necessary information.

- Select the cost card and complete it in the same fashion as the first one.

- *Note:* 4 tablespoons will convert to 2 ounces, and sea salt will be assigned a cost of $0.10 in the extension column.

When you are finished, the cost should be $18.27 with a per portion cost of $4.57.

Print a hard copy and continue to the next recipe.

Recipe #3. Breast of Chicken Tarragon, p. 395:

Poached Breast of Chicken with Tarragon Sauce

Yield: 8 Servings		
Chicken breasts, boneless, skinless approx. 8 oz (250 g) each	4	4
Whole butter	1½ oz.	45 g
Salt and white pepper	TT	TT
White wine	4 oz.	120 g
Chicken stock	1 pt.	450 ml
Bay leaf	1	1
Dried thyme	1/4 tsp.	1 ml
Dried tarragon	1 tsp.	5 ml
Flour	1 oz.	30 g
Heavy cream	4 oz.	120 g
Fresh tarragon sprigs	as needed	as needed

Note: Chicken stock is not on the inventory list. Ingredients not on the list need to be entered onto the cost card manually, that is, under "QTY" type "16," under "UNIT" type "oz," under "IN-GREDIENTS" type "chicken stock," under "INVOICE COST" type "1.25," under "QTY" type "128" and under "UNIT" type "oz." The recipe cost and extension will be figured for you. What has just happened is that chicken stock at a cost of $1.25 per gallon has been put on the cost card manually.

- Assign a cost of .10 for bay leaf, .10 for thyme, and .10 for tarragon.
- For flour, use "all-purpose" and for heavy cream, use "whipping cream."
- Assign a cost of .10 for tarragon sprigs.

When the recipe is completed, the total should be $6.79 with a portion cost of $0.85.

Print a hard copy and continue on to the next recipe.

Recipe #4. Veal Marsala, p. 327:

Veal Marsala

Yield: 6 Servings		Method: Sautéing
Veal scallops, pounded, 3 oz. (90 g) each	12	12
Salt and pepper	TT	TT
Flour	approx. 2 oz.	approx. 60 g
Clarified butter	2 oz.	60 g
Olive oil	2 oz.	60 g
Dry Marsala	6 oz.	170 g
Brown veal stock	4 oz.	120 g
Whole butter	1½ oz.	45 g

- For veal, use "veal, sliced."
- For flour, use "all-purpose."
- For butter, use "unsalted."
- Veal stock needs to be handled manually at a cost of $1.25 per gallon (128 ounces).

The cost should be $24.10 and a per portion cost of $4.02. Print a hard copy and continue to the next recipe.

Recipe #5. Braised Short Ribs of Beef, p. 303:

Braised Short Ribs of Beef

Yield: 8 8-oz. (230-g) Servings		Method: Braising
Flour	4 oz.	120 g
Salt	1 Tbsp.	15 ml
Pepper	1 tsp.	5 ml
Dried rosemary	1/2 tsp.	2 ml
Short ribs of beef, cut in 2-in. (5-cm) portions	6 lbs.	2.7 kg
Vegetable oil	1 oz.	30 g
Onion, chopped	6 oz.	170 g
Celery, chopped	4 oz.	120 g
Brown beef stock	24 oz.	700 g
Roux	as needed	as needed
Salt and pepper	TT	TT

- Assign a cost of .10 for salt, .10 for pepper, .10 for rosemary, .10 for roux, and .10 for salt/pepper TT.

- Beef stock will be $1.25 per gallon (128 ounces) and will have to be entered manually.

CHAPTER FOUR

Pricing the Menu

OBJECTIVES   By the completion of this chapter, the reader should be able to:

- Explain the makeup of an income statement including the interrelationships of controllable and noncontrollable cost and their effect on sales and profits.
- Describe several of the important markup methods, including the factor method, markup on cost, gross markup, ratio method, and the TRA method, as well as the relationship each has with the others.
- Explain the concept of psychological pricing and its importance in selecting the final menu price.
- Explain the menu precost method for selling price, cost, and amount of items sold.

IMPORTANT TERMS

Income statement	Sales
Food cost	Gross profit
Controllable costs	Noncontrollable costs
Profit	Factor method
Markup on cost method	Gross markup method
Ratio method	TRA method
Psychological pricing	Menu precost

INTRODUCTION

Now that the proper cost has been figured for the listings on the menu, the next determination is the selling price. Prior to the discussion of selling price, one point should be made clear: the object of any business is to make a profit. There should be no argument over this point; it is fact. Far too many managers lose sight of this and, consequently, do not develop a profit mentality. To be sure, many factors go into achieving earnings. Certainly sales are important because sales must exceed costs before a profit can be realized. Menu items that do not cater to customers' desires result in lost sales and, consequently, lost profit. Controls are important, for without them waste and theft eliminate any profit potential. The menu selling price, however, is the starting point on which profit is built. It is the key ingredient in making a profit. Without the proper selling price, all the promotions and all the controls will not assist in producing earnings. If the selling price is too high, sales will be lost. If the selling price is too low, profit will be lost. In an earlier chapter we said that "everything starts with the menu." In this chapter "profit starts with the menu."

Some food service operations such as hospitals, in-plant feeders, and schools are not required to make a profit, but only to break even or make budget. Those managers need also to recognize the importance of proper selling price, for without it, it is fruitless to expect to break even or make budget, in spite of other management factors such as controls.

UNDERSTANDING THE INCOME STATEMENT

To understand fully the relationship between the menu selling price and profit, it is necessary to examine an income statement. While it is not the purpose of this text to explain accounting, it is necessary to have some basic knowledge of the subject to determine how much to charge for an item.

Referring to the income statement in Figure 4.1, assume that Harry Cheatum and Sammy Steele owned a restaurant named the Cheatum & Steele. The first line on the income statement is sales. The figure for sales is calculated by multiplying the selling price of each item times the number of units of that item sold and then totaling the sales for all the items on the menu. If Harry and Sammy sold 30,000 hamburgers over a year's time at a selling price of $1 each, their total sales of hamburgers would be $30,000. If they sold 20,000 orders of french fries at $.50 an order, their total sales for french fries would be $10,000. Their combined sales of these two items would be $40,000. The other $460,000 sales shown on the income statement would be made up of other items on the menu, figured in like fashion, that is, the number of units sold per item times the selling price, with sales of all the items totaled.

FIGURE 4-1. Cheatum & Steele Restaurant income statement year ending 19XX.

THE AMOUNT OF MONEY BROUGHT IN FROM THE SALES OF MENU LISTINGS	SALES	$500,100	100%
	LESS: COST OF FOOD SOLD		
DOLLAR VALUE OF FOOD ON HAND AT THE BEGINNING OF THE PERIOD	OPENING INVENTORY	$8,250	
FOOD BOUGHT DURING THE PERIOD	PLUS: PURCHASES	168,500	
	EQUALS: TOTAL AVAILABLE	176,750	
DOLLAR VALUE OF FOOD ON HAND AT THE END OF THE PERIOD	LESS: CLOSING INVENTORY	7,480	
THE DOLLAR AMOUNT OF FOOD THAT WAS USED DURING THE PERIOD	COST OF FOOD SOLD	169,270	34%
THE AMOUNT OF MONEY MADE ON THE COST OF FOOD	GROSS PROFIT	$330,830	66%
PAYROLL OF HOURLY AND MANAGEMENT PERSONNEL PLUS FRINGE BENEFITS AND PAYROLL TAXES	LABOR EXPENSE	172,380	35%
OTHER COSTS THAT MANAGEMENT CAN CONTROL SUCH AS SUPPLIES	OTHER CONTROLLABLE EXPENSES	48,960	10%
OTHER COSTS THAT MANAGEMENT HAS NO CONTROL OVER SUCH AS RENT OR INSURANCE	NON-CONTROLLABLE EXPENSES	76,290	15%
TOTAL OF ALL EXPENSES (I.E., LABOR, CONTROLLABLE, AND NON-CONTROLLABLE	TOTAL EXPENSES	$297,630	60%
GROSS PROFIT LESS TOTAL EXPENSES. THE AMOUNT OF MONEY MADE BEFORE INCOME TAXES ARE PAID	PRE-TAX PROFIT	$33,200	06%

Notice on the income statement that figures are expressed in both dollars and percentages. Both of these are important in the analysis of the income statement. Dollars are what is brought in (in terms of sales) and expended (in terms of costs) and what is left over (in terms of profit). Percentages put the dollar numbers on an even scale for comparative purposes from period to period. For example, if an expense line such as labor went up, it could be acceptable if sales went up also in a corresponding manner. It would not be acceptable if the expense went up and sales did not or if sales dropped. Analysis of percentages makes it possible to relate cost directly to what happened to sales. Therefore, on an income statement, sales are always 100 percent and cost percents are compared with sales. Look at sales as a whole, and expenses and profit as parts of the whole. To obtain a percentage for a cost line, divide the cost in dollars by sales in dollars. The result is that line's cost percentage. The same holds true for profit. Simply divide profit in dollars by sales in dollars to obtain a profit percentage.

FIGURE 4.2.   Sales, expense, profit chart. The entire circle represents sales at 100%. The various costs and profit are parts of the whole, equaling 100% (sales).

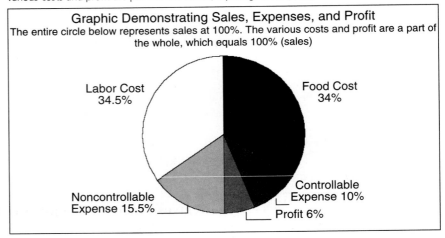

The next line on the income statement, cost of food sold, is figured by taking opening inventory plus purchases minus closing inventory, which equals cost of food sold.

$$
\begin{array}{l}
 \text{Opening Inventory} \\
\underline{+ \text{ Purchases}} \\
= \text{Food Available for Sale} \\
\underline{- \text{ Closing Inventory}} \\
= \text{Cost of Food Sold}
\end{array}
$$

To simplify matters, let's assume that Harry and Sammy sold only one item—strip steaks. If they started off with 30 steaks at a cost of $4 each, they would have an opening inventory of $120 (30 steaks × $4). During the day, they purchased 100 more, also at a cost of $4. Their purchases would be $400 (100 steaks × $4). This would then give them 130 steaks available for sale at a cost of $520 (130 steaks × $4 = $520 or $120 + $400 = $520). At the end of business they counted the steaks and found they had 10 left or $40 worth. Subtracting this from the available steaks for sale of 130 or $520 value, their cost of food sold would be 120 steaks (units) or $480. The formula would then look like this:

Opening Inventory	$120
+ Purchases	+ 400
= Food Available For Sale	$520
− Closing Inventory	− 40
= Cost of Food Sold	$480

Note. Cost of food sold could be a misnomer. If someone stole a steak and if Sammy burned a steak and had to throw it away, these two steaks would show up in cost of food sold even though in actuality they were not sold. I sometimes feel that the title "cost of food sold" should be changed to something like "cost of food used." One client whom I had consulted for called it "food gone" which is a very appropriate title. One would hope that it had gone to the cash register rather than the trash can.

To figure the food cost percent, take food cost in dollars and divide it by sales in dollars and the result is food cost percent. Again, Costs or expenses are expressed in percentages in order to provide a means for easy comparison. In the case of the steaks, the food cost is $480. In the income statement (Figure 4.1) the food cost is $169,270. By themselves, these numbers are meaningless. If, however, we say that the steaks have a 34-percent food cost and the income statement has a 34-percent food cost, we can make some rationalizations regarding cost. Even though the dollar costs are drastically different, the percents are the same. By using percentages we are simply taking the ratio of dollar costs to dollar sales, which gives a more meaningful discussion of costs.

The next line, gross profit, is the amount of money that the Cheatum & Steele Restaurant made from its raw ingredients. Gross profit is determined by subtracting cost of food sold from sales.

	Sales
−	Cost of Food Sold
=	Gross Profit

To figure the gross profit percent, take gross profit in dollars and divide by sales in dollars. If you subtract the food cost percent from the sales percent, the result will be the same.

Gross Profit %	Sales %
Sales $ ⟌ Gross Profit $	− Food Cost %
	= Gross Profit %

66%	100%
$500,000 ⟌ $333,730	− 34%
	66%

The next line, labor expense, is the total payroll for the Cheatum & Steele Restaurant. In some operations, this is broken down into management salaries, hourly personnel payroll, payroll taxes, FICA, and fringe benefit expenses. Fringe benefits would include employees' hospitalization insurance, life insurance, vacation and holiday pay, company-paid retirement benefits, and so on. Labor expense and food cost added together are known as prime cost because these two expenses together are the largest expenses that are controlled by management. To figure labor expense percent, divide labor expense in dollars by sales in dollars.

$$\text{Sales \$} \, \overline{) \, \begin{array}{c} \text{Labor Expenses \%} \\ \text{Labor Expense \$} \end{array}} \qquad \$500,000 \, \overline{) \, \begin{array}{c} 34.5\% \\ \$172,380 \end{array}}$$

The next line, other controllable expenses, includes such items as paper goods, dishmachine detergents, and cleaning supplies. This category is quite often broken down into separate lines on an income statement. These are all the expenses that can be controlled by management.

The next line, noncontrollable expenses, includes all those fixed expenses which management has little if any control over. This would include such items as utilities, rent, insurance, or property taxes.

The next line, total expenses, is figured by adding together all the expense lines except food cost (in other words all expenses below gross profit) and then subtracting this figure from gross profit. The result is profit before depreciation and taxes. To figure profit percent, divide profit in dollars by sales in dollars or add all the expense percents and subtract from gross profit percent. To put all this into perspective, let's review the following facts:

- FACT—All restaurants are in business to make a profit.
- FACT—All restaurants have costs.
- FACT—In order for a restaurant to make a profit, sales must exceed costs.

As we saw earlier, sales are nothing more than the selling price times the number of items sold. Therefore, the key to profit is determining the correct selling price. To do this we need to charge a price that not only will cover the cost of goods (food cost), but also will cover all of our other expenses *and* produce a profit. There is a misconception that abounds in our industry that selling price is dependent solely on the cost of ingredients or is based only on the cost of ingredients and labor. Wrong! The selling price must cover not only food and labor costs, but all other expenses and profit as well. To do otherwise will put you on a collision course for disaster.

MARKUP METHODS

With an understanding of where profit comes from and the interrelationship of expenses to sales, the various methods of marking up costs to determine a selling price can be explored. A multitude of formulas are available to assist the restaurant manager in determining what should be charged for an item. Some are simple, some are complicated, and some make absolutely no sense at all. Out of this multitude of formulas, the more popular ones are those that have passed the test of time. These are excellent in assisting management to determine a fair selling price, and are the ones explored here.

THE NO-METHOD METHOD

Perhaps the most popular method of determining what to charge for an item (although few managers admit to doing it) is simply charging what the competition charges. This method, as such, is foolhardy because no two restaurants are alike. Style, decor, location, rent, utilities, insurance, labor costs, and so on all change from location to location. To charge the same price for an item as a competitor charges ignores these differences, and profitability becomes a hit-or-miss proposition. Certainly, with a large investment in a restaurant, a more scientific approach, one that assures a profit margin, is in order.

While the no-method method appears to violate the statement that only worthy formulas will be presented, it is mentioned for two reasons. First, it is popular, and, second, it has its place when used correctly, which is discussed later.

THE FACTOR METHOD

Perhaps the simplest formula to use is the *factor method*. In this method, it is necessary to have predetermined what the food cost should be. Therefore, it should be used only in established restaurants where past performance indicates that the gross profit (food cost minus sales) is sufficient to cover all expenses and profit. If this is the case, then this formula can be used. To obtain the selling price, take the desired food cost percent and divide it into 100 percent. The result is the factor. Next, take the factor and multiply it by the item cost (from the cost card) of the menu listing. The result is the menu selling price of that item (Figure 4.3). Once the factor has been de-

FIGURE 4-3. Factor method.

1. Determine desired food cost percent.
2. Divide this number into 100. (100%)
3. The result is your factor.
4. Multiply the factor times the cost of the meal or item.
5. The result is the selling price of that meal or item.

Example: Desired food cost %—34%
Meal cost—$2.18

$$.34 \overline{\smash{\big)}\ 1.00} \quad 2.94 \text{ (factor)}$$

$2.18 meal cost
× 2.94 factor
$6.41 selling price

termined, it is unnecessary to repeat step 1 each time a selling price is needed. Simply multiply the item cost by the factor to determine what to charge on the menu for that item. If all controls are effective and the costs remain constant, the desired food cost percent will be accurate. Should the costs of that item increase or decrease, it will be necessary to multiply the new cost by the factor to determine a new selling price that would reflect the change in cost.

THE MARKUP ON COST METHOD

Another simple method, very similar in nature, is the *markup on cost method.* Take the food cost of the item and divide it by the desired food cost percent. The result is the selling price to be charged for that item (Figure 4.4). As in the factor method, it must be a known fact to management that the desired food cost is adequate to obtain a satisfactory gross profit to cover all other expenses and achieve a profit.

FIGURE 4.4.   Markup on cost method.

1. Determine your desired food cost percent.
2. Divide this percent into the cost of the meal or item.
3. The result is the selling price of that meal or item.

Example: Desired food cost %—34%
Meal cost—$2.18

$$\begin{array}{r} 6.41 \text{ selling price} \\ \text{(food cost \%)} \quad .34 \overline{\smash{\big)}\ \$2.18 \text{ meal cost}} \end{array}$$

THE GROSS MARKUP METHOD

The third system to be examined is the *gross markup method.* Unlike the previous methods which used only food cost to determine the selling price, the gross markup method takes into account all expenses and profit as well as food cost to determine a selling price. Marking up a menu item in relation to its food cost is an adequate way to ensure profitability if the assumption that the gross profit covers all costs and profit is true. However, in the present economy where escalating labor and fixed costs (such as insurance, rent, and utilities) are the rule, many restaurateurs believe that, when determining a selling price, the total income statement must be taken into account to ensure profitability.

To figure the gross markup method, first take the gross profit in dollars and divide this figure by the number of customers served. The result is the contribution rate per customer. Second, take the food cost of the item and add this to the contribution rate per customer. The result is the selling price. Several things have happened here. First, by using gross profit, all of the costs (except food) have been accounted for, as well as profit. If this is confusing, refer back to the income statement to see that gross profit represents not only food cost minus sales, but also represents all other expenses plus profit; thus all expenses and profit, as well as the item cost, are accounted for in this markup formula. The second thing that has happened here is that all of the other expenses and profit (gross profit) has been divided equally among all the customers (gross profit in dollars divided by number of customers).

FIGURE 4.5. Gross markup method.

1. Take gross profit in dollars from your income statement.
2. Determine the number of customers served.
3. Divide the gross profit dollars by the number of customers served.
4. The result is the cost per customer.
5. Add the cost per customer to the cost of the meal or item.
6. The result is the selling price.

Example: Gross profit dollars—$330,730
Number of customers served—75,000
Meal cost—$2.18

$$\frac{4.41 \text{ cost per customer}}{75,000 \,|\, \$330,730 \text{ gross profit}}$$

4.41 cost per customer
+ 2.18 meal cost
6.59 selling price

Note: Cost per customer also includes profit.

Since all of the labor expense, other controllable expense, noncontrollable expense, and profit (gross profit) are taken into consideration and are divided equally among all customers, this method could also be known as the "quasi-communistic" approach to the restaurant business. Nevertheless, it is an excellent way to determine the selling price on a menu where all items are in the same price range.

As can be seen, the gross markup method tends to average prices more toward a median than does the factor method, which has a higher margin for a low-cost item and a lower margin for a high-cost item (Figure 4.6). Therefore, to use the gross markup method, the entire menu must be in the same general item-cost range. Some strange things can happen when using the gross markup method on

FIGURE 4.6. Gross markup method vs. factor method.

Meal	Cost	Selling Price	
		G.M.M.	F.M.
Prime Rib	$4.15	$8.55	$12.20
Strip Rib	$3.95	$8.35	$11.60
Fried Chicken	$1.80	$6.20	$ 5.30
Broiled Fish	$2.10	$6.50	$ 6.15
Rack of Lamb	$3.55	$7.95	$10.45

Note: Figures from previous examples were used (i.e., $4.41 cost per customer in the gross markup method and 2.94 for the factor in the factor method). Notice the tighter spread between the highest and lowest selling price using the gross markup method.

a menu with a wide range of costs. Consider some of the strange pricing that would result from using this method on a coffee shop menu, which has a wide item-cost range (Figure 4.7). Because this method is most appropriate for operations with a tight item-cost range, it is also very useful in table d'hote restaurants where one price is charged for all entrees, as well as for all you can eat buffets and/or salad bars.

FIGURE 4.7. When not to use the gross markup method!

Item	Cost	Cost per Customer	Selling Price
Coffee	$ .10	$4.41	$4.51
Apple Pie	$ .40	$4.41	$4.81
BLT	$ .60	$4.41	$5.01
Shrimp Cocktail	$1.75	$4.41	$6.16

THE RATIO METHOD

The fourth method is the *ratio method*. Like the gross markup method, it also takes into account all expenses and profit. To obtain a selling price using the ratio method, you must have a valid income statement because the numbers used to develop the ratio are total expenses. These can be either monthly or yearly figures; however, yearly figures will be more accurate in determining the proper markup. To obtain a selling price using the ratio method, first take the sum of labor cost, other controllable costs, noncontrollable costs and profit (these equal gross profit) and divide these costs by the cost of food sold in dollars. The result is your ratio. To the ratio add 1.00 (sales as a percent). Multiply this figure by the item cost (Figure 4.8). Once this multiplying factor has been developed, it can be used repeatedly to determine selling prices as long as the desired results are maintained on the income statement.

FIGURE 4.8. Ratio method.

1. Obtain cost of food sold in dollars from the income statement.
2. Add all other expenses and profit in dollars.
   (The result is the same figure as gross profit.)
3. Divide all other expense and profit by cost of food sold.
4. The result is your ratio.
5. Add 1.00 to the ratio.
6. Multiply this by the cost of the meal or item.
7. The result is the selling price.

Example: Cost of food sold in dollars—$169,270
All other expenses and profit—$330,730
Meal cost—$2.18

$$\frac{1.95}{169,270 \overline{)330,730}} \text{ ratio}$$

1.95 ratio
+ 1.00
2.95

2.95
× $2.18 meal cost
$6.43 selling price

THE TRA METHOD

The last method discussed was developed by the Texas Restaurant Association and, consequently, is known as the *TRA method.* This method, like the previous two, takes into account in determining a selling price all expenses and profit. To figure the selling price of an item, add together labor cost percent, controllable expense percent, noncontrollable expense percent, and profit percent. The result is cost percent without food. Take the cost percent without food and subtract it from 1.00 (sales). The result is the food cost percent. Divide the cost of the item by the food cost percent to obtain the selling price.

FIGURE 4.9.   Texas Restaurant Association Method.

1. From your income statement, take labor cost in percent, operating cost in percent (both controllable and noncontrollable), and profit in percent.
2. Add the three figures together.
3. Subtract this number from 1.00.
4. The result is the divisor.
5. Divide the cost of the meal by the divisor.
6. The result is the selling price.

Example: Meal cost—$2.18
Figures taken from the income statement (Figure 4.1).

Labor Cost %	35% or .35
Operating Cost %	25% or .25
Profit %	6% or .06
	66% or .66 cost without food

$$1.00$$
$$-\ .66$$
$$.34 \text{ divisor}$$

selling price

$$.34\overline{)\$2.18} = \$6.41$$

Assume you wanted to increase your profit to 8 percent, the new selling price would be as follows:

Labor Cost	.35
Operating Cost	.25
Profit	.08
	.68

$$1.00$$
$$-\ .68$$
$$.32 \text{ divisor}$$

$$.32\overline{)\$2.18} = \$6.81 \quad \text{new selling price necessary to increase profit by 2\%}$$

SIMILARITIES AND DIFFERENCES

By now it should be apparent to the astute reader that with one exception the selling prices are all similar (the one exception being the gross markup method). The reasoning behind this is simple. In order to obtain a certain selling price that will achieve a profit, an appropriate amount must be charged that will cover the cost of the item and allow enough money left over to offset other costs and profit.

What is happening in the factor, markup on cost, ratio, and TRA methods is that costs (other than food) and profit are divided in direct relation to the selling price. In other words, a hamburger costing $.70 and selling for $2.10 would contribute $1.40 toward labor, overhead, and profit, while a grilled cheese sandwich costing $.40 and selling for $1.20 would contribute $.80. In the gross markup method, however, labor, overhead, and profit are divided equally among all customers, not in a direct relationship between cost and selling price. For example, in the gross markup method, assume that $.40 was the cost distribution per customer that would make the selling price $1.60 for the hamburger and $1.30 for the grilled cheese. In this method, once all customers ordering from the full menu are served, all expenses and profit are covered.

Another thing to note is that, in the factor method and the ratio method, the item costs are multiplied by relatively the same number, and in the markup on cost and the TRA methods, the item costs are divided by relatively the same divisor. In all four of these cases, the selling price is pretty much the same. Interesting, isn't it? What has happened is that we have looked at the same numbers in different ways but have come up with the same answers.

SELECTING A METHOD

These are but a few of the many methods used to obtain menu selling prices. The proper one to use is the one that management feels most comfortable using. In some cases, corporate policy dictates by telling its management team to multiply the item food cost by a certain factor or divide the item food cost by a certain percentage. Normally, this is for the individual units to determine a selling price for specials, as the regular menu is priced in the corporate office. Many operators prefer the TRA method because it forces them to look at the complete financial picture. Once it is ascertained that a particular food cost will cover all expenses and profit, the formula is no more time consuming than the markup on cost or the factor methods. It is important to remember that management is responsible for the total profitability of the restaurant, not just for achieving an arbitrary food cost.

What should a restaurant's food cost be? Jack Miller, in a report on menu pricing, tells the story of why a 40-percent-food cost was chosen as the preferred operating figure. In the year 500 B.C., on the road to Rome, someone built a restaurant; the first customer was an accountant. The accountant happened to stop to have dinner and afterward said, "Say, I think you have a pretty good thing going. It looks like this restaurant business may develop into something that will spread all over the world. How would you like it if I kept books for you?" The restaurateur had no one working on the books, and so hired the accountant/customer to keep the books for the first month of operation. At the end of the month, the accountant came back to the restaurant operator and reported, "You have a 40 percent food cost." The restaurateur asked, "Is that good?" The reply was, "That is very good." So from that time forward it has been accepted that all food service operations should maintain a 40-percent food cost.[1]

Many food service managers still cling faithfully to this theory. Ask a restaurant owner or manager what food cost should run and you will receive an answer from 20 percent to 50 percent. The correct answer to this question is, "It depends." It depends on many factors that are peculiar to that particular restaurant.

For a consultant, the TRA method is the preferred procedure in order to be certain that all costs and profits are covered when determining the correct selling price for the menu. But the method used is not as important as the idea that some rational method be adopted. As stated earlier, charging what the competition charges is not a rational method. However, there is a point when checking the selling prices of the competition does become important and that is after it has been established that your selling price is sufficient to cover all of your costs and profits. At this point in time, it is prudent to determine whether an item at a particular selling price is competitively priced in the market. It should also be decided whether the selling price is within the existing price range of the present menu and within the demographic market range.

PSYCHOLOGICAL PRICING

Once a rational selling price has been determined using the aforementioned steps, the job is not complete. The next consideration is psychological pricing. What has been determined so far is the restaurant's needs, in other words, how much money the restaurant needs to charge to cover expenses and profit. Psychological pricing theories take into account the customer—how the customer reacts to certain pricing structures. Psychological pricing has a long history in retailing; however, only recently has it been incorporated into food service pricing. Studies conducted at Purdue University and Cornell University have given insight into some interesting facts as they pertain to restaurant pricing.

One of the primary theories behind psychological pricing is the *odd cents price*. This pricing reduces the restaurant customers' resistance to buy because it gives the illusion of a discount. Instead of

[1]From Jack Miller, *Menu Pricing,* p. 58. Reprinted by permission of Van Nostrand Reinhold, New York.

charging $1.50 for an item, charge $1.49 and the customer will perceive this as a better price-value relationship. When using odd cents pricing, the two best ending figures to use are 9 and 5. This holds true for selling prices under $7. With prices in the $7 to $10 range, the best ending figure to use is 5. When dealing with prices over $10 the best ending figure is not an odd cents one but rather a 0. The reasoning behind this is that, in a restaurant with prices over $10, the illusion of a discount would tarnish the establishment rather than enhance it because selling prices over $10 are primarily confined to finer restaurants.

Another factor in psychological pricing is the importance of the left-hand digit and the distance between two prices. In other words, the customer will perceive a greater distance between 69 and 71 than between 67 and 69 even though the distance is the same (two cents). This is of particular importance to the restaurateur when price increases are being contemplated. The decision to break a price barrier by increasing the left-hand digit should be made anticipating a possible unit-sales decrease of that item.

A third factor in psychological pricing is the length of the price or the number of digits in the price. As in the left-hand digit theory, the customer also perceives distance here. In other words, greater distance is perceived between $9.99 and $10.25 than between $9.55 and $9.99, even though there is a $.26 difference between the first set of numbers, and a $.44 difference between the second set. Again, this strategy is of particular importance when increasing prices.

The decision when to break a dollar barrier is a crucial one. Many restaurant managers maintain that, when this occurs, the price should be held below the dollar barrier as long as is economically possible, and when an increase is taken that breaks this barrier, a substantial increase should be taken to offset previous losses when the increase was not taken. This makes sense in that, after a barrier is broken, the customer resistance to the price is the same whether it is close to or far from the barrier. In other words, if the selling price of an item should be $1, it would be wise to hold it at $.99 for as long as possible and then increase it to $1.10.[2]

It is important to recognize that the price ranges given earlier are only suggested parameters. When to use or not use psychological pricing depends on the image that management is attempting to portray for the food service establishment. Most fast food operations use psychological pricing, as these operations are very competitive and want the image of high value and low cost. Many coffee shops use it, as they also are highly competitive and want to portray value. Some theme and ethnic restaurants use psychological pricing and some don't, depending on the type of demographic market

[2]Kruel, Lee M. "Magic Numbers: Psychological Aspects of Menu Planning" *Cornell Quarterly*, August 1982 © Cornell University. Used by permission, all rights reserved.

FIGURE 4.10. Responses to questions regarding value of meals compared to price.*

	Fast Food	Moderately Priced	Higher Priced
Overall	5.85	7.26	6.44
Male	5.74	7.14	6.28
Ages 18-24	6.04	7.28	6.89
Ages 25-34	5.47	7.10	6.21
Ages 35-44	5.53	7.00	5.59
Ages 45-54	6.23	7.35	6.65
Ages 55 and over	5.85	7.16	6.56
Female	5.97	7.38	6.60
Ages 18-24	5.86	7.35	6.78
Ages 25-34	5.70	7.42	6.58
Ages 35-44	5.54	7.11	6.56
Ages 45-54	6.15	7.34	5.91
Ages 55 and over	6.38	7.55	6.90
Income			
Less than $20,000	6.10	7.50	6.79
$20,000-$29,999	6.20	7.32	6.31
$30,000-$39,999	5.41	7.30	6.64
$40,000-$59,999	5.93	7.23	6.54
$60,000 and over	5.47	7.09	6.01
Single	5.93	7.27	6.54
Under age 45	5.79	7.22	6.43
With children	**	**	**
Without children	5.67	7.13	6.45
Age 45 and over	6.23	7.40	6.78
With children	**	**	**
Without children	6.22	7.39	6.67
Married	5.81	7.26	6.37
Under age 45	5.54	7.18	6.28
With children	5.74	7.25	6.36
Without children	**	**	**
Age 45 and over	6.12	7.35	6.48
With children	**	**	**
Without children	6.11	7.40	6.61
Region			
Northeast	5.67	7.32	6.59
North Central	5.72	7.22	6.19
South	6.08	7.37	6.63
West	5.79	7.07	6.30

*On a 10-point scale where 1 = "strongly disagree" that meals are a good value and 10 = "strongly agree."

**Insufficient data.

Source: Courtesy of National Restaurant Association.

they are trying to reach. Fine dining establishments tend to shun the idea; they are trying to create an image of quality and luxury that does not lend itself to discounts.

Another factor to recognize is that psychological pricing can change the selling price that was determined by one of the markup formulas described earlier. This type of adjustment is not at all unusual. Every item on the menu does not have an identical food cost percentage or markup. The reason for this is the price-value relationship.

PRODUCT MIX

The selling price, as determined by management, must be perceived by the customer as being a good value. Consequently, different categories on the menu have different food costs assigned to them.

Why then would one go to all the trouble of figuring a selling price using one of the formulas, when in fact that price is probably going to change anyway?

Just because a restaurant desires, for example, a 35-percent food cost, not every item on the menu is marked up to give that specific cost. The 35-percent food cost would come from an aggregate of all items sold at their various costs. This is known as *product mix*. It is the product mix, the actual number of items sold at their various markups, that makes up cost of food sold on the income statement. Let us suppose, for example, that we opened a stand that sold nothing but tamales and we had a selling price that gave us a 35-percent food cost. As long as we purchased properly, had no waste, controlled our costs, and had no theft, we would in all probability end up with a 35-percent food cost. However, our customers got thirsty eating our tamales, so we added cola to our menu at a 12-percent cost. Selling both items reduced the 35-percent figure. As a matter of fact, the more cola we sold, the lower the composite food cost would be. The number of tamales and cola sold would be our product mix.

To determine the product mix of a menu, refer to the left-hand side of the chart in Figure 4-13, "Current Product Mix." The left-hand column lists the menu. In the next column under "# Sold," put the number of each entree sold. In the third column, put the cost of each item, which is obtained from the cost cards. The fourth column is the selling price, whichis copied from the menu. The fifth column is the food cost percentage, which is obtained by dividing the item's cost by the item's selling price. Then take the food cost in dollars times the number sold and put this figure int he "Total Cost" column. The next step is to take the selling price times the number sold and put this figure in the "Total Sales" column. Next, total the sales column and the cost column. Finally, divide the total cost by the total sales, the result being the composite food cost percent for the menu. *Do not add the food cost percent column and divide by five.* The composite food cost percentage for the menu is the product mix.

FIGURE 4.11. Food cost percent by menu categories.

Listed below are some typical ranges for food cost percent on an average menu.

Appetizers	20%–60%
Salads	30%–45%
Entrees	30%–60%
Sandwiches	25%–45%
Desserts	20%–50%
Beverages	5%–30%

FIGURE 4.12. Pam's tamale cart.

Item	Number Sold	Cost	Selling Price	Total Cost	Total Sales
Tamales	100	.12	.40	12.00	40.00
		%	.30		
		sales⌐cost	$40⌐$12.00		
Food Cost % – 30%					

With Cola Added to Menu

Item	Number Sold	Cost	Selling Price	Total Cost	Total Sales
Tamales	100	.12	.40	12.00	40.00
Cola	50	.06	.35	3.00	17.50
Totals				15.00	57.50
		%	.26		
Food Cost % – 26%		sales cost	$57.50 $15.00		

MENU PRECOST

The final step in determining new menu selling prices is the menu precost, which is very similar in nature to a product mix. The only difference is that a product mix tells what the present food cost percentage should be in the restaurant and the menu precost tells what is likely to occur to the food cost in the future. In order for either of these methods to be successful, it is obvious that careful records must be kept by management. The number of each item sold is critical if these numbers are to have any meaning. This information can be obtained by tallying the guest checks or by reading the printout if the restaurant has a data processing or point-of-sale register. Another critical piece of information is the food cost of each item. Cost cards must be kept up to date if the product mix or the menu precost is to have any validity.

Refer to Figure 4.13 and look on the right side of the chart that is labeled menu precost. The first step is to change the selling prices of those items that are to be altered. The second step is to anticipate the number to be sold based on the price change. If the selling price is increased substantially, the number sold could conceivably drop dramatically. If the price increase is slight, the number sold may not change at all. If the selling price is decreased, the number sold could well increase. It is important here to predict, as accurately as possible, what is likely to occur so that the precost will be a valid management tool on which to base decisions. After these steps are completed, divide the item cost by the projected selling price to get the food cost percentage. The next step is to take the item food cost times the projected number sold and put this figure in the total cost column. Then, take the selling price times the projected number sold

FIGURE 4.13. Example of product mix and menu precost.

			Correct Product Mix				Menu Precost					
	# Sold	Cost	Selling Price	Food Cost %	Total Cost	Total Sales	Total Forecast	Cost	Selling Price	Food Cost %	Total Cost	Total Sales
Prime Rib	110	4.15	10.95	38%	457	1.205	100	4.15	11.50	36%	415	1.150
Strip Steak	75	3.95	9.95	40%	296	746	85	3.95	Same	40%	336	846
Fried Chicken	190	1.80	4.85	37%	342	921	190	1.80	5.45	33%	342	1.035
Broiled Fish	130	2.10	6.50	32%	273	845	130	2.10	Same	32%	273	845
Rack of Lamb	60	3.55	10.50	34%	213	630	60	3.55	Same	34%	213	630
Total				36%	1.580	4.347				35%	1.579	4.506

In the above example, the current food cost is 36 percent. By increasing the selling price of prime rib and fried chicken the cost is lowered to 35 percent. Notice the change in forecast. It is anticipated that prime rib will drop 10 orders because of the increase, with customers shifting their selection to strip steak. Fried chicken remained unchanged because it is still the lowest-priced item on the menu.

and put this figure in the total sales column. Total the sales column and the cost column and divide the projected total costs by the projected total sales; the result is the projected food cost percent (projected product mix). Do not take the percentage column and divide by 5. If the percentage meets the expectations or the desired standard, then all that is left to do is to implement the changes. If not, it is necessary to go back and institute further changes until the desired food cost percentage is achieved.

CONCLUSION

Determining the correct selling prices on a menu, as you can see, is a time-consuming and exacting science. It is imperative that accurate records, such as cost cards and income statements, are kept. If they are not, the results could be disastrous. Remember, profit starts with the menu. If the correct selling price is not established, all of the work and effort that goes into managing a successful enterprise is wasted. The person who decides what to charge by matching what competition charges will eventually have a for sale sign in the window. The astute manager who runs the business like a professional will enjoy success. It's just that simple!

QUESTIONS

1. Explain in your own words
   a) Gross profit
   b) Psychological pricing
   c) Product mix
   d) Menu precost

2. When analyzing financial statements and discussing costs, why are percentages used rather than dollar figures?

3. Given the following data, figure the selling price of an item that costs you $1.19 using
   a) The factor method
   b) The markup on cost method
   c) The gross markup method
   d) The ratio method
   e) The TRA method

Sales	$765,000
Cost of food sold	224,500
Gross profit	?
Labor expense	198,750
Other controllable expenses	74,000
Noncontrollable expenses	85,500
Total expense	?
Pretax profits	?

   Number of customers served 200,000.
   Assume all costs are desired costs.

4. Using the product mix and menu precost chart (Figure 4.13) on page 94, give the new food cost percent, assuming the following changes on the precost side of the chart.
   Prime rib—cost drops to $3.95
   Strip steak—cost increases to $4.15
   Fried chicken—same
   Broiled fish—increase selling price to $6.75
   Rack of lamb—delete
   Rack of lamb will be replaced with stuffed baked pork chops with a cost of $2.25, a selling price of $7, and anticipated forecast of 100 units sold.

5. As a food and beverage director of a large downtown hotel, tell when and how you would use psychological pricing in the following units under your control. Defend your answer.
   a) Coffee shop—moderately priced
   b) Fast food operation—street level, outside entrance, local customers as well as guests
   c) Fine dining—roof top, high priced

6. Using the income statement in this chapter, write the word formulas for each line item.

Software Applications

Select PRICING from the menu plan. The income statement from the textbook is illustrated on the screen. Any number in any of the blue boxes can be changed. By changing these numbers, you can see what different numbers will do to the profitability of a restaurant. For example, if the sales are changing, what happens to costs and profit? What if labor goes up (or down)? Spend some time playing with this section; it is very interesting.

On the upper left part of the screen, put the cursor on "FILE" and drag downward to markup methods. The first one is the factor method. We will use all the methods to complete this exercise and will also use the cost cards developed in Chapter 3. Since the cost cards were for the entree only, a cost of $2.00 will be added to each of the entrees for accompanying items.

For the **factor method,** assume that we want a food cost of 40%. Move the cursor to "DESIRED FOOD COST" and put in the number ".40" (it is imperative that the decimal be used; otherwise you will get 4,000%). Next select the cost card for Carolina Ribs. The cost was $2.88. To this add $2.00 for the accompanying items, for a total meal cost of $4.88. Move the cursor to "MEAL COST" and type in "4.88." The selling price should appear as $12.20.

For the **markup-on-cost method,** assume a 45% food cost and use the cost card for shrimp ($4.57 + 2.00 = $6.57 for the complete meal). Place the numbers in the appropriate boxes, and the selling price should be $14.60.

Next, for the **gross markup method,** assume that the gross profit for the restaurant was $330,830 and the number of customers served was 46,150. Using the cost card for the Chicken Tarragon and adding $2.00 for accompanying items, figure the selling price. It should be $10.02.

The **ratio method** will use the Veal Marsala cost card plus $2.00. Assume that the cost of food sold in dollars is $200,040 and that all other expenses and profit total $300,060. The selling price for this item should be $15.05.

For the **TRA method,** use the beef rib cost card plus $2.00 for accompanying items. Assume that labor cost is 30%, operating cost is 35%, and profit is 10%. The selling price should be $10.76.

Print a hard copy of all these selling prices.

CHAPTER FIVE

Menu Analysis

OBJECTIVES By the completion of this chapter, the reader should be able to:

- Analyze a menu for profitability.
- Apply menu engineering to menu analysis.
- Apply menu scoring methods to menu analysis.

IMPORTANT TERMS

Stars
Puzzles
Menu engineering
Aesthetic analysis

Plow horses
Dogs
Menu scoring

INTRODUCTION

Now that the menu has been priced, this chapter explains how to evaluate it. When measuring a menu to see whether it is successful, two criteria must be met in order to declare it a winner: one, it must be profitable in terms of individual item profitability; and, two, the most profitable items must be those that are selling the best. For evaluating menus, several systems are available. Two of the most widely used methods are presented in this chapter and another technique, product mix, was presented in the previous chapter. The reason these systems are popular is that they systematically break down a menu's components to analyze which items are making money and which items are selling. This analysis then leads management to make decisions as to which menu items to leave alone, which to increase or decrease in selling price, which ones to promote, and which ones to eliminate.

STARS, PLOW HORSES, PUZZLES, AND DOGS

The first method, called menu engineering, was developed by Donald Smith, Ph.D., Westin Hotels Distinguished Professor at Washington State University. This method rates the menu by measuring each entree as to its profitability (gross profit) and its sales. It then combines these measurements and places each menu item into one of four classifications:

1. stars
2. plow horses
3. puzzles
4. dogs

One point to understand before delving into menu engineering is the theory of contributing margins. In using this method, the contribution margin (CM) of each item is determined. To figure this, take the total food cost (FC) of each item and subtract it from the selling price (SP). The result is the contribution margin. Thus, the formula looks like this:

$$SP - FC = CM$$

If contribution margin looks familiar, it is. The contribution margin is exactly the same as an item's gross profit. A point to remember when figuring the food cost is that it is a *total* food cost; that is, the cost of the item plus garnish cost, plus any accompaniments served with that entree such as salad, potatoes, rolls, butter, and so on.

FIGURE 5.1. Contribution margin in dollars vs. food cost in percent.

	Steak Dinner	Fish Sandwich	Coffee
Selling price	$15.00	$4.00	$0.75
Cost	$7.50	$1.00	$0.15
Food cost %	50%	25%	20%
Cont. margin $	$7.50	$3.00	$0.60

In the above example, coffee has the lowest food cost but is also contributing the least amount in terms of real dollars to the profit picture.

Notice in the accompanying illustration that the relationship between food cost percent and contribution margin in dollars is not consistent. In other words, an item that has a high contribution margin in dollars does not necessarily have a low food cost in percent. Too often, management is led to believe that low food cost percents are the primary objective. Not so. As one cynical wag put it, you don't take percents to the bank, you take money.

USING MENU ENGINEERING

This example illustrates how menu engineering works in actual practice. Johnny's Grill is a table specialty restaurant with 10 items on its dinner menu. Figure 5.2 shows how menu engineering is used to analyze Johnny's menu for a 30-day period.

1. First, the manager lists all menu entrees in column A. Only entree items are listed. Appetizers, desserts, and other side items are not listed. Do not list alcoholic beverage sales on this list. While the ratio of food to beverage sales is a key to successful merchandising in most restaurants, the analysis of beverage sales should be done separately. Although these purchases are separated for the menu analysis, the successful manager is always concerned with the guests' total expenditures. Daily specials should also be analyzed separately. Listing purchases of daily specials by themselves makes their impact on the menu more easily identified. If the manager's suggestive selling program is effective, daily specials should be popular and have relatively high contribution margins.

2. The total number of purchases for each item is listed in column B. Note: All purchases are listed on a per-person basis or covers sold. This number can be obtained from the point-of-sale (POS) data or from a tally sheet showing the number of items purchased by each guest on the guest's check.

3. Each item's sales are then divided by the total number of purchases (3,000 in this case) to determine that item's menu mix percentage, column C—mix %.

FIGURE 5.2. Stars, plow horses, puzzles, & dogs

A Entrees	B Purch.	C Mix % Cat.	D Mix Total	E Selling Price	F Food Cost	G Cont. Margin	H Rev.
ITEM 1	170	06%	LOW	$5.95	$2.10	$3.85	$1012
ITEM 2	450	15%	HIGH	$6.25	$2.60	$3.65	$2813
ITEM 3	350	12%	HIGH	$4.50	$1.25	$3.25	$1575
ITEM 4	380	13%	HIGH	$4.95	$1.55	$3.40	$1881
ITEM 5	80	03%	LOW	$6.10	$3.00	$3.10	$ 488
ITEM 6	410	14%	HIGH	$5.50	$1.80	$3.70	$2255
ITEM 7	290	10%	HIGH	$5.85	$2.45	$3.40	$1697
ITEM 8	320	11%	HIGH	$4.85	$1.60	$3.25	$1552
ITEM 9	440	15%	HIGH	$5.25	$1.50	$3.75	$2310
ITEM 10	110	04%	LOW	$4.95	$1.60	$3.35	$ 545
TOTALS	3000						

4. In column D, each item's menu mix percentage is categorized as either high or low. Any menu item that is lower than 70 percent of the menu mix average percentage is considered low. Any item that is 70 percent or above average is considered high. Note: On this 10-item menu, each item is 10 percent of the mix (1.00/10 = 10%). Therefore, 10 percent represents the menu mix average percent. On a 20-item menu the average would be 5 percent (1.00/20 = 50%) where 5 percent is the menu mix average percent. For Johnny's 10-item menu, we multiply 10 percent times 70 percent to get the desired menu mix percentage rate of .07, or 7 percent. Therefore, any item selling 7 percent or higher is considered high. Any item selling less than 7 percent is low.

5. Each item's selling price is listed in column E. Note: The selling price is obtained from the menu.

6. Each item's standard food cost is listed in column F. Note: An item's standard portion cost is obtained from the cost card and is composed of the standard recipe cost, garnish cost, and the cost of accompanying items. Not all items, however, necessarily have all three cost components.

7. The contribution margin for each item is listed in column G. Note: Contribution margin is determined by subtracting the item's standard food cost (column F) from its selling price (column E).

8. In column H, the total menu revenue is recorded. Note: Total menu revenue is determined by multiplying the number of purchases of each item (column B) by its selling price (column E).

9. In column I, list the total item food cost. Note: Multiply each item's standard food cost (column F) by the number of items purchased (column B) to obtain total food cost (column I).

I Total Food Cost	J Total Cont. Margin	K Cont. Margin %	L Cont. Mgn.	M Class. Cat.	N Decision
$ 357	$ 655	06%	HIGH	PUZZLE	LOWER S.P. TO $5.75
$1170	$ 1643	16%	HIGH	STAR	LEAVE IT ALONE
$ 438	$ 1138	11%	LOW	PLOW HORSE	RAISE S.P. TO $4.75
$ 589	$ 1292	12%	LOW	PLOW HORSE	LEAVE IT ALONE
$ 240	$ 248	02%	LOW	DOG	ELIMINATE IT
$ 738	$ 1517	14%	HIGH	STAR	LEAVE IT ALONE
$ 711	$ 986	09%	LOW	PLOW HORSE	REDUCE PORTION
$ 512	$ 1040	10%	LOW	PLOW HORSE	RAISE TO $5.25
$ 660	$ 1650	16%	HIGH	STAR	LEAVE IT ALONE
$ 176	$ 369	04%	LOW	DOG	ELIMINATE IT
	$10538		AVE.C.M. $3.51		

10. The total menu contribution margin is listed in column J. Note: This is determined by multiplying each item's contribution margin (column G) times the item's total number of purchases (column B).

11. In column K, the contribution margin percentage for each item is listed. Note: This is determined by dividing each individual item's contribution margin (column J) by the total menu contribution margin which is the total of column J, $10,538.

12. Each item's contribution margin is categorized as either high or low in column L, depending on whether or not the item exceeds the menu's average contribution margin. Note: The menu's average contribution margin is determined by dividing the total contribution margin ($10,538), the total of column J, by the total number of items sold (3,000), the total of column B. The average contribution margin for Johnny's Grill is $3.51. Any item whose contribution margin is greater than $3.51 is categorized as high, and any item whose contribution margin is lower than $3.51 is listed as low.

13. Use all the data gathered to classify each item into categories in column M. Note: Each menu item is classified as a star, plow horse, puzzle, or dog. These classifications are explained in the following section.

14. In column N list the decisions made on each item. Note: Decisions to retain, reposition, replace, or reprice are discussed after the explanation of the four classifications.

THE FOUR KEY MENU CATEGORIES

When accurate information has been gathered and analyzed for each menu item as was done in Figure 5.2, the items are then categorized for decision making. All menu items can be grouped into four categories: stars, plow horses, puzzles, and dogs.

Stars. Menu items high in both popularity and contribution margin. Stars are the most popular items on the menu. They may be signature items.

Plow Horses. Menu items high in popularity but low in contribution margin. Plow horses are demand generators. They may be a lead item on the menu or a signature item. They are often significant to the restaurant's popularity with price-conscious buyers.

Puzzles. Menu items low in popularity but high in contribution margin. In other words, puzzles yield a high profit per item sold, but they are hard to sell.

Dogs. Menu items low in popularity and low in contribution margin. These are losers. They are unpopular and they generate little profit.

HOW TO USE THE CATEGORIES

Once all the menu items have been grouped into one of the four key categories, it is time to make decisions. The category for each item must be analyzed and evaluated separately.

Stars (popular and profitable). Rigid specifications for quality, quantity, and presentation of all star items must be maintained. They should be located in a highly visible position on the menu. Test them occasionally for price rigidity. In other words, are guests willing to pay more for these items and still buy them in significant quantity? The super stars of the menu—the highest-priced stars—may be less price sensitive than any other items on the menu. If so, these items may be able to carry a larger portion of any increase in cost of food and labor.

Plow Horses (popular but less profitable). These items are often an important reason for a restaurant's popularity. Because they are less profitable, or maybe even unprofitable, one solution may be to increase their price. However, this should be done very carefully. If plow horses are highly price sensitive, then attempt to pass on only the food cost increase of the item to the menu price. In addition, determine the direct labor cost of each plow horse to establish its labor and skill intensiveness. If the item requires high skills or is labor intensive, consider a careful price increase, or, if it is only marginally profitable, drop it from the menu and make a substitution for it. Another possibility would be to consider placing the plow horse's increase onto a super star item. When increasing the price, always test for a negative effect on demand (rigidity). Make any price increase in stages (from $4.55 to $4.75, then $4.95) and remember psychological pricing. If it is necessary to increase prices, again, pass only the additional cost. Do not add more.

If the item is an image maker or signature item, hold its current price as long as possible in periods of high price sensitivity. On the other hand, if the listing is a nonsignature item with a low contribution margin, move the plow horse to a lower profile position on the menu. Attempt to shift demand to more profitable items through merchandising and menu positioning.

Another solution might be to reduce the item's standard portion without making the difference noticeable. You can try adding value to the item through table d'hote packaging. In other words, merchandise the plow horse by packaging it with side items to increase its contribution margin. Another option is to use the item to create a "better-value alternative." For example, prime rib can be sold by the inch, and steaks can be sold by the ounce. This offers guests an opportunity to spend more and get more value.

Puzzles (unpopular but very profitable). One of the best solutions to helping out a puzzle is to decrease its price. While this concept is foreign to many managers and totally unacceptable to others, consider that the item may have a contribution margin that is too high and is facing price resistance. In other words, the customer does not perceive it as a fair value. Or, leave its price alone and feature it at a discounted price in advertising or as a daily special. Care must be taken, however, not to lower the contribution margin to a point where the puzzle draws menu share from a star.

Another option is to reposition the puzzle and feature it in a more popular location on the menu. Additionally, merchandise it by using table tents, chalkboards, or suggestive selling. Rename it. A puzzle's popularity can be affected by what it is called, especially if the name can be made to sound familiar. Remember that a puzzle is not selling well but is making a lot of money. If sales can be substantially increased without decreasing the price, the item could easily become a star.

Limit the number of puzzles you allow on your menu. Puzzles can create difficulties in quality consistency, slow production down, and cause inventory and cost problems. You must accurately evaluate the effect puzzle items have on your image. Do they enhance your image? A final option is to take them off the menu, particularly if a puzzle is low in popularity, requires costly or additional inventory, has poor shelf life, requires skilled or labor-intensive preparation, and is of inconsistent quality.

Dogs (unpopular and unprofitable). Eliminate all dog items if possible. Food service operators are often intimidated by influential guests to carry a dog item on the menu. The way to solve this problem is to carry the item in inventory (assuming it has a shelf life), but not on the menu. The special guest is offered the opportunity to have the item made to order on request. Charge extra for this service. Raise the dog's price to puzzle status. Whenever possible, replace dogs with more popular items. This is an area where the restaurant can take advantage of hot, trendy, or cutting-edge listings. When replacing dogs, add items that will immediately become stars.

Some items in the dog category may have market potential. These tend to be the more popular dogs, and may be converted to puzzles by increasing prices. Another detail to consider is that the menu may have too many items. It is not unusual to discover a number of highly unpopular menu listings that have little, if any, relation to other more popular and profitable items held in inventory. Do not be afraid to terminate dogs, especially when demand is not satisfactory.

MAKING DECISIONS

Using the foregoing explanations, the menu can now be analyzed and an attempt made to improve it. Before starting, however, remember that menu planning is both a science and an art. The scientific part has just been completed. The numbers tell an accurate story of what actually happened: what sold and what didn't, what made money and what didn't. By using this scientific knowledge, changes can now be made both rationally and logically. Making changes is where the art of menu planning comes in. This deals with the future and cannot be quantified as the past can. All the concepts previously discussed in this text, plus industry experience, now come into play. Many options are available and different managers will exercise different ones. Although many of the options could be solutions to the menu's problems and make it a success, some will not and will actually make it worse. The decisions made have a direct impact on the success of the menu.

Item #1.   A puzzle. High contribution margin, but very low unit sales. Lowering the selling price to $5.75 could increase unit sales.

Item #2.   A star. Leave it alone.

Item #3.   A plow horse. Lowest selling price on the menu as well as lowest contribution margin, which in turn is the best price-value relationship. If the selling price is carefully increased to $4.75, the item is still the lowest priced but the contribution margin increases.

Item #4. A plow horse. Probably signature item of the restaurant based on high number sold. An increase in selling price would break the $5 barrier. A decrease in portion size or change in formula could ruin sales. Leave it alone.

Item #5. A dog. Eliminate it and replace with a new and exciting menu item.

Item #6. A star. Leave it alone.

Item #7. A plow horse. By reducing the portion of this item and its cost to $2.20, the contribution margin would increase. Assuming a minimal drop in sales, this item would become a star.

Item #8. A plow horse. Try breaking the price barrier by packaging it with a side item and selling it for $5.25. Cost would increase to $1.85.

Item #9. A star. Leave it alone.

Item #10. A dog. Eliminate it and replace it with a trendy new item.

Once a change has been put into effect by producing a new menu, it remains to be seen whether the change has been positive or negative. After the new menu has had a solid trial run for a month or more, another menu engineering test should be run. This is the report card. Are sales up? Is profit up? Are there more stars and fewer dogs? Are further changes, along with some refinement, needed? If so, then back to the drawing board. If not, then leave it alone for a while. If it's not broke, don't fix it.

A menu engineering test should be run periodically. A more trendy, cutting-edge restaurant would conduct the test more often as its market is in a constant state of flux. A theme, ethnic, family restaurant or fast food operation would conduct the test less often. One thing in life is constant and that is change. By utilizing menu engineering, management can stay in touch with changing food costs, market conditions, customer demographics, and customers' eating habits.

MENU SCORING

Another method of evaluating menu profitability is menu scoring. This method was developed by Michael Hurst, Professor of Restaurant Management at Florida International University, a restaurant owner and past president of the National Restaurant Association. This method was devised to ascertain whether menu changes (that is, additions, deletions, and price adjustments) actually improved the profitability of the menu by comparisons of a menu score. One advantage of this method is that it is quick to complete because it does not track every menu item.

To determine a menu's score simply follow these steps.

A) Determine the entree items on the menu that contribute a major portion of sales income and select those to be evaluated. Unless the income from sandwiches, salads, beverages, or other listings is significant, do not include these. List the items selected under column A.

B) Prepare a menu count for the number of each item sold for the period to be evaluated. Place the counts in column B.

C) List the selling price from the menu for each item tested in column C.

D) Calculate the food cost for each item to be evaluated or obtain the cost from the item's cost card. List the cost in column D.

E) Calculate the item's food cost percentage by dividing the item food cost by the item selling price and put this percentage in column E.

F) Calculate the menu score as follows:
1. Total the item sales dollars by taking the number of items sold times the item selling price to get the total sales of each item. Put this number in column F. Column B times column C = column F.
2. Total the item food cost dollars by multiplying the number sold times the item food cost to get the total cost of each item. Put this number in column G. Column B times column D = column G.
3. Total the sales dollars for all items to be evaluated (column F), total the food cost dollars for all items to be evaluated (column G), and total the number of items sold of those to be evaluated in the period (column B).
4. Figure the composite food cost by dividing the total cost of the item (column G) by total sales (column F). Put the composite food cost at the bottom of column E. Note: Do not total the food cost percent of each item (column E) and divide by the number of items in the test, as this will give you an average food cost, not a composite.
5. The dollar meal average is obtained by taking total sales dollars (column F) and dividing it by total number of items sold (column B).
6. Gross profit percentage of items evaluated during the period is figured by subtracting the composite food cost percent (bottom number under column E) from sales in percent (always 100%).
7. Average gross profit dollars per meal is arrived at by multiplying the average sale times the gross profit percentage. Step 5 times step 6.
8. To obtain the percentage of the menu being tested, take the total number of items sold in the test (total of column B) and divide this number by the total number of customers served in the restaurant during this period.

9. The menu score is figured by multiplying the gross profit dollar average by the percentage of the menu being tested. Step 7 times step 8 equals the menu score (Step 9).

The higher the score is, the more profitable the menu will be. This method not only takes into account how many of certain items were sold, but it also takes into account what their contributing profit was. In other words, the more items were sold that have high gross profits, the more profitable the menu would be and, therefore, the higher would be the score it received. The reverse is also true in that if a high number of items that were sold that have a lower gross profit, the less profitable the menu would be and consequently the lower its score would be. Other scenarios would include a low number of items sold with a high gross profit and low number of items sold with low gross profits. This should all sound vaguely familiar by now.

One menu score by itself doesn't tell anything because scores need to be compared against each other to determine whether the menu is increasing in profitability. Also, scores need to be compared with each other in the same operating unit. A menu score in one restaurant cannot be compared with a menu score in another restaurant because there are too many variables involved.

FIGURE 5.3. Menu scoring exercise.[1]

A Item	B # Sold	C Item Sell Price	D Item Food Cost	E FC %	F Total Sales	G Total Cost	
Totals							

STEP 4.
$$\frac{\text{TOTAL COST}}{\text{TOTAL SALES}} = \text{COMP. FOOD COST}$$

STEP 5.
$$\frac{\text{TOTAL SALES}}{\text{\# ITEMS SOLD}} = \text{DOLLAR MEAL AVERAGE}$$

STEP 6.
SALES %
$$\frac{- \text{FOOD COST \%}}{\text{GROSS PROFIT}}$$

STEP 7.
AVERAGE SALE
$$\frac{\times \text{GROSS PROFIT \%}}{\text{GROSS PROFIT \$}}$$

STEP 8.
$$\frac{\text{TOTAL MEALS TESTED}}{\text{TOTAL MEALS SOLD}} = \text{\% OF MENU BEING TESTED}$$

STEP 9.
GROSS PROFIT $
$$\frac{\times \text{\% MENU UNDER TEST}}{\text{MENU SCORE}}$$

[1]Reprinted with permission from *Management By Menu, Second Edition*, by Lendal H. Kotschevar. Copyright © 1987 by the Educational Foundation of the National Restaurant Association, Chicago, Il.

WHICH METHOD TO USE

As can be seen, whichever method is used, both accomplish basically the same thing. They tell management what is selling, what is not, what is profitable and what is not. They give management the tools to work with to implement change successfully. They force management to look at the menu in terms of profitability, and profitability can mean only one thing to the restaurateur—success.

Different corporations or chains will probably use one or the other or even the product mix concept covered in Chapter 4. If no method is dictated, use whichever is the most comfortable.

COMPUTER APPLICATIONS

Both of these methods, as well as product mix, are easily programmed on a personal computer using any one of a number of spreadsheets such as Excel, Claris, or Lotus, to mention but a few. Several companies have done the programming and integrated one of these analysis methods with other features to give management a complete set of menu controls. Some of these companies are Sweetware, At Your Service, and Menu Pro. Although some of them utilize menu engineering or a similar concept, they do not all employ the same terms used here. Regardless of the terms, the results are the same.

CONCLUSION

Menu analysis is important. If demographic studies, internal capacities, cost cards, and markups have been executed correctly, the score should be a good one. Analysis should be done using either the Smith or Hurst methods to ascertain the profitability of the menu. If the analysis shows a poor menu, management needs to regroup and make improvements. If, on the other hand, it shows that a good menu has been produced, the first step has been taken toward running a successful and profitable operation. It's just that simple!

QUESTIONS

1. Using the following data, develop a star, plow horse, puzzle, and dog chart as well as a menu scoring chart (using four of the six entrees).

Entree	Purchases	Selling Price	Cost
Item I	$150	$9.95	$4.70
Item II	300	7.25	2.90
Item III	250	8.75	3.50
Item IV	500	6.95	2.45
Item V	50	7.50	3.60
Item VI	400	8.95	2.70

2. Complete a star, plow horse, puzzle, and dog marketing grid for the foregoing data.

3. Improve the menu using the concepts learned in this chapter. Defend all of your changes.

4. Redo the star, plow horse, puzzle, and dog chart, as well as your menu scoring chart, to see whether the changes have improved your menu.

5. Explain stars, plow horses, puzzles, and dogs in terms that would help the wait staff improve their selling of the menu you have developed.

- Click on the Analysis box from the menu plan page, and the menu engineering spreadsheet will appear.
- On the upper left-hand of the screen is a plus (+) box and a minus (−) box. Select the + box and add spaces on the spreadsheet until you have five lines.
- Enter the five entrees that you have completed cost cards for and have determined selling prices for (from Chapters 3 and 4) under the entree heading. Abbreviate the names as follows:
  Carolina Ribs
  Shrimp
  Chicken
  Veal Marsala
  Short Ribs
- Next, enter the amount of the purchase for each item. Assume that purchases were as follows:
  Carolina Ribs   90
  Shrimp   85
  Chicken   235
  Veal Marsala   80
  Short Ribs   210
- Notice that the program determined whether the listings were categorized as either high or low.
- Enter the selling prices that may have been modified from the cost cards as follows:
  Carolina Ribs $12.25
  Shrimp $14.60
  Chicken $10.00
  Veal Marsala $15.00
  Short Ribs $10.60 (This was lowered for competitive reasons.)
- Enter the food cost for each item. This is obtained from the cost card-cost per portion plus $2.00 for accompanying items. In other words, it is the same cost that was used on markups.
- Notice that the software program has just completed the spreadsheet.
- Next, categorize each item as to star, plowhorse, puzzle, or dog. Hold off on the decision column for a moment.
- Move the cursor to the "FILE" icon on the upper left-hand part of your screen and scroll down to menu scoring.

- Type in the five entrees, number sold, sell price, and item food cost. Use the same items and numbers that were used on the menu engineering exercise. In the box labeled "Total Meals Sold," put "1200."
- Notice that the menu score has been figured.

Now it is time to make changes and improve the menu. **(Don't forget to print your original.)** Go back to menu engineering and make a decision for each entree. Raise or lower selling prices or drop items. If an item is dropped, it must be replaced with another item. For new items, research and develop a recipe for the new item by consulting cook books. Do a cost card, select a markup method, and determine a new selling price.

Under the column "number sold," be realistic. If a price has increased, there will probably be less sold. If a selling price decreases, there will probably be more sold. A new item will probably take away from other items. Keep the total number sold constant at 700. In other words, if one item sells more, then another must sell less.

Plug all the changes you have made into a new menu engineering and menu scoring exercise. Are there improvements?

CHAPTER SIX

Nutrition

OBJECTIVES   By the completion of this chapter, the reader should be able to:

- Explain the impact of nutrition on menu writing.
- Explain the food pyramid.
- Describe various nutrients and their importance.
- Explain nutritional issues affecting menu design.

IMPORTANT TERMS

Type A lunch
Calories
Absolute claim

The basic four
Registered dietitian
Implied claim

INTRODUCTION

Everyone knows, or should know, the value of nutrition to a person's health and well-being. Most people when cooking at home tend to follow guidelines that result in a nutritionally balanced meal. However, for whatever reason, many of these same people choose to ignore nutritional guidelines when selecting their food away from home. Maybe it's the speed factor at lunch with a double cheeseburger, large fries, and a cola or the celebration factor of a night on the town and "I don't care how many calories or fat grams are in this." The menu writer must remember that while there are nutritional fanatics and junk food fanatics, with everyone else in between, there appears to be a definite shift toward more sound nutritional behavior. The fact is that more people are jogging, exercising, and participating in sports, with the result being a welcome improvement in the diet. Today, a larger segment of society is selecting natural foods with healthier methods of preparation. Nevertheless, while high fat/high calorie foods are on the decline, this is not to say that these items should be stricken from the menu; they still sell.

RESPONSIBILITY

The nutritional responsibility of food service managers with regard to menu listings varies greatly. Their responsibility to the nutritional well-being of their customer also varies. The basis of this variation is dependent on how often a person would frequent the food service establishment. A sliding scale, shown in Figure 6.1, can be developed with restaurants being on the low end and noncommercial food service operations being on the high end. The category of restaurants could be subdivided into a customer's frequency of visits with a high-priced fine dining operation at the low visit end, a mid-priced theme or ethnic restaurant in the middle, and a mid-low priced cafeteria or family restaurant on the high visit end.

Managers of high-priced fine dining operations would have the lowest degree of responsibility. However, that is not to say that they

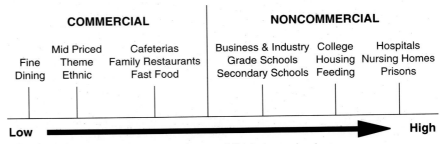

FIGURE 6.1. Management's nutritional responsibility in menu planning.

would have no responsibility at all. Some consideration has to be given to those customers who desire well-balanced healthy meals. Healthy entrees can blend quite easily into the menu alongside the heavier-sauced, high-calorie, high-fat listings. Healthy food does not have to be bland or dull. Quite to the contrary, many chefs are incorporating cooking techniques that emphasize fresh local or regional foods as well as reformulated recipes that greatly lower or even eliminate fats.

A mid-priced theme or ethnic restaurant would have a slightly higher degree of responsibility as repeat customers tend to frequent these establishments more often. Many national chains have listed nutritious items alongside their traditional and signature items with a great degree of success. How far to go with healthy listing depends on customer demographics. Menu analysis, covered in Chapter 5, shows quickly what is selling and what is contributing the most toward profit. If the analysis indicates that nutrition is selling, expand those listings. If not, then cut back on the slow-moving healthy items; however, don't totally eliminate them. Some customers, although they may be fewer in number, still desire and even demand nutritional food away from home.

Cafeterias, family restaurants, and fast food operations, being on the lower end of the pricing scale, have the greatest obligation of the restaurant segment to offer nutritious food to their customers. This group has the greatest frequency of visits by consumers as well as the greatest number of regular customers; that is, people who eat in one particular restaurant day after day. In these operations, healthy menu listings are less of a courtesy and more of a responsibility to the restaurant manager regarding the nutritional well-being of customers. While it is almost mandatory that every establishment in this segment list at least some healthy meals on the menu, it is the customers' right to choose what they please. If they enjoy high-fat, high-calorie food, then so be it; at the very least, the restaurant has met its obligation. The restaurant industry as a whole may not be able to change behaviors, but can accommodate them.

For those who are involved in noncommercial food service operations, the nutritional responsibility increases. This noncommercial category can be broken down into two segments: noncaptive and captive food services. Noncaptive food services, such are those in factories, offices, primary or secondary schools, etc., need to be very aware, not only of nutrition, but of balanced diets as well. Most of the patrons in this segment depend on these establishments for at least one or more of their daily meals. Quite often, that meal is the only nutritionally balanced meal of the day that they will receive. In these operations, the services of a dietitian are quite often utilized to assure that the meals follow accepted nutritional standards. In the primary and secondary school system, the Type A lunch program, discussed later, is followed to assure school children of receiving a nutritionally balanced meal. Whether or not professional help is given in the form

FIGURE 6.2.   A good example of nutritional responsibility to the customer. The nutritional content of the entire menu is listed in this handout. (*Courtesy of Taco Bell Corporation, Irvine, California*)

TACO BELL™

NUTRITIONAL INFORMATION

Item	Serving Ounces	Calories	% Calorie Reduction	Calories from Fat	Total Fat (gms)	% Fat Reduction	% Daily Value **	Saturated Fat (gms)	% Daily Value **	Cholesterol (mgs)	% Daily Value **	Sodium (mgs)	% Daily Value **	Carbohydrates (gms)	% Daily Value **	Dietary Fiber (gms)	% Daily Value **	Sugars (gms)	Protein (gms)	% DAILY VALUE: Vitamin A	Vitamin C	Calcium	Iron	DIABETIC EXCHANGE: Starch/Bread	Meat***	Fat	Vegetable	Milk	Fruit
TACOS																													
Taco	2 3/4	170		90	10		15	4	20	30	10	280	12	11	4	1	4	0	10	4	0	6	4	1/2	1	1			
Soft Taco	3 1/2	210		90	10		15	4 1/2	23	30	10	530	22	20	7	2	8	1	12	4	4	8	6	1	1	1			
Taco Supreme®	4	220		120	13		20	6	30	45	15	290	12	13	4	2	8	2	11	6	6	8	6	1	1	1 1/2			
Soft Taco Supreme®	4 3/4	260		120	14		22	7	35	45	15	540	23	22	7	2	8	2	13	4	6	10	6	1 1/2	1	1 1/2			
DOUBLE DECKER™ Taco	5 1/2	340		130	15		23	5	25	30	10	700	29	37	12	8	32	1	16	4	0	10	10	2	1	2 1/2			
DOUBLE DECKER™ Taco Supreme®	6 3/4	390		170	18		28	8	40	45	15	710	30	39	13	8	32	3	16	6	6	15	10	2	1	3 1/2			
Steak Soft Taco †	5	200		60	7		11	3	15	25	8	500	21	18	6	1	4	1	14	4	0	8	8	1	1	1			
BLT Soft Taco †	4 1/4	340		210	23		35	8	40	40	13	610	25	22	7	2	8	3	11	4	6	10	4	1	1	4			
Kid's Soft Taco Roll-Up	3 3/4	290		140	16		25	8	40	50	17	790	33	20	7	2	8	1	16	20	0	20	6	1 1/2	1	2			
BURRITOS																													
Bean Burrito	7	380		110	12		18	4	20	10	3	1140	48	55	18	12	48	2	13	30	2	15	15	3	1	1 1/2			
Burrito Supreme®	8 3/4	440		170	18		28	8	40	45	15	1220	51	50	17	8	32	3	19	30	8	15	10	3	1	3			
BIG BEEF Burrito Supreme®	10 1/4	520		210	23		35	10	50	70	23	1450	60	52	17	9	36	3	26	30	8	15	15	3	2	3			
7-Layer Burrito	10	540		210	24		37	9	45	25	8	1310	55	65	22	14	56	4	16	10	10	20	15	4	1	3			
Chili Cheese Burrito	5	330		120	13		20	6	30	35	12	880	37	37	12	4	16	2	14	60	0	15	8	2	1	2			
Chicken Club Burrito †	7 3/4	540		280	31		48	10	50	65	22	1290	54	43	14	4	16	5	22	4	10	15	8	2 1/2	2	4			
Bacon Cheeseburger Burrito †	8 1/4	560		270	30		46	12	60	85	28	1360	57	43	14	4	16	4	29	10	8	15	15	2 1/2	3	3			
SPECIALTIES																													
Tostada	6 1/4	300		130	14		22	5	25	15	5	700	29	31	10	11	44	1	11	35	4	15	10	2	1	1 1/2			
Mexican Pizza	7 3/4	570		330	36		55	11	55	50	17	1050	44	41	14	6	24	1	21	45	8	25	20	2 1/2	2	5			
BIG BEEF MexiMelt®	4 1/2	300		150	16		25	8	40	50	17	860	36	21	7	2	8	1	16	30	6	20	6	1	2	1 1/2			
Taco Salad with Salsa	19	840		470	52		80	15	75	75	25	1670	70	62	21	13	52	8	32	150	40	25	35	3	3	7	2		
Taco Salad w/Salsa without Shell	16	420		190	21		32	11	55	75	25	1420	59	29	10	13	52	8	26	150	35	25	25	1	3	1	2		
Cheese Quesadilla †	4 1/4	370		180	20		31	12	60	55	18	730	30	32	11	1	4	1	16	60	0	45	10	2	2	1			
Chicken Quesadilla †	5 3/4	420		190	22		34	12	60	85	28	1020	43	33	11	1	4	2	24	60	2	45	10	2	3	1			
BORDER WRAPS™																													
Steak FAJITA WRAP™	7 3/4	460		190	21		32	6	30	35	12	1130	47	48	16	3	12	2	20	4	4	15	10	3	2	1 1/2			
Chicken FAJITA WRAP™	7 3/4	460		190	21		32	6	30	45	15	1220	51	49	16	3	12	4	18	4	6	15	6	3	2	1 1/2			
Veggie FAJITA WRAP™	7 3/4	420		170	19		29	5	25	20	7	920	38	51	17	3	12	2	11	8	4	15	6	3	1	1 1/2	1		
Steak FAJITA WRAP™ Supreme	9	510		230	25		38	8	40	45	15	1140	48	50	17	3	12	4	21	4	10	15	10	3	2	2 1/2			
Chicken FAJITA WRAP™ Supreme	9	500		230	25		38	8	40	55	18	1230	51	51	17	3	12	5	19	4	10	15	8	3	2	2 1/2			
Veggie FAJITA WRAP™ Supreme	9	460		210	23		35	8	40	30	10	930	39	53	18	3	12	4	11	8	10	15	6	3	1	2 1/2	1		
BORDER LIGHTS™																													
LIGHT Chicken Burrito	6 1/4	310	29	70	8	50	12	2	10	25	8	980	41	41	14	3	12	3	18	40	4	20	6	2 1/2	1	1			
• Chicken Burrito	6 1/4	400		140	16		25	5	25	55	18	720	30	45	15	1	4	2	19	25	4	20	20	3	1	2			
Light CHICKEN Burrito Supreme®	8 3/4	430	28	120	13	50	20	3	15	55	18	1410	59	52	17	3	12	4	25	35	10	15	8	3	2	1			
• CHICKEN Burrito Supreme®	8 3/4	550		230	26		40	9	45	95	32	730	30	50	17	1	4	2	30	25	15	20	20	3	3	2			
LIGHT Chicken Soft Taco	4 1/4	180	39	45	5	55	8	1 1/2	8	25	8	660	28	21	7	2	8	3	13	20	8	10	4	1 1/2	1				
• Chicken Soft Taco	4 1/4	250		100	11		17	3 1/2	18	45	15	380	16	23	8	0	0	1	15	15	8	10	10	1 1/2	1	1			
LIGHT Kid's Chicken Soft Taco	3 1/2	180	33	45	5	55	8	1 1/2	8	25	8	590	25	20	7	1	4	2	13	6	2	10	4	1 1/2	1				
• Kid's Chicken Soft Taco	3 1/2	240		100	11		17	3 1/2	18	45	15	320	13	21	7	0	0	0	15	4	0	10	10	1 1/2	1	1			
NACHOS AND SIDES																													
Nachos	3 1/2	310		160	18		28	3 1/2	18	5	2	540	23	34	11	3	12	2	2	6	0	10	0	2		3			
BIG BEEF Nachos Supreme	6 3/4	430		210	24		37	7	35	40	13	720	30	43	14	9	36	3	12	4	6	10	10	2 1/2	1	3 1/2			
Nachos BellGrande®	10 3/4	740		350	39		60	10	50	40	13	1200	50	83	28	17	68	4	16	6	6	20	15	5	1	6			
Pintos 'n Cheese	4 1/2	190		80	8		12	4	20	15	5	690	29	18	6	10	40	0	9	30	2	15	10	1	1	1/2			
Mexican Rice	4 3/4	190		90	10		15	4	20	15	5	510	21	20	7	0	0	0	6	35	0	10	4	1 1/2		1 1/2			
Cinnamon Twists	1	140		50	6		9	0	0	0	0	190	8	19	6	0	0	0	1	4	0	0	2	1		1			
SAUCES AND CONDIMENTS																													
Green Sauce	1	5		0	0		0	0	0	0	0	150	6	1	0	0	0	0	0	8	4	0	0	*Free Food					
Guacamole	3/4	35		25	3		5	1/2	3	0	0	140	6	2	1	1	4	0	0	0	2	0	0			1			
Hot Taco Sauce	1/3	0		0	0		0	0	0	0	0	85	4	0	0	0	0	0	0	6	0	0	0	*Free Food					
Mild Taco Sauce	1/3	0		0	0		0	0	0	0	0	75	3	0	0	0	0	0	0	6	0	0	0	*Free Food					
Nacho Cheese Sauce	2	120		90	10		15	2 1/2	13	5	2	470	20	5	2	0	0	2	2	6	0	4	0	1/2		2			
Picante Sauce	1/3	0		0	0		0	0	0	0	0	110	5	1	0	0	0	0	0	0	2	0	0	*Free Food					
Pico de Gallo	3/4	5		0	0		0	0	0	0	0	65	3	1	0	0	0	1	0	15	6	0	0	*Free Food					
Red Sauce	1	10		0	0		0	0	0	0	0	260	11	2	1	0	0	0	0	25	0	0	0	*Free Food					
Salsa	3	25		0	0		0	0	0	0	0	490	20	5	2	0	0	3	1	130	15	4	0				1		
Cheddar Cheese	1/4	30		20	2		3	1 1/2	8	5	2	45	2	0	0	0	0	0	2	2	0	6	0			1/2			
Pepper Jack Cheese	1/4	25		20	2		3	1	5	5	2	105	4	0	0	0	0	0	1	6	0	4	0			1/2			
Sour Cream	3/4	40		35	4		6	2 1/2	13	10	3	10	0	1	0	0	0	1	1	0	0	0	0			1			
Non-Fat Sour Cream	3/4	20	50	0	0	100	0	0	0	0	0	55	2	2	1	0	0	0	1	15	0	4	0	*Free Food					
Fat Free Cheddar Cheese	1/4	10	67	0	0	100	0	0	0	0	0	50	2	0	0	0	0	0	2	6	0	6	0	*Free Food					
DRINKS																													
Pepsi-Cola®	16	200		0	0		0	0	0	0	0	47	2	51	17	0	0	55	0	0	0	0	0						
Diet Pepsi®	16	0		0	0		0	0	0	0	0	47	2	0	0	0	0	0	0	0	0	0	0	*Free Food					
Mountain Dew®	16	227		0	0		0	0	0	0	0	93	4	61	20	0	0	61	0	0	0	0	0						
Slice®	16	200		0	0		0	0	0	0	0	73	3	53	17	0	0	52	0	0	0	0	0						
Dr. Pepper®	16	208		0	0		0	0	0	0	0	8 1/2	1	52	17	0	0	52	0	0	0	0	0						
Lipton® Brisk Iced Tea Unsweetened	16	0		0	0		0	0	0	0	0	60	3	0	0	0	0	0	0	0	0	0	0	*Free Food					
Lipton® Brisk Iced Tea Sweetened	16	140		0	0		0	0	0	0	0	60	3	40	14	0	0	40	0	0	0	0	0						
Coffee (Black)	12	5		0	0		0	0	0	0	0	5	0	1	0	0	0	0	0	0	0	0	0	*Free Food					
2% Lowfat Milk	8	110		40	4 1/2		7	2 1/2	12	15	5	115	5	11	4	0	0	10	8	15	4	30	0					1	
Orange Juice	6	80		0	0		0	0	0	0	0	0	0	18	6	0	0	18	1	0	110	2	0						1 1/2
BREAKFAST																													
Fiesta Breakfast Burrito †	3 1/2	280		140	16		25	6	30	25	8	590	25	25	8	1	4	1	9	15	0	8	4	1 1/2	1	2			
Country Breakfast Burrito †	4	270		130	14		22	5	25	195	65	690	29	26	9	1	4	1	8	25	0	10	6	1 1/2	1	2			
Grande Breakfast Burrito †	6 1/4	420		200	22		34	7	35	205	68	1050	44	43	14	2	8	2	13	50	0	10	10	3	1	2 1/2			
Double Bacon & Egg Burrito †	6 1/4	480		250	27		42	9	45	400	133	1240	52	39	13	2	8	2	18	45	0	15	10	2 1/2	1	4 1/2			
Breakfast Cheese Quesadilla †	5 1/2	390		200	22		34	10	50	280	93	940	39	32	11	1	4	0	15	80	0	35	15	2	1	3			
Breakfast Quesadilla with Bacon †	6	460		250	28		43	12	60	295	98	1130	47	33	11	1	4	1	20	80	0	35	15	2	2	3			
Breakfast Quesadilla with Sausage †	6	440		240	26		40	12	60	290	97	1010	42	33	11	1	4	0	17	80	0	35	15	2	2	3			

g = gram   mg = milligram

• Typical product not sold in stores. This information is provided for comparison purposes only.

† Available at participating Taco Bell® locations.

*Free food = Free food based on portion size. Each food has less than 20 calories or less than 5 grams of carbohydrates.

***Based on a medium fat meat exchange.

**Percent Daily Values are based on a 2,000 calorie diet. Your daily values may be higher or lower depending on your calorie needs:

Calories:		2,000	2,500
Total Fat	Less Than	65g	80g
Sat Fat	Less Than	20g	25g
Cholesterol	Less Than	300mg	300mg
Sodium	Less Than	2,400mg	2,400mg
Total Carbohydrate		300g	375g
Dietary Fiber		25g	30g

BORDER LIGHTS™ menu items contain at least 50% less fat than typical products. Typical product nutrition information based on representative database. Substitution of ingredients may alter fat content. Although this data is based on standard portion product guidelines, variation can be expected due to seasonal influences, minor differences in product assembly per restaurant and other factors. Except for limited time offerings or test market items, menu products as of this printing are included in this brochure. Product data is current as of date of publication. If you have any questions about Taco Bell® and nutrition or are particularly sensitive to specific ingredients or foods, please contact us at 1-800-TACO-BELL.

FIGURE 6.2. *(Continued)*

of a consulting or staff dietitian, the manager of this type of food service needs to be, not only aware of, but educated in, the fundamentals of nutrition. The health and well-being of a large number of people depend on the menu being balanced and nutritionally sound.

In those operations that fall into the captive audience segment, the situation changes dramatically. Here the food service manager has a direct responsibility to the patrons for every meal being nutritionally balanced. In hospitals, nursing homes, institutions, prisons, and so forth, the clients have no choice; they have to dine in that food service. If menu choices are not offered, they either eat what is put in front of them or don't eat. Where a choice is available, it is up to the food service manager to ascertain that every food group is represented on the menu, that a choice is offered in one or more of the groups, and that the client has chosen the appropriate number of foods from each group, thus assuring that the client will receive a balanced meal. In captive-audience operations, help is probably at hand. In most states or provinces, by law, a registered dietitian (RD), who is a member of the American or Canadian Dietetic Association, is on staff to handle nutritional issues. Some jurisdictions allow for a consulting dietitian where the food service operation is smaller. In a number of establishments, the manager and RD are one and the same. Many years of training, both academically and on the job, are necessary to become a Registered Dietitian. In addition to normal or regular diets, special diets need to be handled to accommodate people with specific restrictions.

No matter what area of restaurant or food service management that you are involved in or intend to become involved in, nutrition will always play a role—sometimes less, sometimes more. The more patrons depend on management to meet their nutritional needs, the more management needs to know.

BASICS OF NUTRITION

While it is beyond the scope of this text to give a complete course in nutrition, there are some basics that every restaurant or food service manager should know. Nutrition is the study of food: its chemical makeup, and how that makeup relates to health and growth.

Calories are the amount of energy contained in food. Calories are also the unit of measure for the energy needs of the body. Thus, if we ingest more calories than are required for the body's energy needs, we store them as fat and, as a result, gain weight. Conversely, if we burn more than we ingest, the body uses the stored calories and we lose weight. Nutrients are the matter in food that provide energy (calories) and foster the growth of the body, as well as maintain the well-being of the body. The six groups of nutrients include carbohydrates, lipids, proteins, vitamins, minerals, and water. Of these, energy (calories) is provided by carbohydrates, lipids, and protein. Vitamins regulate the body's processes. Minerals and water also regulate the body's processes but promote growth and maintenance as well.

CARBOHYDRATES

Carbohydrates are the primary source of energy or calories for the body. They are broken down into two categories, simple and complex. Simple carbohydrates are natural sugars and refined sugars. They include such entities as granulated sugar, honey, and corn syrup, among many others. Simple carbohydrates are also prevalent in such foods as milk, yogurt, some fruits, some vegetables, and in lesser amounts in bread and cereals. Large amounts are found (of course) in cakes, pies, puddings, candy, and cookies.

Complex carbohydrates include starch and fiber. Starch is broken down in the digestive tract, while fiber is not. Starch is found in such foods as flour, pasta, dried beans and peas, vegetables, and some fruits such as bananas. Fiber is found in oats, barley, whole wheat, and brown rice, as well as rice, beans, and some fruits and vegetables. Carbohydrates as a source of energy are an important part of every diet. Complex carbohydrates should be consumed regularly and should constitute 45 percent of daily caloric intake.

LIPIDS

The term lipid refers to fats, oils, cholesterol, and lecithin. The term *fat* is normally applied if the lipid is solid at room temperature and *oil* if it is a liquid at room temperature. As a rule fat comes from animals and oil from plants. The majority of lipids found in food can be broken down into fatty acids which are known as saturated, monounsaturated, and polyunsaturated.

Foods containing saturated fat include meat, poultry, fish, dairy products, and lards to name a few. Monounsaturated products include oils such as olive, canola, peanut, and other nut-based oils. Polyunsaturated fats are found in other oils including fish, corn, soybean, sunflower, safflower, and sesame oils. The difference in these fatty acids is significant in that mono- and polyunsaturated fats decrease cholesterol levels, while saturated fats increase cholesterol levels. Cholesterol level is important because a person with a higher cholesterol level has a greater risk of heart disease or stroke. In spite of this fact, cholesterol is not all bad. It is used by the body to aid in the digestion of fat, as well as to manufacture cell membranes and sex hormones.

Lecithin, although listed as a nutrient, is not essential in terms of ingestion, as the body manufactures almost all of what it needs. Its importance lies in the fact that it keeps the fats emulsified and is also an important element of the cell membrane. An important fact to remember about the lipid family is that the amount of fats, oils, and cholesterol that is consumed should be curtailed to 30 percent of the daily caloric intake. Another important fact to remember is that many lipids are used as ingredients in products and are therefore unseen. Out of sight, out of mind. In addition to keeping track of lipids in obvious things such as meat, poultry, or dairy products, it is also important to check the ingredients in such things as cakes, pies, salad dressings, sauces, etc.

PROTEIN

The importance of protein as a nutrient becomes evident when you consider that it is responsible for forming collagen, maintaining water balance, forming antibodies, and keeping the blood neutral. It is extremely important in repairing the body after surgery or if the body is infected or burned. During this time additional protein is required as it is during pregnancy and in infancy.

Protein is present in both plants and animals and is prominent in the structure of both. Animal protein in the diet comes from meat, seafood, poultry, and dairy products; plant protein comes from cereal grains, vegetables, legumes, nuts, and seeds. Nutritionists recommend that the amount of protein consumed daily be divided equally between meat protein and plant protein. Meat contains more protein than plants and also contains iron and other nutrients, but it is also high in fat. Although plants contain less protein, they are high in starch, fiber, vitamins, and minerals and are low in fat. People living in developed countries for the most part receive adequate protein in their diets; however too many are consuming more protein than is needed, resulting in obesity. The recommended intake of protein is between 10–12 percent of daily caloric intake.

VITAMINS

Vitamins are nutrients that the body needs in very small amounts. Don't be fooled into thinking that, since only a small amount is necessary, they are not important. Although the body manufactures a few vitamins, the majority are obtained from food. Since they have no calories, they do not provide any energy except for the fact that they are involved in the metabolism of energy. Vitamins are classified as fat soluble and water soluble.

Fat-soluble vitamins come from foods that contain fat and are stored in the body until needed. They include vitamins A, D, E, and K. Vitamin A is involved in cell development as well as growth, healthy skin, the immune system, and the protective lining in many organs. In children it is important for bone and teeth development. Vitamin A is found in many foods including dark green vegetables and dark orange fruits and vegetables, liver, fortified dairy products, and fortified cereals. Vitamin D is somewhat different from the other vitamins in that the body manufactures most of it. It is responsible for ensuring that there is adequate calcium in the system to build bones and teeth. Sources of vitamin D are limited to egg yolks, fish liver oil (an all-time favorite), and milk that is fortified with vitamin D. Vitamin E's role is as an antioxidant that prevents oxidant damage to blood cells, cell membranes, and DNA (also known as the genetic code). As vitamin E does its work, it is destroyed and must be replaced. Vitamin E can be found in legumes, nuts, seeds, green leafy vegetables, whole grain cereals, and vegetable oils.

Water-soluble vitamins, unlike fat-soluble vitamins, are not stored in the body and therefore must be constantly replaced, but not in excess. Water-soluble vitamins include vitamin C and the B complex vitamins. Vitamin C, also known as ascorbic acid, is responsible for forming collagen whose function is to give bones, teeth, muscles, cartilage, and blood vessels their strength and support. It also acts as an antioxidant much like vitamin E. The best food from which to obtain vitamin C is citrus fruits and tomatoes. It is also available in potatoes, green and yellow vegetables (especially broccoli), cantaloupe, and strawberries.

Vitamin B1 (thiamine), vitamin B2 (riboflavin), and vitamin B3 (niacin) combine to release energy from carbohydrates, fats, and proteins. Additionally, thiamine is involved with the nervous system; riboflavin with healthy skin and good vision; and niacin with healthy skin as well as the proper functioning of the nervous system and digestive tract. Thiamine can be found in nuts, seeds, enriched breads and cereals, and liver, with the best source being found in pork. Riboflavin's sources include milk products, organ meats, eggs, and enriched breads and cereals. Niacin is available from meats, poultry, fish, and enriched breads and cereals.

Vitamin B6 is involved in protein metabolism as well as in the making of red and white blood cells. It can be found in organ meats, meat, poultry, and fish. Folate, also known as folic acid, is needed to form DNA, new cells, red blood cells, and white blood cells. Sources for folate are green leafy vegetables, organ meats, legumes, orange juice, meats, poultry, fish, whole grain breads and cereals. Vitamin B12's function is to convert folate into its active form so that it can form DNA. Vitamin B12 is found only in animal foods including meat, poultry, fish, shellfish, eggs, and milk products. Pantothenic acid and biotin are both involved in energy metabolism and are found in many foods. Meat, eggs, cheese, some vegetables and legumes are all good sources.

MINERALS

Minerals are divided into two groups, major minerals that are needed by the body in larger amounts and trace minerals that are needed in smaller amounts. Major minerals include calcium, phosphorus, sodium, potassium, chloride, magnesium, and sulfur. Calcium and phosphorus are both essential in building strong bones and teeth. In addition calcium helps the blood to clot, the muscles to contract, and nerves to transmit pulses. Phosphorus contributes to the formation of DNA and some enzymes and aids in the release of energy in fat, protein, and carbohydrates. Calcium is found in good quantities in milk, yogurt, and cheese. Lesser sources include salmon, sardines, several leafy green vegetables, and calcium-fortified foods. Phosphorus is found in milk and milk products, meat, poultry, fish, eggs, legumes, and whole grain foods. Sodium, potassium, and chloride are known as electrolytes and are responsible for maintaining water balance by moving it around the body. Sodium is found mainly in salt as well as in many processed foods to which sodium is added when they are manufactured. Sources for potassium are many, including vegetables, fruits, meat, poultry, fish, milk, legumes, and grain. Chloride, like sodium, is found primarily in salt.

Trace minerals include copper, fluoride, iodine, iron, selenium, and zinc. Copper, along with iron, forms hemoglobin and, in addition, helps form collagen. It is also part of many enzymes that are important to the body. Copper is found in organ meats, whole grain breads and cereals, legumes, nuts, and dried fruits. Fluoride is essential in developing teeth so that they are resistant to cavities. The major source of fluoride is drinking water. Iodine is necessary for the thyroid gland to work properly and is needed only in small amounts. It is found primarily in iodized salt. Iron is a significant part of the red blood cells and is also important in making oxygen available for muscle contraction. The best source for iron is liver, but it is also found in meats, seafood, egg yolks, enriched breads and cereals, green leafy vegetables, legumes, and dried fruit. Selenium helps prevent oxidation damage to tissues and is found in seafood, liver, and eggs. Zinc is involved in many functions, including DNA metabolism, wound healing, bone formation, development of sexual organs, tissue growth, taste, appetite, and the storage and release of insulin. It can be found in meat, poultry, and shellfish.

WATER

Water is used by the body for many functions including digestion, absorption, circulation, excretion, transporting nutrients, building tissue, and maintaining body temperature. Most of the cells rely on water as it brings nutrients to them and removes waste materials. The amount of water that should be ingested is controlled by thirst. When blood becomes concentrated, the body calls for water. The primary source for water? You guessed it. Water.

THE FOOD PYRAMID

Prior to developing the food pyramid, the United States Department of Agriculture in 1958 developed the basic four to act as a guideline in food selection for an average healthy person. It contained four groups of food and indicated how many servings daily of each group adults should eat if they wanted to consume 1200 calories. The four groups are as follows:

Meats and meat substitutes	2 servings daily
Milk and milk products	2 servings daily
Fruits and vegetables	4 servings daily
Grains	4 servings daily

By following the basic four pattern, adults would receive 80 percent of their recommended daily allowance (RDA) of nutrients as recommended at that time. Since then the RDA nutrient list has more than doubled, and many of the items now listed in it were not accounted for in the basic four food groups. In addition, it did not account for foods such as mayonnaise, margarine, or baked desserts, among others, all of which have a high fat and sugar content. To rectify the situation, in 1992, the basic four model was revised to resemble a pyramid.

The food guide pyramid more accurately reflects the amounts of each food group a person should consume. Similar to the basic four, it contains the grain group, including examples such as bread, cereal, rice, and pasta. It adds a group by breaking the fruit and vegetable group into two separate groups. The pyramid contains the milk group as well as the meat group, in which poultry, fish, dry beans, eggs, and nuts are included. The last group includes fats, oils, and sweets which were missing from the basic four, thus giving the food guide pyramid six food groups.

Another change is that, for each group, a range of servings is recommended rather than a rigid number. Thus, individuals can decide the number of calories that is right for them and choose the proper number of servings for each group on the pyramid. The pyramid is constructed so that the group with the most servings recommended (grains, 6 to 11) is at the bottom. The fruit group (2 to 4 servings) and the vegetable group (3 to 5 servings) share the next level up. This is followed by the meat group (2 to 3 servings) and the milk group (2 to 3 servings) sharing the next level. Fats, oils, and sweets top off the pyramid with no servings recommended but adding the admonition to use sparingly.

Why is all of this important? First, these recommendations should be followed to help insure your own good health and, second, the menu writer needs to be acutely aware of what is healthy and what is not. As discussed earlier, for the food service manager

Food Guide Pyramid

A Guide to Daily Food Choices

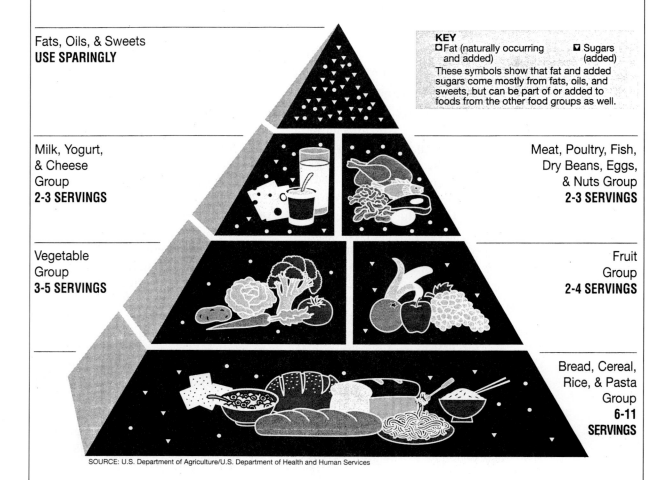

Fats, Oils, & Sweets
USE SPARINGLY

KEY
□ Fat (naturally occurring and added)   ▉ Sugars (added)
These symbols show that fat and added sugars come mostly from fats, oils, and sweets, but can be part of or added to foods from the other food groups as well.

Milk, Yogurt,
& Cheese
Group
2-3 SERVINGS

Meat, Poultry, Fish,
Dry Beans, Eggs,
& Nuts Group
2-3 SERVINGS

Vegetable
Group
3-5 SERVINGS

Fruit
Group
2-4 SERVINGS

Bread, Cereal,
Rice, & Pasta
Group
**6-11
SERVINGS**

SOURCE: U.S. Department of Agriculture/U.S. Department of Health and Human Services

Use the Food Guide Pyramid to help you eat better every day. . . .the Dietary Guidelines way. Start with plenty of Breads, Cereals, Rice, and Pasta; Vegetables; and Fruits. Add two to three servings from the Milk group and two to three servings from the Meat group.

Each of these food groups provides some, but not all, of the nutrients you need. No one food group is more important than another — for good health you need them all. Go easy on fats, oils, and sweets, the foods in the small tip of the Pyramid.

To order a copy of "The Food Guide Pyramid" booklet, send a $1.00 check or money order made out to the Superintendent of Documents to: Consumer Information Center, Department 159-Y, Pueblo, Colorado 81009.

U.S. Department of Agriculture, Human Nutrition Information Service, August 1992, Leaflet No. 572

FIGURE 6.3.   The food guide pyramid showing the six food groups and the number of servings you should have per day from each group. (*Courtesy of the United States Department of Agriculture, Washington, DC*)

How to Use The Daily Food Guide

What counts as one serving?

Breads, Cereals, Rice, and Pasta
1 slice of bread
1/2 cup of cooked rice or pasta
1/2 cup of cooked cereal
1 ounce of ready-to-eat cereal

Vegetables
1/2 cup of chopped raw or
  cooked vegetables
1 cup of leafy raw vegetables

Fruits
1 piece of fruit or melon wedge
3/4 cup of juice
1/2 cup of canned fruit
1/4 cup of dried fruit

Milk, Yogurt, and Cheese
1 cup of milk or yogurt
1-1/2 to 2 ounces of cheese

Meat, Poultry, Fish, Dry Beans, Eggs, and Nuts
2-1/2 to 3 ounces of cooked lean
  meat, poultry, or fish
Count 1/2 cup of cooked beans,
  or 1 egg, or 2 tablespoons of
  peanut butter as 1 ounce of lean
  meat (about 1/3 serving)

Fats, Oils, and Sweets
LIMIT CALORIES FROM THESE
especially if you need to lose weight

> The amount you eat may be more than one serving. For example, a dinner portion of spaghetti would count as two or three servings of pasta.

How many servings do you need each day?

	Women & some older adults	Children, teen girls, active women, most men	Teen boys & active men
Calorie level*	about 1,600	about 2,200	about 2,800
Bread group	6	9	11
Vegetable group	3	4	5
Fruit group	2	3	4
Milk group	**2-3	**2-3	**2-3
Meat group	2, for a total of 5 ounces	2, for a total of 6 ounces	3 for a total of 7 ounces

*These are the calorie levels if you choose lowfat, lean foods from the 5 major food groups and use foods from the fats, oils, and sweets group sparingly.

**Women who are pregnant or breastfeeding, teenagers, and young adults to age 24 need 3 servings.

A Closer Look at Fat and Added Sugars

The small tip of the Pyramid shows fats, oils, and sweets. These are foods such as salad dressings, cream, butter, margarine, sugars, soft drinks, candies, and sweet desserts. Alcoholic beverages are also part of this group. These foods provide calories but few vitamins and minerals. Most people should go easy on foods from this group.

 Some fat or sugar symbols are shown in the other food groups. That's to remind you that some foods in these groups can also be high in fat and added sugars, such as cheese or ice cream from the milk group, or french fries from the vegetable group. When choosing foods for a healthful diet, consider the fat and added sugars in your choices from all the food groups, not just fats, oils, and sweets from the Pyramid tip.

FIGURE 6.3. *(Continued)*

who deals with a captive audience, it is imperative; and for the food service manager whose audience is not captive, it is very important. For the restaurant manager it is important. Figure 6.3, although designed by the USDA for family meal planning, gives an excellent checklist that should be used professionally by food service managers as well as restaurant managers.

NUTRITIONAL ASPECTS OF MENU PLANNING

As discussed in Chapter 1, the menu writer needs to be acutely aware of whom they are writing the menu for. Several different factors of demographics are encompassed when discussing nutrition in relation to the menu. For example, some ethnic or religious groups do not eat certain foods or food groups. An illustration of this would be that people from the Pacific Rim have diets that are extremely low in fat. People following kosher diets do not eat pork or shellfish and keep dairy and meat separate. Regional preferences come into play with coastal people eating more fish and shellfish and inland people eating more beef, pork, and lamb. Balanced and nutritionally sound diets are more prevalent among educated middle- and upper-income people than they are with uneducated lower-income people. However, age is the most predominant category in discussing menu planning, demographics, and nutrition.

To facilitate the discussion on menu planning and nutrition, age is broken down into children, adolescents, adults, and older adults. This grouping has special ramifications for managers depending on which group(s) predominates in their demographic base.

CHILDREN

Children are perhaps the most challenging age group for a menu writer to contend with. They are starting to seek their independence as well as their identity and often use food to express it. They have their favorites such as hamburgers, pizza, hot dogs, fried chicken, french fries, and peanut butter. While their parents often opt for nutritionally sound meals, children resist. To add to the confusion, when dining out, children more often than not determine the restaurant. As a result, the menu writer has to walk a very fine line. Perhaps the solution is to give the children what they want so that they are happy and satisfied and will drag the parents to your restaurant every time the family eats out. The key is to modify the nutritional content of their selections. For example, on children's plates use extra lean ground beef, low-fat hot dogs, vegetable pizzas with low fat mozzarella, baked rather than fried items, and low-fat peanut butter. Make sure the parents know that you are looking out for the nutritional well-being of their children. The children are happy, the parents are happy, and your accountant is happy.

For those food service managers concerned with feeding primary and secondary school age children, the Type A lunch becomes the model for menu planning. Enacted in 1946 by Congress, the National School Lunch Act provides cash assistance for schools who choose to participate in this program. It also provides for the school to receive surplus food commodities, as well as consultation regarding food purchasing, equipment, and management of the school lunchroom. In order to receive this assistance, the school must operate on a nonprofit basis, provide free or reduced-price lunches to children of poverty-level families, not discriminate in any way, and serve a nutritious Type A lunch.

FIGURE 6.4. Nutrition education as well as an appealing display of nutritional food is important in elementary school feeding. (*Photographs courtesy of Marriott Management Services*)

FIGURE 6.4. (*Continued*)

The makeup of the Type A lunch is as follows:

1. Fluid milk, 1/2 pint, served as a beverage.
2. Protein-rich food, such as 2 oz. cooked or canned lean meat, fish, poultry; 2 oz. cheese; 1 egg, 1/2 cup cooked dry beans or peas; 4 tablespoons peanut butter; or an equivalent of any combination of these in a main dish.
3. Vegetables and fruits, at least 3/4 cup, consisting of two or more servings. One serving of full-strength juice may be counted as not more than 1/4 cup of the requirement.
4. Whole-grain or enriched bread (1 slice), or muffins, cornbread, biscuits, or rolls made of enriched or whole grain flour.
5. Butter or fortified margarine, 1 teaspoon, as a spread, as a seasoning, or in food preparation.

Note. It is also necessary to provide a Vitamin C–rich food daily as well as a Vitamin A–rich food at least twice a week.

ADOLESCENTS

Inasmuch as writing menus for children is difficult because they have to be written to please both the children and the parents, adolescents are striking out on their own. Thus, in the case of adolescents the menu writer need satisfy only one group. However, being between childhood and adulthood, adolescents are a confusing lot (in more ways than just menus). Many adolescents, because of nutrition education at home and school, are breaking their childhood habits and becoming more cognizant of the relationship between nutritionally sound meals and snacks and good health. Still others cling to the old habits of diets laden with fats and sugars. In asserting their independence, adolescents eat some meals away from home and many times skip meals altogether. Since fast food is one of their favorite groups of restaurants, nutritionally balanced, low-fat, low-sugar choices should be made available in these venues. Traditional fast food menu offerings such as hamburgers, fries, pizza, and fried chicken should still be on the menu, as many adolescents continue to order them. While the latter are high sources of fat, they still have many of the necessary nutrients. Remember that it is not the restaurant industry's responsibility to enforce nutrition—only to offer a choice for its patrons.

Adolescents, as they pass from childhood to adulthood, go through an amazing stage of physical development. They gain 20 percent of their adult height, 50 percent of their adult weight, and 50 percent of their bone growth. At this stage of development, males add more bone and muscle tissue than females, who put on more fat. Thus, adolescents need increased amounts of calories, proteins, calcium, iron, vitamins, carbohydrates, and zinc.

ELEMENTARY SCHOOL MENU - SIX WEEK CYCLE
REVISED 3/27/97

MONDAY	TUESDAY	WEDNESDAY	THURSDAY	FRIDAY
Cheese Pizza or BBQ Rib on a Bun Oven Baked Fries Steamed Broccoli/Cauliflower Mix Pineapples/Maraschino Grapes	Taco Salad w/Tortilla Chips or Chicken Parmesan Sandwich Lettuce Salad Steamed Corn Strawberry Shortcake	Turkey Fritter on a Bun or Beefy Italian Dunkers Fresh Vegetables w/Dip Steamed Green Beans Fruity Gelatin Chocolate Chip Cookies	Chicken Nuggets w/Corn Bread or Meatball Sandwich Mashed Poatoes w/Gravy Marinated Vegetables Chilled Cherries	French Toast w/Sausage or Breakfast Burrito Tri Tators California Mix Vegetables Chilled Applesauce
Hamburger/Cheeseburger on a Bun or BBQ Chicken Glazers w/Muffin Crinkle Cut Fries Steamed Carrots Pear Slices	Cheese Ravioli w/Italian Sauce or Lettuce & Tomato Salad Steamed Peas Shape Up	Hot Dog on a Bun or BBQ on a Bun Skin-on Wedge Cut Fries Steamed Mixed Vegetables Orange Wedges Brownie	Nachos w/Seasoned Meat & Cheese Sauce or Turkey & Cheese Melt Fresh Garden Salad Steamed Corn Chilled Mixed Fruit BIRTHDAY CAKE	Pizza or Crispy Chicken Chef Salad w/Crackers Lettuce & Tomatoes Fresh Vegetables Peach Cobbler
Chicken Nuggets w/Roll or Fish & Cheese Sandwich Oven Baked Fries Steamed Cauliflower Cherry Crisp	Chicken Patty on a Bun or Burrito w/Cheese Sauce Tator Tots Three Bean Salad Orange Slices	Macaroni & Cheese w/Mini Corn Dogs or Breaded Steak on a Bun Steamed Green Beans Fresh Vegetable Relishes Pineapple w/Mandarin Oranges	**School Planned Celebration**	Taco Salad in Tortilla Bowl or Chicken Pot Pie w/Biscuit Fresh Garden Salad Steamed Corn Chilled Peaches
Pizza or Teriyaki Chicken Chunks w/Muffin Steamed Peas Marinated Vegetables Spiced Apples	French Toast w/Sausage or Quiche w/Blueberry Muffin Tri Tators Winter Mix Vegetables Applesauce	BBQ Rib on a Bun or Baked Potato w/Meat Toppings Broccoli w/Cheese Sauce Baked Potato Half Strawberries & Bananas	Chicken Nuggets w/Roll or Pizza Burger Mashed Potatoes w/Gravy Steamed Carrot Coins Pear Slices w/Maraschino Grapes	Lasagna w/Meat Sauce or Turkey Gems School Made Roll Lettuce Salad California Blend Vegetables Mixed Fruit Apple/Cinnamon Struedel Cake
Turkey Fritter on a Bun or Hot Ham & Cheese Sandwich Carrot & Celery Sticks Steamed Corn Pineapple Tidbits Chocolate Chip Cookies	Chicken Strips w/Roll or Bierock Steamed Carrots Broccoli, Cheese & Rice Casserole Chilled Strawberries	Pepperoni Pizza or Tuna Salad on Wheat Bread Creamy Cole Slaw Fresh Vegetables w/Dip Orange Wedges	Hamburger/Cheeseburger on a Bun or Corn Dog Potato Salad Baked Beans Grapes	Soft Shell Taco or BBQ Chicken Glazers w/Corn Bread Lettuce Salad Steamed White Rice Mixed Fruit Chocolate Pudding
Chicken Nuggets or Meatloaf Muffin Mashed Potatoes w/Gravy Steamed Cauliflower	Turkey Sticks w/Roll or Pigs in a Blanket Criss-Cut Potatoes Steamed Mixed Vegetables Sliced Peaches Marshmallow Squares	French Toast w/Sausage or Breakfast Pizza Oven Baked Tri Tators Fresh Vegetables w/Dip Juice Bar	Italian Spiral Noodle & Meat Sauce or Chef's Salad Roll Lettuce & Tomatoes Seasoned Green Beans Fresh Orange Slices	Grilled Cheese w/Soup or Rotisserie Chicken Nuggets w/Corn Bread Fresh Lettuce Salad California Mixed Vegetables Sliced Pears Chocolate Ice Cream Cup

FIGURE 6.5. An example of an elementary school lunch menu. (*Courtesy of the Blue Valley School District, Shawnee Mission, Kansas*)

In addition to these Entrees, the following choices are offered each day:

Cold Sandwich

Peanut Butter & Jelly Sandwich

Salad Bar

Steamed Vegetables

Fresh Vegetable

Chilled Assorted Fresh Fruit

Chilled Fruit Cup

<u>Juice</u>	<u>Milk</u>
Apple	Whole
Grape	2% White
Orange	Skim White
	Skim Chocolate

A-La-Carte Breakfast also offered every day.

MIDDLE SCHOOL

MONDAY	TUESDAY	WEDNESDAY	THURSDAY	FRIDAY
	Turkey Fingers w/Roll or Hot Ham & Cheese Sandwich 1	Soft Shell Taco or BBQ Chicken Glazers w/Roll 2	Chicken Nuggets w/Muffin or Beef CharSteak w/Muffin 3	**Parent Conferences NO SCHOOL** 4
Royals Home Opener Pizza or Hot Dog on a Bun 7	Chicken Breast Tenders w/Roll or Bierock 8	Italian Spaghetti w/Meat Sauce & Garlic Bread or Fish & Cheese Sandwich 9	**Staff Development NO SCHOOL** 10	**District Staff Development NO SCHOOL** 11
Cheese Pizza or BBQ Rib on a Bun 14	Taco Salad w/Tortilla Chips or Rotisserie Chicken Nuggets w/Roll 15	Baked Turkey Fritter on a Bun or Tuna Salad on Wheat 16	Chicken Nuggets w/Corn Bread or Meatball Sandwich 17	*Italian Bar* Pasta Bar or Beefy Italian Dunkers 18
Sausage Pizza or BBQ Chicken Glazers w/Corn Bread 21	Chicken Patty on a Bun or Meat Loaf w/Roll 22	Cheese Ravioli w/Italian Sauce or Breaded Steak Sandwich 23	Chicken Nuggets w/Roll or Pizza Burger 24	*Mexican Bar* Nachos w/Seasoned Meat & Cheese Burrito 25
Pepperoni Pizza or Chicken Parmesan w/Spaghetti 28	Macaroni & Cheese w/Mini Corn Dogs or BBQ on a Bun 29	Taco Salad in a Tortilla Boat or Corn Dog 30		

FIGURE 6.5. *(Continued)*

Blue Valley Schools
Food and Nutrition Services

BREAKFAST MENU

January-May 1997

MONDAY	TUESDAY	WEDNESDAY	THURSDAY	FRIDAY
<u>Breakfast Prices</u> Students $.80 Adults $.95		*Offered Daily:* **Cereal & Graham Crackers** **Chilled Fruit** **Toaster Pastries**	**Milk** **Juice**	
<u>WEEK 1</u> Breakfast Pizza	Cinnamon Raisin Biscuit	Bagel w/Cream Cheese	French Toast Sticks w/Syrup & Jelly	Breakfast Pocket
<u>WEEK 2</u> Toasted English Muffin w/Jelly	Peanut Butter & Jelly Sandwich	Pancakes w/Syrup or Jelly	Sausage Biscuit	Cinnamon Pita
<u>WEEK 3</u> French Toast Sticks w/Syrup or Jelly	Eggo Waffles w/Syrup	Cinnamon Raisin Biscuit	Breakfast Pizza	Scrambled Eggs & Tri Tators
<u>WEEK 4</u> Breakfast Burrito	Sausage Biscuit	Toasted English Muffin w/Jelly	Cinnamon Pita	Biscuit & Gravy

*******Note: See Back of Menu for More Information*******

FIGURE 6.5. *(Continued)*

ADULTS

As adolescents become adults, the growth pattern slows and, along with this change, the need for calories decreases. There is a wide divergence of opinion as to the age at which this starts to occur, with variations due to genetics, environment, and previous nutritional habits. Some suggest that many of the organ systems "max out" in the late twenties and mid-thirties, including the digestive system which is responsible for absorbing and metabolizing nutrients.

Adults should closely follow the food guide pyramid discussed earlier along with the recommended caloric intake for their age, sex, height, and physical activity. A wide variety of foods is recommended, including additional servings of fruits, vegetables, breads, pasta, and cereals. Eating less fat and fatty foods, including saturated fat and cholesterol as well as reducing the intake of sugars and sweets are recommended.

Menu planners need to be aware of these needs and to have a good understanding of the food guide pyramid. Every menu, regardless of whether it is a fast food operation; a family, theme, or ethnic restaurant; a cafeteria; a fine dining establishment; or a captive or noncaptive food service—in other words every menu—must have a selection(s) that would enable its customers to order a meal that would encompass, not only the pyramid, but their individual caloric need as well.

OLDER ADULTS

This is the fastest-growing segment of the population today. Restaurant and food service managers must be educated as to the wants, needs, and nutritional requirements of this age group.

Older adults (those 65 and over) have rapidly changing health needs. Most of them have at least one chronic disease or disability and half of them are on medication. Over half have lost their teeth and/or are wearing dentures, and most have lost much of their ability to taste, including saltiness and sweetness. The digestive system has also slowed down. At this stage of life, because they have less physical activity, their need for calories has lessened, while at the same time their need for vitamins and minerals has increased. As a result, they need to pack their calories with nutrients, not fats and sugars.

Management needs to take these factors into account when writing menus. Portions need to be smaller. A common complaint heard among senior citizens is that they must pay a high price for portions that are too large. Many restaurants have been reluctant to offer smaller portions along with lower selling prices, as the average check and table turnover are what make up sales. To lower the selling price and therefore the check average could spell disaster should it cause sales to drop. Many restaurants have solved this dilemma by offering seniors smaller portions and lower prices during their off-peak hours. This works out well for both parties, as the dining room is full when it used to be empty, and seniors tend to eat earlier anyway.

In addition to smaller portions, menus need to address other problems such as chewing by offering a choice of tender, chopped, or ground meats as well as soft fruits, vegetables, and salads. Choices other than fried foods, foods high in fat content, and sugars should be made available. Dessert offerings such as fruit, frozen yogurt, and low-fat or fat-free ice cream or custards are excellent, as they not only have less fat and sugar but have additional nutrients as well. Less spicy foods should also be made available.

Don't eliminate traditional menu listings or even trendy items, as many of these can fit the criteria given. Also, keep in mind the statistics: half of older adults are on medication and/or have dentures; the other half are not. Although many are on medication and their digestive systems have slowed down, this doesn't mean that they can't or won't enjoy some of the more traditional menu fare.

NUTRITIONAL MENU LISTINGS

Given the brief overview on nutrition, the question then becomes: how far should the industry go in accommodating those people who desire more nutritional menu listings or require special diets or cooking procedures? As stated earlier, captive-audience food services must provide them and noncaptive-audience food services should provide them. Restaurants on the other hand are divided.

Consider some facts. In survey after survey, when restaurant patrons were asked whether or not they chose nutritious meals when dining out, many were totally noncommittal, that is, they would eat what they wanted. Some were on the border line, that is, they could take or leave the more nutritious selections, and some were totally committed to ordering nutritious offerings only. With exceptions, for the most part the groups were fairly even, that is one-third, one-third, and one-third. Another fact is evident after reading numerous surveys over the past few years: that is, that the latter group, those totally committed to nutrition, is slowly but surely increasing.

Therefore it would be safe to say that a trend is developing and that healthful eating habits are not a fad. With one-third (and growing) of total patrons demanding nutritious meals and another one-third leaning, the conclusion should be evident that all restaurants regardless of whether they offer fast food or fine dining or something in between should offer some nutritious listings on their menu, leaving the other listings for those patrons who order whatever they want. In other words, satisfy everyone.

To set up a series of healthful menu listings, carefully review the federal guidelines established by the Food and Drug Administration as given in Figure 6.3. Compare the restaurant's present menu for possible listings that meet those guidelines. There could already be several selections that comply. These could be listed as healthful choices and boxed in to draw attention to them, or left where they are on the menu and identified with a mark to indicate healthfulness. Start with the obvious, soups and salads, then review the descriptive terminology on appetizers, entrees, and sandwiches. If the terms *baked, broiled, grilled,* or *steamed* appear, then compare the item with the guidelines to see whether it qualifies as a healthful choice. If the investigation comes up with some healthful listings, then all that is left to do is merchandise them.

If the list needs to be augmented or comes up with nothing, then the research begins. Consult trade journals, healthy cookbooks, or the food section of the local paper. Although some of these recipes are for small-batch cookery, they can probably be converted easily. Another approach is to modify some of the recipes presently used in the establishment to qualify as healthful under federal guidelines.

Start with only a few selections in each category as this should not be a major overhaul of the menu, only an attempt to gain new customers and/or satisfy some of the present clientele. As always, monitor the results of these changes and all of the other listings to ascertain what is profitable and what is selling. (How to do this is covered in Chapter 5, Menu Analysis.) Let the selections either stay or be removed, the healthy offerings either expanded or reduced, based on the facts presented in the analysis.

INCREASING HEALTHFUL MENU LISTINGS IN PRODUCTION

Many times, with only a slight variation in an ingredient or a change in cooking methods, an existing menu selection can become a healthful menu selection. This, however, should only be attempted if there is no noticeable change in either the taste, texture, or appearance of the product. For example, a fine dining, white-tablecloth restaurant would not want to substitute skim milk for heavy cream in its signature crab bisque. They may, however, opt to offer a clear consommé as an alternative. On the other hand, a family restaurant may want to change to skim milk and flour rather than a roux and homogenized whole milk in order to merchandise a cream of broccoli soup as "lighter." Which of the following suggestions to use to modify recipes should be left to the experts: the chef, culinary staff, and management. The success of the modification will ultimately be decided by the customer.

The following is a list of just a few possible recipe and preparation modifications for menu listings to increase the number of healthful menu listings in a restaurant or food service.

Menu Changes and Adoptions

Offer soups based with defatted stocks in addition to cream soups. Add low-fat or fat-free salad dressings to the menu in addition to regular dressings.

Serve dressing in a separate vessel.

In addition to offering fried veggies as appetizers, offer raw or marinated vegetables.

Add frozen yogurt, sherbet, or sorbet to supplement ice cream.

Offer egg substitutes such as Egg Beaters® in addition to eggs.

Increase the listings of fish, seafood, and boneless skinless chicken breast on the menu.

Also increase pasta and rice dishes on the menu.

Reduce salt in recipes, check results for flavor.

Avoid packaged foods and frozen entrees as they are usually high in sodium.

Read the label on soup bases; if salt is the first ingredient, change brands.

Use wine, stock, juices, or water rather than fat when sautéing.

Try thickening sauces, soups, and gravies with a starch rather than a roux which contains fat.

Use flavored vinegars with less oil when making oil and vinegar-based dressings.

Baste meats with citrus juices, wine, or broth rather than fat.

Preparation Methods

The nutritionally preferred methods for cooking are broiling, grilling, barbecuing, steaming, and microwaving. Acceptable methods include roasting, if the product is placed on a rack; sautéing, if a nonstick skillet is used along with a nonfat spray; pan broiling, if the fat is removed during the cooking process; and stir-frying, if a minimal amount of oil is used. Unacceptable methods are braising and boiling—as fat stays with the meat and nutrients are lost if vegetables are being boiled—frying or deep-fat frying.

NUTRITION LABELING LAWS

In 1990, Congress enacted the Nutrition Labeling and Education Act. Its purpose was to require nutritional information on the label of practically all foods and to insure that nutrition-related claims would be used responsibly as well as have consistent meanings throughout the marketplace. It is this latter requirement that concerns most of the restaurant industry.

Although the law exempts restaurants from providing nutrition information on their menus, the FDA rules have a significant effect on how the nutritional attributes of foods and menu listings are communicated to customers. Although the law was passed by Congress, the FDA (the Food & Drug Administration) administers the law by passing and enforcing regulations. As a matter of interest, the law passed by Congress was 15 pages long and the regulations put forth by the FDA encompass over 4,000 pages.

Three types of nutritional claims that restaurants could use on their menu or in advertising are regulated by the FDA. If any of these three are used, they must meet the specific FDA definition for that claim.

Absolute Claim

An absolute claim is a statement made about the exact amount or range of a nutrient in a food. "Low-fat" and "calorie-free" are ex-

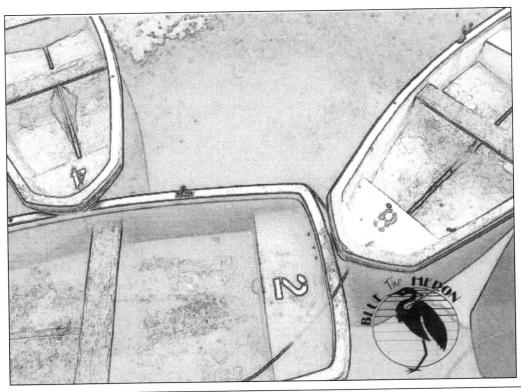

APPETIZERS

Asiago Spinach and Artichoke Dip (Chef's Favorite)
$6.85
Three cheeses, spinach and artichokes baked in a crusty French bread boule. Offered with lemon and spicy Buffalo sauce.

Feta Cheese Puffs
$5.45
Feta cheese, cream cheese and spinach, breaded and fried to a golden brown. Accompanied with a spinach confetti salad, and served with marinara sauce for dipping.

Loaded Potato Strips
$5.45
Idaho potatoes are hand scooped, then the skins are sliced into strips, deep fried and piled high. Topped with melted Colby cheese, chopped bacon, and green onions. Served with sour cream.

Baguette Spinach Loaf
$5.95
French baguette bread covered with fresh spinach, garlic, Asiago cheese and butter, then baked until hot and crusty. Served with marinara sauce for dipping.

Fiesta Dip
$7.45
Spicy chicken, black olives, guacamole, green onions, sour cream and tomatoes smothered in Colby and Jack cheeses. Served with tortilla chips and salsa.

Buffalo Portobello Mushroom Steak
$6.95
Wood-grilled portobello mushroom basted with our special Buffalo sauce, accompanied with carrots and celery, and Blue Cheese dressing.
Without the dressing.

Pot Stickers
$5.75
Five fried Chinese dumplings filled with a pork stuffing, served with our famous Sesame Ginger Vinaigrette Dressing. Known in the Far East as *yakimandu* or *gyoza.*

Szechwan BBQ Wings
$6.95
Chicken wings, lightly coated with Szechwan BBQ sauce. Served with a fortune cookie.

Tequila Shrimp
$7.95
Ten wood-grilled shrimp, basted with our tequila-lime butter. Accompanied by black bean-corn relish and salsa.

Dining à la Heart
The Dining à la Heart Program is sponsored and endorsed by NASSER, SMITH & PINKERTON CARDIOLOGY, INC., The Heart Center of Indiana.
Indicates the menu item is lower in fat, cholesterol and sodium to comply with Dining à la Heart guidelines.

Hot   Extra Hot   Firebrand

FIGURE 6.6. An excellent example of integrating healthful listings into regular menu offerings.
(*Courtesy of the Blue Heron Restaurant, Indianapolis, Indiana*)

❤ House Salad
$3.25
Mixed greens with tomato, cucumbers, carrots, Pepper Jack cheese, red onion, croutons and your choice of dressings.

Southwestern Cobb Salad
$6.95
House greens topped with spicy chicken, red and yellow tomatoes, black olives, black bean-corn relish, green onion, and Colby and Pepper Jack cheeses. Served with salsa and Ranch dressing.

Trio Salad
$7.25
Can't make up your mind? Try our three-salad combination – chicken salad, broccoli-pasta salad, and spinach confetti salad.

❤ *Caramelized Pecan-Orange Salad
$5.65
House greens are piled high with Mandarin oranges, toasted caramelized pecans, red onion, and chunks of Feta cheese. Tossed with our Balsamic Vinaigrette dressing.
Our chef's favorite.
Add a wood-grilled chicken breast for $1.95
❤ * Without chicken

Chicken Salad
$6.75
Diced plump chicken breast, tossed with toasted pecans, chunks of pineapple, raisins and onion, and stuffed into a large tomato. Served with a fat-free fruit muffin.

Caesar Salads
Traditional classic $4.25

With wood-grilled chicken breast
$5.95

Dressings
House (*Raspberry-Balsamic Vinaigrette), Honey Mustard, Bleu Cheese, Ranch, Thousand Island, Fat-Free Catalina, *Balsamic Vinaigrette, and *Sesame Ginger.
❤ * All vinaigrette dressings

❤ Wood-Grilled Chicken Salad
$7.95
Strips of chicken breast, salad greens, grilled tomato wedges, mushrooms, cucumber, green onion, red onion, red pepper, and Sesame Ginger Vinaigrette dressing.

French Onion Soup
Cup $3.25
Bowl $3.75
Topped with croutons and Swiss cheese.

Soup of the Day
Cup $2.45
Bowl $2.95
Ask your server for today's selection.

Soup and Salad Combination
$5.45
A bowl of our Soup of the Day served after our house salad, with your choice of dressings.

Soup and half a Chicken Salad Sandwich
$5.95

Cordon Bleu Sandwich
$6.45
Wood-grilled or deep-fried chicken, topped with ham and Swiss cheese.

Portobello Mushroom Sandwich
$8.25
Grilled portobello mushrooms, layered with tomatoes, spinach, caramelized onions, and Jack and smoked Gouda cheeses. Served on a baguette with trio mustard for dipping.

Chicken Salad Sandwich
$5.50
Our fresh chicken salad, served on thick-sliced, toasted, whole-wheat bread.

Burgers
Hamburger $4.95
A full half-pound of fresh ground beef, wood grilled to perfection.

Cheeseburger $5.35
Smothered in American cheese.

Megaburger $6.50
A feast of Southern fixin's. Bring your appetite!

Baguette Burger $5.75
Rolled in chopped onions, wood grilled, and served on crusty baguette bread with Swiss cheese.

Roman Burger $6.50
Topped with pepperoni, ham, marinara and cheese.

❤ Pork Tenderloin
$6.25
Center-cut tenderloin, wood grilled or deep fried.
❤ * If wood grilled

❤ * Turkey Club
$6.45
Layered with honey-smoked turkey, spinach, bacon, Swiss cheese, tomato, and cranberry mayonnaise on crusty baguette bread.
❤ * Without bacon

Chicken Salad Quesadilla
$6.25
Served with salsa and sour cream.

♪ ❤ * Buffalo Chicken Sandwich
$5.95
Wood-grilled chicken breast, basted with our unique spicy Buffalo sauce. Topped with shredded lettuce, carrots, and Bleu Cheese crumbles. Bleu Cheese dressing on the side.
❤ * Without the dressing

♪♪♪ Maui Sirloin Sandwich
$7.45
Certified Black Angus sirloin steak marinated in a pineapple teriyaki glaze, and topped with chipotle and tomatillo salsa.

❤ Grilled Salmon Sandwich
$8.25
Atlantic salmon, wood grilled and served with a cucumber-lemon dressing.

Voodoo Chicken Sandwich
$5.95
Grilled chicken breast, topped with Voodoo sauce, green onion and Jack cheese.

♪ Hot   ♪♪ Extra Hot   ♪♪♪ Firebrand

Sides
Redskin Potatoes	$1.50
Honey-Smoked Mushrooms	$1.75
Seasoned Fries	$1.50
❤ Vegetables	$1.75
Broccoli-Pasta Salad	$1.95
Rice	$1.25
❤ Black Bean/Corn Relish	$1.50

FIGURE 6.6. *(Continued)*

All dinners are accompanied with a house salad and fresh-baked Gonnella bread straight from Chicago. Caesar salad may be substituted for house salad for an additional 75 cents.

DINNERS

Fresh Fish Specialties
Ask your server about our changing daily specials. Our chefs and staff strive to present these offerings as the signature to our menu.

Hawaiian Chicken
$10.95
Plump chicken breast marinated in a pineapple teriyaki glaze, then wood grilled. Served with chipolte salsa on the side, rice and house vegetables.
Chipolte is very hot!

Mexican Chicken
$12.95
Grilled chicken breast basted with roasted garlic butter atop a bed of rice and covered with Colby and Monterey Jack cheeses, tomatoes and guacamole. Served with black bean-corn relish, salsa and sour cream.

Cajun Vegetable Wrap
$10.95
Peppers, onions, mushrooms, carrots, spinach, tomatoes and Jack cheese wrapped in a baked Cajun flour tortilla. Served over rice with our black bean-corn relish and salsa.

Tequila Shrimp
$16.95
Twenty wood-grilled shrimp, basted with our tequila-lime butter. Served with rice and vegetables.

Petite Salmon
$13.50
Fresh Atlantic salmon, wood grilled and covered with a trio mustard sauce. Served over rice with house vegetables.

Cajun Pork Chops
$14.95
French-style, center-cut loin chops are grilled with Cajun spices then nestled in marinara sauce, and served with rice and caramelized onions.

About Our Menu
Our menu is designed to have something for everyone, from fresh seafood to great sandwiches, salads, pastas, chicken, meats, our daily specials, and weekend breakfast items. We make our own salad dressings, sauces and marinades, and use only top-grade cuts of meat. We are able to fly in our seafood overnight, fresh from the Florida coast. Realizing healthy is in, we offer several tasty, heart-healthy items. Please try something new and exciting at The Blue Heron, while relaxing and enjoying our scenic waterfront atmosphere.

Hot   Extra Hot   Firebrand

Don't stop here! More dinners on next page...

DINNERS

Cajun Shrimp Penne Pasta
$15.85
Gulf shrimp and penne pasta blended with peppers, mushrooms, onions and fresh herbs, then tossed in a Cajun red sauce.

Lemon Chicken Penne Pasta
$12.65
Chicken strips, red peppers, green onions and fresh herbs are tossed with penne pasta in a light lemon cream sauce.

Seafood Fettuccine
$15.95
Shrimp, snow crab meat, mushrooms, and green onions, sautéed in an Asiago cream sauce.

Cajun Chicken Fettuccine
$12.95
Cajun-seasoned chicken strips sautéed with mushrooms, green onions, and red pepper in a Parmesan cream sauce.

Fettuccine Alfredo
$10.95
Sautéed with mushrooms in a Parmesan cream sauce.

Portobello Pasta
$12.95
Portobello and button mushrooms, red peppers and fresh herbs. Tossed with trottole pasta in a tomato, roasted garlic and parmesan cream sauce.

House Steak
$13.95
Certified Black Angus sirloin is marinated in a Kentucky Bourbon whiskey marinade and wood grilled. Served with honey-smoked mushrooms and redskin potatoes.

Filet Mignon
$18.95
Choice, aged tenderloin is basted with roasted garlic butter and wood grilled to your specifications. Served with honey-smoked mushrooms and redskin potatoes.
Butterflied if ordered blackened or cooked beyond medium.

New York Strip
$16.95
Basted in roasted garlic butter and cooked to your desired temperature over a wood grill. Served with honey-smoked mushrooms and redskin potatoes.

Sirloin and Tequila Shrimp
$18.95
Certified Black Angus marinated in Kentucky Bourbon and wood grilled with tender shrimp marinated in our tequila-lime butter.

Pasta Aegean
$12.65
Red and yellow tomatoes, pepperoncini peppers, Feta cheese, fresh herbs, spinach, red onions, black olives and garlic. Tossed with olive oil and trottole pasta.

Gratuity is included for parties of 10 or more. Reservations accepted for any size group.

Hot   Extra Hot   Firebrand

All dinners are accompanied with a house salad and fresh-baked Gonnella bread straight from Chicago. Caesar salad may be substituted for house salad for an additional 75 cents.

FIGURE 6.6. *(Continued)*

amples of absolute claims. While definitions of these terms are not required on the menu or in the advertisement, the food must meet specific criteria. (For the specific criteria, see appendices in the back of the text.)

Relative or Comparative Claim

A relative or comparative claim is a statement that compares the amount of nutrient in a food with the amount of that nutrient in a referenced food. For example, claims such as "light," "reduced," or "less" are relative claims. The referenced food (that food to which the claim is being compared) may be the restaurant's regular product; another restaurant's product; a value obtained from a valid database; an average of national or regional brands; or a market-based norm. Although definitions of these terms are not required on the menu or in the advertisement, the food must meet specific criteria.

Implied Claim

An implied claim is a statement that implies that a nutrient is present or absent in a food. Quite often an ingredient is used to imply a nutrient. For example, "high in oat bran" implies that the product is high in fiber. Remember that an implied claim refers to a nutrient. If an ingredient is added or deleted from an item, it is not an implied claim, for example, "contains no MSG." It is quite apparent that there are some gray areas in these claims and the FDA has determined that it will rule on a case-by-case basis. Therefore good judgment should be used when writing a menu listing.

"Free": calorie free; sugar free; cholesterol free, etc.
"Low": low sodium; low calorie; low fat; low cholesterol, etc.
"Light" or **"lite"**: light entree; lite dressing; light fare; lite bites, etc.
"Reduced" and **"less"**: reduced fat; less calories; reduced cholesterol; less sodium, etc.
"Lean" or **"extra lean"**: such as lean hamburger; extra lean roast beef, etc.

HEALTHY MENU

FIGURE 6.7.   FDA menu rules: What to watch out for.

CONCLUSION

When writing menus, make them interesting as well as nutritional. Good variety, popular items, and nutritionally balanced menus properly prepared and served go a long way toward making customers happy. It's just that simple.

QUESTIONS

1. Discuss the difference in writing menus for a captive audience as opposed to a commercial restaurant.

2. Discuss the role of nutrition in menu planning for:
   a) Commercial restaurants
   b) Semicaptive food service
   c) Captive food service

3. Explain and give examples of the basic four.

4. Write a one-week menu for a:
   a) Type A lunch for a grade school
   b) College dormitory

5. Make a list of the current nutritional issues that exist in menu design for:
   a) free-standing restaurants
   b) institutional feeding
      1. schools
      2. healthcare facilities
   c) international travelers

CHAPTER SEVEN

Menu Content

OBJECTIVES   By the completion of this chapter, the reader should be able to:

- Identify the categories that are used on menus and differentiate *when* each is used.
- Explain the criteria that are used to determine specific menu listings.
- Explain the importance of utilizing descriptive terminology to explain and sell menu listings.

IMPORTANT TERMS

Menu categories	Variety
Texture	Shape, size, and color
Menu listings	Balance
Plate composition	Descriptive terminology
Negative terminology	Composition

INTRODUCTION

All menus, regardless of size or complexity, are broken down into various categories. The number of categories used on a menu is determined by the needs and desires of that particular establishment. Such factors as style, decor, type of service, price range, and area demographics are all taken into consideration when determining which and how many categories will appear on a menu.

The traditional categories for menu writing are appetizers, soups, salads, cold entrees, hot entrees, sandwiches, vegetables, side dishes, starches, desserts, cheeses, fruits, and beverages. In a high-ticket, fine dining restaurant all of these categories could be used, while in other operations only several would be used. The following is an explanation of each of these categories.

APPETIZERS

To many people, appetizer is a combination of two words—*appetite* and *teaser*. Indeed, that is the true intent of an appetizer—to tease the palate and awaken the digestive system to want more. Because of the nature of appetizers (stimulating the palate), the portion size is small. They are usually sharp to the taste. If the particular food used is bland, it is served with a tangy, sharp, pungent sauce. Appetizers may be served hot or cold. The type of food used varies, ranging from fruits and vegetables to meat, seafood, and poultry. See Figure 7.1.

SOUPS

In many food service operations, particularly those with limited menu listings, soups and appetizers are included in the same category with one being served in lieu of the other. Like appetizers, they can be served either hot or cold, although in North America hot soups are definitely preferred. There are three different bases: clear, thick, and special. Clear soups include consommes, broths, and variations that occur when various vegetables and/or meats are added to them. Thick soups include chowders, bisques, creams, purees, and potages and have endless varieties when fruits, vegetables, meats, seafoods, or poultry are added. Special soups, sometimes referred to as national soups, include minestrone and vichyssoise among others. There is probably no other sector of modern-day cookery in which variations and individualism are more prevalent than in the preparation of soups. The possibilities are endless. Many a smart operator has chosen this category to utilize leftovers to create a high-selling, high-profit menu item. See Figure 7.2.

```
┌─────────────────────────────────────────────────────┐
│                                                       │
│                  FIRST COURSES                        │
│                                                       │
│               GOAT CHEESE TERRINE                     │
│        spiced pepper sauce & balsamic glaze … seven   │
│                                                       │
│              CHILLED SELECT OYSTERS                    │
│       smoked red pepper mignonette … market price     │
│                                                       │
│                      SOUP                             │
│     saffron, sweet onion and penn cove mussels … seven│
│                                                       │
│               COLD SMOKED AHI TUNA                    │
│    cucumber wasabi vinaigrette & daikon sprouts … nine│
│                                                       │
│                 5-SPICED OYSTERS                      │
│         banana curry & roasted apple … eight          │
│                                                       │
│           THE ULTIMATE SEAFOOD SAMPLER                │
│   a trio of hot oysters, gravlax & smoked tuna … fourteen│
│                                                       │
│          COFFEE & ORANGE DUSTED QUAIL                 │
│      bittersweet chocolate sauce & bok choy … ten     │
│                                                       │
│              TEQUILA-CURED GRAVLAX                    │
│   chickpea fritter, marinated cukes & tomato … nine   │
│                                                       │
│        PAN-SEARED HUDSON VALLEY FOIE GRAS            │
│        spiced pear puree & fresh mango … fourteen     │
│                                                       │
│                 SEARED SCALLOPS                       │
│      tomato, grilled fennel & citrus broth … eleven   │
│                                                       │
└─────────────────────────────────────────────────────┘
```

FIGURE 7.1.   An example of an appetizer menu.

SALADS

Salads basically come in two sizes, an accompanying salad or an entree salad. Reference here is made to accompanying or side salads with the large entree varieties being covered in the following section. In most food service operations, accompanying salads are served prior to the main entree. However, in fine dining restaurants with a more traditional style of service, they are served after the entree as a means of cleansing the palate. Where they are served prior to the meal, they may take the place of an appetizer and/or soup, or they may be served in addition to these. Salads in this category are usually made with fresh, crisp vegetables, but can also contain fruit. Meat, seafood, and poultry are normally not used in accompanying

PALM TERRACE RESTAURANT

◊ ◊ ◊ ◊ ◊

APPETIZERS

Norwegian Smoked Salmon Roll filled with
Potato, Sevruga Caviar, and Fresh Herbs in Sour Cream
$12.50

Casserole of California Vineyard Snails in a Merlot Wine and Garlic Sauce
$12.00

"Salad Gourmande"
Louisiana Crayfish, Grilled Sea Scallops, Foie Gras, Asparagus, and
Wild Mushrooms on a bed of Mesclun and Herbs, Banyuls
Wine Vinegar and Truffle Oil Dressing
$13.00

Quick Fried Quail over Frisée Salad with Roasted Garlic and Truffles
$14.00

Maine Lobster Croustillant with an Oriental Salad
$13.00

Polenta and Farm Goat Cheese Tarte with
Glazed Onion and Fresh Tomatoes with Basil Oil
$11.00

Sautéed Fresh Duck Foie Gras with Grapes in a Black Muscat Wine Sauce
$16.50

California Baby Field Greens with Aged Red Wine Vinaigrette
$8.50

A Sauté of Spring Wild Mushrooms in Brioche, Madeira Wine infusion
$13.00

FIGURE 7.1.   *(Continued)*

SOUP

Chilled Vine Ripe Tomato Soup with Lobster Medallions and Basil Sauce
$9.50

Fresh Green Asparagus Soup with Morel and White Asparagus
$8.50

The Palm Terrace is pleased to provide Italian mineral water for our guests.
FONTE LIMPIA NON-CARBONATED MINERAL WATER *(1000 ml)* **$4.50**
SAN PELLEGRINO SPARKLING MINERAL WATER *(750 ml)* **$4.50**
TYNANT ORIGINAL NATURAL SPRING WATER *(25 fluid oz.)* **$5.50**

FIGURE 7.2. An example of a soup menu.

SALADS

CARAMELIZED PEAR & HAZELNUTS
field greens & cider vinaigrette … six

ROASTED BEET & SHALLOT VINAIGRETTE
tossed with field lettuces … six

MEDITERRANEAN CEASAR
smoked mussels & clams … eight

FRESH SPINACH
warm, brown butter & goat cheese vinaigrette … seven

DUNGENESS CRAB & FENNEL
with citrus & tarragon … nine

A gratuity of 17% will be added to parties of 6 or more
Monique Andrée Barbeau—Executive Chef
William Belickis—Chef du Cuisine

FIGURE 7.3. An example of a salad menu.

salads due to cost factors. Rarely does a restaurant or food service skip this category, the reasons being twofold. Salads are popular because of their healthy ingredients. They also have a low cost, giving them a high gross profit. Most operations opt for the popular tossed salad, giving it a variety of names to entice the customer. Smart restaurateurs offer a variety, and, depending on the season and locale, the variety is endless. *Clean, crisp, well chilled,* and *colorful* are passwords that make this category successful in any operation. See Figures 7.3 and 7.4.

COLD ENTREES

The predominant listing in the cold entree section in most food service operations is the ever famous chef's salad. However, the selection shouldn't stop here. In warmer climates year round, and northern areas in the summer, cold entrees can be a welcome addition and change to the menu. The variety of cold plates and entree salads is limitless. Crisp greens topped with grilled chicken or seafood are very popular. Fresh fruits chilled and colorfully arranged on a platter served with a fruit sherbet or chicken salad present another alternative. Cold meat and cheese platters offer an excellent means to utilize leftover roasts. A tomato stuffed with either chicken, shrimp, or tuna salad; a chilled seafood platter featuring shrimp and crab—the list goes on and on. Consult your recipe books. Use your imagination to create new and exciting cold entrees that add variety and interest to your menu.

Salads

HOUSE SALAD *seasonal greens, fresh mushrooms, croutons, roasted nuts, feta cheese and tomato. Tossed with a honey-balsamic vinaigrette* 3.95

A SALAD OF FRESH SPINACH *crisp bacon, croutons, sweet red onion and hickory-smoked almonds with a warm bacon dressing* 5.95

A SALAD OF SLICED TOMATOES AND RED ONION
herb vinaigrette . . . . 2.95   *with bleu cheese* 3.95

CAESAR SALAD *garlic, olive oil and parmesan cheese* 4.95

GRILLED SEA SCALLOPS & SHRIMP SALAD *seasonal greens, double-smoked bacon, Fontina cheese and bell pepper with an herb vinaigrette* 7.95

GRILLED CHINESE CHICKEN SALAD *seasonal greens, assorted bean sprouts, mushrooms, snow peas and toasted almonds with a light sesame dressing* 6.95

FIGURE 7.4. An example of a salad menu.

HOT ENTREES

The listings for hot entrees are considerable. For this reason, they are broken down into the following subcategories or groups: meat, poultry, fish and seafood, extenders, and nonmeat entrees.

Meat

This being the largest group within the hot entree category, the possibilities for menu listings are endless. Beef, veal, pork, lamb, and variety meats offer a wide choice for the menu writer. Combine this with the various cookery methods—roasting, braising, steaming, broiling, barbecuing, smoking, grilling—and the door is wide open for many exciting menu offerings. See Figures 7.5 and 7.6.

The most popular offering in this group is beef. In practically every survey taken on the likes and dislikes of the American population, beef always scores high. Pork runs second with lamb running third. Current trends are changing these ratings, with pork increasing slightly while beef is decreasing slightly. Also on the increase are chicken, fish, and seafood.

The predominant reason behind these changes is the consumer's increasing awareness of the relationship of diet to overall health and the reduction of fat intake. The beef industry, however, is now producing a leaner product and the ratings are changing again.

Steaks & Combinations

*Served with vegetable and your choice of
roasted garlic mashed potatoes and gravy, wild rice pilaf, steamed new potatoes.*

To continue with our tradition of excellence, along with our seafood, we offer Certified Angus Beef. Only top of the line and choice grades are labeled and sold under the Certified Angus Beef trademark. Carefully aged and cut to our rigid standards, the C.A.B. label is your guarantee of fresh Certified Angus Beef, never frozen.

FILET MIGNON (*8 oz.*) *16.95*

KANSAS CITY STRIP (*14 oz.*) *11.95*

FILET MIGNON (*6 oz.*) **& BROILED OR STEAMED LOBSTER TAIL** *26.95*

FILET MIGNON (*6 oz.*) **& JUMBO FRIED SHRIMP** *19.95*

FILET MIGNON (*6 oz.*) **& MARYLAND-STYLE CRABCAKE** *19.95*

In consideration of all our guests, cigar and pipe smoking is permitted.

FIGURE 7.5. An example of a hot entree category with a steak subheading.

Analyze any menu and odds are beef will be the predominant listing among the meat groups. Taste is the foremost criterion, but keep in mind that pork and lamb are not allowed in some religions, thus eliminating them from the diet of these people regardless of taste. Do not, however, preclude that, since beef is so popular, it should be listed to the exclusion of other meats. People opt for diversity as they get bored eating the same things and will readily order tantalizing meats other than beef.

Poultry

Poultry has always been and will continue to be a popular food. Chicken is the most popular in this group, ranking second behind beef in the overall listing of entrees. Very close to chicken is turkey. Other game birds such as duck, quail, and pheasant rank lower, but can add excitement to any menu. Frying chicken was the number one method of preparation; however, frying has been replaced by baking, broiling, grilling, and smoking as these methods help reduce fat and calories. Roasting turkey is the traditional method of preparation for this item, which is often served with dressing or stuffing. Smoked turkey is an excellent preparation alternative. Game birds are normally preferred roasted or smoked.

Fish and Seafood

This group is the rising star in the hot entree category. Low in fat and cholesterol, rich in protein, and light in taste, it is increasing in popularity daily. While batter-dipped deep frying has been the accepted method of preparation, broiling and baking are becoming increasingly popular. It's no wonder. Why cover up delicate taste with a fried batter that adds calories and fat? The types and species of fish and seafood are endless and, consequently, so are the menu listings. There is hardly a section of the world where freshwater fish is not available. In the coastal regions, freshwater as well as saltwater fish and seafood are readily available. Fresh fish and seafood can be flown inland, giving endless variety to a menu. See Figure 7.7.

Extenders

More commonly known as casseroles, extenders can run the gamut from low cost to high. They incorporate as their main ingredient any of the aforementioned groups. Sometimes they are made from fresh ingredients, and at other times they are prepared from leftovers. Extenders that use low-cost ingredients are an excellent way to keep costs down in an institutional-type food service or to offset high-cost items in a restaurant that demands a good product mix. The variety of extenders is endless. Using the

MEAT AND POULTRY

Roasted Half Free Range Chicken
with a Confit of Garlic and Shallots and a Medley of Vegetables
$25.00

Sautéed Magret of Moulard Duck with
Pineapple in a Vanilla Scented Szechwan Pepper Sauce
$26.00

Medallions of Loin of Veal with Fresh Oregon Morels and Asparagus
$28.00

Medallions of Beef Tenderloin in a Light Roquefort and Aged Red Shallots
$28.00

Oven Roast Loin of Spring Lamb in Moroccan Spice Crust
with a Vegetable and Lemon Couscous
$29.50

Roasted Rib of Beef "Marchand de Vin," Vegetables Bouquet
$56.00   **(2 Persons)**

Any entree can be prepared plain broiled, grilled, or poached without sauce upon request.

GRATUITY IS NOT INCLUDED, 15% IS CUSTOMARY IN THE UNITED STATES FOR GOOD SERVICE.

FIGURE 7.6. An example of a hot entree section with a combination meat/poultry subheading.

many ingredients available, one can follow standardized recipes or release the imagination with personalized variations.

Nonmeat Entrees

Eggs and cheese are the primary sources of nonmeat hot entrees. Comparatively low in cost, they are excellent sources of protein. Although eggs predominate on the breakfast menu, they can also be a welcome addition to a lunch or dinner menu with such listings as quiches or omelets. Another hot entree which is quite popular is pasta covered with numerous meatless sauces or combined with

FISH AND SEAFOOD

Roasted Sea Scallops with Verjus Ravigote Dressing,
Fresh Field Salad, and Root Vegetable Chips

$27.00

Sautéed Dover Sole Filets with Dungeness Crab Meat Millefeuille
in a Lobster Sauce and Tarragon Oil

$28.00

Seared Canadian Salmon Filets and Root Vegetable filled Smoked Salmon Ravioli
with Green Lentils in a Fine Herb Vinaigrette

$28.00

Northern Atlantic Black Sea Bass Filets with
Caribbean Fruits in a mild spicy sauce

$27.00

Fresh Atlantic Turbot cooked in a Potato Crust
with Porcini Mushrooms and a Merlot Wine Sauce

$28.00

Grilled Gulf Shrimp in a Roast Garlic Sauce and Red Chili Oil

$26.00

FIGURE 7.7. An example of a seafood menu.

sauteed fresh vegetables. People who follow a vegetarian diet and lifestyle are increasing in numbers and are prime potential customers for this category with offerings such as vegetable plates, as well as entrees and extenders made with nonmeat ingredients.

SANDWICHES

One of the more popular categories, sandwiches, is found on most menus, the only exception being in a fine dining establishment. Served hot or cold, they are made from a multitude of ingredients including meat, poultry, fish, seafood, cheeses, and vegetables, not to mention the many condiments and spreads that accompany them. Almost every menu that lists sandwiches includes the most popular listing anywhere, the hamburger.

Specialties

*Our Specialties are served with vegetable and your choice of
roasted garlic mashed potatoes and gravy, wild rice pilaf, steamed new potatoes or shoestring fries.*

FIRE ROAST "FLATTENED" CHICKEN *with roasted garlic mashed potatoes,
natural gravy and fresh vegetable saute* *10.95*

SAUTEED FRESH SEA SCALLOPS *with chef's seasoned butter* *15.75*

TRIO COMBO *crisp-fried shrimp, scallops and jumbo lump crabcake with a trio of sauces* *16.95*

GRILLED SHRIMP & SCALLOP PASTA *spicy tomato sauce and cream. With vegetable* . . . *13.95*

SHELLFISH CIOPPINO *fresh fish, sea scallops, Maine Mussels and Gulf Shrimp
in a red wine tomato-herb sauce. Garlic cheese toast* *14.95*

LOBSTER TAIL *broiled or steamed* *19.95*

JUMBO SHRIMP *crisp-fried. With traditional cocktail sauce* *15.95*

JUMBO LUMP MARYLAND-STYLE CRABCAKES *17.95*

MIXED GRILLE *jumbo sea scallops and shrimp over sauteed savoy spinach and grilled
Mahi Mahi with tomato-basil salsa.* *16.95*

FIGURE 7.7. *(Continued)*

VEGETABLES

This group used to be an integral part of every menu. In the 1970s, they started disappearing from the product listing of many restaurants. However, vegetables continued their popularity on noncommercial food service menus. Recently, vegetables have made a comeback on restaurant menus and are presently very popular both as an accompaniment and as an entree. Vegetables, for the most part, are low cost, nutritious, well accepted by customers, low in calories, and, when properly prepared, very colorful additions to any plate.

SIDE DISHES

This is the miscellaneous part of the menu. If the restaurant desires to sell an item and doesn't know where to list it in the other categories, it ends up here. Normally, side dishes are nothing more than a list.

ENTREES

SAFFRON & SUMAC-DUSTED DEMI RACK OF LAMB
barley & black-eyed peas, port & mango … twenty-eight

PAN-SEARED SALMON
black olive basil jus & potato fennel casserole … nineteen

SEASONAL FISH
artichoke chervil broth, fingerling potatoes & asparagus … twenty-one

GRILLED OREGON RABBIT
herb spaetzle, roasted carrots & madeira … eighteen

GRILLED RARE AHI TUNA
kimchee salad & pickled vegetables … twenty-two

FULLERS' SIGNATURE VEGETARIAN ENTREE
eighteen

CERVENA VENISON
sage gnocchi & red onion jam … twenty-three

EAST COAST SCALLOPS
english pea jus & ginger risotto … twenty-two

STILTON & GRILLED ENDIVE STUFFED BEEF TENDERLOIN
mushrooms & truffle oil … thirty

ROASTED SONOMA SQUAB
truffled israeli cous cous, pearl onions & wild mushrooms … twenty-four

SIDES
Truffled Israeli Cous Cous
Ginger Risotto
Potato Fennel Casserole
Honey-Glazed Carrots
Grilled Fennel
three

The chef will prepare a tasting menu for your table for forty-eight dollars
per person
Please ask your server for this evening's courses

It is our pleasure to meet your special requirements

FIGURE 7.8. An example of a mixed entree menu.

Pastas & Sandwiches

GRILLED CHICKEN & PASTA *spicy red pepper cream sauce tossed with linguine. Garlic cheese toast* *11.95*

GRILLED BREAST OF CHICKEN *melted mozzarella and crisp hickory smoked bacon on a toasted roll with dill-mustard mayonnaise. With cole slaw and French fries* *6.95*

LINGUINE & SHRIMP *tossed in a light broth with fresh basil and diced tomatoes. Garlic cheese toast* *12.95*

CHEDDAR BURGER *grilled fresh ground chuck on a toasted roll. With cole slaw and French fries* *5.95*
    With crisp hickory-smoked bacon strips *6.95*

FRESH FISH SANDWICH *mesquite-grilled on a toasted roll. Served with cole slaw and French fries. Your server will tell you today's fresh fish selection* *4.95*

FIGURE 7.9. An example of a combination entree/sandwich section of a menu.

However, consider for a moment what they really are and what they can mean to sales. Add-ons, when properly merchandised on a menu, can mean more business. Items that a customer would normally not consider ordering, when sold by calling attention to them, result in a higher check average and, consequently, higher sales.

STARCHES

Starches are one of the low-cost, high-profit categories of the menu and as such should be properly merchandised. They include such foods as potatoes, pastas, and rice. With proper use of this category, a smart restaurant manager can increase profits. In many cases, customers prefer starches to other selections and, as a result, these items will continue to be popular.

DESSERTS

This is the easiest category in which to obtain add-on sales, if (and that's a big if) they are properly merchandised. Desserts are items that not only require a prominent menu listing, but additionally require suggestive selling. They are rarely ordered as a matter of course. Not only should they be predominantly merchandised on the menu, but also via table tents, prominent lobby displays, and on rolling carts. A well-rounded selection is important, including pastries, baked goods, ice creams, sherbets, sorbets, puddings, mousses, gelatins, fresh fruits, and on and on. See Figure 7.10.

PALM TERRACE RESTAURANT

◊ ◊ ◊ ◊ ◊

DESSERT
$8.00

ANIS CREME BRULEE
Star Anis Flavored Custard with a Caramelized Crust

PASSION FRUIT SOUFFLE
*A rich Custard flavored with fresh Passion Fruit Juice folded into an Italian Mousse
then baked and served with a Mango Coulis*

FRENCH APPLE TART
With Caramel Sauce and Vanilla Ice Cream

CHOCOLATE CARACAS
*Fine Chocolate Sponge Cake layered with a Chocolate Mousse and Caramelized Butter
covered with an Italian Meringue and served with a Rum Crème Anglais*

CREPES SUZETTE
*Warm Crêpe filled with Banana Ice Cream surrounded by Citrus Fruit,
a Grand Marnier Orange Sauce, and Banana Spice Infusion*

"MINESTRONE" OF FRESH TROPICAL FRUIT
*Tropical Fruits sitting on a Spiced Tomato and Vanilla Infusion Broth,
served with a Fromage Blanc Ice Cream and a Crispy Cookie*

SORBETS AND ICE CREAMS

◊ ◊ ◊ ◊ ◊

FIGURE 7.10. An example of a dessert menu.

CHEESES

This category is used only in the finer restaurants. Although cheese is an important ingredient in items in other categories, its listing as an exclusive item is limited. When used in this way, the cheese cat-

---

Desserts

SOUR CREAM APPLE PIE *with walnut streusel topping*. *3.95*
  With ice cream. . . . . *Add .50*

HOMEMADE NEW YORK-STYLE CHEESECAKE. *3.75*
  With fresh strawberries in sauce. . . . . *Add .50*

CARROT CAKE. *3.75*

CHOCOLATE EXTREME CAKE *with coconut cream anglaise*. *3.95*

DEEP DISH KEY LIME PIE. *3.95*

FRESH BERRIES . . . . *market*

"HAAGEN DAZS" VANILLA ICE CREAM
with chocolate chip cookie. *2.95*

FIGURE 7.10. *(Continued)*

egory should contain a well-rounded assortment. Brie, Gouda, Edam, Bleu, and Camembert are a few of the many popular varieties. They can be sold either as an assortment of several varieties or as a single entity, where the customer chooses from a listing. Many times cheese is listed in conjunction with fruits. When so listed, only fresh fruits are appropriate.

FRUITS

Ever popular on institutional menus, fruits are also widely used on restaurant menus, particularly for breakfast. With excellent availability either as a canned, frozen, or fresh product, fruits can add variation to any menu. Fresh fruit plates for luncheon or light supper menus, in conjunction with other cold entrees, listed as an alternative to desserts or featured as a garnish, add color and taste alternatives for your customers.

BEVERAGES

Customers are so conditioned to purchasing a beverage with their meal that this category just deserves a mention. Listing the popular selections and their selling prices will normally suffice. Space in this section should be reserved for merchandising specialty beverages that produce a high check average as well as high gross profit. See Figure 7.11.

DESSERT WINES

CHÂTEAU RIEUSSEC, SAUTERNES
$8.50 *per glass*

MOSCATO d'ORO, ROBERT MONDAVI
$7.00 *per glass*

ALEXIS LICHINE, SAUTERNES
$5.00 *per glass*

FIGURE 7.11. An example of a beverage section of a menu.

LISTINGS

Deciding which categories to use is more or less a personal choice; there are no iron-clad regulations governing exactly how many categories should be on a specific type of menu. There is, however, a general rule of thumb that the higher the average selling price, the more categories should be used. For example, fast food normally utilizes sandwiches, sides, and beverages, while on the opposite end of the spectrum, fine dining uses most, if not all, of the 13 categories.

Once the decision has been made as to how many and which of the categories to use, the next step is to determine the specific listings to be presented in each of those categories. This cannot be done in a haphazard manner based on personal likes and dislikes. Many factors need to be taken into account. First and foremost are the demographics of the trade area, as the popularity and the selling price of the item must fit the customer's wants and needs. The restaurant or food service operation must be able to produce the items properly from the standpoint of equipment as well as the capabilities of the production and service staff. The item must also fit the commitment to offering nutritious, well-balanced meals.

When these criteria have been satisfied, the listings are then assembled and go through another series of tests before being placed on the final menu. These would include ascertaining that variety, balance, and composition are all included. Many people call this exercise *menu patterning*. By using this method, the menu writer is assured of meeting all the desired criteria.

VARIETY

It is very important that each category included in the menu have variety within its listings. Variety takes on many different connotations in connection with menus. There should be variety in temper-

FIRST COURSES

GOAT CHEESE TERRINE
spiced pepper sauce & balsamic glaze ... seven

CHILLED SELECT OYSTERS
smoked red pepper mignonette ... market price

SOUP
saffron, sweet onion and penn cove mussels ... seven

COLD SMOKED AHI TUNA
cucumber wasabi vinaigrette & daikon sprouts ... nine

5-SPICED OYSTERS
banana curry & roasted apple ... eight

THE ULTIMATE SEAFOOD SAMPLER
a trio of hot oysters, gravlax & smoked tuna ... fourteen

COFFEE & ORANGE-DUSTED QUAIL
bittersweet chocolate sauce & bok choy ... ten

TEQUILA-CURED GRAVLAX
chickpea fritter, marinated cukes & tomato ... nine

PAN-SEARED HUDSON VALLEY FOIE GRAS
spiced pear puree & fresh mango ... fourteen

SEARED SCALLOPS
tomato, grilled fennel & citrus broth ... eleven

SALADS

CARAMELIZED PEAR & HAZELNUTS
field greens & cider vinaigrette ... six

ROASTED BEET & SHALLOT VINAIGRETTE
tossed with field lettuces ... six

MEDITERRANEAN CAESAR
smoked mussels & clams ... eight

FRESH SPINACH
warm brown butter & goat cheese vinaigrette ... seven

DUNGENESS CRAB & FENNEL
with citrus & tarragon ... nine

A gratuity of 17% will be added to parties of 6 or more

Monique Andrée Barbeau - Executive Chef
William Belickis - Chef de Cuisine

FIGURE 7.12. The complete menu of Fullers Restaurant located in the Seattle Sheraton Hotel and Towers, Seattle, Washington.

ENTRÉES

SAFFRON & SUMAC-DUSTED DEMI RACK OF LAMB
barley & black-eyed peas, port & mango
twenty-eight

PAN-SEARED SALMON
black olive basil jus & potato fennel casserole
nineteen

SEASONAL FISH
artichoke chervil broth, fingerling potatoes & asparagus
twenty-one

GRILLED OREGON RABBIT
herb spaetzle, roasted carrots & madeira
eighteen

GRILLED RARE AHI TUNA
kimchee salad & pickled vegetables
twenty-two

FULLERS' SIGNATURE VEGETARIAN ENTREE
eighteen

CERVENA VENISON
sage gnocchi & red onion jam
twenty-three

EAST COAST SCALLOPS
english pea jus & ginger risotto
twenty-two

STILTON & GRILLED ENDIVE STUFFED BEEF TENDERLOIN
mushrooms & truffle oil
thirty

ROASTED SONOMA SQUAB
truffled israeli cous cous, pearl onions & wild mushrooms
twenty-four

SIDES

Truffled Israeli Cous Cous
Ginger Risotto
Potato Fennel Casserole
Honey-glazed Carrots
Grilled Fennel
three

*The chef will prepare a tasting menu for your table for forty-eight dollars
per person
Please ask your server for this evening's courses*

It is our pleasure to meet your special requirements

FIGURE 7.12. (*Continued*)

FIGURE 7.13. The complete menu of the Bristol Bar and Grill. (*Courtesy of Gilbert/Robinson Inc., owner and operator of The Bristol.*)

Appetizers

FRESH OYSTERS *today's selection, half dozen* 5.95
COCKTAIL OF JUMBO SHRIMP *with tangy cocktail sauce and fresh horseradish* 6.95
SCAMPI SAUTE *in seasoned garlic butter* 5.95
STEAMED MAINE MUSSELS *in white wine broth* 5.95
ESCARGOT *baked in seasoned garlic butter* 5.25
SWORDFISH SOFT SHELL TACOS *with spicy sour cream,*
tomato-basil and avocado salsas 5.95
CRISP FRIED CALAMARI *with Anaheim chili aioli* ....*half order 3.75* 5.95
CLAM CHOWDER *New England-style* ....*cup 2.95* ....*bowl 3.95*
CREOLE GUMBO *spicy New Orleans-Style* ....*cup 2.95* ....*bowl 3.95*

Salads

HOUSE SALAD *seasonal greens, fresh mushrooms, croutons, roasted nuts,*
feta cheese and tomato. Tossed with a honey-balsamic vinaigrette 3.95
A SALAD OF FRESH SPINACH *crisp bacon, croutons,*
sweet red onion and hickory-smoked almonds with a warm bacon dressing 3.95
A SALAD OF SLICED TOMATOES AND RED ONION
herb vinaigrette ....2.95   *with bleu cheese* 3.75
CAESAR SALAD *garlic, olive oil and parmesan cheese* 2.95
GRILLED SEA SCALLOPS & SHRIMP SALAD *seasonal greens, mushrooms,*
double-smoked bacon, Fontina cheese and bell pepper with an herb vinaigrette 9.95
GRILLED CHINESE CHICKEN SALAD *seasonal greens, assorted julienne vegetables,*
bean sprouts, mushrooms, snow peas and toasted almonds with a light sesame dressing 7.95

Pastas & Sandwiches

GRILLED CHICKEN & PASTA *spicy red pepper cream sauce*
tossed with linguine. Garlic cheese toast 8.50
GRILLED BREAST OF CHICKEN *melted mozzarella and crisp hickory-smoked bacon*
on a toasted roll with dill-mustard mayonnaise. With cole slaw and French fries 7.95
LINGUINE & SHRIMP *tossed in a light broth with fresh basil*
and diced tomatoes. Garlic cheese toast 9.25
CHEDDAR BURGER *grilled fresh ground chuck on a toasted roll.*
With cole slaw and French fries 6.95
    With crisp hickory-smoked bacon strips ....*Add .25*
FRESH FISH SANDWICH *mesquite-grilled on a toasted roll. Served with*
cole slaw and French fries. Your server will tell you today's fresh fish selection 8.95

Desserts

SOUR CREAM APPLE PIE *with walnut streusel topping* 3.95
    With ice cream ....*Add .50*
HOMEMADE NEW YORK-STYLE CHEESECAKE 3.75
    With fresh strawberries in sauce ....*Add .50*
CARROT CAKE 3.75
CHOCOLATE EXTREME CAKE *with coconut cream anglaise* 3.95
DEEP DISH KEY LIME PIE 3.95
FRESH BERRIES ....*market*
"HAAGEN DAZS" VANILLA ICE CREAM
with chocolate chip cookie 2.95

This space is used for "Daily Fresh Sheet"

Specialties

Our Specialties are served with vegetable and your choice of
roasted garlic mashed potatoes and gravy, wild rice pilaf, steamed new potatoes or shoestring fries.

FIRE ROAST "FLATTENED" CHICKEN *with roasted garlic mashed potatoes,*
natural gravy and fresh vegetable saute 10.95
SAUTEED FRESH SEA SCALLOPS *with chef's seasoned butter* 15.75
TRIO COMBO *crisp-fried shrimp, scallops and jumbo lump crabcake with a trio of sauces* 16.95
GRILLED SHRIMP & SCALLOP PASTA *spicy tomato sauce and cream. With vegetable* ..13.95
SHELLFISH CIOPPINO *fresh fish, sea scallops, Maine Mussels and Gulf Shrimp*
in a red wine tomato-herb sauce. Garlic cheese toast 14.95
LOBSTER TAIL *broiled or steamed* 19.95
JUMBO SHRIMP *crisp-fried. With traditional cocktail sauce* 15.95
JUMBO LUMP MARYLAND-STYLE CRABCAKES 17.95
MIXED GRILLE *jumbo sea scallops and shrimp over sauteed savoy spinach and grilled Mahi Mahi with*
tomato-basil salsa 16.95

Steaks & Combinations

Served with vegetable and your choice of
roasted garlic mashed potatoes and gravy, wild rice pilaf, steamed new potatoes or shoestring fries.
To continue with our tradition of excellence, along with our seafood, we offer Certified Angus Beef. Only top of the U.S.D.A. prime
and choice grades are labeled and sold under the Certified Angus Beef trademark. Carefully aged and cut to our rigid quality specifications,
the C.A.B. label is your guarantee of fresh Certified Angus Beef, never frozen.

FILET MIGNON *(8 oz.)* 17.95
KANSAS CITY STRIP *(14 oz.)* 19.95
FILET MIGNON *(6 oz.)* **& BROILED OR STEAMED LOBSTER TAIL** 29.95
FILET MIGNON *(6 oz.)* **& JUMBO FRIED SHRIMP** 18.95
FILET MIGNON *(6 oz.)* **& MARYLAND-STYLE CRABCAKE** 19.95

In consideration of all our guests, cigar and pipe smoking is permitted only at the bar.

FIGURE 7.13. *(Continued)*

PALM TERRACE RESTAURANT

◊ ◊ ◊ ◊ ◊

APPETIZERS

*Norwegian Smoked Salmon Roll filled with
Potato, Sevruga Caviar, and Fresh Herbs in Sour Cream*
$12.50

Casserole of California Vineyard Snails in a Merlot Wine and Garlic Sauce
$12.00

*"Salad Gourmande"
Louisiana Crayfish, Grilled Sea Scallops, Foie Gras, Asparagus, and Wild Mushrooms
on a bed of Mesclun and Herbs, Banyuls Wine Vinegar and Truffle Oil Dressing*
$13.00

Quick Fried Quail over Frisée Salad with Roasted Garlic and Truffles
$14.00

Maine Lobster Croustillant with an Oriental Salad
$13.00

*Polenta and Farm Goat Cheese Tarte with
Glazed Onion and Fresh Tomatoes with Basil Oil*
$11.00

Sautéed Fresh Duck Foie Gras with Grapes in a Black Muscat Wine Sauce
$16.50

California Baby Field Greens with Aged Red Wine Vinaigrette
$8.50

A Sauté of Spring Wild Mushrooms in Brioche, Madeira Wine infusion
$11.50

SOUP

Chilled Vine Ripe Tomato Soup with Lobster Medallions and Basil Sorbet
$9.50

Fresh Green Asparagus Soup with Morel and White Asparagus Flan
$8.50

The Palm Terrace is pleased to provide Italian mineral waters for our guests:
FONTE LIMPIA NON-CARBONATED MINERAL WATER *(1000 ml)* $4.50
SAN PELLEGRINO SPARKLING MINERAL WATER *(750 ml)* $4.50
TY NANT ORIGINAL NATURAL SPRING WATER *(25 fluid oz.)* $5.50

FIGURE 7.14. The complete menu of the Palm Terrace Restaurant located in the Palazzo Hotel, U.S. Virgin Islands.

FISH AND SEAFOOD

Roasted Sea Scallops with a Verjus Ravigote Dressing,
Fresh Field Salad, and Root Vegetable Chips

$27.00

Sautéed Dover Sole Filets with Dungeness Crab Meat Millefeuille
in a Lobster Sauce and Tarragon Oil

$28.00

Seared Canadian Salmon Filets and Root Vegetable filled Smoked Salmon Ravioli
with Green Lentils in a Fine Herb Vinaigrette

$28.00

Northern Atlantic Black Sea Bass Filets with
Caribbean Fruits in a mild spicy sauce

$27.00

Fresh Atlantic Turbot cooked in a Potato Crust
with Porcini Mushrooms and a Merlot Wine Sauce

$28.00

Grilled Gulf Shrimp in a Roast Garlic Sauce and Red Chili Oil

$26.00

MEAT AND POULTRY

Roasted Half Free Range Chicken
with a Confit of Garlic and Shallots and a Medley of Vegetables

$25.00

Sautéed Magret of Moulard Duck with
Pineapple in a Vanilla Scented Szechwan Pepper Sauce

$26.00

Medallions of Loin of Veal with Fresh Oregon Morels and Asparagus

$28.00

Medallions of Beef Tenderloin in a Light Roquefort and Aged Red Port Sauce

$28.00

Oven Roast Loin of Spring Lamb in Moroccan Spice Crust
with a Vegetable and Lemon Couscous

$29.50

Roasted Rib of Beef "Marchand de Vin", Vegetables Bouquetière

$56.00   (2 Persons)

Any entree can be prepared plain broiled, grilled, or poached without sauce upon request

GRATUITY IS NOT INCLUDED, 15% IS CUSTOMARY IN THE UNITED STATES FOR GOOD SERVICE.

FIGURE 7.14.   *(Continued)*

PALM TERRACE RESTAURANT

◊ ◊ ◊ ◊ ◊

DESSERT
$8.00

ANIS CREME BRULEE
Star Anis Flavored Custard with a Caramelized Crust

PASSION FRUIT SOUFFLE
A rich Custard flavored with fresh Passion Fruit Juice folded into an Italian Meringue,
then baked and served with a Mango Coulis

FRENCH APPLE TART
With Caramel Sauce and Vanilla Ice Cream

CHOCOLATE CARACAS
Fine Chocolate Sponge Cake layered with a Chocolate Mousse and Caramelized Bananas,
covered with an Italian Meringue and served with a Rum Crème Anglaise

CREPES SUZETTE
Warm Crêpe filled with Banana Ice Cream surrounded by Citrus Fruit,
a Grand Marnier Orange Sauce, and Banana Spice Infusion

"MINESTRONE" OF FRESH TROPICAL FRUITS
Tropical Fruits sitting on a Spiced Tomato and Vanilla Infusion Broth,
served with a Fromage Blanc Ice Cream and a Crispy Cookie

SORBETS AND ICE CREAMS

◊ ◊ ◊ ◊ ◊

DESSERT WINES

CHÂTEAU RIEUSSEC, SAUTERNES
$8.50 per glass
MOSCATO d'ORO, ROBERT MONDAVI
$7.00 per glass
ALEXIS LICHINE, SAUTERNES
$5.00 per glass

FIGURE 7.14. *(Continued)*

ature, cooking methods, textures, shapes, sizes, and color—each with special meaning when applied to certain categories. The following sections explore some specific examples.

Temperature

Temperature variation applies to several categories. Vegetables and starches are normally served hot, while salads, cheeses, and fruits are normally served cold. Appetizers, soups, entrees, sandwiches, beverages, and desserts, on the other hand, should contain a variety of both hot and cold offerings. These listings are almost always exclusively hot or cold. With so many choices, temperature variety should be given.

Cooking Methods

Regardless of whether an item is served hot or cold, chances are that it has gone through some kind of a cooking process. Some exceptions to this would be raw fruits, vegetables, marinated fresh fish and seafood, and steak tartar. The smart menu writer would assure that there is a variety of cooking methods in each category. Let's analyze the key categories where different methods can be employed. Deep-fat frying for breaded vegetables, boiled and chilled shrimp or crab claws, and fresh, raw, sautéed, and steamed items comprise a few of the methods available for the appetizer section. Sandwich fillings could be deep fried, grilled, broiled, and roasted (some hot, some cold). For hot entrees the methods are endless; braised, sautéed, fried, roasted, baked, deep fried, grilled, and smoked, to name a few. Cold entrees would follow basically the same methods. Desserts could be frozen, baked, fresh, cooked, and chilled. With all of these methods of food production available, the menu should have plenty of variety.

Texture

Foods have many textures and including a variety of these textures is important when selecting various listings to place on the menu. For example, a solid, chewy texture is found in meats such as steaks or roasts. A soft, mushy texture is inherent in whipped potatoes or puddings. Casserole items might tend to have a liquid texture for their bases as would listings that contain a sauce. Cooked vegetables, if they are properly prepared, have a slight crispness to them, while raw vegetables have a definite crunch. A diversity of these and other textures available throughout a meal makes it a more enjoyable experience than a meal with only one or two textures.

Shapes and Sizes

Shape and size appeal to the eye. An attractively presented plate appeals to a customer more than a boring plate and, psychologically, tastes better too. An entree of medallions of beef, pommes Anna, and sliced zucchini squash would contain all circles and as such would not be very appealing. In addition to varying the shapes and sizes on a menu, remember that the shape of food should always be natural. With the proliferation of prefabricated foods on the market, it is easy for the menu planner to forget this fact. For example, a fish square on a plate is not nearly as attractive as a fillet.

Color

Although shape and size are important, color will do more for eye appeal than anything. Consider this: if a menu is properly prepared with a variety of shapes, sizes, and color, the plate would need no garnish. The result would be less labor to prepare the plate and less food cost. Many beautiful, bright, vivid colors occur naturally in foods and these should be used to create an advantage. Unfortunately, many dull, bland colors are also inherent in foods. It would not be prudent to eliminate these foods, as many of them are quite popular. A careful blend is the key to a colorful plate. Take, for example, a simple pork chop. If we were to serve this with potatoes au gratin, buttered corn, and a ramekin of applesauce, we would have dull like you wouldn't believe. But by substituting wild rice pilaf, baby LeSeur peas, and cranberry-orange relish, we create a plate with substantially more eye appeal than its predecessor.

Balance

Balance takes on several different connotations when used in conjunction with menu planning. The same criteria that were used in association with variety would be used when discussing balance. Each category listed on the menu should have, within itself, satisfactory variety. This variety should have balance, that is, one or more listings each for variation in temperature, cooking methods, textures, shapes, sizes, and color. To illustrate balance, analyze the hot entree category of the menu.

Balance of items in hot entrees would include meat, poultry, and fish/seafood. Breaking this down further, it would be necessary to have a balance of meats, that is, beef, veal, pork, and lamb. Likewise, poultry could include chicken, turkey, and possibly game such as quail or pheasant. Fish and seafood should also have balance. Including some or all of these items automatically gives variety and balance. However, if one particular type of item were used to the exclusion of the others, the menu would become one-dimensional. An exception to this, of course, would be a specialty restaurant where one type of food would be predominant. A steak house, for instance, offers mainly beef, although other selections may be offered as well. Notwithstanding this exception, the rule would be to have a balanced variety within specific categories.

Temperature within the hot entree category would be a nonentity as it would be assumed that all hot entrees would be served hot. Different cooking methods, on the other hand, should be considered. In the section on variety, roasting, broiling, grilling, and braising were discussed. Not only is it important to have a variety of cooking methods, it is also important to strike a balance among them.

Texture balance is also important. Entrees of solids such as steaks and roasts, semi-solids such as croquettes and loafs, and extenders such as stews and casseroles, should be listed in a balanced manner. Shapes, sizes, and colors should also be handled similarly.

COMPOSITION

Composition refers to the makeup of the plate itself. Consideration of composition needs to be taken into account when writing menus for a captive audience. Banquets, institutions, school lunches, and food service operations in which the customer has no choice are all areas where composition becomes important. In operations where customers can choose which items they prefer, composition is then taken out of the hands of the menu writer.

In considering plate composition, all the criteria heretofore mentioned must be taken into consideration. The plate should have variety and balance. Various cooking methods should be used. Textures are important. We would not want, for example, a plate of chicken á la king with scalloped potatoes and harvard beets all running together. Shape, size, and color also come into play. All of this needs to be analyzed carefully before writing a menu.

DESCRIPTIVE TERMINOLOGY

Descriptive terminology is used on a menu for two reasons: first, to explain a product, and, second, to sell that product. Although these functions would appear to be among the duties of the service personnel, don't count on it. A case in point: the other evening, while dining in a fine restaurant, the maitre d' commented while seating us that the waiter would explain the chef's selection for the evening as well as the soup du jour. The waiter did neither, nor was a wine offered or even suggested, and no attempt was made to sell a dessert. The waiter did not know the contents of several of the dishes. The point is, unfortunately, that service personnel cannot be counted on to sell or explain, no matter how well trained they are. Sometimes they're swamped, sometimes they forget, and sometimes they don't care. The menu must do it. If both the menu and the service personnel sell and explain, that's a plus.

EXPLAINING

Quite often some of the menu items are confusing to customers. If they don't understand what a particular dish is made of, they won't order it. Although the majority of your customers understand most of the listings, some won't. The assumption must be made that *all* of the customers won't understand *any* of the listings and, therefore, all listings should be fully described. All too often restaurant owners and managers, because they see the same items over and over, forget that there may be some confusion among some customers.

For example, take an item like beef stroganoff. Ask a group of people what it is. Very few will be able to answer you. Simply listing beef stroganoff on the menu will not get the job done. Many people will avoid ordering it not knowing that the ingredients could be some of their favorite foods and that they would thoroughly enjoy this dish, if it were properly explained. Next, ask a group of chefs how they prepare beef stroganoff. Prepare yourself for a difference of opinion. Some use tenderloin tips; others, stew beef; still others use miscellaneous cuts from leftovers. How much and what kinds of spices? Some use more, some less. How do they serve it? En casserole, over buttered noodles, with or without caraway seeds? With wide noodles, or narrow, dumpling style? Odds are, you won't get two identical answers. That's one of the things that makes our industry so great—individuality. Even if your customers know what beef stroganoff is, they do not know how your restaurant or your chef prepares it. It must be explained to them in order for that item to sell.

Take an item that 99.94 percent of the population knows and understands. Steak. Simply listing steak doesn't tell customers everything they need to know about that item. What kind of steak? Strip. *Strip steak.* What style of strip steak? New York. *New York strip steak.* How is it cooked? Broiled. *Broiled New York strip steak.* How is it broiled? Charcoal. *Charcoal broiled New York strip steak.* What is its size? 12 oz. *Charcoal broiled 12 oz. New York strip steak.* Now we have a menu listing. All of these questions go through customers' minds when making decisions. If the menu doesn't answer these questions, they will ask the service personnel with delay and possibly confusion. Anticipate these problems when writing the menu. Describe fully and accurately each menu listing. As we will discuss in Chapter 8, accuracy is a must.

SELLING

Once the item is described, the task of writing the menu is partially complete. Next, the selling of that item must be accomplished. To have a truly complete menu listing, the item must be fully described as well as romanced in order for it to sell.

For a listing to sell, it must sound so good that the customer can't pass it up. To do this, adjectives are used profusely. Here simple wording is not enough. Use a complete sentence, maybe two, to sell the item. For instance, the steak in the previous example becomes:

Fish, Birds and Meat

Asparagus Napoleon
crispy potatoes, roasted tomato, asparagus and potato sauce $18

Sauteed Red Snapper
crab-hash and black bean sauce $26

Grilled Duck Breast and Confit Leg
potato mashers and roasted olive sauce $27

Trio of East Coast Seafood
grouper, sea scallops and shrimp ravioli $28

Grilled Missouri Ostrich
garlic cream, parsley puree and wilted greens $30

Sesame Coated Beef Tenderloin
broccoli, soba noodles and sake $28

Sauteed Alaskan Halibut
roasted bell pepper, saffron onion puree and sage olive oil $25

Grilled Amish Chicken
lemon grass, mushrooms and water chestnuts $22

Orecchietta Pasta and Wild Mushrooms
olive oil, herbs and aged parmesan $20

Grilled Veal Loin and Foie Gras
celery root puree, sweetbreads, hazelnuts and Madeira sauce $29

Grilled asparagus with roasted red bell peppers $5
Creamy potato au gratin $5
Sauteed wild mushrooms with port glaze $7

Make Your Mother's Day Brunch Reservation in Advance at 426-1133
Executive Chefs: Debbie Gold and Michael Smith
Cigarettes, Pipes and Cigars May Be Enjoyed in the Lounge

Vegetables, Salads, and Starters

Broccoli - White Cheddar Soup
broccoli and croutons $5

Seared Hudson Valley Foie Gras
belgian endive and crispy potato napoleon $15

24K Gold Saffron Risotto
grilled basil shrimp $12

Beluga Caviar
served tableside with buckwheat blini and traditional accompaniments $40

Pan Fried Gulf Oysters
Corn cream, arugula and roasted red peppers $12

Laura Chenel Cabecou Cheese
marinated mushrooms, field greens and black pepper cracker $10

Blue Crab and Frisse Salad
radish sprouts, cucumbers and ginger vinaigrette $11

Grilled Fennel and Radicchio Salad
prosciutto and lavander vinaigrette $8

Smoked Salmon Tortellini
goat cheese cream $9

Mary's Greens
Missouri young lettuces with sliced shallots, caper berries, pinenuts and focaccia crackers $6

Caesar Style Salad
spears of romaine, aged goat cheese, and a trio of tapanade croutons $7

Loose Leaf Spinach and Caramelized Pear Salad
honey glazed walnuts, gorgonzola and balsamic vinaigrette $8

For Off Premise Catering Needs, Contact American Catering 426-1172
American Restaurant Gift Certificates Available

FIGURE 7.15.   The theme of the American Restaurant in Kansas City, MO is American bounty. Notice how the items, headings and descriptive terminology carry out this theme. (*Courtesy of the American Restaurant, Kansas City, MO*)

NEW YORK STRIP STEAK
A generous 12 oz. portion of USDA Choice well-marbled beef carefully charcoal broiled to your specifications.

Thus we have a complete menu listing. It both explains and sells the item.

Writing descriptive terminology on menus is not easy, nor is it easily taught. It comes primarily from experience, both in the industry and the classroom. Students often ask why they need liberal arts in addition to the technical courses. Here is a perfect example. Skills learned in a communications or creative writing class go a long way in aiding people who must write menus as part of their job. Appendix A contains some key words used in menu writing. Take these, add some of your own, and go to work. Practice makes perfect, and you will soon find that this task is in reality very easy.

An often-asked question is that if every item on the menu is written in such a way that the customer cannot pass it up, won't this be confusing? The answer to that is an emphatic, NO! Customers immediately eliminate items they personally dislike. Even if you are a Pulitzer Prize–winning writer you will not convince people to order lamb if they do not like lamb. From a correctly written menu, customers can choose from several items they "cannot pass up." They will select one listing with the intention to return to try the others. Thus, a properly written menu has a residual effect: repeat business. Of course, the item selected must be properly prepared and must meet customers' expectations.

Most menus are written with descriptive terminology limited strictly to entrees. Appetizers, soups, side orders, and desserts are simply listed. This is a mistake, as the definition of descriptive terminology is to explain and sell. When people come into a food service establishment, they are probably going to order some entree regardless of how it is written or described. What needs to be sold are the add-ons, those items that increase the average check. By using descriptive terminology to sell appetizers, soups, side orders, and desserts, we accomplish just that. Thus, it is not enough to write just part of the menu; we must do a complete job. Descriptive terminology should be used throughout the entire menu, including all the the headings or category listings. Choose headings that tie into the theme of the restaurant.

NEGATIVE TERMINOLOGY

All too often menus contain wording that can best be described as negative terminology. Although written in a positive framework, some terms still have negative overtones. They have a negative psychological effect on customers and, therefore, destroy all the positive effects the menu writer has attempted to convey. Some examples of negative terminology are: *Roquefort dressing, 50¢ extra. Fifteen percent gratuity will be added to your check. No shoes, no shirt, no service.* Don't undo all of the positive selling by a negative comment.

CONCLUSION

It's mind boggling. By now the reader is likely to be saying, "I didn't know writing a menu could be this complicated." Let's review. Pick the categories that you want to serve. Draw up a list of items that you want to sell in each category. Check for variety, balance, and composition. Make changes where necessary. Once the listings are complete, explain and sell those items using descriptive terminology. It's just that simple.

QUESTIONS

1. Meeting all the criteria in the chapter, write out six menu listings for each of the 13 categories.

2. Define in your own words the following terms as they apply to menu planning.
   a) Variety
   b) Texture
   c) Size and shape
   d) Color
   e) Balance
   f) Composition

3. Rewrite the following menu listings using descriptive terminology. Consult a recipe book if you are unfamiliar with the items.
   Fruit Compote
   Shrimp Cocktail
   Sauerbraten
   Roast Loin of Pork
   Finnan Haddie
   Lobster Newburg
   Peas
   Duchess Potatoes
   Chef's Salad
   Strawberry Mousse

4. Write a section of a menu focusing on variety, balance, and composition.

5. List resources you will use to develop descriptive copy. Where will you look?

CHAPTER EIGHT

Truth in Menu

OBJECTIVES   By the completion of this chapter, the reader should be able to:

- Explain the importance of accurately describing menu listings.
- Explain the eleven sections of the accuracy in menu position paper adopted by the National Restaurant Association.

IMPORTANT TERMS

Representation of:
Quantity
Price
Product identification
Merchandising terms
Preparation
Visual presentation

Quality
Brand names
Point of origin
Preservation
Verbal presentation
Nutritional claims
"Truth in menu"

INTRODUCTION

In the preceding chapter, descriptive terminology was presented as an important element in creating menus. Equally important is the *truth in menu* concept. Also known as *accuracy in menu offerings* and *truth in dining*, it concerns itself with accurate menu listings. An overzealous menu writer, using flowery descriptive terminology, could (and many do) unwittingly mislead the customer.

Because of misleading menu listings on the part of unscrupulous or naive operators, some states have enacted legislation to thwart such maneuvers. California, for example, created legislation in 1974 to prohibit inaccurate menu listings. The law is enforced on a county-to-county basis. Thousands of cases, involving chains as well as independent operators, have been prosecuted and the owners fined as a result of this bill. The city of Chicago also enacted similar legislation with like results.

In a speech before the International Society of Restaurant Association Executives, Dr. Bailus Walker outlined a survey taken in Washington, DC. Results of a review of 350 menus in various restaurants in that city clearly pointed out that many contained violations. Over 85 percent of the restaurants that listed beef as "prime" could not substantiate that claim. One hundred percent listed shrimp as fresh when it was, in fact, frozen. Fifty percent of the restaurants listed delicatessen products as kosher when they were not.[1] The list goes on and on. Because of enacted legislation in some states and impending legislation in many others, as well as in Congress, the National Restaurant Association decided to face up to the problem. An Accuracy in Menus position paper was prepared and adopted in February 1977. Over the years since its inception, it has become the guideline that most restaurants and food service operations follow. Accuracy in Menus contains 11 sections. There are:

Representation of Quantity
Representation of Quality
Representation of Price
Representation of Brand Names
Representation of Product Identification
Representation of Points of Origin
Representation of Merchandising Terms
Representation of Means of Preservation
Representation of Food Preparation
Representation of Verbal and Visual Presentation
Representation of Dietary or Nutritional Claims

[1]Walker, Bailus Jr., Ph.D., M.P.H., *A Survey of the Accuracy of Menus in Public Eating Establishments in the District of Columbia.*

The following is a reprint of the Accuracy in Menus paper.

ACCURACY IN MENUS

Introduction

Every food service operator is acutely aware that success is based upon providing customer satisfaction. A keystone in this effort is the accurate representation of the products served. This truthful representation involves not only the printed menu, but also photographs, graphic illustrations, and other printed materials, as well as verbal depiction by employees.

The founders of the National Restaurant Association recognized this in 1923 when adopting its Standards of Business Practices. These standards have been repeatedly endorsed and employed by NRA members in the conduct of their business. In February 1977, the NRA Board of Directors reaffirmed the position by adopting the statement "Accuracy in Menus" (reproduced on pages 178–179).

This publication has been developed to assist the food service operators in properly representing the foods offered for sale in their restaurant. The specific types of errors are limitless and this guide describes some of the most likely kinds of mistakes.

The ultimate responsibility for accuracy in representing your menu offerings rests with you. Creativity and appealing merchandising is in no way restricted, but description and phrases must accurately reflect the food served. Be certain you can substantiate your written and spoken words with product, invoice, or label.

Representation of Quantity

Proper operational procedures should preclude any concerns with misinformation on quantities. Steaks are often merchandised by weight, and the generally accepted practice of declared quantity is that prior to cooking.

Obviously, double martinis are twice the size of the normal drink, and if jumbo eggs are listed they are exactly that—as "jumbo" is a recognized egg size. Petite and super-colossal are among the official size descriptions for olives. However, the use of terms such as *extra large salad* or *extra tall drink* may invite problems if not qualified. There is no question about the meaning of a "three-egg omelette" or "all you can eat." Also, remember the implied meaning of words— a bowl of soup contains more than a cup of soup.

Representation of Quality

Federal and state standards of quality grades exist for many restaurant products including meats, poultry, eggs, dairy products, fruits, and vegetables. Terminology used to describe grades includes Prime, Grade A, Good, No. 1, Choice, Fancy, Grade AA, and Extra Standard.

Care must be exercised in preparing menu descriptions when these words are used. In certain uses, they imply certain quality. An item appearing as "choice sirloin of beef" connotes the use of USDA Choice Grade Sirloin of Beef. One recognized exception is the term *prime rib*. *Prime rib* is a long established, well-understood, and accepted description for a cut of beef (the "primal" ribs, the 6th to 12th ribs) and does not represent the grade quality, unless USDA is used in conjunction.

Because of our industry's volume use of ground beef, it is well to remember the USDA definition: ground beef is just what the name implies. No extra fat, water, extenders, or binders are permitted. The fat limit is 30 percent. Seasonings may be added as long as they are identified. These requirements identify product ground and packaged only in federal- or state-inspected plants.

Representation of Price

If your pricing structure includes a cover charge, service charge, or gratuity, these must be appropriately brought to the customer's attention. If extra charges are made for requests such as "all white meat" or "no-ice drinks," these should be stated at the time of ordering.

Any restrictions when using a coupon or premium promotion must be clearly defined.

If a price promotion involves a multiunit company, clearly indicate which units are participating.

Representation of Brand Names

Any product brand that is advertised must be the one served. A registered or copyrighted trademark or brand name must not be used generically to refer to a product. Several examples of brand names of restaurant products are:

> Armour Star Bacon, Sanka, Log Cabin Syrup, Coca-Cola, Seven-Up, Swifts Premium Ham, Pepsi-Cola, Starkist Tuna, Ry-Crisp, Jell-O, Heinz Catsup, Maxwell House Coffee, Chase and Sanborn Coffee, Kraft Cheese, Tabasco Sauce, Ritz Crackers, Seven and Seven, Miracle Whip.

Your own "house" brand of a product may be so labeled even when prepared by an outside source, if its manufacturing was to your specifications. Containers of branded condiments and sauces placed on a table must be the product appearing on the container label.

Representation of Product Identification

Because many food products are similar, substitutions are often made. These substitutions may be due to nondelivery, availability, merchandising considerations, or price. When such substitutions are made, be certain these changes are reflected on your menu. Common substitutions are:

Maple syrup and maple flavored syrup
Boiled ham and baked ham
Chopped and shaped veal patty and veal cutlet
Ice milk and ice cream
Powdered eggs and fresh eggs
Picnic-style pork shoulder and ham
Milk and skim milk
Pure jams and pectin jams
Whipped topping and whipped cream
Turkey and chicken
Hereford beef and Black Angus beef
Peanut oil and corn oil
Beef liver and calves liver
Cream and half & half
Nondairy creamers or whiteners and cream
Ground beef and ground sirloin of beef
Capon and chicken
Standard ice cream and French-style ice cream
Cod and haddock
Noodles and egg noodles
Light meat tuna and white meat tuna
Pollock and haddock
Flounder and sole
Cheese food and processed cheese
Cream sauce and nondairy cream sauce
Bonito and tuna fish
Roquefort cheese and bleu cheese
Tenderloin tips and diced beef
Mayonnaise and salad dressing
Margarine and butter

Representation of Points of Origin

A potential area of error is in describing the point of origin of a menu offering. Claims may be substantiated by the product, by packaging labels, invoices, or other documentation provided by your supplier. Mistakes are possible as sources of supply change and availability of product shifts. The following are common assertions of points of origin:

Lake Superior Whitefish	Bay Scallops
Idaho Potatoes	Gulf Shrimp
Maine Lobster	Florida Orange Juice
Imported Swiss Cheese	Smithfield Ham
Danish Bleu Cheese	Wisconsin Cheese
Louisiana Frog Legs	Alaskan King Crab
Colorado Brook Trout	Colorado Beef
Florida Stone Crabs	Long Island Duckling
Chesapeake Bay Oysters	

There is widespread use of geographic names used in a generic sense to describe a method of preparation or service. Such terminology is readily understood and accepted by the customer and its use should be restricted.

Examples are:

Russian dressing	French toast
New England clam chowder	Country fried steak
Irish stew	Denver sandwich
Country ham	French dip
French fries	Swiss steak
Danish pastries	German potato salad
Russian service	French service
English muffins	Manhattan clam chowder
Swiss cheese	

Representation of Merchandising Terms

A difficult area to define clearly as right or wrong is the use of merchandising terms. "We serve the best gumbo in town" is understood by the dining-out public for what it is—boasting for advertising's sake. However, to use the statement "We use only the finest beef" implies that USDA Prime Beef is used, as a standard exists for this product.

Advertising exaggerations are tolerated if they do not mislead. When ordering a "mile-high pie," a customer would expect a pie heaped tall with meringue or similar fluffy topping, but to advertise a "foot-long hot dog" and to serve something less would be an error. Mistakes are possible in properly identifying steak cuts. Use industry standards such as provided in the National Association of Meat Purveyor's *Meat Buyer's Guide.*

"Homestyle," "homemade style," or "our own" are suggested terminology rather than "homemade" for describing menu offerings prepared according to a home recipe. Most food service sanitation ordinances prohibit the preparation of foods in home facilities.

If using any of the following terms, be certain you can qualify them.

Fresh daily	Corn-fed porkers
Fresh roasted	Slept in Chesapeake Bay
Flown in daily	Finest quality
Kosher meat	Center cut ham
Black Angus beef	Own special sauce
Aged steaks	Low calorie
Milk-fed chicken	

Representation of Means of Preservation

The accepted means of preserving food are numerous, including canning, chilling, bottling, freezing, and dehydrating. If you choose to describe your menu selections with these terms, they must be accurate. Frozen orange juice is not fresh, canned peas are not frozen, and bottled applesauce is not canned.

Representation of Food Preparation

The means of food preparation is often the determining factor in the customer's selection of a menu entree. Absolute accuracy is a must. Readily understood terms include:

Charcoal broiled	Deep fried
Sauteed	Barbecued
Baked	Smoked
Broiled	Prepared from scratch
Roasted	Poached
Fried in butter	

Representation of Verbal and Visual Presentation

When your menu, wall placards, or other advertising contain a pictorial representation of a meal or platter, it should portray the actual contents with accuracy. Examples of visual misrepresentations include:

- The use of mushroom pieces in a sauce when the picture depicts mushroom caps.
- The use of sliced strawberries on a shortcake when the picture depicts whole strawberries.
- The use of numerous thin-sliced meat pieces when the picture depicts a single thick slice.
- The use of five shrimp when the picture depicts six shrimp.
- The omission of vegetables or other entree extras when the picture depicts their inclusion.
- The use of a plain bun when the picture depicts a sesame-topped bun.

Examples of verbal misrepresentation include:

- If a waiter asks, "Sour cream or butter with your potatoes?" when, in fact, an imitation sour cream or margarine is served.
- A waitress responds, "The pies are baked in our kitchen," when, in fact, they are purchased prebaked institutional pies.

Representation of Dietary or Nutritional Claims

Potential public health concerns are real if misrepresentation is made of the dietary or nutritional content of food. For example, "salt-free" or "sugar-free" foods must be exactly that to assure the protection of customers who may be under particular dietary restraints. "Low calorie" or other nutritional claims, if made, must be supportable by specific data.

To list menu items accurately should be a priority with all professional food service managers, whether or not it is law in your jurisdiction. Not to do so can result in customers' dissatisfaction and, consequently, lost sales. The original intent of misrepresenting a menu listing to obtain increased sales backfires when the patron discovers that what was ordered was not what was received.[2]

Some critics of Accuracy in Menus maintain that it takes away from the ability to sell via the use of descriptive terminology. This could not be further from the truth. Thousands of words are available to describe, romance, and sell food. Use them. Whet the customers' appetites with what they are going to get, not what they think they are going to get.

A POSITION STATEMENT OF THE NATIONAL RESTAURANT ASSOCIATION

The food service industry has long recognized the importance of accuracy in describing its products, on menus and through visual or

---

[2]*Accuracy in Menus*, National Restaurant Association, Washington, DC, February 1977.

oral representation, both on ethical grounds and from the stand-point of customer satisfaction. The National Restaurant Association incorporated standards of accuracy in all representations to the public in its Standards of Business Practice, originally adopted by the Association in 1923. We reaffirm and strongly support the principles therein expressed.

"Truth in dining" or "truth in menu" laws and ordinances have been proposed in some government jurisdictions and, in few cases, adopted, in the belief that representations on restaurant menus present a unique problem in consumer protection. The National Restaurant Association believes that such legislation is unnecessary as federal, state, and many local governments have laws and regulations prohibiting false advertising and misrepresentations of products, and providing protection from fraud. In an industry such as ours, where economic survival depends upon customer satisfaction, misrepresentation is most effectively regulated by the severe sanction of customer dissatisfaction and loss of patronage.

To be equitable, the complexity of such legislation would be staggering. It is conceivable that standardized recipes for each menu listing would be required if regulatory refinement followed its logical course. The problems of enforcement and proof, if due process is observed, would be monumental, if not impossible.

The "truth in dining" movement is not confined to the proposition that restaurant menus be absolutely accurate in their representations. Legislation and ordinances have been proposed that would require the identification of a specific means of preservation, method of preparation, or statement of food origin. Such requirements could unjustly imply that certain foods, processes, or places of origin are unwholesome or inferior.

Government action must be confined to problems where its intervention can be effective and at a cost commensurate with the benefits to be gained. Adopted February 1977.[3]

CONCLUSION

Descriptive terminology is important for explaining and selling menu listings; however, the menu writer should not be caught up in overstating the case. Accurate menu descriptions result in a satisfied customer receiving the product expected. Accuracy also improves the confidence of the public toward the restaurant industry. Tell the truth. It's just that simple.

---

[3]*Position Statement of the National Restaurant Association.* National Restaurant Association, Washington, DC, February 1977.

QUESTIONS

1. Discuss why truth in menu is important to an individual restaurant and the industry as a whole.

2. In your own words, describe and analyze each of the 11 truth in menu concepts.

3. In your own operation (or one in which you work), list all truth in menu violations or potential violations.

4. Analyze the menus of several competitors. See if you can spot any potential truth in menu violations.

5. List the legal issues that could come up if a restaurant violates the "truth in menu" concepts.

6. Write an in-house policy to avoid creating aspects of a menu that mislead the guest.

CHAPTER NINE

Menu Layout and Printing

OBJECTIVES By the completion of this chapter, the reader should be able to:

- Describe the various styles of menu covers and explain their importance to the overall ambiance of the restaurant.
- Explain the proper layout techniques for the headings, subheadings, listings, and descriptive terminology for food and alcoholic beverage listings.
- Describe the basic principles of printing techniques and terminology needed to communicate with the printing staff.
- Explain the issues related to the desktop publishing of a menu.

IMPORTANT TERMS

Menu cover
Menu layout
Institutional copy
Type styles
Leading
Lowercase
Desktop publishing

Lamination
Prime space
Clip-ons
Points
Uppercase
Proof

INTRODUCTION

At this stage of menu development, the hard work is over and, for most people, the fun is about to begin. With the layout and printing of the menu, imagination and artistic talents can go wild. Of course, certain criteria must be followed, but overall the possibilities are endless, limited only by one's daring or lack thereof.

COVER

The cover of the menu is vital to the aesthetic strategy of the restaurant in that it should immediately convey the establishment's overall theme to the customer. That old adage you can't tell a book by its cover does not apply here. Conversely, what the customer wants to know about a particular restaurant should be conveyed by the cover. Clues as to theme, price range, decor, and cooking style should all be at least hinted at by the cover. It is the symbol of identity and ties together the various nuances of the restaurant.

STYLE OF COVERS

A multitude of menu cover styles is available from which to choose. Some of the more popular types are padded, custom designed, insert, laminated, and paper. The most expensive are the padded and custom-designed covers.

Padded Covers

Padded menu covers are made with either a light board or very heavy cardboard. This is then covered with a plastic material resembling leather, and filled with material to give it a padded effect. These covers are quite heavy. Some variations, such as suede, velvet, and real leather, are available in addition to imitation leather. Because of the special materials used, the printing on these covers is limited to a logo and/or the name of the establishment. The inside of these menus consists of heavy, linen-type paper on which the various listings are printed and held in place by a ribbon, cord, or stick tape going down the center fold of the cover. These inserts are changed as often as the listings and selling prices dictate. Although padded covers are very expensive, they are durable and will last a long time when properly cared for. Changes to the menu are made on the inserts only and one cover can go through many insert changes. Normally padded covers are limited to fine dining establishments and exclusive clubs.

Custom Designed Covers

These covers have a special shape or design rather than the typical rectangle. Their patterns are limited only by the designer's imagination. The variations in size, shape, and material are so numerous that, unfortunately, they can't all be listed.

Although these types of menu covers are great conversation pieces for customers and convey the theme appropriately, it should be remembered that they are more expensive than the norm. Oftentimes materials such as wood or metal rather than paper or cardboard are used, adding even more expense to the project. Even if paper or cardboard is used, the special cutting process necessary to obtain an unusual shape or size involves a more costly process than does a standard square or rectangle. However, the uniqueness of such a design might well outweigh the cost when measured against the increase in sales which results from such a bold and imaginative menu.

Insert-Type Covers

Insert-type covers are widely used and are less expensive than the previous two types. They follow the same principle as padded covers in that the cover is used repeatedly while the insert is changed as often as the menu items and prices dictate. The primary difference between the padded cover and the insert-type cover is in the material used—a heavy cardboard, which can be selected from several different styles including imitation velvet, leatherette, or a glossy finished card stock. These covers can either be produced by your local printer or purchased from one of several national companies that specialize in menu cover design. The user can choose among many stock designs or have a customized design drawn by one of the company's artists. Obviously, a stock design would be less expensive, but remember that the cover is a reflection of the restaurant's theme and decor. If a suitable stock design is compatible with the theme and decor, fine. If not, it would be well worth the extra money to have it custom designed. Remember that the cover will be used many times and the dollars spent will become infinitesimal with use, especially in light of a menu that properly reflects the theme for your restaurant.

Laminated Covers

Laminated covers are very popular in informal settings, such as coffee shops. Lamination is a process in which the menu, usually a durable cardboard, is covered with a clear plastic coating in order to protect it. Thus, when a menu becomes soiled or greasy, it can simply be wiped off and used over again. With this process the entire menu, cover and inside, is printed on the cardboard. It can be folded in the middle, creating a four-page menu, or in thirds, creating in effect a six-page menu.

SPECIALTIES

BURGERS & MORE

SOUP & SALAD

STARTERS

Tater Skins   3.95
Crisp fried tater skins under Jack and Cheddar cheeses, bacon bits and scallions.

Chicken Quesadillas   4.95
Two grilled tortillas filled with spicy chicken, melted Jack and Colby cheese. Served with guacamole, sour cream and salsa.

Onion Rings   2.50
A hefty portion of steak cut, batter fried rings.

'shrooms   2.25
Jumbo mushroom caps filled with herbs, garlic and cheese. Breaded and fried. Served with creamy horseradish dip.

Buffalo Chicken Wings   2.95
Hot and spicy wings cooked just right then served up with a Bleu cheese dip.

Santa Fe Dip   2.95
Crispy corn tortillas topped with spiced ground beef, refried beans, diced tomatoes and onions, smothered with a Cheddar cheese sauce.

Chicken Fingers   5.25
White meat chicken strips breaded and fried to a golden brown. Served with a tangy BBQ sauce.

Mozzarella Stix   2.95
Six luscious Mozzarella stixs breaded and fried. Served with marinara sauce.

Flautas   4.95
Shredded beef and spicy chicken rolled in a corn tortilla then fried to perfection. Served with salsa and sour cream.

Crestwood Tid Bits   3.95
Tater skins, nachos and flautas. A great combination.

FIGURE 9.1.   A unique menu presentation with each category folding down and the drink and dessert categories on the back. (*Courtesy of the Crestwood Country Club, Pittsburg, Kansas*)

Chimichanga 9.95

Your choice of beef, chicken or seafood blended with cheese, scallions and mild sauce in a golden fried flour tortilla. Topped with lettuce, diced tomato and guacamole.

Sizzling Fajitas 8.95

Char-grilled beef or chicken with bell peppers, red onion, guacamole, sour cream, Cheddar cheese and mild salsa. Served on a sizzling platter. Beef, chicken or combination.

Southwestern Torte 7.95

Spicy ground beef, cheese and a special Rio Grande sauce layered between corn tortillas, baked then topped with lettuce and diced tomato. Served with refried beans and salsa.

Shrimp and Fettuccine Primavera 10.25

White Gulf Shrimp sauteed with fettuccine noodles, vegetables and garlic in a white wine sauce topped with Parmesan cheese.

Straw and Hay 8.50

Green and white pasta tossed with green peas, prosciutto ham in a three cheese sauce.

Flying Angel 8.95

Grilled marinated chicken breast combined with diced tomato, sweet peppers, mushrooms, onion and herbs on a bed of angel hair pasta.

TAKEN TO FLIGHT

Chicken Breast Dijon 8.50

Charbroiled boneless chicken breast cooked to perfection and delightfully topped with a Dijon mustard and white wine sauce.

Cashew Chicken 8.50

Tender strips of boneless chicken breast breaded, deep fried and topped with our special sauce, cashews and chives nested on a bed of rice pilaf.

Chicken Cordon Bleu 8.95

Boneless chicken breast breaded with fresh bread crumbs then filled with ham and Swiss cheese, baked in our own Cheddar cheese sauce.

FROM LAND AND SEA

Kansas City Strip 8 oz. 10.95 / 12 oz. 12.95

The finest U.S.D.A. prime beef. Carefully charbroiled to your specification.

Chopped Sirloin 7.95

7 oz. of lean ground beef, charbroiled and garnished with an onion ring.

Chicken Fried Steak 7.25

Lightly hand breaded, country fried and topped with cream gravy.

Jumbo Gulf Shrimp 9.95

Deep fried to perfection or broiled with herbs. Served with cocktail sauce or tartar sauce.

Pittsburg Filet 6 oz. 10.95 / 8 oz. 12.95

The Pride of Pittsburg, juicy choice tenderloin cut to order and charbroiled to your satisfaction.

Beef Bourguignon 10.25

7 oz. of tenderloin tips blended with onion, mushrooms and bordelaise sauce then finished with burgundy wine.

Baby Beef Liver Lyonnaise 6.95

Dusted in flour then sauteed with julienne strips of onion and green pepper.

Filet of Sole 8.95

7 oz. of white boneless sole broiled with lemon pepper and lemon juice to flaky perfection.

All entrees are served with a house salad or soup, the appropriate potato, vegetable du jour, and our homemade rolls.
May we suggest a loaf of cinnamon bread to enhance your dining pleasure.

FIGURE 9.1. *(Continued)*

BURGERS & MORE

Crestwood Burger   3.95
5 oz. of lean ground beef cooked the way you like.
Served on a toasted bun with fries.
Topped with bacon or cheese add 25¢ each.

Teriyaki Burger   3.95
Our 5 oz. patty broiled with teriyaki sauce, served on a
toasted bun, accompanied by stir fry vegetables.

Mushroom Burger   4.25
Sauteed mushrooms, onions and melted Swiss cheese
top our charbroiled burger on a toasted bun. Served with
fries.

California Burger   4.95
A butter toasted bun topped with 5 oz. of lean ground
beef. Charbroiled to your liking. Dressed with cool
avocado slices and alfalfa sprouts. Served with fries.

Club Sandwich   4.95
Triple decker of bacon, turkey, lettuce, tomato on toasted
whole wheat. Served with a juicy dill spear and fries.

Hot Stacked Beef & Cheese   5.95
Sliced roast beef with sauteed onions, mushrooms and
melted Swiss cheese on a Hoagie bun, served with Au
Jus and fries.

Grilled Ham & Cheese   4.25
Lean shaved ham with your choice of cheese on whole
wheat bread with fries.

Reuben Sandwich   4.95
Lean corned beef, sauerkraut and Swiss cheese on
buttered grilled rye bread. Served with fries.

Chicken Breast Sandwich   6.95
A tender grilled chicken breast topped with bacon and
Monterey Jack cheese on a Kasier roll. Served with fries.

Crestwood Omelet   4.25
A fluffy three egg omelet with your choice of three
ingredients, country fries and toasted whole wheat.

Build a Pizza   3.50
Start with a 6 inch crust topped with sauce and a blend
of cheese and you pick everything else you want 25¢
per item.

American Cheese	Mushrooms	Bell Pepper	Pepperoni
Swiss Cheese	Onions	Sausage	Black Olives
Cheddar Cheese	Tomatoes	Ham	Ground Beef

Cakes for all occasions are made upon request. Contact us for all of your catering needs. We provide the best for you for all private parties, weddings and receptions.

FIGURE 9.1. *(Continued)*

SOUP & SALAD

French Onion	Cup	1.25
Sauteed onions simmered in rich beef stock and sherry, topped with a crouton and melted cheeses. | Bowl | 1.95 |

Soup of the Day	Cup	1.95
Made in our kitchen daily from the freshest ingredients. | Bowl | 2.50 |

Cinnamon Bread   Mini .50
Bill's homemade cinnamon bread baked   Large 1.50
daily into mini loaves or large for the
whole family.

Cobb Salad   4.95
Cold crisp iceberg lettuce tossed tableside with tomato, egg, cheese, black olives, ripe avocado and your choice of dressing.

Monterey Seafood Salad   5.25
Flaked salmon, bay shrimp, artichoke hearts, sliced mushrooms, black olives and wedges of tomato on a bed of mixed greens.

Crestwood Chef Salad   4.25
Thin sliced ham, breast of turkey, black olives, hard boiled egg, Swiss and American cheeses on a bed of crisp mixed greens.

Seafood Salad Supreme   5.25
Freshly tossed lettuce accompanied by baby bay shrimp and crabmeat with tomato wedges, sliced egg and a ring of green pepper.

Taco Salad   4.25
Iceberg lettuce topped with seasoned ground beef, diced tomato, cheese, guacamole and sour cream in an edible shell. Served with salsa.

Fresh Fruit Salad   4.25
A bountiful array of seasonal fruits served with our sensational poppy seed dressing.

Pasta Salad   4.25
Bow tie pasta tossed with peppers, broccoli, cauliflower, carrot strips, sundried tomato in a special balsamic vinegar dressing.

FIGURE 9.1.   *(Continued)*

SPECIALTY DRINKS

Lime Daiquiri
Strawberry Daiquiri
Pina Colada
Strawberry Colada
Crestwood Surfer
Butter Nip
Snowshoe
Fuzzy Navel
Attitude Adjuster

Rich, thick ice cream drinks served tall with special blends of liqueurs.

Kansas Tumbleweed
California Pink Squirrel
Italy's Golden Cadillac
Brandy Alexander
Grasshopper

BOTTLED BEERS

DOMESTIC

				IMPORTED
Bud	Busch Light	Coors Dry	Michelob Light	Corona
Bud Light	Coors	O'Douls	Michelob Dry	Heineken
Bud Dry	Coors Light	Michelob	Miller Light	Moosehead
Busch				

PREMIUM WINES

*We carry a fine selection of wines to enhance your dining pleasure.
Ask your server for our complete wine list.*

Wine By The Glass . . . . . California Taylor . . . . Chablis   Burgundy
                                                White Zinfandel   Chardonnay

                               Riunite . . . . Lambrusco   Rosato
                                                              Bianco

BEVERAGES

Pepsi, Diet Pepsi, Teem 75
Iced Tea 60
Hot Tea 60
Coffee, regular and decaf 60
Milk 75
Hot Chocolate 60
Perrier 1.25

AFTER DINNER DRINKS

Served in warm snifters for the best aroma and flavor.

Grand Marnier 3.50
  A fine cognac with a hint of orange
B & B 3.50
  A delicate balance of Benedictine liqueur and fine French brandy.
Drambuie 3.50

SWEETS

Cheesecake 2.50
  Classic New York style. Rich and creamy, with fruit topping.

Turtle Pie 2.95
  Rich Praline Pecan ice cream in a chocolate cookie crust, layered with tawny carmel, garnished with a rippling fudge border and pecan halves.

Ice Cream 95

? ? At the whim of the chef, we may have a special dessert today. Ask your server.

Gourmet Cake 3.25
  A changing variety of deluxe gourmet cakes. All are rich and luscious. Ask about today's selection.

Sherbert 95
  Cool and delightful, orange, lime or pineapple.

Crestwood Sundae 3.25
  Combine two scoops of vanilla ice cream, cover with hot fudge sauce and warm caramel and top it off with whipped cream, nuts, maraschino cherry and a French cookie.

CRESTWOOD COUNTRY CLUB, Pittsburg, Kansas 66762
WILLIAM H. ASKEW, Executive Chef

FIGURE 9.1.   *(Continued)*

Although the laminated menu is durable, it is a fairly expensive process. Therefore, this style should be used only in restaurants where the listings are permanent and price changes are not anticipated with any regularity. If this is the case, because of its extended use, the cost becomes quite reasonable over the long run.

Paper Covers

The paper cover and menu have become commonplace in many restaurants. The primary reason for this is the low cost. Once the cost of setting the type is paid for, making minor changes and printing additional copies are relatively inexpensive. At a time when food costs are fluctuating rapidly, selling prices on the menu, as well as menu listings, can be changed with a relatively reasonable printing charge. If the restaurant prints its own menus using a computer, word processing program, and inkjet or laser printer, the cost becomes practically zero.

A new operation, in particular, would be wise to print its first menu on paper until best-selling listings are determined. Another advantage to paper menus is that they are economical enough to be given away to customers. In fact, they are a very reasonable means of advertisement and when they become soiled or greasy, they can simply be discarded. Thus, established restaurants, as well as new ones, find this particular style to their liking.

Selection of a Cover

The type of menu cover chosen will depend on several factors: the type of restaurant involved, the style of service, the price range of that restaurant, and the cost of the cover. A fine dining restaurant or private club could opt for an elegant menu with a padded cover, while a fast food operation would prefer a giveaway style printed on paper. Certainly, cost enters the picture based on the budgetary restrictions set aside for menu printing. Whichever avenue is pursued, choose or design a cover that has style, that ties together the theme of the restaurant, and reflects its decor.

THE LAYOUT

Once the cover has been chosen, attention should be given to the layout of the inside of the menu. There is a right way and a wrong way to accomplish this.

The first consideration is the sequence of the headings. The headings are merely the names of the various categories covered in Chapter 7. They are:

- appetizers
- soups

- salads
- cold entrees
- hot entrees
- vegetables
- sandwiches
- side dishes
- starches
- desserts
- cheeses
- fruits
- beverages

Selecting Category Names

After the decision is made as to which categories will be used, the names of these categories or headings are listed on the menu. The majority of restaurants simply use the name of the category as its heading, but with a little imagination and foresight, these can be changed to offer variety or to tie in with the theme of the restaurant. For example, instead of using the word *Appetizers* as a heading, why not use *Starters* or *Before the Feast*. One restaurant with a racing theme headed *appetizers* as "Gentlemen—Start Your Engines."

With some imagination, a standard generic menu can become an individualized piece of work, one that excites the customer into looking at all the categories and, consequently, ordering additional items. The longer the customers read the menu, the more likely they are to order a meal complete with opening and closing selections.

Whether the proper name of a category or an imaginative one is used, the sequence of the headings must be in or close to the order given in the foregoing list. This creates a smooth flow to the menu and leads the reader on a logical course to choose a meal. Exceptions to this rule are possible, however, as one may opt to place sandwiches before entrees or soups before appetizers. Categories can also be combined, such as soups and appetizers. Even if certain headings are changed, the smooth flow rule must never be violated.

Subheadings and Listings

Occasionally it is necessary to list subheadings under main headings—most likely in the entree category. Under the entree headings, subheadings might include, but not be limited to, meat, poultry, fish, and seafood. Under the headings and subheadings come the actual menu listings. These should be presented in no particular order; however, like items should be grouped together. For example, under the heading *entrees*, subheading *beef*, the steaks would be listed together rather than mixed throughout the beef category. Do not list items in direct or inverse relation to selling price. In other words, avoid listing items with the most expensive first and going on down with the least expensive last. The reverse is also true. Products arranged by price will cause customers to think in terms of price rather than taste and, in turn, will lower the average check of the establishment.

Under each listing on the menu is the descriptive terminology for that listing. As previously discussed, descriptive terminology is used to explain and sell the product and the product must be described truthfully and accurately. Many menus do not recognize this fact, leaving the customer confused and undecided prior to ordering and angry if what is received is not what was anticipated.

If the headings and listings on the menu are written in a foreign language to tie in with the theme, it is mandatory that the descriptive terminology be written in English unless of course the foreign language predominates in that area. Some restaurants take on a snobbish attitude assuming that the customer who doesn't understand their particular cuisine doesn't belong there in the first place. Don't drive customers away with this attitude. Use accurate, descriptive terminology on your menu.

Be Creative with Alcoholic Beverage Listings

Alcoholic beverages baffle many menu writers. Some stick them in some unused space on the menu, while others, not knowing what to do, totally ignore the problem—blissful ignorance. Alcoholic beverages, if sold at an establishment, can impact business in three significant ways. First, and most important, they are among the highest gross profit items sold in the restaurant. Second, they relax the customer and break down inhibitions, which in turn makes the meal more enjoyable. Third, they can cover up delays in seating and service. A famous restaurateur once said that giving a customer a drink was like giving a baby a rattle. Of course, this theory can and has been overdone, with some operations holding guests in the bar with a half-full dining room with the result a disgruntled rather than satisfied customer.

With the profit to be made on alcoholic beverages, the obvious solution is to get them on the menu. In placing them, the same criteria used to arrange the food category headings would apply. That is, they should be listed in proper sequence with a smooth flow to guide the customer through the meal. Three menu categories should be considered for alcoholic beverages: before-dinner drinks, wine with the meal, and after-dinner drinks.

Before-Dinner Drinks. Before-dinner drinks would be listed on the menu prior to the appetizer section . In addition to listing popular items such as highballs, some creative house specialty drinks, also known as *blender* or *umbrella drinks*, should be listed. These bring a higher selling price and, consequently, a higher gross profit. Merchandise them in special glasses with unusual garnishes. Feature them on the menu with appealing pictures.

Wine. Wine, one of the fastest growing alcoholic beverage sales in America, is still misunderstood by many people. Because of this fact, descriptive terminology is imperative—primarily to explain. Tell about the flavor, whether it is light or heavy, sweet or dry, to assist the customers in making a selection they will enjoy. Since wines are consumed primarily with the meal, they should be listed immediately adjacent to the entrees. Inasmuch as education is a primary goal, perhaps a selected wine could be listed with each entree. Alternatively, a wine list could point out those wines that would add enjoyment to a particular entree. Some establishments, rather than list the wines with the entrees on the regular menu, opt to have a separate wine list, with guests making their own decisions.

The point is that the menu must encourage the customer to order wine by breaking down the resistance due to lack of knowledge. The menu should inform, educate, and lead customers to a proper selection.

After-Dinner Drinks. After-dinner drinks would obviously be listed adjacent to or after desserts. The same theory would apply here as applied to the before-dinner drinks. In addition to listing the obvious, try some blended ice cream creations that can become house specialties and properly merchandise them for added profit.

At the beginning of this section on alcoholic beverages, it was stated that they do three things. Consider one more—they are add-ons. By handling them correctly on your menu, they can increase the average check. Be careful not to overdo it, however. While the discussion has been focused on ways to increase sales by selling alcoholic beverages, it must be done in a responsible manner. Enticing customers to become intoxicated is not the point. Enticing them to have a good time and enjoy themselves is. Proper menu merchandising will accomplish the latter, while responsible bar service will ensure that the former does not happen.

PUTTING IT ALL TOGETHER

The menu is now starting to take shape. The categories have been decided, the headings and subheadings chosen, the listings selected, and the descriptive terminology written. Assuming the order is correct, the menu flows along, leading the customers to the choices they will select.

Stephenson's
Home of the famous

Old Apple Farm Daiquiri

For your drinking pleasure we have created this rum drink —
served in a frosted, king size glass —
plenty of authority in this drink.
Your choice of Plain, Apple, Strawberry, Peach or Banana

Farm Size Martini's and Manhattan's

Old Apple Farm Fresh Fruit Wine Punch

This is the way they used to make punch — delicious!
Glass or Carafe

Stephenson's Missouri Apple Wine
Made from apples grown right here on our farm.
Glass or Bottle

Marquerita
The Apple Farm version of the famous
Tequila drink South of the border.

Open every day — 11:30 a.m.
Come as late as 10:00 p.m. Monday thru Thursday
11:00 p.m. Friday and Saturday
9:00 p.m. Sunday
for complete service

FIGURE 9.2. Excellent merchandising of high gross profit "add-on" drinks. Before-dinner drinks are on the cover with after-dinner drinks on the back. The wine list is an insert in the middle of the entree section. (*Menu courtesy of Stephenson's Old Apple Farm Restaurant, Kansas City, Missouri*)

After Dinner

Coffee Calypso

A secret ingredient and topped with whipped cream.

Florentina

This is Galliano liqueur blended with french vanilla ice cream into a delicate, delicious dessert drink.

Hot Cider in Tuaca Liquor	**Sambucca**
Cherry Heering	**Grasshopper**
Galliano	**Black Russian**
Kuhlua	**Brandy Alexander**
Brandy	**Irish Coffee**
Creme de Menthe	**Rusty Nail**
Courvoisier V.S.O.P.	**Stinger**
Bailey's Irish Cream	**Drambuie**

To Our Guests:

As expenses continue to rise we have to adjust menu prices from time to time. We still, however, want to give you the best value possible without sacrificing quality or quantity.

Our object, as always, is to be one of Americas finest restaurant and one our community is justly proud. We pledge as in the past to cook everything from scratch. We smoke our own meats and poultry over hickory and apple wood. We do our own baking, making hot light yeast rolls, fresh apple pie and dumplings. We make our own sauces, salad dressings, relishes, apple butter and squeeze our own cider.

We purchase the finest ingredients, meat, produce and supplies available. We will continue to serve you with friendly, polite, gracious service in a pleasant, casual and comfortable surroundings.

We always hope you will have a memorable visit and think of Stephenson's as a place you would want to take friends. If there is anything we can do for you please let us know.

Rick Stephenson, Manager

FIGURE 9.2.   *(Continued)*

May We Suggest a Bottle of Wine?

Champagnes and Sparkling Wines

Bin #		Bottle
32	**Korbel Brut**	21.00
	A most popular sparkling wine	
33	**Domaine Chandon Blanc de Noir**	23.00
	Deliciously fruity sparkling wine	
34	**Moet Dom Perignon (Vintage) (French)**	105.00
	True French champagne at its umcompromising best	
35	**Villa Banfi Asti Spumante (Italy)**	16.00
	Sparkling light and delicate	
36	**Freixenet**	13.00
	A white sparkling wine from Spain	

Red Table Wines

Bin #		Bottle
26	**Baron Phillipe De Rothschild Mouton Cadet**	15.00
	Light and fruity	
27	**Louis Jadot Beaujolais Villages**	15.00
	A versatile wine that enhances steaks and chops	
28	**Inglenook Cabernet Sauvignon**	16.00
	Medium bodied with excellent balance	
29	**Beaulieu Vineyard Cabernet Sauvignon**	15.00
	This rich elegant wine is praised for its depth of flavor and intense bouquet	
30	**Robert Mondavi Cabernet Sauvignon**	28.00
	Classically styled California Cabernet Sauvignon showing a supple texture and elegant flavor	
31	**Fetzer Zinfandel**	12.00
	Medium bodied red wine with a spicy characteristic and a fruity bouquet	

Rose Table Wines

Bin #		Bottle
24	**Lancers Rose**	10.00
	Light, semi-dry and fruity	

Stephenson's Missouri Apple Wine

Made from apples grown right here on our farm

Glass	Bottle
2.95	8.95

White Table Wines

Bin #		Bottle
10	**Simi Chardonnay**	23.00
	Prized by wine lovers the world over, a stylishly dry and complex wine	
11	**Robert Mondavi Chardonnay**	25.00
	Exhibiting a unique depth of flavor	
12	**Chateau Ste Michelle Chardonnay**	19.00
	A dry complex wine	
13	**Inglenook Sauvignon Blanc**	15.00
	A soft, crisp taste	
14	**Robert Mondavi Fume Blanc**	17.00
	A rich fruity aroma, full bodied	
15	**Chateau Ste Michelle Gewurztraminer**	12.00
	A crisp, dry, medium bodied wine	
17	**Simi Chenin Blanc**	13.00
	Light bodied and semi dry	
18	**Baron Phillipe De Rothschild Mouton Cadet Blanc**	15.00
	Delicate, dry and crisp	
19	**Kendall-Jackson Sauvignon Blanc**	15.00
	Crisp, fresh and fragrant	
20	**Louis Jadot Pouilly Fuisse**	34.00
	A distinct, rich quality	
21	**Rudolf Muller Piesporter Goldtropfchen Qba**	15.00
	Light, gold in color	
22	**Blue Nun Liebfraumilch**	11.00
	Light, fruity and semi dry	
23	**Sutter Home White Zinfandel**	11.00
	Blush-colored with a fresh bouquet.	

A Glass or Carafe of Wine
Special Premium Wines by the Glass

Chateau Ste Michelle Chardonnay	4.25
Rudolf Muller Piesporter	4.25
Blue Nun Liebfraumilch	3.75
Sutter Home White Zinfandel	3.75
Louis Jadot Beaujolais	3.75
Inglenook Cabernet Sauvignon	4.25
Freixenet	3.75

House Wines - Robert Mondavi

	Glass	Carafe
California Sauvignon Blanc	3.25	9.95
California Gamay Rose	2.95	8.95
California Cabernet	3.95	12.95

FIGURE 9.2. *(Continued)*

Using Prime Space

When placing all of this on the menu itself, one more factor needs to be taken into consideration—prime space. When customers open the menu, the spot that their eyes hit first is known as the *prime space.* Studies have shown that the customer is more likely to order what is seen first. Thus, the prime space on the menu becomes an extremely important merchandising area. Many people are ignorant of this fact, because few menus use it to advantage. The prime space is determined by the type of menu. On a two-page menu, it is located in the middle of the right-hand page. On a three-page or a single menu, it is in the center of the upper third of the menu. Figure 9.3 illustrates this.

Since this is the predominant area, it stands to reason that the menu writer should place the item that they most want to sell in this spot. Quite naturally this item should be popular and bring the restaurant a high gross profit. If the listing is unpopular, it would defeat the purpose. Customers who do not like sauteed lamb kidneys will not buy them, no matter how well they are merchandised. Also, if the restaurant does not realize a good profit margin from a listing, then why display it in the predominant area? One more thing: Do not waste this space to list the house specialty. Use it for something else that you want to sell. If the restaurant is famous for prime rib, the customer already knows that. Don't use prime space to state the obvious.

Boxes or borders should be used to outline and accentuate those items that you most want to sell. They should always be used in prime space, but can be used elsewhere on the menu as well. A word of caution: don't overdo borders as they tend to lose their effectiveness. A maximum of three boxes per page should be used.

With the criteria stated for prime space, it should be fairly obvious that an entree would be listed. When discussing a high-gross-profit item, we are talking about dollar gross profit, not percent. To get the menu to flow properly, with the correct order of categories, and to end up with the entree section in the prime space is sometimes quite tricky. Often it takes work and imagination to make this happen. The result will pay dividends to the person who perseveres.

Using Leftover Space—Institutional Copy

With the menu properly laid out, the next point of business becomes what to do about the leftover space. This space can be used for institutional copy—stories about the restaurant, the area, or an explanation of the theme. This copy goes hand in hand with the cover of the menu. Institutional copy ties all the loose ends together to make the restaurant, its theme, location, and the meal a total experience for the customer. It can be written on the back of the menu, toward the front, or interspersed throughout. Good institutional copy separates an ordinary, mundane food list from an outstanding menu.

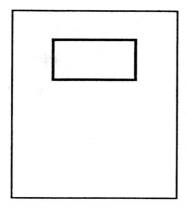

Prime Space on a One Page Menu

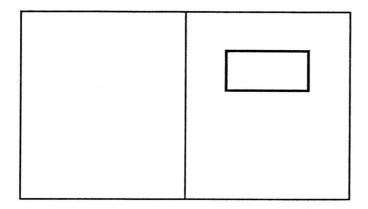

Prime Space on a Two Page Menu

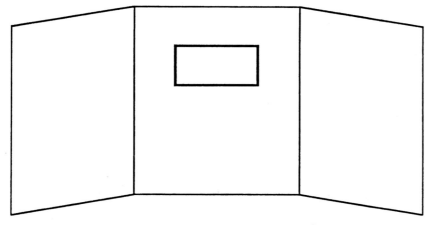

Prime Space on a Three Page Menu

FIGURE 9.3. Proper use of prime space.

EVENING FARE

Christiana Campbell's TAVERN

Giving Satisfaction to TRAVELERS and TOWNSPEOPLE with a Taste for SEAFOODS

APPETIZERS

Captain *Rasmussen's* Clam CHOWDER
1.95

Cherrystone CLAMS on the Half Shell
One-Half Dozen   One Dozen
4.95   8.25

Colonial PASTY
A Mixture of MEATS and SPICES
in a Pastry SHELL
2.50

SOUP of the Day
1.75

Blue Point OYSTERS on the Half Shell
One-Half Dozen (offered seasonally)
6.95

ENTRÉES

SMALL TENDERLOIN AND CRAB IMPERIAL
Backfin CRAB Imperial and
Broiled Tenderloin of BEEF
served with Russet POTATOES, a Pumpkin FRITTER,
and a VEGETABLE
21.25
Suggested WINE: Bin No. 84 (Red) or No. 194 (White)

THE GLOUCESTER DINNER
Captain *Rasmussen's* Clam CHOWDER
Southern Skillet-Fried CHICKEN
served with *Virginia* HAM, a Pumpkin FRITTER,
and a VEGETABLE
Choice of BEVERAGE   Choice of ICE CREAM
18.45
Suggested WINE: Bin No. 93

A MADE DISH OF SHRIMPS, SCALLOPS, AND LOBSTER
SHRIMPS, SCALLOPS, and LOBSTER combined with
Fresh MUSHROOMS, TOMATOES, Green PEPPERS,
and ONIONS
sautéed in SHERRY and served with RICE
20.45
Suggested WINE: Bin No. 122

CHESAPEAKE BAY JAMBALAYA
A Combination of SCALLOPS and SHRIMPS
braised in a Spicy Tomato SAUCE
and served over RICE
18.95
Suggested WINE: Bin No. 47

CHRISTIANA CAMPBELL'S CRAB CAKES
served with *Virginia* HAM,
Russet POTATOES, and a
VEGETABLE
18.95
Suggested WINE: Bin No. 98

WALLER STREET SELECTION

The CHEF'S nightly Choice
Priced daily

BROILED RIB EYE STEAK
served with Braised Sliced Fresh
MUSHROOMS, Baked POTATO, and a
VEGETABLE
18.75
Suggested WINE: Bin No. 19

MRS. *CAMPBELL'S* SEAFOOD PLATTER
A Combination Platter of Fried SHRIMP,
SCALLOPS, and Broiled FLOUNDER with CRAB Imperial,
Russet POTATOES, and a VEGETABLE
20.25
Suggested WINE: Bin No. 105 or No. 159

CHICKEN *CHRISTIANA*
Fillet of CHICKEN Breast with
CRABMEAT and White Wine SAUCE
served with a VEGETABLE
17.45
Suggested WINE: Bin No. 93

All Selections are served with

Campbell's Cabbage SLAW   SPOON BREAD   Drop BISCUITS   Sweet Potato MUFFINS

BEVERAGES

Hot COFFEE or Hot TEA 1.25   Iced TEA or LEMONADE .95
Serving *Christiana Campbell's* Tavern Orange Pekoe TEA

Please, NO SMOKING inside the Tavern.

4/93

FIGURE 9.4.   Excellent use of prime space on a one-page menu. The two featured entrees are highlighted by boxes on the upper part of the page. (*Menu courtesy of Christiana Campbell's Tavern, Colonial Williamsburg, Williamsburg, Virginia*)

FIGURE 9.5.   A menu from the Victoria Dining Room with institutional copy on the inside front cover. (*Courtesy of Chateau Lake Louise, Alberta, Canada*)

Using Clip-ons

Clip-ons are used on menus in all styles of restaurants. While some operations disdain the use of clip-ons, the degree of success with such an advertising medium depends on how they are used. Clip-ons are predominant on low- to moderate-priced menus, but are also seen on high-priced menus. The rationales behind using clip-ons are many. They can be used to test new products to see whether they will sell. They can be used to feature either low-priced specials or high-gross-profit items. In operations that feature fresh items such as fish and seafood, they can be used to list the catch of the day. They are an excellent means of selling leftovers, which otherwise could not be merchandised on a predetermined printed menu.

If it is the restaurant's philosophy that clip-ons are a good merchandising tool, then proper planning for them must be executed when the menu is arranged. All too often, clip-ons cover up important listings on the menu. Few customers lift up a clip-on to see what is underneath; therefore, those items cannot be expected

Victoria
Dining Room

JEWEL OF THE ROCKIES

Lake Louise was discovered by the late Tom Wilson in 1882. Tom was at that time emplc
Maj. Rogers who was surveying for the Canadian Pacific Railway which was under constr
at that time. Lake Louise was named after Princess Louise, in 1884, who was the wife
Lorne, the Governor General of Canada, and also the daughter of Queen Victoria. The te
Louise during the year averages 1 degree celcius to 5 degrees celcius. The altitude of La
feet above sea level. The dimensions of Lake Louise are 1½ miles long, ¾ miles wide; a
The colouring of the lake is due to the depth and the fine mineral deposits of Glacial
carried down from the Victoria Glacier.

The Victoria Glacier is 6 miles from the Chateau Lake Louise. The upper Glacier is 200 tc
while the lower Glacier is 400 to 500 feet in depth. Lake Agnes is located 2½ miles by trail
at an altitude of 6,885 feet. There is a Tea House at the lake which was built in 1908. T!
reconstructed in 1981. A trail from the Chateau takes you to the Tea House, and can ei
horse ridden. The Plain of Six Glaciers is 4 miles from the Chateau Lake Louise at an alti
This site also boasts a Tea House which was built by the Chateau Lake Louise in 1925, a
by foot or on horse back.

There have been four different buildings of the Chateau. They are as follows:

Original Chateau built	1890
Chateau burned completely	1892
Chateau rebuilt	1893
Wooden building constructed	1900
Paynter Wing constructed	1913
Wooden building burned	1924
Barrett Wing constructed	1925
Major Exterior Renovations	1985
Glacier Wing constructed	1987

FIGURE 9.5.   *(Continued)*

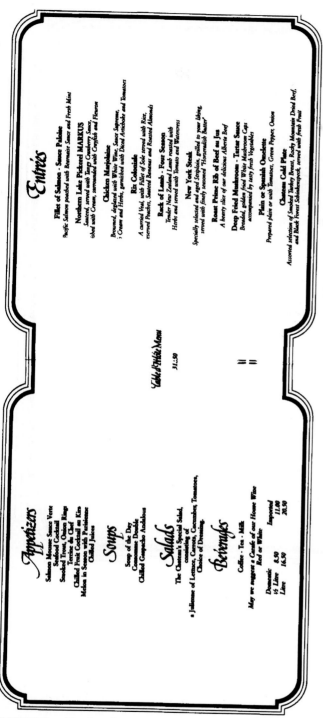

FIGURE 9.5. *(Continued)*

Desserts

Kahlua Parfait
Today's Pie, plain or à la mode
Canadian Cheddar Cheese with Grapes & Biscuits
Black Forest Cake
Vanilla or Chocolate Cheese Cake
Passion Fruit Cake
Fresh Fruit in Season

Special Coffees

Monte Cristo   4.75
Rich black coffee together with Kahlua (¾ oz.),
Curacao (¾ oz.) and fresh cream.

Blueberry Tea   4.75
Take a little break from coffee and try fine Earl Grey tea
with Grand Marnier (¾ oz.), Amaretto (¾ oz.), and fresh cream.

Spanish   4.75
The perfect blend of smooth Brandies (1 oz.), Kahlua (½ oz.),
coffee and fresh whipped cream.

Irish   4.75
The old country traditional of Irish Whiskey (1 oz.),
Irish Mist (½ oz.), coffee and fresh whipped cream.

The Princess Louise Coffee   5.00
The perfect blend of Grand Marnier, Amaretto and Kahlua
with special blend coffee, fresh cream and shaved chocolate.

FIGURE 9.5. *(Continued)*

to sell well. When planning a menu that will use clip-ons, the space underneath them should have either some artwork or institutional copy. Do not leave the space blank. If you do not use the clip-ons during a particular day or meal period, the menu will look incomplete to the customer. Clip-ons should be printed on the same type of paper as the menu and should use the same style of type. They may be bordered to attract attention and should always be clean and fresh, never dirty or greasy.

PRINTING THE MENU

Once the style and overall layout of the menu have been determined, the next step is to have it printed. Many decisions must be made which will affect the final outcome. First and foremost a reliable printer must be selected, as the printer's knowledge and expertise will not only speed up the process but also dictate the quality of the finished product. This is important as all of the previous efforts will have been for naught if the menu is not properly printed.

The printing industry is a large one. Select a printer who has experience with menus. Analyze the firm's work. Develop a strong line of communication so that each person knows exactly what is to be done. As previously stated, many decisions must be made, including the paper to be used, the size and shape, the style of type, and the artwork.

Paper

The paper or paperboard chosen for the menu will normally run 30 percent of the finished cost, but could run as high as 50 percent, depending on the product selected. The characteristics of the paper influence, to a large degree, the finished appearance of the menu. Since there is an almost infinite number of possibilities affecting paper characteristics, it is important that the menu planner work closely with the printer in selecting the proper paper. Several factors need to be considered: weight, strength, color, and coating.

Paper is manufactured and identified by its basis weight, that is, the weight in pounds for 500 sheets of the basic size for that particular grade. For example, book paper varies in basis weight from 50 to 100 pounds. Do not confuse weight with strength. Although weight has some bearing on strength, the strength of paper is more dependent on the fiber used. Generally speaking, stronger papers have more long pulp fibers than do papers of lesser strength. Color is important as it affects the readability of the color of type used.

Type is most easily read on a soft white paper. The type of coating also affects the final outcome of the menu. Although some papers are not coated at all, finishes are available from dull to very glossy and everything in between. Do not confuse laminated menus with those printed on high gloss paper. Lamination is a process that takes place after the menu is printed to give it protection and durability.

After the paper is selected, one more consideration must be made—size. Paper used for printing purposes comes in large sheets of varying sizes. On selecting a particular type of paper, inquire into the size of the sheets that are available. Compare the proposed size of the menu to the most economical size sheet available. Normally several menus can be printed on one sheet of printing paper. It is entirely possible that, by changing the size of the menu slightly, more menus can be printed using fewer sheets. This is important because, as stated earlier, the paper can equal up to 50 percent of the cost. For example, a common size printing sheet is 17½″ by 22½″. If you desire to have a menu page that measures 9″ by 11″, you could print one 2-page menu per sheet. If, on the other hand, the menu page were reduced 1/2″ to 8½″ × 11″, two 2-page menus could be printed, thus reducing your paper cost by 50 percent. This is shown in Figure 9.6.

This is but one example. Because many sizes of printing sheets are available, consult the printer about the desired size of the menu versus the size of the printing sheets for the most economical approach. Sometimes aesthetics need to be measured against cost. If it is vitally important that the menu be a certain size or take on a particular shape to emphasize a theme, then cost should be less a factor and design should dominate your planning.

Color

In conjunction with the paper selected for the menu, a decision must be made with regard to color. Of course, the basic black ink on white paper is least expensive. However, for a very slight increase in cost, colored ink on colored paper could be used. The cost increases as the number of colors increases because additional press runs must be made. To achieve various colors, a printer uses four basic inks (colors). As the menu goes through the press, each run with a different ink, different colors are produced. Thus the four basic inks produce virtually every imaginable color. The overall aesthetic value of the menu is greatly influenced by the proper selection of paper color and the combinations of inks.

Type

Many different styles of type are available. To simplify matters, the most common are classified as old style, modern, transitional,

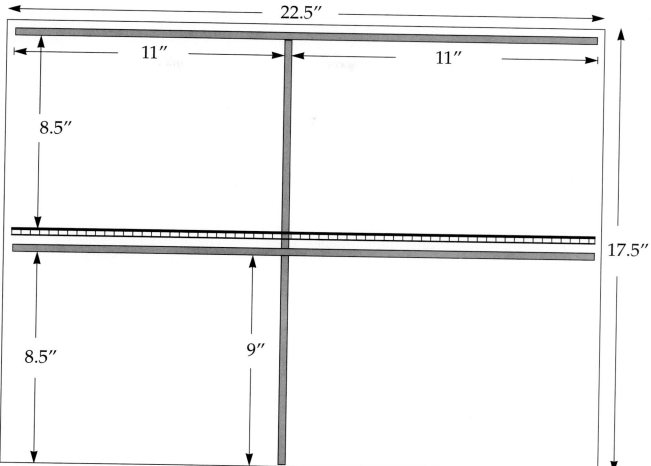

FIGURE 9.6. Illustration showing how a large sheet of printing paper is reduced to smaller sizes. Notice how a common size will give more menus per page.

square serif, sans serif, script, text letters, and decorative types. Although these classifications in no way cover all of the styles, this is a useful breakdown that covers a wide variety of types.

Old style is patterned after letters used on classical Roman inscriptions. It is a very readable style of type because the letters are open, wide, and round. This would be an excellent choice for the descriptive terminology and the institutional copy on the menu.

Modern is a class of type that refers to its style as opposed to the time it was developed. It has a much greater degree of mechanical perfection than the old style type. It is also a good choice for menus that have a multitude of words in the copy.

Transitional combines the first two classes—old style and modern. Although most of the characteristics of old style have been retained, it is less sturdy. As in the case of the first two classes, it is an excellent choice for the wordier portions of the menu.

Square serif is a contemporary style of type with a blocked or square look to it and more uniform strokes. This class should be used in category headings or for the listing of items. It should not be used for institutional copy as it is difficult to read in larger blocks of text.

Sans serif, while similar to square serif, is cleaner and has a simpler design. It is a comparatively new type and is useful for headings and product listings.

Script is a style of type used to simulate handwriting or hand lettering. It is commonly used on invitations or announcements. As far as menus are concerned, it is very popular for category headings.

Text letters resemble the hand-drawn letters of early scribes. The styles are quite often selected for religious documents, certificates, and diplomas. These would be an excellent choice for restaurants that have an Old World theme such as seafaring or Old English. They should, however, be used only for category headings or product listings as this style is difficult to read when used for menu copy.

Decorative types are designed to express different moods; they may appear eccentric at times. Primarily used to command attention, they are a good choice to headline boxed or bordered items on the menu. They can also be used for headings and listings.

Type selection should be carefully considered. The styles chosen can reinforce the theme of the restaurant as carried out on the menu. Limit the selection to one or two styles: one for headings and item listings, and one for copy. Too many classes of type on one menu make it appear cluttered and confusing. Check with your printer to see what styles are available.

In addition to selecting the styles of type, other decisions must be made regarding the printing of the menu. They include the size of the type, letter spacing, and leading.

The *size of type* is measured in points, with 72 points equaling an inch. Normally, type is available from 6 to 72 points. When selecting the size of type for a menu, 12 points should be considered the minimum, and then only for institutional copy or for descriptive terminology. While 12 points is relatively large for copy, it should be remembered that most restaurants have a lighting level that is more conducive to dining and atmosphere than it is to reading. Headings and item listings should be 18 points or more. In addition to selecting the size of type, a decision must be made as to whether to use uppercase, lowercase, or both. *Uppercase* is printers' terminology for capital letters, *lowercase* refers to small letters.

Another consideration is the letter spacing and leading. *Letter spacing* is just what the name implies, the amount of space between letters. Spacing affects readability. It also allows you to fill an empty

Avant Garde
Baskerville
Bellevue
Blippo Black
Bookman
Brittanic
Broadway
Brody
Brush Script
Century Schoolbook
Chaucer
City Medium
Clarendon
Clearface Gothic
Cooper Black
Copperplate
Eurostile
Flare Gothic
Frugal Sans
Garamond

Gill Sans
Goudy
Helvetica
Hobo
Kauflinn
Korinna
Mural Script
Old Towne
Optima
Palatino
Park Avenue
Sans Extended
Souvenir
Square Serif
Tekton
Times New Roman
University Roman
Vivante
Windsor
Zapf Chancery

FIGURE 9.7. Type styles.

area of the menu. It is best to leave letter spacing to the judgment of the printer. *Leading,* on the other hand, is the amount of space between the lines. Like type size, it is also measured in points. Again, because of the amount of light in most restaurants, three points of leading is recommended.

Artwork

Another decision to be made is whether or not to employ artwork on the menu. Many menus have no artwork at all, using strictly printed copy, while others use art quite extensively. Because artwork increases the cost of the menu, you should decide whether the use of artwork will enhance the overall impression of the menu. Certainly it could be used to enhance the theme of the restaurant or to highlight certain areas of the menu or both. However, is it cost effective?

Larger printing firms have artists on their staffs who can provide this service. If a small printing firm is used, the artwork will have to be supplied. This can be obtained from a commercial art firm or a freelance artist. It is generally helpful if the artwork supplied to the printer is camera-ready copy.

The Proof

Now the printer goes to work. The menu is laid out and typeset according to specifications. The result is a *proof*—a copy of what the menu will look like. Examine the proof carefully. Check for spelling, accurate phrasing, punctuation, and correct pricing. Any errors that are not detected and corrected will appear on the final menu. Avoid massive changes as these will add to the cost. If the work to this point was performed accurately with good communication with the printer, the changes should be minor in nature. Remember, it is imperative to check for accuracy before approving the proof for final printing.

After the proof has been approved, the last decision to be made is how many menus should be printed. While approximately 30 percent of the menu cost is in paper, about 50 percent of the cost is in typesetting the menu, press preparation, and run(s). Since this is a one-time cost, it stands to reason that the greater the number of menus you print, the lower the cost for each menu will be. However, don't be misled by false economies. For example, if you need 100 menus at a cost of $3 each ($300 total), don't order 1,000 at a cost of $1.50 each ($1,500 total).

Although the quantity to order varies from operation to operation, depending on specific circumstances, some rules of thumb can be established. In restaurants where revisions due to fluctuating prices or item changes are not anticipated for a period of six months or longer, two and a half times the number of seats would be the normal amount to purchase. In restaurants where revisions are made on a more frequent basis, such as seasonally, two times the number of seats would be the norm. There are exceptions to this rule, and knowledge of the operation is essential if modifications are to be made. For example, if the menus were laminated, less would be needed due to the added durability.

The reason for printing more menus than seats is that menus get soiled, torn, and stolen. There is little that can be done to correct

APPETIZERS

Chicken Fingers
Lightly breaded and seasoned chicken breast tenderloin deep-fried to a golden brown. Served with barbecue sauce or honey-mustard dressing. $3.45

Deep-Fried Mushrooms
Plump and juicy breaded mushrooms, fried light and golden. Served with country ranch dressing for dipping. $2.45

Seasoned French Fries
Our famous French fries, seasoned to perfection. $1.45

Mozzarella Cheese Sticks
Breaded and deep-fried golden brown and served with marinara sauce for dipping. $3.25

Country Onion Rings
Cut large, breaded with our special batter and fried golden. $1.95

SOUPS

Old-Fashioned Calico Bean Soup ❤
A Country Kitchen® specialty. A hearty combination of seven different beans, smoked ham and special seasonings.
Cup $1.25   Bowl $1.75

Soup of the Day
Ask your server for today's selection
Cup $1.25   Bowl $1.75

Chili
Hearty chili prepared with just enough spices. Topped with cheddar cheese and served with crackers.
Cup $1.95   Bowl $2.45

Soup and Salad
A bowl of Calico Bean Soup® served with our tossed green salad. $3.25

Soup and Sandwich
A bowl of Calico Bean Soup® served with today's featured sandwich. $4.25

SALADS

Grilled Chicken Breast Salad ❤
A mound of crisp garden greens topped with grilled marinated chicken breast, tomatoes, green onions, mushrooms, green peppers and croutons. Served with your choice of dressing and a dinner roll. $5.45

Taco Salad
Spicy taco meat, cheddar cheese, tomatoes, black olives, onions, sour cream and guacamole served over crisp garden greens in a giant tortilla shell. Served with salsa and a dinner roll. $5.25

Country Club Salad
Salad greens topped with chunks of turkey and ham. Garnished with egg and tomato wedges, shredded cheddar cheese and bacon. Served with your choice of dressing and a dinner roll. $4.95

Beef or Chicken Fajita Salad ❤
Grilled seasoned beef or chicken strips, cheddar cheese, black olives, green peppers, green onions, tomato, guacamole and sour cream on crisp garden greens. Served with tortilla chips, salsa and your choice of dressing. $5.45

Salad Bar (Where Available)
Salad bar as a meal in itself. $4.50
With any sandwich. $1.75
With entrée as substitute for tossed salad. $.95

❤ Indicates Country Kitchen® specialties.
Right Choice™ – For guests concerned about a healthy diet.
- Less than 400 calories.
- Less than 100 mg. cholesterol.
- Less than 1000 mg. sodium.
- Meets guidelines without French fries.

SANDWICHES

All of our sandwiches and burgers (excluding All-American Hot Sandwich) are served with seasoned French Fries and pickles.

Deluxe Clubhouse
A triple-decker of sliced turkey, ham, crisp bacon, Swiss cheese, tomatoes and lettuce. Served with mayonnaise on your choice of toast. $5.45

Country Clubhouse
A triple-decker with sliced turkey, crisp bacon, lettuce and sliced tomatoes. Served with mayonnaise on your choice of toast. $4.95

French Dip ❤
Thinly-sliced roast beef served on a French roll. Accompanied by au jus for dipping. $5.25

Philly Beef and Cheese ❤
Thinly sliced beef grilled with onions and mushrooms served on a French roll with lots of melted mozzarella cheese. $5.45

Reuben Sandwich
The classic combination of corned beef, Swiss cheese, sauerkraut and Thousand Island dressing served on grilled caraway rye bread. $5.25

Barbecued Chicken Sandwich
Boneless chicken breast, grilled and topped with barbecue sauce, Swiss cheese and bacon. Served on a toasted Kaiser roll. $5.25

Smothered Chicken Melt
Grilled chicken breast smothered in mozzarella cheese, onions, tomatoes and mushrooms on grilled Parmesan sourdough. $5.25

Fish Fillet
Lightly breaded fish fillet, fried golden brown and topped with American cheese. Served on a French roll with lettuce and tartar sauce. $4.95

Chicken Breast Sandwich ❤
Grilled chicken breast, on a toasted Kaiser roll with lettuce and tomato slices. Served with mayonnaise. $4.95

Chicken Bacon Melt
Grilled chicken breast smothered in American cheese, topped with bacon and tomato on grilled Parmesan sourdough. $5.25

All-American Hot Sandwiches ❤
Your choice of roast beef, meat loaf or sliced turkey mounded on fresh bread. Served with mashed potatoes and gravy. $4.25

BURGERS

Country Boy® ❤
Our famous double-decker hamburger served on a toasted roll with cheese, tomato, lettuce and special sauce. $3.95

Classic Hamburger ❤
A third-pound of ground beef topped with lettuce, tomato and mayonnaise. Served on a toasted Kaiser roll. $4.25
With Swiss, cheddar or American cheese add $.20
With bacon add $.70

Barbecue Burger
Our beef hamburger topped with grilled ham, Swiss cheese, lettuce and tomato. Served with barbecue sauce. $4.65

Mushroom Cheeseburger ❤
The classic beef hamburger topped with American and Swiss cheese, mushrooms, lettuce, tomato and mayonnaise. $4.65

Patty Melt
An all-time favorite. A beef hamburger topped with American cheese, Swiss cheese and sautéed onions. Served on grilled caraway rye bread. $4.65

❤ Indicates Country Kitchen® specialties.
Right Choice™ – For guests concerned about a healthy diet.
- Less than 400 calories.
- Less than 100 mg. cholesterol.
- Less than 1000 mg. sodium.
- Meets guidelines without French fries.

FIGURE 9.8. Notice how the artwork on this menu ties in with the decor of the restaurant. (*Menu and photograph courtesy of Country Kitchen, Country Hospitality Corporation, Minneapolis, Minnesota*)

FOR OUR SENIOR GUESTS

Specially planned smaller portions for those over sixty. For dinner, each meal (excluding pasta dish) includes your choice of potato or rice pilaf, vegetable of the day, a cup of soup or tossed green salad and a warm dinner roll.

One Egg Any Style
With two strips of bacon, toast and juice. $2.95

A Short Stack of Pancakes
Our famous pancakes with warm syrup, sausage and juice. $2.95

French Toast
Thick slices of French bread and grilled golden. Served with crisp bacon, warm syrup and juice. $3.25

A Cup and a Half
A cup of our soup and today's hot sandwich. $3.25

Hamburger
With seasoned French fries. $3.40

Spaghetti with Meatballs
Served with garlic toast. $3.95

Country Fried Chicken
Two pieces, crisp and tender. $4.25

Roast Turkey Dinner
With sage stuffing and cranberry sauce. $4.25

Fillet of Fish
Served with tartar sauce. $4.25

Chopped Beef Steak
A third-pound of ground beef topped with a golden onion ring. $4.25

Baked Meat Loaf
Topped with rich gravy. $4.25

Indicates Country Kitchen® specialties.
Right Choice™ — For guests concerned about a healthy diet.
♥ Less than 400 calories.
♥ Less than 100 mg. cholesterol.
♥ Less than 1000 mg. sodium.
♥ Meets guidelines without French fries.

KIDS' MEALS

For kids under 10, we have special reduced portions. Each meal includes choice of small juice, soft drink or a special dessert.
Kids' beverages are served with a fun collectible, re-useable, spill resistant cup which is yours to take home.

BREAKFASTS

Lil' Stack
Piping hot Country Kitchen® pancakes served with crisp bacon and warm syrup. $2.25

Cakes and Egg
One farm-fresh scrambled egg, crisp bacon and pancakes served with warm syrup. $2.25

Kids' French Toast
Two slices of French bread dipped in egg batter and grilled golden. Served with crisp bacon and warm syrup. $2.25

LUNCH AND DINNER

Grilled Cheese Sandwich
An American cheese sandwich grilled golden brown. Served with crisp seasoned French fries. $2.25

Kids' Burger
Our special hamburger served on a toasted bun with seasoned French fries. $2.25

Spaghetti with Meatballs
Kids favorite! Served with a slice of toast. $2.25

Fillet of Fish
A golden flaky fish fillet served with seasoned French fries and toast. $2.25

Country Fried Chicken Strips
Tender chicken filet strips deep-fried and served with seasoned French fries, choice of dipping sauce and toast. $2.25

Corn Dog
The original corn dog, served with seasoned French fries. $2.25

Peanut butter and jelly sandwich
Everyone's favorite sandwich, made with Smucker's peanut butter and grape jelly, served with seasoned French fries. $2.25

Each meal (excluding pasta and stir fry dishes) includes a choice of potato or rice pilaf, today's vegetable, a warm dinner roll and a salad.

CHICKEN

Smothered Chicken
Boneless chicken breast, grilled with onions and mushrooms and covered with melted mozzarella cheese. $6.25

Grilled Chicken
Marinated, boneless chicken breast grilled to perfection. $5.95

Country Fried Chicken
Our special recipe. Fried crisp and golden on the outside, moist and tender on the inside. $5.95

Chicken Parmigiana
Tender boneless chicken breast, served over pasta and topped with marinara sauce and mozzarella cheese. Served with a salad and garlic toast. $6.25

Chicken Finger Dinner
Six chicken fingers, lightly breaded and deep-fried. Served with honey-mustard or barbecue sauce. $5.45

SEAFOOD

Shrimp Scampi
Shrimp sautéed in garlic flavored sauce and served over pasta. Accompanied by a salad and garlic toast. $6.25

Rainbow Trout
Tender boneless rainbow trout fillet, butterflied and grilled to perfection. Served with tartar sauce. $6.45

Country Breaded Shrimp
Lightly dusted shrimp deep-fried to a golden brown. Served with tangy cocktail sauce. $5.95

Fillet of Fish
Lightly breaded fried fish fillets. Served with tartar sauce. $5.95

STEAKS

New York Strip Steak
U.S.D.A. Choice 10 oz. strip steak grilled to your liking. Garnished with onion rings. $9.95

Rib Eye Steak
U.S.D.A. Choice 8 oz. rib eye steak, grilled to your liking. Garnished with onion rings. $8.95

Top Sirloin Steak
U.S.D.A. Choice 6 oz. top sirloin steak, grilled to your liking. Garnished with onion rings. $6.95

SPECIALTIES

Beef or Chicken Stir Fry
Specially seasoned beef or chicken stir fried with oriental vegetables on a bed of rice pilaf. Served with teriyaki sauce, salad and warm dinner roll. $5.95

Old-Fashioned Meat Loaf
A Country Kitchen® favorite. Baked and topped with rich gravy. $5.45

Country Turkey Dinner
Sliced breast of turkey with cranberry sauce. Served with our delicious stuffing and gravy. $5.45

Country Fried Steak
Select beef, pounded thin, lightly breaded and fried golden. Served with country gravy. $5.75

Spaghetti with Meatballs
The classic Italian favorite! Served with a salad and garlic toast. $4.95

Baked Lasagna
Lasagna noodles layered with ricotta cheese and a classic-style tomato sauce with sausage; topped with mozzarella cheese. Served with a salad and garlic toast. $5.95

Indicates Country Kitchen® specialties.
Right Choice™ — For guests concerned about a healthy diet
♥ Less than 400 calories.
♥ Less than 100 mg. cholesterol.
♥ Less than 1000 mg. sodium.
♥ Meets guidelines without French fries.

FIGURE 9.8. *(Continued)*

Farm Fresh
"Top to the Morning"

OMELETTES

Our omelettes are made with three eggs and served on a bed of seasoned hash browns, accompanied by toast and jelly.

Simply Eggs™ Garden Omelette ♥
Stuffed with broccoli, tomato, mushrooms, onions and green peppers. $4.95

Western Omelette
Sautéed ham, onions and bell peppers combined with eggs and American cheese and topped with cheese sauce. $4.95

Ham and Cheese Omelette ♥
Fresh ham and cheese combined into the classic omelette and topped with cheese sauce. $4.95

Mushroom and Cheese Omelette ♥
Sautéed mushrooms and American cheese folded into an omelette and topped with cheese sauce. $4.75

PANCAKES

Best Pancakes in Town ♥
Our famous pancakes are light and fluffy with a hint of sugar and vanilla. Served with your choice of bacon, ham or sausage and warm syrup.
Full stack. $4.25
Short stack. $3.75

Cakes and Eggs
Two eggs, two pancakes and two slices of crisp bacon. Served with warm syrup. $3.75

Blueberry Pancakes ♥
Our light fluffy pancakes filled with blueberries and cooked golden. Served with your choice of breakfast meats and warm blueberry compote or syrup. $4.75

JUICES

Chilled Orange, Grapefruit, Tomato or Apple Juice $.95

SKILLET BREAKFASTS

Farm Skillet ♥
Seasoned hash browns, topped with two eggs, sausage, onions and green peppers. Served with toast and jelly. $4.75

Skillet Scramble ♥
Two scrambled eggs and grilled ham served on a bed of seasoned hash browns, topped with tangy cheese sauce. Served with toast and jelly. $4.75

Fiesta Skillet ♥
Seasoned hash browns combined with taco meat, topped with two eggs, shredded cheese, diced tomatoes and green peppers. Served with a side of salsa, sour cream, toast and jelly. $4.75

Double-Up Skillet ♥
Two eggs, two strips of bacon and two slices of French toast on a bed of seasoned hash browns. Served with warm syrup. $4.75

Southern Skillet ♥
An old favorite! Sausage patties on biscuits, with two eggs. Served with country sausage gravy on the side. $4.75

♥ Indicates Country Kitchen® specialties.
Right Choice™ – For guests concerned about a healthy diet.
● Less than 400 calories.
● Less than 100 mg. cholesterol.
● Less than 1000 mg. sodium.
● Meets guidelines without French fries.

Sweet Taste
DESSERTS
AND
BEVERAGES

BEVERAGES

Soft Drinks
Free refills. $.95

Milk $.95

Coffee
We serve a bottomless cup of the best coffee in town. Regular or decaffeinated.

Iced Tea
Free refills. $.85

Hot Tea
Free refills. $.85

Lemonade
Free refills. $.95

Hot Chocolate
Free refills. $.85

BEER AND WINE
(Where Available)

Country Kitchen® Marks of Quality

We use only Grade AA eggs, real dairy Half and Half creamers, Grade A garden vegetables and U.S.D.A. Choice steaks. We proudly serve such nationally famous quality brands as Heinz Ketchup, Smucker's jams and jellies, Uncle Ben's Rice, Oscar Mayer meats and more. In the interest of your health, we also serve 2% lowfat milk and all of our fried and grilled foods are cooked with cholesterol-free oils.

Give a Gift That's Always In Good Taste

Country Kitchen® restaurant Gift Certificates make an excellent, thoughtful gift for any occasion – holidays, birthdays, anniversaries or as business gifts. They can be redeemed at any participating Country Kitchen® restaurant in the U.S., Canada or Puerto Rico. To purchase, see the cashier or ask your server.

DESSERTS

Down-Home Apple Dumpling ♥
A tangy, sweet apple, baked in a pastry shell and topped with cinnamon sauce and served a la mode with cinnamon or vanilla ice cream. $1.75

Hot Fudge Cake ♥
Creamy vanilla ice cream layered between slices of rich chocolate cake. Drizzled with hot fudge sauce, crowned with whipped topping. $1.75

Pecan Pie $1.45

Special Recipe Pies – *Baked Fresh Daily*
Fruit pie, served hot. $1.35
A la mode. $1.75
Cream pie. $1.45

Ice Cream Sundaes
Two scoops of ice cream covered with your choice of hot fudge, butterscotch, chocolate or strawberry sauce. Topped with whipped topping. $1.75

Strawberry Twinkie® Shortcake ♥
A tender cream-filled Twinkie,® sliced and topped with vanilla ice cream, sweetened strawberries and whipped topping. $1.95

Hot Fudge HoHo® ♥
Two cream-filled HoHos® topped with vanilla ice cream, hot fudge and whipped topping. $1.95

Twinkie and HoHo are registered trademarks of The Continental Baking Company.

♥ Indicates Country Kitchen® specialties.
Right Choice™ – For guests concerned about a healthy diet.
● Less than 400 calories.
● Less than 100 mg. cholesterol.
● Less than 1000 mg. sodium.
● Meets guidelines without French fries.

FIGURE 9.8. *(Continued)*

FIGURE 9.8. (*Continued*)

COUNTRY CLASSICS

Country Eggs
Two eggs any style, seasoned hash browns, toast and jelly. $2.95

Everybody's Favorite
Two eggs any style, seasoned hash browns, toast and jelly. Served with your choice of bacon, ham, sausage or a grilled beef patty. $4.45

Country French Toast
Thick slices of French bread dipped in egg batter and grilled golden. Served with bacon, ham or sausage and warm syrup. $4.45

Simply Eggs™ Breakfast ♥
Scrambled Simply Eggs' served with fresh fruit and a warm muffin. $4.75

Country Fried Steak and Eggs
Tender beef, lightly breaded and fried. Served with two eggs, seasoned hash browns, country gravy, toast and jelly. $4.95

Steak and Eggs
Two eggs, seasoned hash browns and two slices of toast and jelly with a 6 oz. U.S.D.A. Choice top sirloin steak. $5.95
With an 8 oz. U.S.D.A. Choice rib eye steak. $7.95
With a 10 oz. U.S.D.A. Choice New York strip steak. $8.95

SIDE ORDERS ♥

Hot or Cold Cereal ♥
Served with fruit, a freshly baked muffin and milk. $3.25

Oscar Mayer Bacon or Sausage ♥ $1.95

Ham ♥ $1.95

Seasoned Hash Brown Potatoes ♥ $1.45

English Muffin ♥ $.95

Giant Sweet Roll ♥
Glazed or caramel, served warm. $1.45

Toast ♥ $.95

Freshly Baked Muffin ♥ $1.25

Fruit Medley ♥
Served with a freshly baked muffin. $3.25

Biscuits and Gravy $2.25

Country Kitchen® restaurant's famous breakfasts are served all day. Ask your server for today's breakfast specials. We serve  products.

For our guess concerned about diet, we offer Simply Eggs'. Simply Eggs™ is a great tasting, real, whole egg product that has 80% less cholesterol than shell eggs. Simply Eggs™ is available as a substitute on any breakfast. Simply Eggs™ is a registered trademark of Michael Foods, Inc.

♥ Indicates Country Kitchen® specialties.
Right Choice™ – For guests concerned about a healthy diet.
♦ Less than 400 calories.
♦ Less than 100 mg. cholesterol.
♦ Less than 1000 mg. sodium.
♦ Meets guidelines without French fries.

FIGURE 9.8. (*Continued*)

the first two problems, but to reduce theft, reproduce a copy of the menu on a regular sheet of paper. These can be used as handouts and are an excellent form of advertisement at a very reasonable cost.

DESKTOP PUBLISHING

An alternative to having a printer create the layout, typesetting, and artwork on your menu would be to use *desktop publishing*. This is becoming more and more popular, particularly with independent restaurants and small chains. Desktop publishing can be very cost effective assuming that the computer system is already being used for other functions such as accounting, inventory, and cost controls.

In addition to saving money on menu setup costs, a computer-developed menu can allow a quick reaction to cost changes in the marketplace, shift menu items as customer demand fluctuates, take advantage of seasonal items, and run holiday or special event promotions. An additional advantage would be to tie the menu to one of several analysis methods (Chapter 5) so that it can be quickly determined what adjustments are needed on your menu mix to improve profitability.

If an entire system (hardware and software) is to be purchased, make sure it will handle the multiplicity of functions that occur in a restaurant, not merely in the menu development. If the hardware is in place, all that is needed is to purchase the software. Two packages will probably be required; one for text, and one for artwork. The menu text can be done on any one of the many word processing programs available. Some of the more popular programs include Microsoft Word, WordPerfect, Quark XPress, and Smart, to name a few. As far as artwork goes, the simplest method is to purchase a clip-art program and simply "cut and paste" the desired clip art to the menu in the appropriate place. If greater control over the artwork is desired and the user has a degree of artistic talent, then a program such as McDraw Pro or Canvas could be selected to complete original drawings for the menu. Only a few of the many programs available have been mentioned, and any computer software dealer can assist in selecting the proper software for a particular brand of computer.

Another factor to consider is the printer, as it will affect the quality of the finished menu more than anything. Four types of printers are available: dot-matrix, letter-quality, inkjet, and laser. The first two do not give high-quality results. Inkjet provides a good outcome, while a laser printer develops a menu that is so close to a typeset menu that the average customer will not notice the difference.

In creating a menu with desktop publishing, the entire project—cover and inside text—can be created in house. Another option is to do just the text and artwork (if applicable) for the inside, and purchase a cover from one of several menu companies that have created covers specifically for computer-developed menus.

IN THE BEGINNING

Baked Brie — $5.25
Point your compass in this direction! Our wheel is topped with toasted pecans and baked to perfection. Served with slices of French bread.

Garlic Broiled Shrimp — $6.25
You'll travel over land and sea for these awesome treats. Five jumbo shrimp broiled in a rich garlic butter sauce. Served with slices of French bread.

Gourmet Round — $5.95
Be adventurous as Marco Polo was!! This eight inch pizza is topped with sundried tomatoes, smoked chunk chicken and fontina cheese.

Smokey Black Bean and Vegetable Soup
Little did Christopher Colombus know that the spices he discovered in the Caribbean would add such wonderful flavor to this hearty black bean, vegetable soup.
cup $2.95
bowl $3.95

Wild Rice Soup
Unsurpassable! This creamy classic unites wild rice, bacon and smoked ham with just a touch of garlic.
cup $2.95
bowl $3.95

Soup of the Day
Ask your server about today's freshly prepared soup.
cup $2.95
bowl $3.95

LIGHT DISCOVERIES
All salads are served with slices of French bread

Super Spinach Salad — $5.95
You have landed and this salad is your reward. Bacon, bean sprouts, mushrooms, green onions, hard boiled eggs, and dry roasted sunflower seeds mixed with our special oil and vinegar dressing.

Curried Chicken and Couscous Salad — $6.95
India's aromatic spice gives this salad its distinctive taste. Sauteed chicken breast combined with couscous, peas, roasted red peppers and golden raisins. Served on a bed of lettuce.

Mandarin Salad — $5.95
New World Cafe's unique discovery of flavors! A light mixture of mandarin oranges, green onions, celery and toasted sweet almonds on a bed of romaine and iceberg lettuce. Tossed with a light house dressing.

Mixed Salad Murcian Style — $6.95
Any true adventurous Spanaird will love this salad. Chilled albacore tuna, tomato, onions and black olives arranged on a bed of bibb lettuce. Sprinkled with chopped eggs and topped with a sherry wine vinegar dressing.

New World Garden Salad — $4.95
Select greens mixed with carrots, red onion and croutons. Served with your choice of dressing. Dressings: Creamy Ranch, Thousand Island, Bleu Cheese, Vinaigrette, Low calorie, French and Italian.

NEW WORLD CAFE

OLD WORLD CHARM
NEW GLOBAL CUISINE

Discovered November 1, 1994

FIGURE 9.9. An example of a menu cover and copy developed using desktop publishing software on a computer.

UNEARTHED TREASURES
Dig into these hearty sandwiches.

All served with your choice of our New World garden salad or cup of soup.

BLT&G (Bacon, Lettuce, Tomato, & Guacamole) $5.95
An exciting and fresh change from the ordinary. A double-decker loaded with crisp bacon, vine-ripened tomato, lettuce, and spicy guacamole.

Smoked Turkey Reuben $6.25
This jewel combines smoked turkey, swiss cheese, and finely shredded cabbage on grilled pumpernickel bread. Served with a side of our specially blended Thousand Island dressing.

Steak Sandwich with Mushroom Gravy $6.95
A sandwich that borders on the sublime. Thinly-sliced, seasoned sirloin over toasted French bread and ladled with a mushroom/wine sauce.

Fresh Tuna Melt Burger $5.95
You've struck it rich!! A large skillet-seared fresh tuna patty covered with Monterey Jack cheese. Garnished with romaine lettuce and tomato and served on a toasted whole wheat bun.

Pesto Chicken Cheese Sandwich $6.25
A real find! Zesty pesto sauce and melted fontina cheese top a charbroiled chicken breast. Served on grilled French bread.

New World Vegetarian Sandwich $5.95
A treasure for the serious vegetable lover. Loaded with grilled lettuce, red onion, tomato and Monterey Jack cheese, this sandwich is served on marbled rye bread.

UNPARALLED ENDINGS

Bittersweet Chocolate Cake $3.95
Expose your palate to chocolate mousse spread between layers of chocolate cake, topped with a smooth chocolate glaze.

Explorer's Tart $3.95
You will find blackberries and raspberries mixed in this double crust tart. Puff pastry dough makes the crust extra light.

Praline Cheesecake $3.25
Indulge the senses. This creamy cheesecake is covered with caramel and topped with pralines.

Amaretto-Laced Ice Cream $2.95
Two generous scoops of vanilla ice cream drizzled with amaretto and sprinkled with amaretto cookies.

UNIVERSAL LIBATIONS

Wines by the glass

Beaujolais Village, Louis Jadot $3.75
Soft and Light with easy-to-like fruit flavors.

Chianti Classico, Ruffino Aziano $3.75
A spicy sensual red with a touch of the Old World

Chardonnay, Jordan $3.50
A chardonnay worthy of its fame. Rich and lush with a taste of oak.

Piesporter Michelsberg $3.50
From the Mosel River Region in Germany. An elegant and fragrant wine.

White Zinfandel, New World Cafe $3.25
A fruity and easy-to-drink California white zinfandel.

Merlot, New World Cafe $3.25
A great merlot with plum berry fruit flavor with hints of currant and spice.

Specialty Coffees

New World Cappuccino $2.75
A rich shot of espresso blended with milk and flavored with just a hint of vanilla.

Jewel of the Land $3.25
The perfect blend of Grand Marnier, Amaretto and Kahlua with special blend coffee, fresh cream and shaved chocolate.

The Irish Blend $2.75
Rich black coffee together with Bailey's Irish Cream Liqueur

OUT OF THIS WORLD CATERING
Contact us for all your luncheon catering needs.
We provide the best for your private parties

FIGURE 9.9. (Continued)

215

FIGURE 9-10. A menu showing the daily specials for the week is another example of desktop publishing. This menu used Design CAD 2-D, Microsoft Word, and MoreFonts for DOS. (*Courtesy of the Hospitality Management Program, Fort Leavenworth Disciplinary Barracks, Leavenworth, Kansas*)

Once the menu has been developed, it is still necessary to have it printed, assuming that a large number of copies are needed. This can be done at a neighborhood quick printing operation if it is a simple print job, or at a printer's if it is a more complicated job requiring several colors. The costs of reproducing the menu will be solely for the printing. What has been saved is the cost of the layout and typesetting. An additional plus is that the menu is exactly the way you want it.

ANALYZING AESTHETICS

One last thing concerning menu layout. If the customer doesn't read the menu, doesn't like the menu, or doesn't order from the menu, the restaurant has gained nothing. The primary objective in all that we do is to please the customer. Therefore the menu must be aesthetically pleasing to the guest. As previously discussed, the menu conveys the theme and sets the mood. It sells and explains. In analyzing aesthetics, the artwork, design, layout, style of type, copy, merchandising, marketing, mechanical considerations, and creativity are all taken into account.

A menu aesthetics checklist, Figure 9-11, takes all of these areas into consideration and rates each of them numerically. Thus management can rate their own menu in terms of style and saleability. Incidentally, menu contests are held annually in many states and provinces as well as at the National Restaurant Show. The criterion used to judge the best menus in most of these competitions is menu aesthetics.

FIGURE 9.11. Menu aesthetics checklist.

Cover
___ Reflects the theme of the restaurant
___ Has imaginative and creative artwork
___ Has unusual shape or design
___ Is constructed of durable stock
___ Gives address, phone, and other pertinent information
___ Is clean

Inside
___ Categories are listed in proper sequence
___ Headings are used to separate categories and are in bold type
___ Listings are worded utilizing descriptive terminology
___ Truth in menu is followed
___ Prime space is properly used for high gross item and is boxed in
___ Type is easily read and is 12 points minimum
___ Wine and cocktails, if applicable, are suggested in the appropriate locations
___ Clip-ons, if used, are printed on the same quality of paper and in the same style of type
___ Clip-ons do not cover regular item listings
___ Psychological pricing is utilized
___ There are no add-on charges (i.e., sour cream or bleu cheese extra)
___ Negative terminology is not used
___ Artwork is used to tie in with the cover and the theme of the restaurant
___ Institutional copy is used to enhance the theme
___ Marketing for banquets, catering, carry outs, and/or delivery is present

CONCLUSION

Once the items have been selected and priced, a critical point is reached—the layout and subsequent printing of the menu. Select a style that fits the restaurant. The cover, the inside layout, and the institutional copy should reinforce the theme and ambiance of the restaurant. Work closely with the printer's staff and use their knowledge and expertise. The result will be a menu of which you can be proud and, more importantly, which sells products and makes a profit. It's just that simple.

QUESTIONS

1. Explain in your own words:
   Lamination
   Headings
   Institutional copy
   Prime space
   Clip-ons
   Points
   Uppercase
   Leading

2. In designing a menu for a coffee shop, theme restaurant, and a fine dining restaurant, tell what type of cover you would design for each operation, what headings and subheadings you would use, and what listing(s) would be merchandised in the prime space. Write the institutional copy.

3. Referring to question 2, tell what style of type and size in points you would use for your headings, subheadings, descriptive terminology, and institutional copy.

4. Based upon your knowledge of computer, list the hardware and software needed to develop a simple menu.

5. Price out a menu to be
   - Typeset
   - Xeroxed
   - Designed

6. How many copies of a menu do you need? What is the proper care of a menu as far as cleaning and maintenance?

CHAPTER TEN

Quick Service Menus

OBJECTIVES   By the completion of this chapter, the reader should be able to:

- Discuss how simplicity impacts a quick service menu.
- Explain how speed, holding qualities, packaging, and minimum handling of products are important in menu planning.
- Explain the importance of standardization of menu items.
- Describe the role of test marketing in menu selection for quick service operations.
- Explain how the menu interrelates with other facets of the quick service industry such as concessions, delis, drive-thrus, and delivery.

IMPORTANT TERMS

Quick Service	Holding qualities
KISS	Standardization
Test marketing	Concessions

INTRODUCTION

When we think of fast food, we most often think of the major players, for example, McDonald's, Pizza Hut, Taco Bell, and so on. Although the dominant force in this segment of the food service industry is in the national and regional chains, many small independent operators compete successfully in this market. In addition to the stereotype of quick service operations, other components compose this part of our industry. Concession stands in sports arenas, small neighborhood delis, drive-thrus, home deliveries, gourmet boxed to go, and hot food take-outs in supermarkets all account for a portion of this segment. Although only a few principles are involved in menu planning for quick service operations, each of them is important.

SIMPLE AND LIMITED

The key to writing a quick service menu is simplicity. The president of a successful quick service chain has a sign behind his desk that says, "KISS"—translated "Keep it simple, stupid." Good advice! Along with *simple* comes *limited.* That is, the menu should be simple to prepare and serve as well as limited in the number of menu items.

The reasons behind keeping the menu simple and limited are many—the most important one being speed. Quick service operations are, for the most part, in the low-price range. With today's high fixed costs and high labor costs, the only way for a restaurant to survive is with equally high sales. Therefore, if the menu has a low selling price, it must depend on a high turnover rate to achieve high volume. Thus, speed becomes important. Without it, high turnover and, consequently, high volume cannot be realized. To realize speed, any item placed on the menu must fit the following criteria. First, it must involve minimum handling by the production staff. Second, it must have the ability to withstand a holding temperature for a period of time and also maintain an acceptable quality level, as most quick service items are precooked. Third, it must require minimum handling by the service staff. If a potential menu item can't be put directly into a bag or box by the service personnel, forget it—it will slow down service.

Although speed is the primary reason for keeping the menu simple and limited, several other factors benefit from this key criterion. One important benefit is a low inventory. With a limited menu, less product will have to be kept in storage than would be the case with an extensive menu. With less inventory, the restaurant has a higher turnover of goods and, consequently, a better cash flow. Also, with a simple, limited menu a lower skill level is necessary for personnel. Thus, a totally unskilled person can be trained in a rela-

101 Bean Co. has been providing the 92nd and Metcalf neighborhood with espresso, specialty beverages and high quality coffee beans for several years. We are now pleased to offer a menu of unique selections for your enjoyment. The selection of soups will be hand-crafted in our kitchen daily. Our sandwiches are made with breads from the best of the local bakers. The sandwich fillings are made with fresh, high quality ingredients and presented with a unique twist for your pleasure.

We at 101 Bean Co. are proud of our food, beverages and service. We offer you guaranteed satisfaction. Please let us know if there is anything we might provide for you.

Box Lunch

For those working lunches or office get-togethers.

Cold sandwich w/ pasta salad & cookie

....	5.25
Add Cup of Soup......................	1.45
Bowl of Soup........................	2.75
Chips....................................	.75

Each Box Lunch includes fresh lettuce & tomato, mayonnaise & mustard packets, napkins & utensils.

Delivery Available for orders over $50.00 with one day's notice.

15% gratuity added to all deliveries.

Specialty Beverages

Espresso	Caffe Latte
Cappuccino	Caffe Mocha
Con Panna	Macchiato
Brevé	Frappé
Italian Sodas	

101 BEAN CO.

9220 Metcalf
Overland Park, Kansas 66212

tel: 642.3267 (64-BEANS)
fax: 913 642.5037

FIGURE 10.1. Another example of the quick service restaurant is the coffee house which utilizes a limited menu. This differentiates it from the coffee shop which has a larger and more diverse menu. The back of the menu is shown on the left and the front of the menu is show on the right. (*Courtesy of the 101 Bean Co., Overland Park, KS*)

All sandwiches served with simple pasta salad, green salad or cup of soup

Bowl of soup with sandwich add $1.00

1/2 cold sandwich available for $1.00 off regular price

Soups

Gourmet Soups
Hand-Crafted Daily with a Variety of Fresh Ingredients.

Cup of Soup $1.45

Bowl of Soup With a Slice of Bread $2.95

Cup of Soup, Small Salad and Slice of Bread $3.95

Bowl of Soup, Small Salad and Slice of Bread $4.95

Quiche

Quiche Lorraine $3.25

With Cup of Soup $4.35

With Green Salad $4.35

Salads

All Gourmet Salads served with a slice of bread

Mediterranean Garden Salad
Romaine, Red Onions, Tomatoes, Black Olives, Feta Cheese and Vinaigrette $4.75

Tuscany Spring Salad
"Spring" Salad Mix, Roasted Walnuts, Feta Cheese, Red Grapes and Honey Balsamic Vinaigrette $4.95

Caesar Salad
Romaine, Croutons, Parmesan Cheese and Caesar Dressing $4.75

Oven Roasted Sandwiches

Italian Croque Monsieur
Provolone, Swiss, Cheddar, Ham and Tart Apple Slices on Italian Bread $4.95

Spicy Italian Po-Boy
Capicola, Salami, Pepper Cheese, Lettuce, Tomato and Mayo on a Hoagie Roll $4.95

Roasted Vegetables with Melted Provolone
Sweet Red Onion, Zucchini, Yellow Squash, Green and Red Peppers, Tomatoes and Herbed Cream Cheese on Focaccia $4.95

Italian Tuna Salad & Provolone on a Hoagie Roll
Finished with Lettuce, Tomato, Red Onion, Pepperocini Pepper Rings and Vinaigrette Dressing $4.95

Calzone
Filled with Italian Sausage, Peppers, Onions, Spicy Tomato Sauce, and Provolone Cheese $5.25

Cold Sandwiches

Tuna Salad on Italian Bread
Tuna Salad with Lettuce and Tomato $4.75

Chicken Salad on Italian Bread
Chicken Breast, Tart Apples, Celery, Scallions and Mayonnaise $4.95

Club Sandwich
Sliced Turkey Breast and Smoked Ham, Cheddar Cheese, Lettuce, Tomato and Mayonnaise on Italian Bread $5.25

Turkey Breast on Italian Bread
Sliced Turkey Breast, Mayonnaise, Spicy Mustard, Lettuce and Tomato $4.95

Pesto Veggie on 9–Grain Bread
Pesto, Herbed Cream Cheese, Tomatoes, Red Onions, Lettuce, Cucumbers and Sprouts $4.45

FIGURE 10.1. (*Continued*) The inside of the menu is shown here.

tively short period of time to produce and serve the menu. The primary benefit from this factor is a lower wage per hour resulting in a lower total payroll. A simple menu also allows these unskilled people to produce an acceptable product that meets the company's standards and the customer's expectations. Finally, a limited menu takes away from customer indecision, which greatly slows down service. There's an old industry story about why a restaurant owner carried only vanilla ice cream. "If I added chocolate, it would take the customer forever to decide." Although this may not be totally valid, it does bear some truth. A limited menu definitely speeds up service.

STANDARDIZATION

Another important criterion in writing quick service menus is the ability of an item to be standardized—one of the key features of chain operations. The independent operator can follow the same approach. Standardization means that the product must be of the same quality and quantity time after time. It must be identical whether a customer orders it in San Francisco or Kansas City. Therefore, when deciding on a menu item, determine how closely that product can be controlled. For example, if an operation were deciding between adding a 4-oz. hamburger to the menu or a 3-oz. roast beef sandwich, in terms of control, they should opt for the hamburger. A preformed 4-oz. hamburger patty can be obtained from any meat packer. With this item, there is no question. A 4-oz. (precooked weight) hamburger will be served each and every time one is ordered. With the roast beef sandwich, on the other hand, many things can go wrong in terms of control. For example, each roast will differ in its fat-to-lean ratio. Each roast has a different weight. As a result, the yield will not be constant. Purchasing a precooked roast would solve part of the problem, but what about portion control? Can the server be counted on to put exactly 3 ounces of sliced beef on a sandwich each and every time? Probably not. Quick service standards need to be precise and exact. If a standard calls for three pickle slices on a sandwich, it doesn't mean two or four; it means three—period! As soon as people start thinking that four pickle slices would be better, they become dangerous to the organization. Each menu item must be explored by the menu writer for possible variations by the staff. The fewer variations that are made, the better will be management's control over the operation.

Finally, we must consider the equipment. As discussed in a previous chapter, the restaurant must have the proper equipment and capacity to produce the item. Consider the following anecdote concerning a well-known quick service chain. This chain decided to add coleslaw to its menu. A formula was developed, costs were established, a selling price was determined, and purchasing specifications were written. The material was sent to the stores in the field. They forgot one thing, however—the equipment necessary to produce the coleslaw. As one executive from this company put it, "Things got so bad, we had managers chopping cabbage on their desks." Although making sure that the proper equipment is available may seem obvious, even the largest companies make mistakes.

TEST MARKETING

Once a tentative decision has been made to add a new item to the menu, the item should be test marketed. After all, a menu is written for customers. It may be perfect for the restaurant, but if the new listing is not accepted, all is for naught. Each quick service chain has certain markets they designate as test markets. Normally these markets are demographically typical of the country as a whole. A new menu item is tested in these areas to determine customer acceptance. If it passes the test, the item is then introduced chainwide. If it fails, it goes on the shelf.

Not only is customer acceptability tested, but also the effect the item has on the total product mix of the store is tested. Assume, for example, that the new item has a lower gross profit than another menu listing and that it takes sales away from that particular listing. This would result in a lower total gross profit. Therefore, the new item, however well received by customers, would be totally unacceptable to the chain. Independent quick service operations, even though they don't have test stores, should also carefully test new items using blackboards, table tents, or point-of-purchase signs before making them a permanent part of the menu.

MARKETING

Once a new menu listing has passed its test, it is marketed throughout the chain. The marketing function in quick service restaurants determines more than anything which items on a menu will sell. Two criteria are used to determine which items to market: those items that have a high gross profit, and new items that will bring new customers into the store. Feature these items in your advertising.

Quick service restaurants started out with only one or two items on their menus. Their efforts were concentrated on expanding their chains across the country. While these chains were expanding, new companies entered the market. This led to overcrowding and, in some cases, market saturation. As this happened, the byword became increased store sales. With expansion less

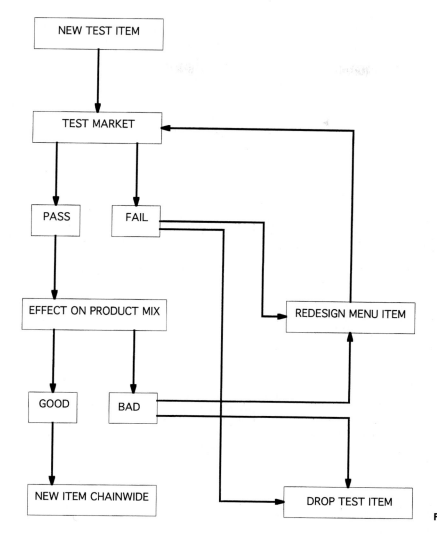

FIGURE 10.2. New item test model.

prevalent in the chain's total sales, the only place left to obtain increases was with each individual store contributing more sales. To achieve this, the quick service companies looked to the menu. Slowly and carefully adding new items to reach a greater market, they increased store sales by menu changes appealing to a broader base. In addition to this, they expanded their hours of operation with the addition of breakfast. At first, only a few chains experimented with this novel idea, then one by one the others fell into line with virtually every quick service restaurant now serving breakfast.

What is a limited menu? That's a good question, because even the experts can't agree. Some chains still cling to the few menu items, while others, even though they classify themselves as quick service, resemble mini coffee shops. How far will the chains go with menu expansion? How far can they go before the concept of simple and limited menus with fast service is destroyed? As of this writing, these questions go unanswered.

One observation, however, is clear. The pendulum swings back and forth. Quick service companies add to and delete from their menus. During one period, the byword is menu expansion. During another period, it is back to basics with limited offerings. Perhaps this youngest segment of the restaurant industry is still trying to find itself.

CONCESSIONS

Food service in sports arenas and stadiums is big business. Many of the newer facilities have fine dining, theme restaurants, and/or catering service to luxury boxes, as well as the familiar concession stands. The concepts of menu planning for the restaurants were covered in a previous chapter, and delivery to private boxes follows the same premises as hotel room service delivery. The concession stands likewise should conform to the same rules for fast food with a few minor additions.

In addition to limited, simple, standardized, and fast, concession stands also need to be concerned with volume. However, their sales must be limited to a very short period of time, as the average ballgame or concert lasts only from 4 to 6 hours. This makes the previously mentioned principles paramount to success. The menu selections must also take into account the fact that people are there for a good time—to have fun—and nutritious, healthful food is not included in the mix. Nachos, popcorn, hot dogs, pizza, ice cream, cotton candy, peanuts, beer, and soda are the staples. It must taste good, be easily packaged, and be sold quickly.

Packaging is very important, not only for the ease of the customer or vendor in delivery to the seats, but in many cases for cost control. Most concessionaires control their costs by strict inventory control. Hot dogs, buns, popcorn boxes, soda and beer cups, packs of peanuts, and the like are all counted prior to and after the event. Closing inventory is subtracted from opening inventory for each item to ascertain what the sales should be by product. The product sales are then added together for total sales, which should equal the cash sales of that particular stand.

DELIS

The term *deli* refers to a small operation that limits its sales to cold meats, salads, breads, and pastries—not to be confused with the large delicatessens found in most major cities that closely resemble a coffee shop or theme restaurant and thus would follow those menu principles.

Delis are, in reality, two businesses in one: quick service and bulk sales. The quick service aspect of the business follows the pre-

FIGURE 10-3. Example of drive-thru service (left) and drive-thru menu (right). (*Courtesy of Taco Bell*)

viously discussed concepts of quick service menu planning with one exception—most of the sandwiches are prepared to order. Salads are, for the most part, packaged to order as well. Thus, speed is less of a factor than quality and the satisfaction of the customers, who are able to choose their own ingredients.

In addition to individually portioned items, bulk sales are an important part of the overall sales mix of a deli. Meats and cheese sold by the pound; salads sold by the pint, quart, or pound; and bakery products sold by the dozen make up a large part of the business. Meat, cheese, and vegetable platters are also sold, and many delis have an extensive catering business as well.

Paramount to menu planning in delis is the ability of the products to retain freshness as well as taste.

DRIVE-THRU, DELIVERY, AND BOXED TO GO

Although three totally different concepts are presented here, they all have two things in common with regard to menu planning: the items selected for the menu must have the ability to be packaged for easy handling, and they must have the capacity to hold temperature and quality over a period of time. While drive-thru and delivery operations are for the most part an extension of existing quick service operations, they offer a new challenge to the menu planner. *Drive-thru* patrons must have access to all the items on the regular menu and, therefore, packaging becomes of utmost importance to the entire menu. While most quick service restaurants have drive-thrus, *delivery*, on the other hand, may or may not be offered by a restaurant depending on whether its menu can withstand holding qualities for a period of 30 minutes or more. Some restaurants that offer delivery may not offer the entire menu for delivery, allowing only those items that have excellent holding qualities to be delivered. While many restaurants do their own delivery, there are some enterprising individuals who have formed companies that will deliver for several restaurants in a particular area, thus giving the customer a selection of places and items from which to choose.

Boxed to go is the newest segment of our industry and caters to the working person who does not have the time or inclination to cook, but would prefer to eat at home rather than in a restaurant. These operations are found in storefronts, supermarkets, and as extensions of established restaurants. In addition to offering menu selections that have holding qualities and can be readily packaged, these items should also be microwaveable.

CONCLUSION

Quick service restaurants should carefully choose menu items for simplicity: simple to prepare, package, and serve. The menu should be limited with careful attention to standardization. The less room there is for error, the better the operation will run.

To summarize previous chapters, the concluding comment has been, "It's just that simple." In this chapter, it is fact. It's just that simple.

QUESTIONS

1. Discuss the relationship among simplicity, sales, and profit in the quick service industry.

2. Choose a quick service restaurant in your area and develop a new menu item using the skills you learned in this chapter.

3. Develop a quick service menu for a new trend or type of cuisine that is not represented in the quick service industry.

4. In your opinion, have the quick service chains gone too far with menu expansion, or is this expansion justified? Defend your answer with concrete examples.

5. Drive-thrus have a variety of layouts. Check out the local menu boards and designs of quick service restaurants. How would you improve upon them? Should the drive-thru menus be limited? Defend your answer.

CHAPTER ELEVEN

Coffee Shop Menus

OBJECTIVES   By the completion of this chapter, the reader should be able to:

- Explain the primary structure for coffee shops regarding pricing, staffing, and complexity of listings.
- Describe the importance of variety and balance in coffee shop menus.
- Generate menus that have the familiar listings as well as innovative and cutting-edge listings.

IMPORTANT TERMS

Moderation
Variety
Three-in-one menu
Club breakfast

Continental breakfast
Balance
Check average

INTRODUCTION

Coffee shop menus are as diverse as the restaurants themselves. Although some offer breakfast items exclusively and are open only during early morning hours, most coffee shops provide breakfast, lunch, and dinner. Some are even open 24 hours a day. In addition to the main meals, many offer snacks, fountain items, and late suppers. In some areas coffee shops are better known as family restaurants. Their size and style vary considerably from the simple, small diner to the heavily decored California coffee shop often seating 200 or more. Although many coffee shops today are free-standing units, an equal number share space in a variety of settings—hotels, truck stops, diners, and shopping malls, among others.

Not surprisingly, coffee shops are often confused with coffee houses because the names are sometimes used interchangeably. There are, however, major differences between the two. Coffee houses do not offer an extensive menu, instead limiting their listings to various types of specialty coffees, teas, imported waters, and sodas. Some have a very confined menu of biscottis, muffins, and other baked goods, while others may have a limited menu of soups, salads, and sandwiches. To avoid confusion, the phrase "coffee shops" is used to describe restaurants with full menus (family restaurants). Coffee house menus are covered in the quick service chapter.

GENERAL PRINCIPLES

If one word had to be chosen to describe coffee shop menus, it would have to be *moderation*. The range of selling prices, the menu items themselves, the skill level of the kitchen and service personnel, and the descriptive terminology are all moderate. However, do not confuse moderate with plain or boring. Nothing could be further from the truth. Coffee shop menus can be exciting and trendy as well as moderate.

Because each coffee shop serves a unique market, the menu writer must know and understand the clientele. The principles presented in this chapter cover the majority of coffee shops and, therefore, a wide range of demographics. Usually, prices are in the low to moderate range. Care must be exercised in this area because we are dealing with a dual-edged sword. The object of the menu listings chosen is to create as high a check average as possible to ensure profitability, but at the same time keep the selling price within the range of the clientele.

The skills of the cooking staff are frequently limited. Therefore, the menu items should not be complicated to prepare. The service personnel, likewise, should not be expected to perform at high levels of achievement or to possess much sales ability. The menu, although simple, must sell the customer. Do not expect your service personnel to do it for you.

One of the objectives in coffee shops is a high table turnover and, therefore, the menu items should mirror this objective. The items should be either ready-to-serve listings or short-order items. *Ready-to-serve items* are prepared ahead by the kitchen staff and are available for service when the customer orders them. Some examples include beef stew, soup, and chicken a la king. *Short orders,* on the other hand, are prepared when the customer orders them and should be cooked within a relatively short period. Examples are eggs, hot cakes, hamburgers (cooked to order), or sandwiches. Even one item on the menu that takes an extraordinary amount of time to prepare or requires extensive handwork could very easily slow table turnover. This is a lose-lose situation both for the coffee shop in decreased sales, and for the customer, who must wait unnecessarily.

Another element to consider in coffee shop menus is the terminology used on the menu. Because the food and setting of a coffee shop are both relatively simple, the menu should be equally uncomplicated. Foreign terms should be avoided and the terminology should be kept modest. This does not mean, however, that descriptive terminology should be avoided. Simple but exciting words that describe and sell should be used, since the menu, not the staff, must create sales. As previously stated, the service staff has limited training, limited experience, and limited time.

Both hospitality management students and patrons frequently observe that coffee shop menus are quite dull and include common items that one can get in any other establishment. Such menus lack imagination. Although coffee shop menus should be simple and uncomplicated, they do *not* have to be dull! When writing the menu, in addition to listing the known sellers that all coffee shops offer, feature some items that are characteristic of the region, as well as new and exciting cutting-edge items. However, interest and excitement must be balanced with simplicity and efficiency. Remember the people involved with the operation—the staff and their skills, the clientele and their potential.

Unusual, new, and exciting items add sales to any coffee shop. If the back-of-the-house skill level is not sufficient, try incorporating some convenience foods for menu variety. Test new items to see whether they will gain customer acceptance. One way to do this is to utilize clip-ons. Another method is taste testing with present customers. Give each one a small sample and note their reactions. If the reactions are favorable, then a new menu item has been created.

BREAKFAST

To investigate the makeup of coffee shop menus, start with breakfast. The general population in the United States is not consistent in its attitude toward this meal. Many people subscribe to the notion that breakfast is the most important nutritional meal of the day; others are content with a cup of coffee to get them going. One thing is certain: People are always in a hurry at breakfast. Whether they overslept, had to take the children to school, or are even on schedule, they must arrive at work on time, and therefore have little time for breakfast. On the other hand, senior citizens have the time to socialize and quite often do so over breakfast. Theirs is a steady market that gives the restaurant a consistent sales volume. Therefore, the menu writer must take into account speed of service and variety in order to cover everyone. Increasing the difficulty of the task is the fact that the majority of breakfast items are cooked to order.

The makeup of the menu should include a la carte items, as well as club breakfasts, which are nothing more than combinations of a la carte items. Club breakfasts or specials are usually complete and should include an appetizer such as a fruit or juice as well as an entree with potatoes, toast, and beverage. Club breakfasts are priced lower as a package than the same individual items ordered a la carte. Because customers have come to expect a value or a price bargain, club breakfasts should always be featured.

Another combination similar to a club breakfast is the continental breakfast, which consists of juice or fruit; Danish, muffin, biscuit, or toast; and coffee or tea. Since nothing is cooked to order on a continental breakfast, it is quick to serve and normally has a lower selling price than a club breakfast, making it a very popular menu item.

The menu itself should be set up in headings utilizing the following categories: juices, fruits, cereals, eggs, meats, griddle cakes, waffles, side orders, bakery items, and beverages.

Juices

The number one selling juice is orange juice and should, by all means, be on every menu. Canned juice is a rather undesirable product and should be avoided. Frozen orange juice, on the other hand, is very tasty, economical, and efficient, and it is used in many operations. In restaurants where customers are willing to pay the extra price, fresh squeezed orange juice is advisable and even mandatory if the location is near an orange-growing region.

Other juices to consider include tomato, V-8, cranberry, pineapple, grapefruit, apple, and prune juice. In addition to these, juice blends such as cranapple, cran-raspberry, and tropical combinations featuring exotic fruits such as papaya, guava, and kiwi might be considered. The extent of variety and the specific types of juices to list on the menu depend on customer demographics. For example, in areas where there are many elderly people, prune juice is an excellent seller. However, in other areas where the population is made up of primarily younger people or blue collar workers, it would be a very slow seller.

Fruit

The fruit category requires considerable planning and common sense. Depending on the type of food service operation and the price range of the menu, fruits listed can be canned, frozen, or fresh. When listing fresh fruits, include only those that are available all year, for example, bananas, apples, oranges, or grapefruit. In some regions a greater selection is available, giving the menu writer a greater latitude of offerings. Nothing is more tacky on the menu than the line "Fresh fruits in season—ask your server." Cantaloupe, honeydew, strawberries, and other fruits with limited seasons would best be offered to the customer by the use of a table tent, a clip-on, or the suggestion of the service staff. Another approach is to list a fresh fruit compote on the menu. Describe it as "a medley of fresh fruits carefully selected by our chef." By not being specific as to the content, the ingredients can change as the seasons change.

Breakfast menus are somewhat mundane, with every operation selling basically the same items. The fruit category is an area where some different items can be added, giving something distinct that the competition does not have. When using fresh fruit, be careful with the types of fruits that are listed and the amount purchased, since they are perishable. Any items that have to be thrown out or discounted will directly affect the food cost of the restaurant.

Cereals

Cereals are listed on the menu as hot or cold. Hot cereals have severely declined in popularity in the past several years although they are still popular with senior citizens. Whether hot cereals are listed on the menu depends on customer demographics and the amount of the product that could be sold. Dry cereals are fairly popular and a wide assortment can be had by ordering the "variety" pack. They are fast and easy to serve and should be used on breakfast specials where speed is of the essence. Cereals can be served with either milk or half and half or, if you are featuring a diet combination, skim milk. If there is an extra charge for half and half, it should be so stated on the menu. An excellent way to increase the average check in a breakfast operation is to add fruit to the cereal. Bananas, which are available year round, are a good choice, but the fruit can also be seasonal, such as strawberries. Cereal might also be added to a continental breakfast of coffee, juice, and a roll. If reasonably priced, it will sell.

Eggs

Eggs are the backbone of breakfast to many people. They can be prepared several ways: fried, sunny-side-up, over easy, boiled, scrambled, shirred, and poached. Check local laws, since some jurisdictions dictate that egg yolks must be thoroughly cooked (hard) to prevent potential salmonella poisoning. Omelets are another popular way to present eggs, as well as an excellent way to increase the average check of the restaurant. Several varieties can be listed on the menu or the customers could create their own if the menu simply lists the basic price of an omelet and, beneath that, the various ingredients to choose from such as ham, sausage, bacon, onion, green pepper, mushroom, and cheese, to name a few. In addition to these items, the egg category on the menu can feature many other exciting items. Eggs Benedict or Florentine, huevos rancheros, or a breakfast taco made up of scrambled eggs, sausage, green pepper, onion, and hash browns, cooked together and folded in a warm flour tortilla, are but a few of the many selections available.

Meat

The meat category should include the three basics—ham, bacon, and sausage. The sausage listing could be either patties or links, with many menus mentioning both. To give some variety to the menu, other meats such as steak, Canadian bacon, Italian sausage, or scrapple—a Pennsylvania Dutch favorite made from pork and cornmeal—could be added. In addition to meat, this category could also include fish such as smoked salmon or lox served with a bagel, cream cheese, sliced tomatoes, and capers.

Waffles and Griddle Cakes

The waffle and griddle cake category also includes French toast. Griddle cakes, also known as hot cakes or pancakes, are relatively easy to prepare and do not take a great deal of time, which is also the case with French toast.

Waffles, on the other hand, are more time consuming because of the equipment involved. Each waffle iron produces only one waffle and, when that is completed, the iron needs recovery time to allow it to return to its proper temperature. Although waffles are very good sellers, the skill level of the kitchen staff and the number of irons need to be sufficient to produce this item adequately. If not, and the restaurant is serving an excellent product with a high level of waffle sales, the kitchen could easily get stacked up with back orders.

Sales appeal can be added to waffles, griddle cakes, and French toast by offering a variety of syrups. Higher check averages can be obtained by offering various fruit toppings such as fresh or frozen peaches, strawberries, or cinnamon flavored apples. Belgian waffles, which require a different formula as well as a different waffle iron, command a high selling price along with a high gross profit.

Bakery

An operation can really excel in the bakery category. Sweet rolls; Danish; doughnuts; coffee cake; hot biscuits with butter and jam or hot biscuits with sausage gravy; cereal muffins such as bran; and fruit muffins such as apple or blueberry greatly increase the sales of any coffee shop. In addition to these are English muffins, croissants, and bagels.

If the operation is large with a bakery, these listings will not be a problem. If the operation is small, a wide variety of convenience foods are available to increase the bakery section on the menu. Many mixes on the market make it relatively easy to produce many of these items. Frozen doughs, which need simply to be thawed, proofed, and baked, are also available.

When writing the bakery section of the menu, do not forget the basic item: toast, which could be either white, whole wheat, or rye.

Side Orders

Side orders incorporate any other items not listed in the other categories. One predominant listing in this category is starches including potatoes (American fried, lyonnaise, and hash browned) or grits. Other miscellaneous items can include cream cheese to go with bagels, sliced tomatoes, or a side order of sausage gravy.

Beverages

Beverages are basically self-explanatory, including coffee (both regular and decaf), Sanka, tea (regular, exotic blends, herbal, and decaf), milk (regular, 2 or 1 percent, and skim), buttermilk, chocolate milk, and hot chocolate.

CLUB BREAKFASTS

Club breakfasts are made up of combinations of a la carte items and should be all-inclusive with the possible exception of beverages. Although some restaurants charge extra for beverages, others include it on the club breakfast. "All-inclusive" means including such items as juice or fruit; potatoes or grits; and toast, bagels, muffins, or English muffins. It is very tacky to have a nice assortment of club breakfasts with the words "hash browned potatoes extra." Club breakfasts should incorporate such listings as eggs, omelets, and hot cakes, waffles, or French toast. All these listings should include a choice of bacon, ham, or sausage.

The menu should also include one relatively fast club breakfast that a customer could be served in a short period of time, for example, scrambled eggs with diced ham, hash browns, toast, jelly, and coffee. Prepared ahead of time, these items are simply plated when the customer orders them.

LUNCH AND DINNER

The next two sections to be examined, lunch and dinner, have many inherent similarities. So their meals will be discussed concurrently. For example, the menu categories are very similar. These include appetizers, soups, salads, entrees, sandwiches, side orders, desserts, and beverages. Whether to include all these listings for both meals depends on several factors.

First, think about the *clientele* that the family restaurant is attempting to serve. If the demographics dictate a predominantly blue collar clientele, the check average will probably be lower than in a coffee shop catering to a white collar clientele with a higher average income. As a result, appetizers, soups, and salads will probably play a diminished role and can possible be combined. Sandwiches will probably outsell entrees and should be so featured. Entrees should be priced on the lower side and the selections generic. Desserts also play a diminished role.

In a coffee shop where a higher *check average* is desired, it is wise to include appetizers, soups, and salads as separate listings, both on the luncheon menu as well as on the dinner menu. Conversely, it might be advisable to drop sandwiches, or at least lessen their role, on the dinner menu since they tend to lower the check average. Entree listings can be less generic with some simple cutting-edge combinations highlighted. Desserts should also be featured to help increase sales.

The *skill level* of the production staff also has a bearing on the number of categories you would use. With the advent of convenience foods, it is simple to include several categories even if the employee skill level is low.

The *operating philosophy* of the restaurant also needs to be considered. If the scope of the operation is limited, then all categories should not be used. If the coffee shop is complete, that is "being all things to all people," then a comprehensive menu should be the goal.

The categories chosen should create balance. Certainly, the menu should be nutritionally balanced. This is imperative in coffee shop menus since many of the customers served are the same patrons day after day. Although the industry's job is not to force nutrition on our customers, there is a responsibility to offer a nutritionally balanced meal. Customers decide for themselves how they wish to eat.

Other balances to consider are hot/cold, textures, and cooking methods. Balance as a whole will be discussed later within each category. When you write a menu, balance forces you to compose an exciting, varied menu. A well-balanced menu will not be dull, repetitious, or uninteresting. To make sure the menu has balance and variety, a menu pattern could be used. This would predetermine the number of items in each category, their color, texture, cooking methodology, temperature, and so on. Menu patterns can be devised for any combination desired, and their use ensures that balance and variety are achieved.

Some general statements on the differences between luncheon and dinner menus are in order. Items on luncheon menus should be lighter in terms of fat content than those on dinner menus. Portion sizes should be smaller and, consequently, the selling price should be lower. The speed of preparation should also be taken into account. While breakfast menus focus on speed, lunch is a divided affair: Some patrons will be in a hurry due to a limited lunch break, while others whose time is not restricted will demand a slower pace. Dinner, on the other hand, is almost always a more leisurely meal.

Appetizers

In analyzing the various categories on the luncheon and dinner menus, start with appetizers. If the appetizer category is used, several selections should be offered—some hot, some cold. Balance should be sought among meat, seafood, fruit, and vegetables. Other food groups, such as cheese, could be included. Avoid using the same cooking technique on all hot items. Too many menus list only a variety of breaded or tempura battered vegetables—all fried. With the ever-increasing health-conscious market, raw vegetables with a dip or a fresh fruit and cheese board are becoming very popular.

Soups

The second category, soups, is closely aligned with appetizers and, in many instances, is combined with it. The number and variety of soups listed depend on your particular operation; however, at least one, a soup du jour, is indispensable. When offering two or more soups, balance a clear soup with a cream or chowder-type soup.

This category is critical to the success of your operation since many coffee shops have built a reputation on the quality of their soups and some have even become famous for a particular soup. Obviously, the best quality is obtained from preparing your own on your premises. Nothing is more insulting to a customer than to offer a bowl of canned soup for $1.90, when they can prepare it themselves at home for 70¢. Let your imagination run wild, creating new and exciting offerings for your customers. Soup is also an excellent food cost item, particularly when the cost is lowered even more by utilizing leftovers. Soups also offer menu versatility when used in combination with sandwiches and salads.

Salads

Salads are rapidly gaining popularity as diet-conscious Americans turn away from fried foods to more lightly prepared offerings. Salads are of primary importance in markets that cater to white collar clientele. Balance in the variety of salads offered is important and could include fruit, vegetable, and meat, poultry, fish, and seafood.

Fresh fruit salads with sherbet are excellent sellers in season. Because of their seasonality, they should be promoted by a table tent or clip-on. The most common salad and the top seller in many coffee shops is the familiar chef's salad which consists of greens topped with ham, chicken or turkey, cheese, and tomato wedges. By all means, this should be on every coffee shop menu. Other entree salads should also be offered. Greens topped with blackened, sautéed, or grilled chicken, served either hot or cold, with a vinaigrette is popular because it is, relatively speaking, low in fat. Grilled fish, such as tuna, along with shrimp or scallops served over tossed greens also fall into this category. Fresh spinach salad and tossed garden greens are also popular.

A word about salad dressings—make them distinctly yours. They are simple to make in large batches and have a good shelf life when properly refrigerated. Avoid factory-made dressings if at all possible, but, if you must use them, at least alter them for individuality. Cold meat platters sell year round. Chicken and tuna salads, whether arranged on a cold plate with other fresh vegetables or stuffed in a ripe tomato, are also good sellers. Try new ideas when building the salad section of your menu. The result will be increased sales.

Entrees

The entree section of the menu is the most important since it contributes the highest gross profit dollars and the entire operation is judged by it. It is critically important that the pricing structure fall within the framework of your demographic guidelines. Balance among the food groups is also important and should contain a variety of beef, veal, pork, lamb, poultry, and seafood, as well as vegetables. The only exceptions occur if one of these happens to be ethnically unacceptable in your trade area. Conversely, one of the groups may predominate your area and the selections would therefore be increased and highlighted on the menu. You must provide a variety of cooking methods, using roasting, broiling, sauteing, pan frying, grilling, and deep fat frying. As previously mentioned, fried and deep fat fried foods should be downplayed, and broiled and baked items given more predominance than in the past.

The entree section food groups can be broken down further into solid, semisolid, and extenders. Typical *solid* entrees include steak, pork or lamb chops, fried or baked chicken, and shrimp or fish filets. *Semisolid* items include meat loaf, Salisbury steak, and ham or chicken croquettes. *Extenders* are casserole items such as beef stew, chicken a la king, ham and beans, and pasta. Each of these has its place on the menu; the solids get a high selling price, increasing the check average but yielding a low gross profit. The semisolids and extenders get a lower selling price, but a higher gross profit. Among the three, the result is a good product mix with a satisfying gross profit.

FIGURE 11.1. A complete coffee shop menu. (*Courtesy of Flagstar Corporation, operators of Denny's Restaurants, Spartanburg, South Carolina*)

Moons Over My Hammy 4.59

The supreme ham and egg sandwich, made with Swiss and American cheese on grilled sourdough. Served with choice of hashed browns or French fries.

Southern Slam 3.89

Two steamy, buttermilk biscuit halves, covered with rich, country sausage gravy and served with two eggs, two bacon strips and two sausage links.

All-American Slam 4.59

Three eggs scrambled with Cheddar cheese. Served with hashed browns, two sausage links, two bacon strips and choice of toast, buttermilk biscuit or English muffin.

Chicken-Fried Steak and Eggs 4.85

A southern specialty. Served with country gravy and hashed browns. Choice of toast, buttermilk biscuit or English muffin.

Day Breaks

You may substitute _____, in any breakfast for an additional 25¢. Low-calorie syrup available upon request.

Look for this symbol for our famous signature entrées.

BEVERAGES

Denny's Mug O'Coffee
Our famous private blend.
Regular or decaffeinated .... .80
Hot Chocolate .... .80
Hot Tea, Herbal Tea .... .80
Freshly Brewed Iced Tea .... .95
Soft Drinks, Lemonade .... .99
Milk:
Regular (10 oz.) .... .80
Large (16 oz.) 1.00
Juice:
Orange, Apple, Grapefruit or Tomato
Regular (10 oz.) .... .89
Large (16 oz.) 1.29

Free refills on coffee, soft drinks, lemonade and tea.

OTHER POPULAR FAVORITES

Two-Egg Breakfast with Ham 4.40
Served with hashed browns and choice of toast, buttermilk biscuit or English muffin.
Two-Egg Breakfast 2.90
With four bacon strips or four sausage links 4.20
Steak and Eggs 5.99
U.S.D.A. Choice top sirloin steak and two eggs, served with hashed browns and choice of toast, buttermilk biscuit or English muffin.

GRIDDLE FAVORITES

Buttermilk Pancakes with Bacon or Sausage 3.45
Three fluffy pancakes served with warm, rich syrup and two bacon strips or two sausage links.
Buttermilk Pancakes 2.55
French Toast with Bacon or Sausage 3.65
Extra thick, batter-dipped and perfectly browned. Served with warm, rich syrup and two bacon strips or two sausage links.
French Toast 2.75
Belgian Waffle with Bacon or Sausage 3.65
A crisp, golden waffle served with warm, rich syrup and two bacon strips or two sausage links.
Belgian Waffle 2.75
Belgian Waffle Supreme 3.35
Covered with strawberry or blueberry topping and whipped cream.

BREAKFAST SIDES

Large Egg	.79	Bagel and Cream Cheese	1.30
Smoked Ham Slice	1.99	Buttermilk Biscuit	.85
Bacon or Sausage	1.95	Biscuit and Sausage Gravy	1.69
Hashed Browns	.99	Grits	.95
Toast or English Muffin	.85	Hot or Cold Cereal	1.10
Hot Cinnamon Roll	.99	Applesauce	.75
Blueberry Muffin	.99	Fresh Fruit in Season	1.00
NEW! Banana-Nut Muffin	.99	Mixed Fruit	1.00

FIGURE 11.1. *(Continued)*

International Slam™ 3.99

Two French toast halves and half of a golden Belgian waffle, served with two bacon strips, two sausage links and two eggs.

Original Grand Slam Breakfast® 3.69

A Denny's original. Two buttermilk hotcakes, two eggs, two bacon strips and two sausage links.

Scram Slam™ 4.89

Three eggs scrambled with Cheddar cheese, mushrooms, green peppers and onions, then topped with diced tomatoes. Served with hashed browns, two sausage links, two bacon strips and choice of toast, buttermilk biscuit or English muffin.

French Slam® 3.89

Four extra thick, batter-dipped halves of lightly browned bread, served with two eggs, two bacon strips and two sausage links.

All omelettes are served with hashed browns and choice of toast, buttermilk biscuit or English muffin.

Harvest Slam™ 3.99

Two whole wheat, apple, nut and spice hotcakes with rich apple topping. Served with two eggs cooked just the way you want them, two strips of bacon and two sausage links.

Veggie-Cheese Omelette 4.89

A fluffy three-egg omelette with sautéed onions, green peppers and sliced mushrooms, add Cheddar cheese and tomato slices, then top it with chopped green onions.

Mexican Omelette 4.99

A three-egg omelette filled with spicy ground beef and Cheddar cheese, topped with diced tomatoes. Served with salsa and sour cream.

Ham 'n' Cheddar Omelette 4.79

Diced ham and Cheddar cheese in a fluffy three-egg omelette.

Chili-Cheese Omelette 4.79

A three-egg omelette filled with Cheddar cheese and chili, then topped with even more chili and cheese.

Cereal Combo 3.55

Hot or cold cereal, with mixed fruit or banana and a regular-size glass of juice. Served with choice of toast, buttermilk biscuit, English muffin, blueberry muffin, banana-nut muffin or bagel.

Ultimate Omelette® 4.95

Three eggs wrapped around sautéed mushrooms, onions, sausage, bacon, green peppers and tomato. Topped with American cheese.

LD63

FIGURE 11.1. *(Continued)*

FIGURE 11.1. *(Continued)*

Salads

Taco Salad   4.99

Spicy ground beef, Mexican-style beans, Cheddar cheese, black olives, tomato, guacamole and sour cream. Served over mixed greens in a crispy tortilla shell. Salsa on the side.
Add bowl of soup... .99

California Grilled Chicken Salad 4.99

A tender breast of chicken, grilled and sliced. Served over mixed greens with fresh cucumber, tomato, Cheddar cheese and chopped nuts. Honey mustard dressing on the side. Served with bread.
Add bowl of soup .... .99

Chicken Melt Slam   5.19

A grilled chicken breast between two slices of Monterey Jack cheese, tomato slices and crisp bacon on grilled sourdough.
Add soup or salad .... .99

Tuna Melt Supreme   4.69

Tuna salad topped with tomatoes and bacon strips, then covered with melted American cheese, all on grilled Parmesan sourdough bread.
Add soup or salad... .99

Look for this symbol for our famous signature crisps.

Roast Beef Deluxe   4.79

Thinly sliced roast beef with sliced tomatoes and melted American cheese on grilled sourdough. Thousand Island dressing on the side.
Add soup or salad ... .99

The Super Bird®   4.79

A Denny's original. Sliced turkey breast with Swiss cheese, bacon strips and tomato slices on grilled sourdough.
Add soup or salad ..... .99

The Club   4.79

The classic triple-decker. With sliced, oven-roasted turkey breast, bacon, lettuce and tomato on toasted white bread.
Add soup or salad .... .99

Megamelt Slam   5.39

Thinly sliced ham and melted American cheese, topped with a layer of sliced roast beef, melted Monterey Jack cheese, mild green chiles and tomato slices, all on grilled sourdough. Served with French fries and coleslaw.
Add soup or salad .... .99

OTHER FAVORITES

Add soup or salad to any of these favorites for only 99¢. All sandwiches and burgers are served with our large-cut French fries and pickle chips.

Grilled Chicken Sandwich   4.60

Grilled breast of chicken, topped with lettuce and sliced tomato on an herb-toasted bun. Honey mustard dressing on the side.

Bacon, Lettuce and Tomato   3.70

Grilled Cheese on Sourdough   2.95

SIDES

NEW! Caesar Salad	1.65	Onion Rings	1.85
Garden Salad	1.65	Coleslaw	.99
Seasoned Fries	1.70	Bowl of Soup	1.65
French Fries	1.45	Bowl of Chili	1.99

Veggie-Cheese Melt   3.35

Fresh tomatoes, cucumber, guacamole and lettuce together with Monterey Jack, Swiss and American cheese on grilled multigrain bread.
Add soup or salad .... .99

FIGURE 11.1.   *(Continued)*

Bowl of Chili   1.99
A hearty bowl of chili topped with shredded Cheddar cheese. Diced onions available on request.

Seasoned Chili Fries   3.09
A heaping basket of seasoned fries topped with chili and shredded Cheddar.

Mozzarella Sticks   3.75
Breaded and golden-fried. Served with a tangy tomato sauce.
Mini Order...   1.99

NEW! Buffalo Wings   3.99
A dozen spicy chicken wings served with celery sticks and your choice of bleu cheese or ranch dressing.
Mini Order 1.99

SOUP of the DAY

DAILY
Vegetable Beef   1.65
A hearty favorite at Denny's. With beef, barley and eight garden vegetables.

MONDAY
Chicken Noodle   1.65
With chunks of chicken, egg noodles, diced onions, celery and chopped parsley.

SIDES

NEW! *Caesar Salad*	1.65
Garden Salad	1.65
Basket of French Fries	1.45
Basket of Seasoned Fries	1.70
Basket of Onion Rings	1.85
Coleslaw	.99

BEVERAGES

Denny's Mug O'Coffee™
Our famous private blend.

Regular or decaffeinated	.80
Hot Chocolate	.80
Hot Tea, Herbal Tea	.80
Freshly Brewed Iced Tea	.95
Soft Drinks, Lemonade	.99
Milk:	
Regular (10 oz.)	.80
Large (16 oz.)	1.00
Juice:	
Orange, Apple, Grapefruit or Tomato	
Regular (10 oz.)	.89
Large (16 oz.)	1.29

Free refills on coffee, soft drinks, lemonade and tea.

Denny's features Coca-Cola® classic and other popular favorites.

Chicken Strips   3.95
A basket of golden-fried chicken strips served with honey mustard dressing or tangy barbecue sauce.
Mini Order 2.49

Sampler   4.79
A delicious sampling of chicken strips, mozzarella sticks and onion rings. Served with a tangy tomato sauce and choice of barbecue sauce or honey mustard dressing.

Quesadilla   2.29
Diced tomatoes and mild green chiles, with melted Cheddar cheese, folded in a hot flour tortilla. Served with a side of sour cream, guacamole and salsa.
Chicken Quesadilla   4.29
Spicy Ground Beef Quesadilla   3.99

FIGURE 11.1.   *(Continued)*

LIGHT LUNCH COMBINATIONS

Served Monday through Friday, 11 a.m. - 2 p.m.

Fresh Garden or Caesar Salad with Bowl of Soup — 2.99

Sandwich with Choice of Bowl of Soup, Garden Salad or Caesar Salad — 3.89

Your choice of garden salad, Caesar salad or bowl of soup (vegetable beef or soup of the day) and one of the following sandwiches: turkey breast on wheat, tuna salad on white or ham and Swiss on rye.

Soups & Starters

We use only 100% soybean oil for frying.

Cocktails, wine and/or beer may be available at this restaurant. Please ask your server.

TUESDAY

Cream of Potato 1.65

Diced potatoes, green peppers, celery, carrots and onions. With a hint of bacon.

WEDNESDAY

Cream of Broccoli 1.65

A creamy combination of broccoli, cheese, celery and onions, flavored with a hint of garlic.

THURSDAY

Cheese 1.65

A delicious surprise. Mild cheese, bacon, diced celery and green onion.

Nachos Supreme 2.99

Crispy tortilla chips topped with spicy ground beef, Mexican-style beans, Cheddar cheese, green onions, diced tomatoes, black olives, guacamole and sour cream. Salsa on the side.

FRIDAY

Clam Chowder 1.65

Our famous prizewinning chowder made with clams and whitefish.

LD63

FIGURE 11.1. (*Continued*)

New York Steak   7.69

Over 1/2 lb. (precooked weight) of grilled U.S.D.A. Choice strip steak. Served with hot vegetable of the day and choice of potato or rice pilaf.

Fried Chicken   6.09

One-half chicken, southern-fried to a crispy golden brown. Served with hot vegetable of the day and choice of potato or rice pilaf.

All entrees are served with bread and choice of soup, garden salad, Caesar salad, coleslaw or fruit.

Dinner At Denny's

*Dinners served from 11 a.m.
Baked potato served from 4 p.m. - 10 p.m. only.*

*We use only 100% soybean oil for frying.
Denny's features Coca-Cola® classic
and other popular favorites.*

Roast Beef Dinner   5.99

The classic American meal. Hot roast beef on white bread, with a generous helping of mashed potatoes, both covered with rich brown gravy. Served with hot vegetable of the day.

Steak and Shrimp   7.79

U.S.D.A. Choice top sirloin with six large, golden-fried shrimp. Served with a zesty cocktail sauce, hot vegetable of the day and choice of potato or rice pilaf.

Liver with Bacon and Onions   5.29

Two slices of beef liver, lightly seasoned and grilled, then topped with onions and two bacon strips. Served with hot vegetable of the day and choice of potato or rice pilaf.

Cocktails, wine and/or beer may be available at this restaurant. Please ask your server.

Roast Turkey and Stuffing   5.99

Sliced, oven-roasted turkey breast, layered over savory stuffing with rich gravy. Served with hot vegetable of the day and choice of potato or rice pilaf. Includes cranberry sauce.

FIGURE 11.1.   (*Continued*)

Chicken Strip Dinner 5.89
Four chicken fillet strips, breaded and golden-fried. Served with hot vegetable of the day and choice of potato or rice pilaf. Honey mustard dressing on the side.

Chicken-Fried Steak 5.79
A southern specialty. Topped with rich country gravy. Served with hot vegetable of the day and choice of potato or rice pilaf.

Stir-Fry Chicken with Vegetables 5.39
Tender chunks of chicken breast, stir-fried with fresh vegetables. Served with rice pilaf and teriyaki sauce.

Spaghetti with Meatballs 5.79
A traditional favorite smothered with our tangy tomato sauce and a generous helping of meatballs.

Spaghetti 4.89
Topped with our tangy tomato sauce.

Grilled Catfish 6.45
Two tender fillets of farm-raised catfish, delicately seasoned with herbs. Served with hot vegetable of the day, tartar sauce and choice of potato or rice pilaf.

Shrimp Dinner 6.85
A dozen large shrimp, lightly breaded and golden-fried. Served with a zesty cocktail sauce, hot vegetable of the day and choice of potato or rice pilaf.

Grilled Breast of Chicken 5.99
A boneless, skinless breast of chicken, seasoned with lemon pepper and dill, then grilled. Served with hot vegetable of the day and choice of potato or rice pilaf.

Grilled Trout 6.35
A tender fillet of trout, delicately seasoned with lemon pepper and dill. Served with hot vegetable of the day, tartar sauce and choice of potato or rice pilaf.

Cod Dinner 5.99
Two fillets of tender cod, lightly battered and golden-fried. Served with hot vegetable of the day, choice of potato or rice pilaf and a side of tartar sauce.

Grilled Halibut 6.85
A tender, grilled halibut steak. Served with hot vegetable of the day, tartar sauce and choice of potato or rice pilaf.

LD63

FIGURE 11.1. (*Continued*)

FIGURE 11.1. *(Continued)*

Chocolate Cake 1.75

Calling all chocolate lovers! Luscious layers of dark chocolate cake, covered with rich chocolate icing.

Ice Cream Shakes 1.99

Here's a friend from the soda fountain days. We'll even give you an extra helping in the malt can. Try chocolate, vanilla or strawberry.

Denny's Banana Split 2.79

Rich chocolate, strawberry and vanilla ice cream smothered in hot fudge, strawberry and blueberry toppings. Crowned with whipped cream and nuts.

Denny's Mug O'Coffee .80

Our famous private blend. Regular or decaffeinated.

Finishing Touches

A la mode, add .75 Whipped topping, add .25
Pie prices and selection may vary by location.
Please ask your server for details.

Hot Fudge Cake Sundae 2.55

Triple-layer chocolate cake topped with a scoop of vanilla ice cream, hot fudge, whipped cream and nuts.

Ice Cream by the Scoop
Chocolate, vanilla or strawberry.
Single.........90
Double.... 1.20

Blueberry Cream Cheese Pie 1.85

LD63

FIGURE 11.1. *(Continued)*

Senior Selections

At Denny's, we believe our senior patrons deserve extra-special attention. That's why we offer a selection of delicious entrees which feature smaller-size portions at reduced prices. And they're all prepared exclusively for customers age 55 and over.

BREAKFAST

You may substitute _____ in any breakfast for an additional 15¢.
Low-calorie syrup available upon request.

Senior Omelette   3.50
A fluffy two-egg omelette filled with chopped onions, tomatoes, bacon and American cheese. Served with hashed browns and toast.

Senior Grand Slam® Breakfast   2.39
A large buttermilk hotcake served with one egg cooked to order, a crispy bacon strip and a sausage link.

Senior Starter   2.35
A large egg cooked the way you like it, served with hashed browns, toast and a crispy bacon strip or a sausage link.

Senior Belgian Waffle Slam®   2.49
One-half waffle, served with one large egg, a strip of crispy bacon and a sausage link.

LUNCH and DINNER

*Dinners are served with bread and your choice of soup, salad, coleslaw or fruit.
We use only 100% soybean oil for frying.*

Roast Beef   4.50
Sliced roast beef served open-faced on white bread alongside a helping of mashed potatoes, all covered with rich brown gravy. Served with hot vegetable of the day.

Fried Shrimp   4.65
Six large shrimp, lightly breaded and golden-fried, served with hot vegetable of the day, rice pilaf and cocktail sauce.

Grilled Catfish   4.50
A tender fillet of farm-raised catfish, delicately seasoned with herbs. Served with hot vegetable of the day, rice pilaf and tartar sauce.

NEW! Cod Dinner   3.85
A lightly battered, golden-fried fillet, served with hot vegetable of the day, French fries and a side of tartar sauce.

Roast Turkey and Stuffing   3.85
Sliced, oven-roasted turkey breast served with savory stuffing and rich gravy. Served with hot vegetable of the day and cranberry sauce.

Half Sandwich and Soup or Salad
Available 11 a.m. - 2 p.m. only   2.90
One-half of a tuna salad sandwich on white bread or one-half of a grilled cheese on sourdough bread with your choice of salad or bowl of vegetable beef or soup of the day.

Grilled Breast of Chicken   4.30
A tender, boneless, skinless breast of chicken. Served with hot vegetable of the day and rice pilaf.

Chicken-Fried Steak   3.75
A southern favorite. Fried to a golden brown and ladled with rich country gravy. Served with mashed potatoes and hot vegetable of the day.

Fried Chicken   3.85
Two tender pieces, southern-fried. Served with mashed potatoes, chicken gravy and hot vegetable of the day.

Sirloin Tips   3.70
Juicy sirloin tips and sautéed mushrooms in a rich brown gravy, ladled over egg noodles. Served with hot vegetable of the day.

Spaghetti with Meatballs   3.45
A traditional favorite topped with our tangy tomato sauce.

Liver with Bacon and Onions   3.55
One slice of grilled, tender beef liver topped with onions and a crispy bacon strip. Served with hot vegetable of the day and mashed potatoes with gravy.

Turkey Sandwich   3.25
Sliced turkey with lettuce and tomato on multigrain bread. Served with French fries or coleslaw.

Denny's is committed to providing the best possible service to all customers regardless of race, creed or national origin.

The above credit cards are accepted at most Denny's locations.

FIGURE 11.1.   *(Continued)*

Sandwiches

The sandwich section is almost as critical in importance as the entree section. Balance within the meat food group—beef, pork, poultry, variety meats, fish—is imperative. And so is a balance of temperature and cookery methods. Sandwiches familiar to your clientele should be featured, but include sandwiches featuring fresh vegetables served with or without cheese or cheese spreads. Variety should also be included, along with new or unusual items on the menu.

Side Orders

The side order section historically has been a miscellaneous area of the menu. If one did not know where to list an item, it automatically went to this section. Consider for a moment what side orders are; they are essentially add-ons. With proper merchandising on your menu, they can substantially increase your check average. Use them to complement your entree and sandwich sections with offerings that are compatible to these listings.

Desserts

The last section to be discussed, the dessert section, is frequently given only passing notice by otherwise good menu planners. In addition to the regular listings that are common to all coffee shops, give this section some flair. Pastries, tortes, eclairs, tarts, and fountain creations can pay dividends to the menu planner with imagination. If the skills of your kitchen staff or the proper equipment is lacking, try convenience foods. If it is properly planned and executed on the menu, you can increase the check average and also create business, particularly during the slack hours.

MENU LAYOUT

The next issue concerns layout. As you can already see, a coffee shop menu is really several menus combined into one, the most common approach in the industry today. As a matter of fact, it is called by many in the industry as a three-in-one menu. While some restaurants utilize a separate menu for each meal, the most common approach in the trade today is to combine all three meals into one printed menu. Certainly, this is the most expedient, as well as the least costly, approach to the problem. In some restaurants, due to equipment contraints or skilled kitchen staff, this method creates a logistical problem in that it might not be expedient to serve breakfast during a lunch or dinner rush. In this case, the breakfast menu is normally printed on the back along with the hours of service. During the breakfast period, the customer is handed the backside of the menu, which shows the breakfast offerings, and during the rest of the day the front side of the menu, which, when opened up, shows lunch and/or dinner listings. The method chosen—one or separate menus—is dictated by the individual needs of the restaurant.

CHILDREN'S MENUS

Children's menus offer the menu writer a challenge. Two forces are at work. The parents want a well balanced, healthful meal, while the children want food that tastes great—in other words, foods high in fat and sugar. Since the children are often the decision makers regarding the destination restaurant, it behooves management to satisfy all parties. As discussed in the chapter on nutrition, you can go about this in a number of ways: extra lean ground beef for the hamburgers, low-fat cheese for the cheeseburgers, low-fat hot dogs, and skim mozzarella for the pizzas and lasagna. This is just a start. There are many other ways a creative manager can write a healthful menu that appeals to children.

Market the concept to the parents. Tell them via institutional copy that the ingredients used to prepare their children's meals are low-fat, low-cholesterol, low-sugar, fresh, natural foods. Give extra plates to parents to share their own meal with the children at no charge. This takes the burden off the menu writer since the parent selects the meal, healthful or not.

Market to children with prizes for clean plates and coloring books to occupy them while they are waiting for their meal. If the restaurant can cover it financially, offer free meals to the children when parents purchase a dinner. Merchandise the menu to appeal to children with artwork and descriptive terminology.

ROOM SERVICE MENUS

An offshoot of the coffee shop menu is the room service menu that is used in all major hotels and in some smaller properties with food service. While there are striking similarities between the two in that they both cover all meal periods and snacks, a few major differences need to be studied.

Probably the most crucial part to room service is the facilities and staffing of this department. Because room service is expensive to maintain with its labor-intensiveness, many operations attempt to cut corners—with disastrous results. Consider the fact that one member of the waitstaff can handle 20 to 30 seats in the coffee shop and turn them over relatively quickly, but it takes one person 10 to 15 minutes to assemble an order and deliver it to one room. The room service delivery should, if properly done, be delivered in a cart that holds the temperature, either heated or chilled, of the prod-

FIGURE 11.2. A room service menu that includes institutional copy marketing the hotel's other restaurants and bars. (*Courtesy of the Doubletree Hotel, Overland Park, Kansas*)

Breakfast

Breakfast is Served

Monday through Friday from 6:30 a.m. to 11:00 a.m.

and Saturday and Sunday from 7:00 a.m. to 11:00 a.m.

Freshly Squeezed Orange Juice or Grapefruit Juice 3.25

Fruit and Vegetable Juices 2.50

Half Grapefruit 2.50

Fresh Seasonal Berries or Melon 3.50

Bakeries & Cereals

Basket of Fresh Baked Muffins 3.25

Wolferman's English Muffin 2.75

Danish Pastry 2.75

Hot and Cold Cereals with Fresh Fruit 2.95

Bagel with Cream Cheese 3.25

The Executive Express

Your Choice of Juice, Freshly Baked Muffin and Croissant.

Served with Whipped Butter, Preserves and Jams, Coffee, Tea

or Decaffeinated Coffee   5.95

The Natural

Low in Cholesterol and Saturated Fats, Naturally!

Birchermeusli 4.75

Oatmeal and cereal with fruits, berries and nuts

Whole Grain Pancakes 5.75

Fresh Fruit or Lite Maple Syrup

Veggie Frittata 6.50

Egg Beaters, Scrambled in Margarine, Crisp Vegetables, and

Lowfat Cheese

A suggested gratuity of 15% and applicable tax will be included.

Touch Extension 36 to Order   8/92

FIGURE 11.2.   *(Continued)*

Eggs & Omelettes

Served with Breakfast Potatoes and Fresh Bakeries

Skillet Eggs 6.75

    Two Eggs Any Style, with Ham, Bacon or Link Sausage

Classic Eggs Benedict 7.50

    Toasted Muffin, Canadian Bacon, Poached Eggs, Hollandaise

Three Egg Omelette 7.00

    Your Choice of Three Items: Ham, Bacon, Pepper

    Mushrooms, Cheddar, Jack or Swiss Cheese

K.C. Steak and Eggs 9.95

Cakes & Waffles

Includes Choice of Bacon, Sausage or Ham Served with

Whipped Butter and Warm Syrup.

Golden Stack 5.75

Short Stack 4.50

Belgian Waffle 6.75

    Any of the Above Topped with Fresh Berries   Add .50

Thick Sliced Cinnamon French Toast 6.50

On The Side

Hash Brown Potatoes 2.25

Link Sausage 3.00

Rasher of Bacon 3.00

Side of Ham 3.00

Canadian Bacon 3.25

One Egg .... 1.75   Two Eggs 2.50

A suggested gratuity of 15% and applicable tax will be included.

Touch Extension 36 to Order   8/92

FIGURE 11.2. *(Continued)*

Beverages

Coffee, Decaffeinated Coffee

    Small Pot (3 Cups) 3.75

    Large Pot (6 Cups) 5.50

Specialty Teas 1.00

    Assorted Flavors

Hot Chocolate, Milk 1.00

A suggested gratuity of 15% and applicable tax will be included.

Touch Extension 36 to Order   8/92

FIGURE 11.2. *(Continued)*

All Day Dining

All Day Dining Available from 11:30 a.m. to 11:00 p.m. Daily.

Starters

K.C. Strip Steak Soup (Our Signature)	Cup 2.95	Bowl 3.75
Baked French Onion		Bowl 3.75
Chef's Kettle (Different Each Day)	Cup 2.75	Bowl 3.50
Shrimp & Sauces		7.95

Jumbo Shrimp with Cocktail and Remoulade Sauce

House Salad	2.95

Salads

Hot and Cold Chicken Salad 8.50

Grilled Chicken Breast, Oriental Greens, Crisp

Rice Noodles, Sweet Hoisin Sauce

Chef's Salad 8.50

Crispy Greens with Julienne Meats and Cheeses, Tomato and Egg

Painter's Pallette 6.95

Seasonal Fruit, Berries with Yogurt Dipping Sauce

Freshly Baked Grain Muffin

Specialties

K.C. Steak Sandwich 9.25

Served Open Face Topped with Dofino Cheese and Crispy Onions

Shrimp Scampy 9.25

Sauteed with Butter, Garlic, Lemon over Cappilini Noodles

A suggested gratuity of 15% and applicable tax will be included.

Touch Extension 36 to Order   8/92

FIGURE 11.2.   (*Continued*)

Sandwiches & Burgers

Served with French Fries

Doubletree Steak Burger 7.25

    One Half Pound Ground Chuck, Cheddar, Jack or Swiss Cheese

Boulevard Chicken Sandwich 7.50

    Grilled Breast on a Seven Grain Bun, Dofino Cheese,

    Avocado and Cilantro Mayonnaise

Jumbo Chicken Salad Croissant 6.75

Overland Park Club 7.50

    Toasted Triple Decker of Ham, Turkey, Bacon, Lettuce,

    Tomato and Swiss Cheese

Reuben Tradition 6.95

    Corned Beef, Swiss Cheese and Sauerkraut

    with Thousand Island Dressing

A suggested gratuity of 15% and applicable tax will be included.

Touch Extension 36 to Order   8/92

FIGURE 11.2.   *(Continued)*

After 5 P.M.

Available 5 p.m. to 11:00 p.m. Daily.

Appetizers & Salads

Louisiana Crab Cakes 7.25

Basil Buerre Blanc

Santa Fe Spinach and Artichoke Dip 6.25

Blue and Gold Corn Chips

Traditional Caesar Salad 4.75

Parmesan Garlic Croutons

Small Garden Salad 2.95

Entrees

Includes Vegetable, Potato, House Salad, Rolls and Butter

K.C. Strip Steak 19.95

14 oz. Broiled or Blackened

Perfect Prime Rib .... 10 oz.   16.95   14 oz.   18.95

Slowly Roasted to Perfection

Roast Long Island Duckling 19.95

Crisp Duckling in Classic Citrus Sauce

Chicken Breast Cordon Bleu 17.50

Freshly Prepared, Herb Butter Sauce

Salmon Fillet 19.95

Broiled with Lemon Butter

Ozark Mountain Trout 17.95

Panned Fried, Almondine

Desserts

Peppermint Ribbon Ice Cream Pie (Our Specialty) 3.95

Triple Chocolate Death 3.95

N.Y. Deli Cheesecake (Fresh Strawberries Optional) 3.95

Dark Chocolate Terrine (Incredibly Rich) 3.95

A suggested gratuity of 15% and applicable tax will be included.

Touch Extension 36 to Order   8/92

FIGURE 11.2. *(Continued)*

Wines

In Addition to Our Wide Selection of Domestic and Imported Wines,

We are proud to Offer the Following House Selections

By the Bottle or by the Glass.

Chardonnay	White Zinfandel	Cabernet Sauvignon
	Select	Premium
Glass	4.00	4.50
Bottle	20.00	22.00

Premium Wine By The Bottle

Cabernet Sauvignon	Chardonnay	White Zinfandel
Charles Krug 28.00	Chateau St. Jean 25.00	De Loach 21.00
Sequoia Grove 32.00	Kendall Jackson 32.00	Robert Mondavi 21.00
Jordan 43.00	Robert Mondavi 34.00	**Champagnes**
Beaulieu Vinyards George De La Tour Private Reserve 64.00	Jordan 39.00	Mumms Cordon Rouge 52.00
Opus 1 95.00	Far Niente 45.00	Moët and Chandon 48.00
		Dom Perignon 130.00

A suggested gratuity of 15% and applicable tax will be included.

Touch Extension 36 to Order

8/92

FIGURE 11.2. *(Continued)*

Hospitality Suggestions

Available from 11:00 a.m. Daily.

Please allow 45 minutes to 1 hour for preparation.

Dip the Chip Buffet (minimum 4 people) .... per person 4.75

  Deluxe Mixed Nuts, Tortilla and Potato Chips with Freshly

  Made Salsa and Bleu Cheese Dip

Deli Platter Sampler (serves 4) 22.50

  Generous Slices of Ham, Roast Beef, Turkey, Salami, Cheddar and

  Swiss Cheese with Appropriate Condiments and Breads

Cheese and Fruit Assortment (serves 4) 20.50

  A Selection of Domestic Cheeses with Fresh Fruit and French Bread

Crudite Tray (serves 4) 17.50

  Garden Fresh Vegetables with a Bleu Cheese Dip

Buffalo Chicken Wings .... per dozen 12.00

  Hot and Spicy with Bleu Cheese Dip

"Iced and Spiced" Shrimp 22.50

  One pound of Peel and Eat Shrimp, Cocktail Sauce and Lemon

  (25-30 shrimp)

Bottled Beer

  Domestic 3.00

  Imported 3.25

Bar Setups 12.50

  Fruit, Olives, Napkins, Ice and 1 Dozen Glasses

Ice

  Bucket 3.00

  Tub 10.00

A Wide Selection of Wines and Spirits are Available

Ask Your Operator for Premium Liquors Available

by the Bottle Complete with Bar Set-ups.

A suggested gratuity of 15% and applicable tax will be included.

Touch Extension 36 to Order   8/92

FIGURE 11.2. *(Continued)*

Enjoy genuine American cuisine at its best. Be it Breakfast, Lunch or Dinner, you will find the atmosphere memorable and the food delightful. Daily, enjoy Perfect Prime Rib, the house specialty or your choice from a wide variety of Steaks, Seafood, or Rotisserie-Roasted Chicken or Duck items. For the morning diner, Hearty Mid-Western Breakfast is Served Daily with a-la-carte or buffet service as you please. Our guaranteed five minute breakfast will help the busy traveler start the day.

Also Enjoy Our Traditional Sunday Brunch.

Butterfly Club

For after-hours relaxation or into-the-evening entertainment, the Butterfly Club is the place to be. Weekday afternoons, our inviting bar offers a complimentary buffet of appetizers, with a different international theme each day of the week.

Evening has a distinctive sound at the Butterfly Club. It sings with live performances of mellow musical favorites each Wednesday through Saturday. Elegance resounds with our delightful selection of special desserts, cordials, fine single-malt scotches, wines by the glass and savory specialty coffees.

FIGURE 11.2. (*Continued*)

Children's Menu

STEPHENSON'S

APPLE FARM RESTAURANT

GRACIOUS COUNTRY DINING

Hey Kids . . .

Don't forget the cider-barrel at the entrance. It is filled with sweet, pure, cold cider made here on the farm from red, ripe, juicy apples and squeezed in our press.

You may have all you like, that is, as long as your parents don't object. Sweet cider is very good for you. In fact, you can drink it in the morning for breakfast instead of orange juice. So, on the way out, get a cup, turn the wooden spigot and have another drink of health.

FIGURE 11.3. A good example of a children's menu written with children in mind. The regular menu from this restaurant can be found in Chapter 7. (*Menu courtesy of Stephenson's Old Apple Farm Restaurant, Kansas City, Missouri*)

Children's Meals

Smokey Wokey - ¼ hickory smoked chicken. Finest in the world. Smoked over hickory wood. . . . 5.25

Little Red Hen - ¼ baked chicken in butter and cream. Tender and delicious. 5.25

The Specialty of the House

Three Little Pigs - Hickory smoked ribs, really cooked over hickory wood. Pick up and eat with your fingers. 5.25

Piggy Wiggy - A hickory smoked pork chop. This is an entirely different flavor in pork chops. . . . 5.25

Porky Pig - ½ center-cut hickory smoked ham - served with honey sauce. 5.25

Fishy Wishy - Fried Jumbo Shrimp. Served with our own shrimp sauce. 7.95

Above meals include your choice of the following: Tossed, frozen or marshmallow salad, baked or french fried potatoes and hot bread.

Kid's Plates

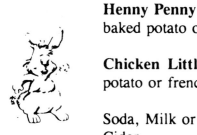

Henny Penny - 2 pieces of hickory smoked chicken, baked potato or french fries and hot bread. . . 4.50

Chicken Little - 2 pieces of baked chicken, baked potato or french fries and hot bread. 4.50

Soda, Milk or Iced Tea 85
Cider 1.25

Mom! If you like, we will be glad to bring you an empty plate so you may share some of your meal with your child.

FIGURE 11.3.   *(Continued)*

uct whereas a tray would suffice in the coffee shop. Thus delivery creates additional expense. Because of its high cost and low sales volume, many operations charge a higher selling price on the room service menu than for the same item on the coffee shop menu, or they might impose a service charge. Sometimes they charge more *and* add a service charge. In spite of the additional revenues, room service still loses money. As a result, some operations simply write it off as a guest service to entice the room rental, which has a very high markup.

Many operations, particularly the smaller ones, simply place a coffee shop menu, with or without higher selling prices, in the rooms. By all means, do not let this suffice for your room service menu. The room service menu should be a limited version of the hotel's coffee shop menu and list only items that fit the following criteria. Due to the fact that the product normally must travel a long distance from the kitchen to the room, offer only items that have good holding qualities. They also should be transported easily. If the equipment is not available to properly hold the temperature, then foods that are highly susceptible to contamination and food-borne illness should be avoided.

In most properties, room service menus, in addition to meals, also list items for parties and small receptions that would take place in the guest's room or suite. Larger functions would be handled by the catering department. Room service listings should include chips and dip, mixed nuts, crudités and canapes, as well as shrimp, meat, and fruit and/or cheese platters. Bottled liquor, mixes, beer, wine, and soda are also included.

CONCLUSION

Throughout this chapter, emphasis has been on balance and variety. If you can gain the patronage of customers with quality, they will eventually look for variety in your menu. Without that, you can lose sales. Try new ideas: Ride the trends. Use your imagination. Give your customers something to look forward to. It's just that simple!

QUESTIONS

1. Differentiate between quick service items and short order items. Explain their importance in coffee shop menu planning.
2. Discuss how you would improve a coffee shop menu that is dull and unimaginative. Be specific.

3. Develop a breakfast menu for a coffee shop located in a truck stop on a major interstate.

4. Develop a lunch and dinner menu for a coffee shop in a luxury hotel.

5. Which is preferable for a coffee shop—a three-in-one menu or separate menus? Defend your answer.

6. Develop a children's menu for a family restaurant.

CHAPTER TWELVE

Theme-Ethnic Menus

OBJECTIVES By the completion of this chapter, the reader should be able to:

- Differentiate the characteristics of theme and ethnic restaurants and menus.
- Utilize descriptive terminology to influence the success of a theme-ethnic menu.
- Describe the elements of design for the menu covers which are critical to tying together the theme of the restaurant.

IMPORTANT TERMS

Theme restaurant
Price range
Descriptive terminology

Ethnic restaurant
Course sequence

INTRODUCTION

Theme restaurants, as well as ethnic restaurants, are difficult to classify due to their diversity. Some theme-ethnic restaurants are nothing more then upgraded fast food outlets with waiter/waitress service, while others are quite intricate, both in style of service and in culinary knowledge. For the most part, however, the skill levels of the staff are greater than for fast food and, in many cases, surpass those of coffee shop personnel. Classification notwithstanding, a common thread runs among these operations when it comes to discussing menus.

GENERAL CHARACTERISTICS OF THEME RESTAURANTS

Theme restaurants are loosely categorized as those operations built around a certain characteristic or idea. This idea, called the *theme*, is followed throughout the operation. The building structure, decor, employee uniforms, and menu design, as well as the food items listed all tie into and augment the theme. Operations that classify themselves as theme restaurants almost always have waiter/waitress service.

The skill level of service in these restaurants is higher than one would find in a coffee shop. Cocktail service is common, requiring a more skilled server. This higher competency level would also hold true for the production staff of independently owned and operated establishments. Most chain-operated theme restaurants have less skilled staff than their independently operated counterparts, and many (if not all) of the menu offerings are either produced in a commissary and delivered to each location or prepared from frozen preportioned products.

In chain theme restaurants, as in quick service operations, it is imperative that the menu planner determine in advance whether a menu item is easily adaptable to uniformity. Two reasons for this prevail: one, the aforementioned skill level, not to mention the ease of training, and, two, a chain's overriding need to have all of its restaurants identical. On the other hand, an independent theme restaurant would, for the most part, prepare menu items from standardized recipes and thus would need kitchen employees with a higher degree of culinary knowledge.

Selling prices in theme restaurants range from moderate to moderately high. Two things result from this fact: one, the average check is higher than in a coffee shop, and, two, there is a slower table turnover. Both of these points are important to the menu writer. The higher check average indicates a wider range of ingredients from which to choose in the makeup of menu items. The slower table turnover indicates a more leisurely meal by the customer, which in

FIGURE 12.1. This restaurant carries the apple farm theme throughout its operation including building, decor, uniforms, and menu. (*Courtesy of Stephenson's Old Apple Farm Restaurant, Kansas City, Missouri*)

turn affords more time in the kitchen for more time-consuming methods of preparation. Also important to remember is that with a slower table turnover, the check average must be higher in order for the restaurant to be profitable.

Many theme restaurants are trendy operations. One trend was hanging plants with various forms of memorabilia attached to brick or stuccoed walls. Art deco is also a popular motif, with its design accents, period lighting, and emphasis on color coordination, including mauve, gray, and taupe. By the time this is read, these trends will have changed to some other design innovation concocted by leading interior decorators. Trendy theme restaurants tend to feature nouveau, regional, fusion, national, or a combination of two or more styles of cooking.

A relative newcomer to the theme restaurant scene is the eclectic North American restaurant. Quite often regional in nature, it uses native fresh ingredients as well as local techniques to produce a product that is purely North American. Fish and seafood from the

A Little About The Apple Farm Restaurant

In 1870, when Highway 40 (Kansas City, Mo) was a mud road, the Stephenson fruit and vegetable farm had its beginning. From a little, one-room stone building, our grandparents sold homegrown produce to folks traveling between Lee's Summit and Independence. Old Timers say the little building was regarded as the half-way point between these two towns.

In 1935, Norman, our older brother, joined father in the orchard business. Since then, the orchard acreage has spread from Lee's Summit to locations in Blue Springs, Grain Valley and Sibley. From these orchards come our fresh apples, peaches, berries and the sweet cider which we serve all year long. Fresh produce from these orchards can also be bought, in season, at Norman's stand next to the restaurant.

Like most early Missouri settlers, our grandparents smoked meats, made apple butter, canned their own fruits and vegetables. And so, on April 16, 1946, when we opened our restaurant in the original stone building, it seemed natural to call it The Apple Farm. We had 10 booths then and served 38 people the first day.

Then, as now, we served old-fashioned hickory smoked meats, home-made apple butter, preserves and relishes, all prepared in our own kitchens in the unique manner that our grandparents had taught us.

Gradually, during seven remodelings, the original stone building has been engulfed. It remains, however, as part of the restaurant's superstructure.

In 1977, due to popular demand we decided to open two new restaurants, since our original restaurant had been expanded to it's capacity. One of the new restaurants is located 8 miles south of the Kansas City International Airport, in Platte Woods, Missouri. The other new restaurant is located in Jane, Missouri, on Highway 71, near Bella Vista, Arkansas.

Again, in 1985, we opened our newest restaurant, The Red Mule Inn. A casual neighborhood style pub and grill just across old U.S. 40 Highway from the Old Apple Farm.

We join the young men and women who are serving you in a warm welcome.

Lee & Loyd
The Twins

Stephenson's
APPLE FARM RESTAURANT
40 HIGHWAY AND LEE'S SUMMIT ROAD · KANSAS CITY · MISSOURI

FIGURE 12.1. *(Continued)*

Pacific Northwest and East Coast; beef from the Midwest; and fresh fruits, vegetables, and spices from Canada, the United States, and Mexico make this one of the newer, exciting ethnic restaurant offerings. Many of these operations are always on the cutting edge of culinary experimentation. This particular style of theme restaurant is rather expensive to operate and maintain, as change always occurs in terms of decor, culinary techniques, and menu listings. Patrons of these trendy styles are quite flighty and will quickly go to another establishment if change is not constant. Closely related to trendy theme restaurants are bistros which have a more stable decor and menu; however they do embrace change from time to time.

Another style of theme restaurant includes those that entertain. Referred to in the industry as "eatertainment" operations, they do more than just sell food and drink. Hard Rock Cafe, for example, has museum-quality artifacts hanging on the walls, as does Planet Hollywood.

Our Famous Apple Fritters

Bowl of 4 . . . . 1.50
Famous here at the Old Apple Farm for years.

Sweet Endings

Hot Apple Pie with Brandy Sauce 2.25
Made from scratch with fresh apples.

Hot Apple Dumpling with Whipped Cream . . 2.75
We think this is one of America's finest apple desserts. Since we grow several thousand bushels of apples each year, naturally we take great pride in the apple desserts we turn out—it's all in there—nothing is spared.

Apple Parfait 2.50
This is apple juice, sugar, butter and spices cooked together with a smidgen of brandy into a delicate delightful fruit sauce and then poured generously over our french vanilla ice cream.

Pecan Nut Ice Cream 1.95
Premium ice cream, especially made for us.

Pecan Nut Pie 2.25
A rich caramel custard filling topped with pure heavy whipped cream and garnished with gobs of Hickory Nut.

Frozen Lemon Dessert 2.50
A very fine whip cream ice box dessert flavored with fresh lemons and served with lemon sauce.

Coconut Cheesecake 2.50

Gold Brick Chocolate Sundae 2.50

Beautiful Private Banquets

Dinner from 12.50   Luncheons from 8.00
(plus taxes & service)

We cater off premise.

15% gratuity will be added to all groups of 8 people or more. If you request separate checks, please allow additional time. Major Credit Cards Accepted, No personal Checks Please.

Apple Farm Dinners

From our Hickory & Apple Wood Smoker

Chicken (1/2) 12.95
The House Specialty. So tender it will fall off the bone.

Brisket of Beef Au Jus 13.95
Cooked long and slow in our oven. Very tender, served with our famous horseradish sauce.

Ribs (1/2 slab) 13.95
Pork Ribs served with Apple Farm B-B-Q Sauce.

Ham Steak 13.95
Center Cut, bone-in, served with wine & honey sauce.

Pork Chops (2) Center-cut. 14.95
Some guests eat these every time they come here.

Half N Half 14.95
Choice of any two: Chicken, Brisket, Ham or Pork Chop.

Baked Chicken 'n' Butter & Cream (1/2) . . 12.95
This is real old-fashioned baked chicken with lots of butter and cream, tender and delicious. Our recipe is in Better Homes and Gardens Cook Book "Famous Foods from Famous Places".

Chicken Livers (sauteed) 12.95
If you are a liver lover you'll love these.

Seafood

Broiled Red Snapper 14.95
Florida Red Snapper Filet broiled in a light wine and garlic butter.

Hickory Smoked Deep Sea Whitefish 13.95
Delicious moist white meat, lightly smoked in butter and lemon.

Jumbo Shrimp (Lightly breaded and French Fried) . 17.95
They're large and they're good, served with our fine shrimp sauce.

Steaks

Broiled Filet Mignon Steak 17.95
Cut from choice loins — Served with a buttery mushroom sauce.

Broiled K.C. Strip Steak 17.95
Served with a buttery mushroom sauce.

Marinated K.C. Strip Sirloin Steak 17.95
We marinate this in a special wine and garlic oil which adds a special delicious flavor to the steak. Served with a buttery mushroom sauce.

The Apple Farmer's Dinner (For the hearty appetite) . 21.95
Brisket of Beef — Ribs — Ham — Chicken

Served with all Dinners: Potato — Casserole Dish — Garnish — Hot Breads and Apple Butter — Farm Relish — Apple Farm Fritter

Salads: Tossed Green , Frozen Fruit or Marshmallow Blue Cheese Dressing .75

Split Dinner for Adult $4.00 Additional. Includes Salad, Potato and Hot Breads.

At the Beginning

Sauteed Chicken Livers 3.75
for the liver lover.

Hickory Smoked Chicken Gizzards 3.75
Delicious — tender as livers.

May be ordered as a dinner 12.95

Fresh Sweet Apple Cider 1.25
from our Mill and Farm.

Our Famous French Onion Soup en Tureen . 2.95
the Chef's own creation — delicious.

Escargots 4.95
In a mild garlic and wine butter sauce.

Stuffed Mushrooms 4.95
With blue cheese and onions, flavored with a touch of wine and garlic.

A Taste of the Farm

Arrive after 6:00 p.m. Sunday
Arrive by 6:00 p.m. Monday through Friday
Arrive after 9:00 p.m. Saturday
Entrees from 6.95

Sunday Chicken Dinner

11:30 a.m. to 9:00 p.m. (includes Chef's Dessert)

(except Holidays)   8.95

Brunch On Sunday

10 a.m. to 2 p.m.

A marvelous treat for all the family!

Adults $10.95, Children 6 through 10 $5.95 under 6 FREE

Coffee, Tea and Milk .85   Pepsi Cola & 7-up .85

FIGURE 12.1. *(Continued)*

The Cider Barrel

We have been making and freezing Apple Cider here for over 40 years. Our large cider mill is located at one of our orchards and from it comes many thousand gallons of cider each year. We supply much of the greater Kansas City trade with our apple cider in season, through the grocery stores. We think the finest apple cider in the world today is the cider you tasted in the barrel in our lobby. It is made with tree-ripened Missouri apples, grown in our own orchards. Our grandfather started growing apples in Jackson County back in 1890. In 1900 there were more apple trees in the state of Missouri than are presently growing in the state of Washington. Late in the fall, we take the right combination of select, tree-ripened Missouri apples and press them into that wonderful old Missouri beverage, sweet, pure, apple cider, then we put it into the freezer for your year-long enjoyment here at the restaurant.

Try our new restaurant north of the river in Platte Woods (8 miles south of the Kansas City International Airport). When in Bella Vista, Arkansas, visit Stephenson's Cider Mill Restaurant on Highway 71. Also, for a casual meal, stop by our Red Mule Inn across 40 Highway from the Old Apple Farm. There you can loosen your tie and relax.

FIGURE 12.1. (*Continued*)

Theme restaurants that adhere to a specific focus such as railroad, nautical, colonial, or sports memorabilia change menus only occasionally and decor rarely. Consequently, they are less expensive to operate and for the most part enjoy a more stable clientele.

GENERAL CHARACTERISTICS OF ETHNIC RESTAURANTS

Although ethnic restaurants are similar to theme restaurants, they are less trendy because they are based on a long-standing cultural tradition. French, Italian, Mexican, Pacific Rim, Cajun, and Greek are some of the more popular ethnic themes. Others not as popular, for example, Caribbean, Thai, Tandouri, and Columbian, just to mention a few, still manage to have very loyal followings with one or two restaurants in larger cities. All these establishments feature dishes of a particular culture, race, or country.

Ethnic restaurants have waiter or waitress service. Those that have self-service would fall into the quick service category as far as menu planning is concerned. Those are covered in Chapter 10. The skill level of the service as well as the production staff of a full-service ethnic restaurant would be the same or higher than that found in a theme restaurant. This competency level would be anywhere from moderate to high. Take, for example, one of the Italian or Mexican chain operations. American-style service, with the menu printed in English, with the majority of items familiar to the average patron, and with cocktail service, would indicate a moderate service skill level. In the kitchen, standardized recipes for those items that are not commissaried, frozen, or from mix would also indicate a moderate talent level.

At the other end of the spectrum, for example, in a nouvelle cuisine French restaurant, the skill level would be extremely high. For the wait staff, the service is French, a very formal style that requires the finish-cooking of menu items to be performed in the dining room on gridons, in full view of the guests. In addition, the service staff must be knowledgeable about wines and proper wine service, as well as about the ingredients and preparation of each menu item, should the guest inquire. This knowledge requires extensive training, making French the most difficult skill level of service to achieve. The production area requires an executive chef and a number of *sous* chefs, depending on the size of the restaurant, who would also be highly trained. Timing is critical in French service; although most of the preparation is done in the kitchen, the meal is finished in the dining room, and must arrive in a timely manner after the guest has finished the previous course.

An example of the middle ground, where the skill level would be moderately high, is an Oriental restaurant. A hybrid Russian/American style of service, in which the service staff first serves the guests, then leaves the remainder of the meal on the table for the guests to serve themselves, is used. In addition to serving the guest, the server must be knowledgeable about the menu, with an awareness of all of the ingredients, spices, and preparation techniques used. The production staff also requires several highly trained individuals with specialized skills in Oriental cooking methods.

Because of the varying degrees of training in the several types of ethnic restaurants, the menu writer must create menus that live up to the expertise expected by the customer, yet stay within the bounds of the competency level of the staff.

The price range of full-service ethnic restaurants varies greatly, from the moderate range all the way to the upper end of the high range. Mexican, Italian, and Oriental are but a few of the ethnic restaurants normally falling into the moderate range. Northern Italian, French, and North American eclectic almost always feature moderate to relatively high prices. As stated earlier, the higher the price range, the higher the check average will be, and the slower the table turnover. In the case of a French restaurant, the table turnover

FIGURE 12.2.   An excellent example of a North American eclectic menu. (*Courtesy of Fedora Cafe and Bar, Kansas City, Missouri and Tyson's Corner, Virginia*)

APERITIFS

The word derives from the Latin *aperio*, meaning "to open" and that is the purpose of an aperitif, to open a meal.

CAMPARI
PERNOD
APEROL
LILLET Red or White
SWEET VERMOUTH Martini & Rossi
or Cinzano
DRY VERMOUTH Martini & Rossi
or Cinzano

SINGLE MALT SCOTCHES

Auchentoshan 10 yr. old
The Glenlivet 12 yr. old
The Glenfiddich 12 yr. old
Glenmorangie 10 yr., 18 yr. old
Dalmore 12 yr. old
Macallan 12 yr., 18 yr., 25 yr. old
Cragganmore 12 yr. old
Sheep Dip 8 yr. old
  Ask about our many other selections

IMPORTED VODKAS

Absolut
Absolut Citron
Absolut Peppar
Finlandia
Stolichnaya Cristall
Tanqueray Sterling
Wyborowa

BOURBONS

Blanton's Single Barrel
Booker Noe
Jim Beam 7 yr. old
Makers Mark
Wild Turkey "Rare Breed"
Baker's 107
Knob Creek
Basil Hayden's

SPECIALTY DRINKS

FEDORA MARTINI Our Grand Martini with your choice of Gin or Vodka
BURNT MARTINI Vodka with a swirl of Scotch
RASPBERRY MARTINI Vodka with a swirl of Chambord
FEDORA MANHATTAN Bourbon and Sweet Vermouth
FRENCH CONNECTION Grand Marnier & Courvoisier married
HARRY'S OLD FASHIONED Simply a Classic!
THE IRISH RASPBERRY Chambord and Bailey's Irish Cream

BEERS AND ALES

Amstel Light – Holland
Bass Ale Draft – England
Beck's Light & Dark – Germany
Boulevard Pale Ale Draft – Kansas City
Boulevard Wheat – Kansas City
Budweiser – U.S.A.
Bully Porter – Kansas City
Guiness Stout Draft – Ireland
Heineken – Holland
Miller Lite – U.S.A.
Steinlager – New Zealand
Warsteiner – Germany

WATERS AND SODAS

Evian – Large or Individual
Perrier – Large or Individual
San Pellegrino
LaCroix – Sparkling, Berry, Lemon, Orange
Chapelle – Peach, Plum, & Pear

CAFE, CAPPUCCINO AND AFTER DINNER DRINKS

WHITE COFFEE Truffles White Chocolate Liqueur and our Three Bean coffee topped with whipped cream and white chocolate shavings
CAPPUCCINO FEDORA Laced with Amaretto and Frangelica
CAPPUCCINO Regular & Decaffeinated
ESPRESSO Regular & Decaffeinated
ST. MORITZ Chambord topped with heavy cream
SEMI FREDDO CAFE White chocolate ice cream and Espresso topped with whipped cream

FIGURE 12.2. (*Continued*)

FEDORA CLASSICS

FIRST COURSES

Hot Artichoke Dip with Crisp Garlic-herb Toast.   5.35
House-cured Salmon: Cucumber Salad and Mascarpone Mousse.   6.95
Golden Fried Onion Crisps served with Malt Vinegar.   2.95
Carpaccio of Beef: Enoki Mushrooms & Parmesan-Garlic Sauce.   5.95

LARGE SALADS

Baby Field Greens & Sliced Tomatoes, Provolone, Genoa Salami
& Fresh Basil with Balsamic Vinaigrette.   7.50
Grilled Romaine "Caesar Salad" with shaved Parmesan & Pan Roasted Croutons.   7.95
Savoy Spinach Leaves, Spiced Pecans, sliced Strawberries, Sweet Red Onions,
& Poppyseed Dressing.   7.25
Salad of Grilled Duck, Spiced Pecans, Enoki Mushrooms & fresh Raspberries
with Raspberry Hoisin Dressing.   8.50

SIDE SALADS

Salad Fedora: House blended Seasonal Greens with Creme Herb Dressing or Balsamic Vinaigrette.   2.75
Greek Salad, Romaine, Spiced Beets, Feta Cheese, Sweet Red Onions, Olives and Oregano Vinaigrette.   2.95
Savoy Spinach Leaves, Spiced Pecans, sliced Strawberries, Sweet Red Onions,
& Poppyseed Dressing.   3.25

SANDWICHES

Fresh Baked Croissant: Stuffed with Virginia Ham & Vermont Cheddar
served with Honey Dijon Sauce.   7.25
Oven Roasted Chicken Club, thinly sliced, with Lettuce, Tomato, Bacon and Garlic Mayonnaise
on Crusted French Bread.   6.95
210 Burger, half pound, char-grilled Chuck Steak burger on a toasted roll.   6.75

MAIN COURSES

Farm House Chicken with Pearl Onions, Mushrooms & Smoked Bacon braised in
a Cabernet Sauvignon Sauce.   10.25
Penne with Roasted Garlic, Plum Tomato Sauce & Fresh Basil.   8.25
Spit-Roasted Baby Chicken, marinated and basted with Lemon, Garlic & Fresh Herbs.   9.95
Spit-Roasted Indiana "Pekin" Duck, with Raspberry Hoisin Sauce.   13.95
Sauteed Calves Liver, Crisp Bacon, Carmelized Onions with Balsamic Vinegar Glaze.   8.95
Fettuccine Alfredo Cream with Three Cheeses & a topping of Prosciutto Ham.   8.95
Blackened Filet Mignon coated with Fedora Cafe's 'Private Blend' of Spices & pan seared.   13.95

PIZZA

Thin Crust, 24" Oval   8.95
Italian Sausage & Roasted Red Pepper: Plum Tomato Sauce & Three Cheese Blend.
Chicken & Pesto: Sweet Basil Sauce, Char-grilled Chicken, Roma Tomatoes & Romano Cheese.
White Pizza: Roasted Garlic, Italian Herbs, Butter & Three Cheese blend.
Pizza Margherita: Tomatoes, Fresh Basil, Garlic, Mozzarella & Romano Cheese.

Calzone with freshly-made Italian Sausage, Four Cheeses, Fire Roasted Red
Peppers, Fried Garlic & Fresh Basil.   8.95

SIDE DISHES

Pomme Frites Fedora Cafe   1.95
Paneed Potato Cakes   2.25
Sauteed Savoy Spinach   2.25
Escalloped Vermont Cheddar Potatoes   2.50

FIGURE 12.2.   (*Continued*)

FRESH SPECIALTIES FOR TODAY

Fedora Cafe strives to offer you the finest FRESH Meats, Fish, Vegetables and Fruits available. We are dependent upon the Weather, Seasons and Air Express Connections. If we are forced, by one or several of these elements to eliminate a selection from our menu, please accept our apologies.

SOUP OF THE DAY
Tomato-Cabbage with Smoked Ham
cup 2.50 bowl 3.50

PASTA
Fusiili with Pancetta
Garden Peas, Mushrooms, Three Cheeses
& Cream 8.95

Seafood Linguine with Romano Cream
-or- a Spicy Red Sauce 10.95

PIZZA
Italian Sausage, Roasted Peppers
& Gorgonzola Cheese 8.95

FRESH FISH
Chilean Swordfish Wood Grilled and
Herb Marinated -or-
Pan Blackened with Cajun Spices
18.50

Atlantic Baby Halibut
Poached in Saffron Fennel Broth
17.95
may we suggest: Buena Vista Sauvignon Blanc
glass 4.50

ENTREES
Wood Grilled Boneless Breast of Duckling
with a Fresh Fig & Orange Sauce
with Moroccan Couscous
18.95
may we suggest: Joseph Drouhin La Foret Rouge
Pinot Noir glass 5.25

VEGETABLES
Green Beans	2.25
Seasonal Fresh Vegetable Medley	1.95
Asparagus	3.50

DESSERTS & BERRIES
Rainier Cherry Almond Tart	3.75
Peaches & Cream Chocolate Gateau	3.50
California Strawberries	2.95
California Raspberries	3.95
Great Lakes Blueberries	3.50

Your Host: Bill Essmann
Your Chef: Dan Palmer

In consideration of other dining guests, cigar and pipe smoking
in the lounge only please.

FEDORA'S NEW PLATES

Penne with Grilled Chicken,
Toasted Almonds, Orange Zest, Garlic, Oregano
and Asparagus in a Chicken Broth. 8.50

Belgium Endive & Chilled Shrimp Platter
sliced Avocado and Pink Raifort Sauce. 9.50

Pecan Crusted Breast of Chicken
with escalloped Vermont Cheddar Potatoes. 11.95

Roasted Native Lamb Chops
with Rosemary Garlic Jus & Eggplant Torte. 17.95

Heartland Grille
Medallions of Filet Mignon & Pork and Lamb Chop
served with East Texas Onion Pudding. 16.95

"U.S.D.A." Prime T-Bone Steak
Char-grilled, served with Roasted Shallot Sauce. 17.95

SWEETS

Profiteroles, Miniature Cream Puffs filled with
Unsweetened Whipped Cream & coated with
Fedora's Hot Fudge Sauce. 2.50

Tartufo, White Chocolate Ice Cream
coated with chunked Ambrosia White Chocolate
with Hot Fudge Sauce. 3.50

Truffle Cake, Flourless, fallen Chocolate Cake
made with Dark Sweet Chocolate. 3.25

Six Nut Caramel Tart baked in Shortbread
Crust, with Butter Pecan Ice Cream. 2.95

Country Cobbler Mixed Berries topped with a
Sweet Buttermilk Crust. 2.75

Creme Brulee with crisp broiled Sugar Crust. 2.25
With Fresh fruit p.a.

Semi-Freddo Cafe:
White Chocolate Ice Cream floating in Freshly
Brewed Espresso with Whipped Cream 3.25

BEVERAGES

Freshly Brewed:
Fedora Three Blend Coffee 1.25
Decaffeinated Coffee 1.25

Iced Tea or Iced Coffee 1.25

Paradise Tropical Iced Tea 1.25

Coke, Diet Coke & Sprite 1.25

© HRG, INC 10/92D

FIGURE 12.2. *(Continued)*

could be as low as 1.5 to 2 times a night. Therefore, the check average would have to be high in order for the restaurant to achieve a profit. The menu writer must recognize that to get a high check average, the customer must perceive a value relationship between the meal and the price paid. Therefore, the menu must be written using unusual, rare, or expensive ingredients prepared and served with a high degree of skill. As one can see, the scope of theme and ethnic restaurants is great, but the principles of menu planning and writing for them share some fairly common roots.

COURSE SEQUENCE

The courses offered in theme and ethnic restaurants and the sequence of those courses are fairly standard as with other types of menus. The major difference is in the number of courses offered. Theme restaurants tend to have a more limited offering than do ethnic operations. Both theme and ethnic restaurants will normally list hot and cold appetizers, salads, entrees, vegetables, starches, desserts, and beverages. Theme restaurants quite often offer sandwiches and side dishes in addition to those categories already mentioned, while ethnic restaurants do not. However, ethnic restaurants such as French or Northern Italian, might opt to add a cheese and fruit course. There are, of course, exceptions to these rules.

The majority of theme and ethnic restaurants use the a la carte menu as opposed to the table d'hôte menu. In all menus written for this style of restaurant, it is imperative to stay within the theme or ethnic origins of the establishment. Only a few, if any, generic dishes should be added to satisfy those in a party whose tastes do not coincide with the particular theme or ethnic origin of the restaurant. Certainly, balance is critical between courses and within courses of theme and ethnic menus. No matter the nationality of an ethnic menu, balance should always be sought even though certain dishes may be omitted due to ethnic or religious beliefs.

DESCRIPTIVE TERMINOLOGY

In no other type of menu is descriptive terminology as critical as it is in theme and ethnic menus. It is, however, for different reasons that terminology becomes critical. In theme restaurants, descriptive terminology is used primarily to sell both the listings and the theme; explanation is the secondary purpose. In ethnic restaurants, descriptive terminology is used primarily to describe and translate; selling is the secondary purpose.

In the case of theme restaurants, the menu is the focal point of the theme. It is the instrument that ties together the decor, the uniforms, the food, and the general ambiance of the establishment. Two criteria are required to accomplish this: the menu design and the descriptive terminology. The physical design of the theme restaurant menu is as critical as the artwork. This, as well as the descriptive terminology, ties the theme together for the customer. A clever menu writer with a good imagination can do wonders with an ordinary theme menu. Many theme restaurants are known as much for their unusual menus as they are for their food and service. This creates an excellent advertising device as well as an excellent word-of-mouth campaign.

When writing a menu for a theme restaurant, first consider the theme itself. Think of words that best describe that theme and list them. Take this list and then work these key words into the descriptive terminology. For example, in writing a menu for a seafood house, a list could be developed using words such as seafaring, nautical, fisherman, catch, net, freshwater, saltwater, cold, icy, and so on. These words would then be used to describe the various menu listings. In addition to having the descriptive listings tie into the theme, the headings of the various categories should do likewise. The institutional copy is critical in describing and romancing the theme; it must use catchy words and phrases. The net effect of constructively used descriptive terminology is a perfect menu that properly coordinates the restaurant's theme.

Ethnic restaurants' use of descriptive terminology takes on a different, although important, role. Here it is used to explain and translate. Many ethnic menus are written in the language of their country or region. *Never* write a menu in a foreign language without an English translation beneath the foreign terminology. Some restaurants, particularly French and Italian, refuse to provide English translations, perhaps to create some aura of elitism. The only thing it accomplishes is to make a majority of patrons uncomfortable. Avoid surprises. Let customers know exactly what they are getting.

OTHER INCOME

Many restaurants, particularly theme, are expanding their horizons to make profit from products other than food and beverage. On the international scene are such names as Planet Hollywood and Hard Rock Cafe. In addition to chains, many local independent entrepreneurs are opting for extra income. Caps, sweatshirts, T-shirts, glasses, mugs—you name it—they are probably selling it. All of the items sold in the establishment have the restaurant's logo and/or name on them. Such merchandising accomplishes two things: it produces profit and it places the name of the establishment in front of the public. Imagine, getting the customer to pay you to advertise your restaurant.

Appetizers

Grilled Shrimp
jumbo gulf shrimp served with dill mayonnaise on a bed of wild greens   8.25

Smoked Lamb Coin
with a fruit compote on a strawberry and passion fruit coulis   7.25

Grilled Littlenecks with Fennel Broth
garnished with roasted garlic sourdough toast   7.25

Grilled Portobello Napoleon
portobello mushroom layered with grilled vegetables and muenster cheese balsamic vinegar   6.95

Soups & Salads

Seafood Bisque
garnished with roasted red pepper puree   3.25

Chef's Soup of the Day   2.95

Baby Spring Lettuce
served with grilled apples and a walnut vinaigrette   4.75

Tossed Salad
with choice of dressing   3.25

FIGURE 12.3. An example of a menu from an upscale restaurant which is operated by the students at Johnson and Wales University. (*Courtesy of Johnson and Wales University, Practicum Properties, Providence, RI*)

Entrees

Fish

Sautéed Trout
with a saffron cream. accompanied with mushroom potatoes and wilted greens   15.95

Pan Seared Scallops
served over a spaghetti of vegetables in a pernod and peppercorn sauce.
accompanied with lemon herb fried potatoes   15.95

Coconut Shrimp
with a strawberry sauce. vegetable cous cous. and broccoli   15.95

Grilled Swordfish Hawaiian
served with pineapple salsa. broccoli flowerettes. and fried plantains   15.95

Game

Spit Roasted Pheasant
tender young pheasant dusted with our own spice blend and served with rice pilaf.
spaghetti vegetables. and red wine sauce   16.50

Pan Seared Venison
served with Cabernet Sauvignon wild mushroom sauce. accompanied by roasted garlic mashed
potatoes. and sweet and sour cabbage   16.50

Steaks

Grilled Porterhouse Steak
served with garlic mashed potatoes and watercress accompanied by a
wild mushroom and caramelized onion sauce   17.95

Rosemary Cured Tenderloin of Beef
cured with fresh rosemary then grilled and served with haystack onions. tomato horseradish cream
twice baked new potato. and wilted greens   16.95

FIGURE 12.3.   (Continued)

❧ Appetizers ❧

Seared Fresh Tuna with Wasabi and Soy...$6.95

Tenderloin of Beef Carpaccio...$7.95

Crab Stuffed Mushrooms Bearnaise...$7.95

Italian Stuffed Mushrooms...$5.50

Sauteed Fresh Mushrooms...$4.95

Cajun Mushrooms...$4.95

Baked Mushrooms Boursin...$6.95

Italian Sausage Marinara...$4.95

Mozzarella Cheese Sticks...$4.95

Garlic Bread...$1.95

Garlic Mozzarella Bread...$3.25

Toasted Ravioli...$4.50

Scampi Saute...$6.95

Bacon Wrapped Grilled Shrimp...$7.50

Charbroiled Gulf Shrimp...$6.95

Cajun Shrimp Skewer...$6.95

Fresh Blue Point Oysters...$5.95

Gulf Shrimp Cocktail...$6.95

Crab and Potato Pancakes Remoulade...$6.95

Grilled Scallops & Bacon...$7.50

Escargot en Croute...$6.95

Escargot and Herb Purse...$7.95

Chicken Breast Strips...$4.95

Potato Skins Parmesan...$2.95

Cajun Potato Skins...$2.95

Bacon & Cheddar Stuffed Skins...$3.95

Mexican Stuffed Skins...$3.95

Italian Stuffed Skins...$3.95

Baked Brie with Apple...$5.95

❧ Soups & Salads ❧

French Onion & Mushroom
    ...cup $2.25   bowl $2.95

Baked French Onion & Mushroom
    ...cup $2.75   bowl $3.50

Soup du jour...cup $2.25   bowl $2.95

Caesar Salad...$4.95 with entree $2.95

Steamed Fresh Vegetable Plate...$6.95

❧ Greenbriar Specialties ❧

Roast Prime Rib of Beef
                    ...regular $15.95 large $19.95

Cajun Grilled Prime Rib...$16.95

Citrus Herb Grilled Prime Rib...$16.95

Beef Tenderloin Oscar...$19.95

Mixed Grill beef, pork & lamb...$19.95

Duck a L'Orange...$13.95

Breast of Chicken Oscar...$14.95

Rack of Lamb...$23.95

Double Frenched Lamb Chops...$23.95

❧ A La Carte ❧

Potatoes Boursin Gratin (serving for 2)...$5.50

As substitute for potato or rice (single serving)...$2.50

Brandy Cream Mushrooms...$4.95

Roasted Jumbo Garlic Bulb...$1.95

❧ Steaks & Chops ❧

Prime Top Sirloin...$12.95

Teriyaki Top Sirloin...$14.95

Whiskey Sirloin...$14.95

New York Strip...16oz. $21.95

Ribeye Steak Gunpowder Crust...$16.95

Filet Mignon...$18.95

Beef Tenderloin Brochette...$14.95

Beef Tenderloin de Burgo...$18.95

London Broil...$10.95

Ground Sirloin...$8.95

Iowa Chop...$12.95

Smoked Pork Chop...$13.95

Cajun Porterhouse Pork Chop...$13.95

America's Cut...$11.95

Medallions of Pork Loin Piccata...$13.95

FIGURE 12.4. An example of a white tablecloth type bistro menu. (*Courtesy of Trostel's Greenbriar Restaurant, Des Moines, IA*)

❧ Poultry ❧

Lemon & Herb Grilled Chicken Breast...$9.95
Teriyaki Chicken Breast...$10.95
Cajun Chicken Breast...$9.95
Chicken Parmesan...$11.95
Chicken Cordon Bleu...$12.95
Chicken Piccata...$11.95
Chicken & Mushroom Marsala...$12.95
Roast Half Chicken Rosemary...$8.95
Chicken Pecan In Champagne Cream...$12.95

❧ Seafood ❧

Broiled Boston Scrod...$9.95
Baked White Fish Almandine...$10.95
Broiled Orange Roughy...$12.95
Shrimp Scampi...$13.95
Charbroiled Shrimp...$13.95
Tempura Fried Shrimp...$13.95
Steamed Alaskan King Crab Legs...Market
Cajun Grilled Shrimp...$13.95
Sauteed Scallops & Mushrooms...$15.95
Grilled Scallops & Bacon...$15.95
Grilled Halibut Lemon Dill Butter...$12.95
Mixed Seafood Grill...$19.95
Lobster Tail...Single/Market   Twin/Market

❧ Always Fresh Fish ❧

Rainbow Trout Almandine...$12.95
Grilled Rainbow Trout...$11.95
Grilled Salmon with Hollandaise...$15.95
Fresh Catch of the Day...Market

All Entrees Accompanied by Soup du jour or Salad, Baked Potato
or Rice Pilaf, Fresh Vegetable, Rolls and Butter.

❧ Pasta ❧

Linguine with Italian Sausage or Meatballs...$11.95
Penne in Tomato Vodka Sauce...$9.95
Linguine Marinara...$8.95
Fettucine Alfredo...$11.95
Fettucine Primavera...$12.95
Chicken Almond Alfredo Fettucine...$12.95
Angel Hair with Garlic Shrimp & Basil...$13.95
Angel Hair with Sausage, Garlic, Fresh Basil
      & Plum Tomatoes...$12.95
Linguine with Clams, Shrimp & Garlic...$13.95

These Entrees Accompanied by Soup or Salad,
Fresh Vegetables, Rolls and Butter.

❧ Twilight Dining ❧

Served for the lighter appetite
from 5:00 to 6:30 p.m. Monday thru Thursday

Lemon & Herb Grilled Chicken Breast...$7.95
Chicken Parmesan...$8.95
Tempura Fried Shrimp...$9.95
One Quarter Fresh Fried Chicken...$6.95
Broiled Whitefish Almandine...$7.95
Broiled Orange Roughy...$10.95
Petite Filet Mignon...$14.95
Ground Beef Sirloin...$7.50
English Cut Prime Rib...$9.95

These Entrees Accompanied by Soup or Salad, Baked Potato
or Rice Pilaf, Fresh Vegetables, Rolls and Butter.

❧   ❧   ❧   ❧   ❧   ❧   ❧

Trostel's Greenbriar accepts reservations for parties of 6 or more.

Banquet facilities or private rooms available.

The customary 15% gratuity will be added to parties of 6 or more.

For your pleasure, cigar and pipe smoking in the bar only.

FIGURE 12.4.   (Continued)

Chef Troy Trostel's
Special Selections

APPETIZER

Tequila Lime Marinated Char-Broiled Shrimp
with Cilantro Cream and Black Bean Salsa
$7.50

ENTREE

Steak Diane
Beef Tenderloin Sauteed with Garlic,
Forest Mushrooms and Brandy, Served with
Horseradish Mashed Potatoes and
Chili Straws
$20.95

DESSERT

Tiramisu
with Amaretto and Espresso Sauces
$6.95

FEATURED WINE

Gundlach-Bundschu Zinfandel
Bottle $25   Glass $5.95

FIGURE 12.4. *(Continued)*

This isn't the only marketing method being used to generate additional income. Some of the better-known, high-traffic restaurants are selling advertising on their menus. Local shops in the immediate vicinity of these restaurants purchase ads on the menu, which the customer reads while contemplating what to order.

CONCLUSION

Theme and ethnic menus are among the most interesting and fun to write. Knowledge of the subject or country is important so that the menu contains unusual items expressing that particular idea or culture. Menu design, as well as descriptive terminology, must be used to incorporate the theme or country with the decor and general ambiance of the restaurant. Knowledge of the interrelationships among staff skill levels, check average, and table turnover is necessary to achieve a profit and give the customer a good price-value relationship. When you have mastered the strategies described in this chapter, you will find that it's just that simple.

QUESTIONS

1. Develop a menu for a theme restaurant. Explain how the building's architecture and decor will carry out this theme.
2. Explain the differences and similarities of theme and ethnic restaurants.
3. Explain the importance of descriptive terminology on theme and ethnic restaurant menus. Give examples to reinforce your explanation.
4. Discuss the different levels of skill, training, and menu price ranges of the various types of ethnic restaurants. Give examples of each in your discussion.
5. Develop a North American eclectic menu for your area using locally grown foods and local cooking techniques.
6. List all the theme restaurants you know that have retail sales within the operation. Make a list of the type of items sold in the restaurant in addition to food.

CHAPTER THIRTEEN

Banquet/Show Menus

OBJECTIVES   By the completion of this chapter, the reader should be able to:

- Explain the function of the sales department.
- Describe how banquets are packaged for selling.
- Describe the elements of a function sheet.
- Explain how to differentiate between banquet menus and show menus.

IMPORTANT TERMS   Function sheet   Over/under guarantees
Long-range pricing   Show menus
Fixed menus   Banquet contract

INTRODUCTION

Banquet and show menus have certain peculiarities that are exclusive to them and that differentiate them from other types of menus. Although there are some minor differences between banquet menus and show menus, the basic principles that apply to one also apply to the other; thus the two types are included in this chapter.

BANQUET ORGANIZATIONAL STRUCTURE

Banquets are handled daily all over the world in operations ranging from small restaurants serving 15 people at a civic luncheon to large hotels serving 1,500 or more guests at a formal dinner, to civic centers serving banquets to several thousand convention delegates. Even in noncommercial operations, as well as not-for-profit food services, banquets are big business. Regardless of size, the same principles apply. Only the logistics change. Proper planning is the key to any successful event.

In order to fully comprehend the principles of writing menus for banquets, the organizational structure, which varies with the size of the establishment, must first be understood. In a small restaurant, one person would book the event and supervise the setup, decoration, preparation, service, and billing. In a large hotel, these functions would be separated among several individuals, each responsible for one particular job. In operations ranging in scope from the small restaurant to the large hotel, these responsibilities would be divided according to the size of the establishment. To clearly delineate each area's function, we approach the execution of a banquet from the point of view of a large hotel.

The first step in the banquet sequence is booking the event. This is handled by the sales department, which, in addition to planning banquets, is also responsible for selling meeting rooms and guest rooms to large groups. The people in the sales department need, among other things, to be expert menu planners. At this stage the actual menu is decided on. Quite often, the hotel's chef, banquet captain, and food and beverage director also have input regarding the menu. When planning the menu, the salesperson takes into account the type of group, their theme, the dollars they wish to spend, the number to attend, and the food groups and type of service desired. These needs are then matched to the facilities the hotel has to offer and the staff skill level. These criteria are discussed in detail later, but for now suffice it to say that these functions happen in the sales department.

Once the details are decided on between the sales department and client, a function sheet or banquet event order is prepared and sent at the appropriate times to the purchasing department, kitchen,

MEETING AND BANQUET FACILITIES

With more than 14,000 square feet of functional meeting space, Doubletree is the ideal choice for meetings of up to 1,000 and banquets of up to 640. The facilities include a variety of meeting rooms, executive conference suites and a tiered lecture theater. Our Convention Service Department will provide complete planning of your housing and meeting arrangements, audiovisual equipment needs and exceptional catering services. We even offer our Meeting Planners Guarantee: If anything doesn't meet your written specifications, you don't pay for it. We do.

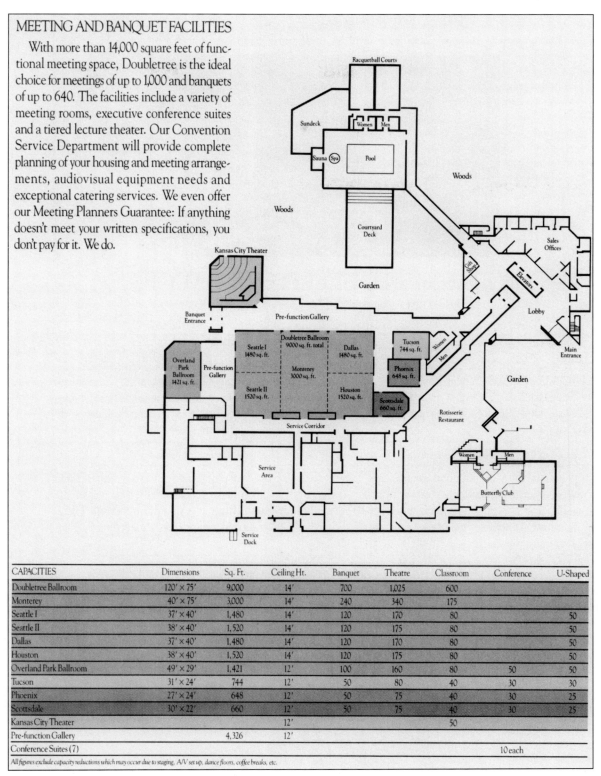

CAPACITIES	Dimensions	Sq. Ft.	Ceiling Ht.	Banquet	Theatre	Classroom	Conference	U-Shaped
Doubletree Ballroom	120' × 75'	9,000	14'	700	1,025	600		
Monterey	40' × 75'	3,000	14'	240	340	175		
Seattle I	37' × 40'	1,480	14'	120	170	80		50
Seattle II	38' × 40'	1,520	14'	120	175	80		50
Dallas	37' × 40'	1,480	14'	120	170	80		50
Houston	38' × 40'	1,520	14'	120	175	80		50
Overland Park Ballroom	49' × 29'	1,421	12'	100	160	80	50	50
Tucson	31' × 24'	744	12'	50	80	40	30	30
Phoenix	27' × 24'	648	12'	50	75	40	30	25
Scottsdale	30' × 22'	660	12'	50	75	40	30	25
Kansas City Theater			12'			50		
Pre-function Gallery		4,326	12'					
Conference Suites (7)							10 each	

All figures exclude capacity reductions which may occur due to staging, A/V set up, dance floors, coffee breaks, etc.

FIGURE 13.1. An advertisement marketing the features of the meeting and banquet facilities of a large hotel. (*Courtesy of the Doubletree Hotel, Overland Park, Kansas*)

DOUBLETREE HOTEL · AT CORPORATE WOODS

10100 College Blvd., Overland Park, KS 66210 • 913-451-6100 • FAX: 913-451-3873

Doubletree Hotels 800-222-TREE • APOLLO • SABRE • DATAS II • PARS • SystemOne

LOCATION

Situated in a wooded, park-like setting, at I-435 and U.S. 69, the Doubletree is right in the heart of the bustling College Boulevard business corridor and less than 20 minutes from Kansas City.

ACCOMMODATIONS

The beautiful, 18-story Doubletree offers 357 executive-tailored guest rooms, including 17 luxurious suites. Non-smoking floors and accessible rooms for individuals with disabilities are also available.

SURROUNDING ATTRACTIONS

At the Doubletree, you're within minutes of dozens of shopping, dining and night life options. Plus, the popular Country Club Plaza, Worlds Of Fun Amusement Park and Kansas City's professional sports events are all just a short drive away.

RECREATION

You'll have plenty of ways to stay in shape or simply relax. You can take a dip in our large, indoor pool. Kick back in the sauna or whirlpool. Or get in a game of racquetball. There are also miles of wooded jogging trails leading directly from the hotel.

DINING/ENTERTAINMENT

At the Rotisserie Restaurant, you'll enjoy classic dining amidst an elegant setting. For live entertainment and a conversational atmosphere, the sophisticated Butterfly Club is the place to be. Plus, Doubletree is surrounded by a variety of other dining choices, all within walking distance.

SERVICE FACILITIES

Laundry and valet services. Instant check in and check out, business services and room service. And, of course, our homemade chocolate chip cookies on your first night.

DOUBLETREE

HOTEL · AT CORPORATE WOODS

1-800-222-TREE

We're waiting to welcome you at over 85 Doubletree Hotels and Canadian Pacific Hotels & Resorts in North America.

FIGURE 13.1. *(Continued)*

banquet service department, and accounting department. This function sheet includes information such as the name of the group, the number to be served, the menu, special setup requirements, billing procedure, and information about any details that differ from normal procedure. The various departments use this data in areas such as purchasing and staffing.

BANQUET MENU PLANNING

The principles of menu planning remain virtually the same for small restaurant banquets or large hotel functions. These principles are:

1. Fixed menu
2. Demographics
3. Theme
4. Staff skill level
5. Pricing
6. Meeting length

FIXED MENU

In banquets, normally the entire menu is fixed. In other words, it is selected by one person or a committee of people during the preliminary planning stage and there is no selection made on the part of the banquet guest. There are, of course, exceptions to this rule, such as in the case of an individual's dietary requirements or religious restrictions. Barring this type of exception, not only is the selection fixed, but the sequence of courses is also fixed. Because the menu is set, all items selected for service at a banquet must be well-liked by the patrons attending that function.

Another factor to consider when selecting courses is that service is simplified and the meeting length shortened if the first course, normally an appetizer, can be preset prior to service. Therefore, a cold appetizer is preferable to a hot one, as it could be set just prior to the guests being seated. However, the wishes of the clients should always be considered over the ease of service. If they prefer a hot appetizer over a cold one, serve it to them.

The sequence of dishes served at banquets has traditionally followed the light-heavy-light sequence. This format was believed to have been developed at the Brown Palace Hotel in Denver, Colorado. This sequence refers to the fat content of each dish. Thus, one would plan a menu starting with a dish that contained little or no fat, then build to a dish that had a higher fat content, and then

ORGANIZATION

CONTACT

MAILING ADDRESS

DOUBLETREE
HOTEL · AT CORPORATE WOODS

BANQUET EVENT ORDER

DAY	MONTH	DATE	YEAR

FUNCTION

FAX #	PHONE	HOME
		BUS.

IN-HOUSE CONTACT (IF DIFFERENT THAN ABOVE)

READER BOARD POSTING (IF DIFFERENT THAN ABOVE)

MENU

EVENT	ROOM	NO. PERSONS	TIME

MEETING ROOM SET-UP

ROOM RENTAL

AUDIO-VISUAL REQUIREMENTS

METHOD OF PAYMENT

BF #: _____   ☐ CASH

_____   ☐ CHECK

CC #: _____   ☐ CREDIT CARD

_____   ☐ DIRECT BILL

ADV DEP REQD: _____

Doubletree Hotel agrees to provide the above as quoted and to make every effort to assure a successful group activity.

By _____   Date _____

I accept the above arrangements and understand the Attendance Guarantee is required by _____ . I understand the attendance guarantee represents the minimum billing and if not received, the above expected figure will be the guarantee.

Accepted By _____   Date _____
CUSTOMER

FIGURE 13.2.   A banquet event order used to communicate a function to all of the hotel's departments, along with an invoice for billing the event. (*Courtesy of the Doubletree Hotel, Overland Park, Kansas*)

DOUBLETREE

185066

GROUP		
FUNCTION		
ROOM	DAY	DATE
BILLING ADDRESS		

COVERS	DESCRIPTION	AMOUNT
EQUIP. RENTAL		
ROOM RENTAL		

BAR		
	FOOD	
	SUB TOTAL	
	BAR	
	SERVICE CHARGE	
SIGNATURE X	TAX	

TOTAL ▶

CUSTOMER COPY - White   FRONT DESK COPY - Green   ACCOUNTING COPY - Blue
SERVICE - Pink   FOOD & BEV. DEPT. - Yellow   MASTER FILE COPY - Gold
110-106

FIGURE 13.2. *(Continued)*

schedule dishes that are successively lower in fat. While this format is still used in more traditional banquets, the majority of banquets today follow the appetizer, salad, entree, vegetable, starch, dessert, beverage format with little or no regard to fat content in any particular course.

DEMOGRAPHICS

Because the menu is fixed, it is important that all dishes selected be popular with the attendees of the banquet. The demographics of the group, therefore, become very important. Particular selections might be eliminated due to religious or ethnic considerations. Still, some groups of highly educated and high-income clients would prefer certain food selections over those that might be preferred by another group with lower education and income. Age is another factor to take into consideration. It would certainly be inappropriate to propose the same menu to teenagers as to a group of senior citizens having a high tea.

THEME

Quite often a group holding a special function requests a theme. This could be a religious or ethnic group celebrating an event, a corporate sales meeting, a club-sponsored fundraiser, or any other reason that brings people together to feast and enjoy each other's company. When this is the case, the banquet should always carry out the theme of the group and/or event. This is done in two ways. First, the room should be decorated following the motif with the table decorations carrying out the subject. Second, the menu should reflect the theme. Therefore, the person responsible for writing the menu should have a vivid imagination and the ability to select foods that will tie the theme and the menu together.

Banquets should be festive affairs and with unrestrictive planning, the menu writer, through decorations and menu selection, can add to the fun and camaraderie of the event. Not only is the selection important, but printed menus placed at each guest's place with descriptive terminology carrying out the theme aid in tying the event together. All too often, unfortunately, banquets are boring, serving roast beef, green beans amandine, etc., etc., etc., when with minimal foresight so much fun could be had planning the menu properly.

SKILL LEVEL

Along with selecting foods that are popular, fitting the demographics of the group involved, and supporting the theme, one other factor should not be overlooked—the skill level of the staff. One could very easily get overzealous planning the menu, but if it cannot be carried out to perfection, it should be scrapped and a new menu prepared. Remember to consider both the production and service staff. Not every kitchen can properly prepare a consommé, a chicken Kiev,

FIGURE 13.3.   A complete set of food and beverage banquet menus, along with the hotel's policies regarding events. Notice the variety of themes that can be used with the "set menus," as well as their policy of developing menus other than the printed ones. (*Courtesy of the Doubletree Hotel, Overland Park, Kansas*)

BETTER THAN COFFEE BREAKS

BETTER THAN COFFEE BREAKS

JOHNSON COUNTY FAIR
Apple Cider, Lemonade, Honey Roasted Peanuts,
Hot Soft Pretzels, Doubletree Chocolate Chip Cookies,
Whole Fresh Fruit and Soft Drinks

COUNTRY STORE
Doubletree Chocolate Chip Cookies,
Assorted Dime Store Candies, Lemonade,
Assorted Soft Drinks

POST TIME/DAY AT THE RACES
Hot Soft Pretzels, Mini Pizzas, Nachos and Cheese, Peanuts,
Popcorn, Non-Alcoholic Beer, and Assorted Soft Drinks

VIP CONFERENCE SETTING
Mineral Waters at Each Setting Along with
Jars of Hard Candies, Pads and Pencils.
(Available for All Set-ups Except Theatre Style)

HIGH TEA
Finger Sandwiches, Crumpets,
Butter, Preserves, Petit Fours,
Chocolate Dipped Strawberries and Specialty Teas

HEALTH FOOD BREAK
Seasonal Fresh Whole Fruits, Fruit Yogurt,
Granola Bars and Assorted Fruit Juices

HOT SUMMER DAY
All Your Favorite Frozen Ice Cream Treats to Include:
Ice Cream Bars, Fudgesicles and Popsicles,
Lemonade, Frozen Candy Bars, Assorted Soft Drinks

SODA FOUNTAIN
Make Your Own Sundae with Vanilla Ice Cream,
Three Sauces, Chopped Nuts, Whipped Cream, Cherries,
Floats and Chocolate Ice Cream Shakes

MOM'S COOKIE JAR
Assorted Freshly Baked Cookies, (3 Kinds)
Brownies, Milk and Assorted Soft Drinks

DOUBLETREE
HOTEL · KANSAS CITY

FIGURE 13.3. *(Continued)*

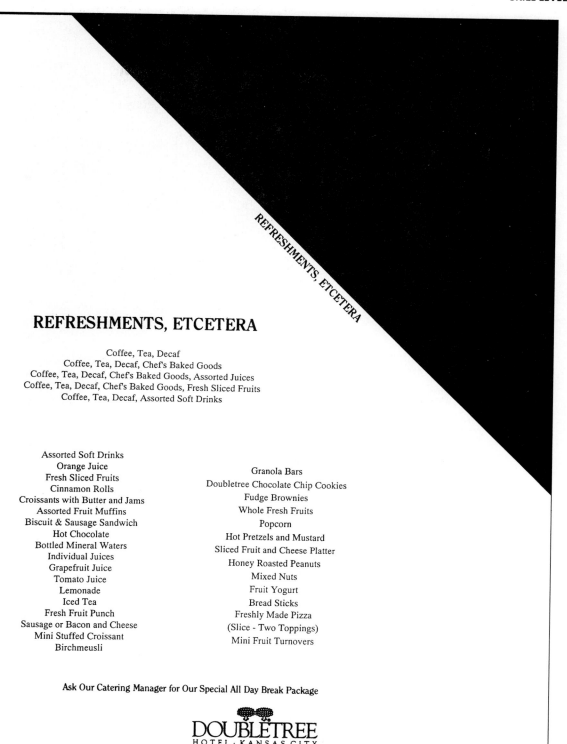

REFRESHMENTS, ETCETERA

REFRESHMENTS, ETCETERA

Coffee, Tea, Decaf
Coffee, Tea, Decaf, Chef's Baked Goods
Coffee, Tea, Decaf, Chef's Baked Goods, Assorted Juices
Coffee, Tea, Decaf, Chef's Baked Goods, Fresh Sliced Fruits
Coffee, Tea, Decaf, Assorted Soft Drinks

Assorted Soft Drinks
Orange Juice
Fresh Sliced Fruits
Cinnamon Rolls
Croissants with Butter and Jams
Assorted Fruit Muffins
Biscuit & Sausage Sandwich
Hot Chocolate
Bottled Mineral Waters
Individual Juices
Grapefruit Juice
Tomato Juice
Lemonade
Iced Tea
Fresh Fruit Punch
Sausage or Bacon and Cheese
Mini Stuffed Croissant
Birchmeusli

Granola Bars
Doubletree Chocolate Chip Cookies
Fudge Brownies
Whole Fresh Fruits
Popcorn
Hot Pretzels and Mustard
Sliced Fruit and Cheese Platter
Honey Roasted Peanuts
Mixed Nuts
Fruit Yogurt
Bread Sticks
Freshly Made Pizza
(Slice - Two Toppings)
Mini Fruit Turnovers

Ask Our Catering Manager for Our Special All Day Break Package

DOUBLETREE
HOTEL · KANSAS CITY

FIGURE 13.3. (*Continued*)

BREAKFAST BUFFETS

$35.00 Service Charge will be Added
for Less than the Minimum Amount

BUFFET I

Assorted Chilled Juices, Fresh Sliced Fruit Platter,
Fluffy Scrambled Eggs, Assorted Cold Cereals, Crisp Bacon,
Sausage Links, Breakfast Potatoes, Chef's Baked Goods,
Country Gravy and Buttermilk Biscuits, Butter, Jellies and Beverages
(minimum of 35 people)

BUFFET II

Assorted Chilled Juices, Fresh Sliced Fruit Platter, Chilled Grapefruit Halves,
Cheese Blintz with Fruit Toppings, Fluffy Scrambled Eggs, Cinnamon French Toast,
Crisp Bacon, Sausage Links, Breakfast Potatoes, Assorted Breakfast Breads,
Syrup, Whipped Butter, Jellies and Beverages
(minimum of 35 people)

BUFFET III
(Healthy Choice)

Vanilla Yogurt with Three Fruit Toppings and Granola, Sliced Fresh Fruits
and Seasonal Berries, Whole Grain Cereal with Skim Milk, Fruit and Bran Muffins,
Baked Buffet Eggs (Egg Beaters), Baked Ham Slices (95% Fat Free),
Assorted Chilled Juices and Beverages
(minimum of 50 people)

BUFFET IV

Assorted Chilled Juices, Eggs Benedict, Fresh Sliced Fruits with Berries,
Pigs in a Blanket with Blueberry Syrup, Medallions of Beef Tenderloin, Lyonnaise Potatoes,
Mini Croissants and Flavored Cream Cheeses, Bagels, Assorted Breakfast Breads,
Whipped Butter, Jellies, and Beverages
(minimum of 50 people)

OMELETTE STATION
Add 3.95 per person

2-HOUR CHAMPAGNE SERVICE
Add 4.00 per person

DOUBLETREE
HOTEL · KANSAS CITY

FIGURE 13.3. *(Continued)*

BREAKFAST

ALL AMERICAN
Fluffy Scrambled Eggs, Choice of: Crisp Bacon,
Ham, Sausage Links, or Canadian Bacon,
Served with Breakfast Potatoes with Fresh Fruit Garnish

COUNTRY BREAKFAST
Fluffy Scrambled Eggs, Buttermilk
Biscuits with Country Gravy, Choice of:
Smoked Ham, Bacon or Sausage Links,
with Fresh Fruit Garnish

BAKED OMELETTE
With Your Choice of Fillings: Ham and Cheese,
Mushroom and Cheese, or Denver Mix,
Breakfast Potatoes with Fresh Fruit Garnish
(maximum of 50 people)

BELGIAN WAFFLE
With Powdered Sugar, Fruit Topping and Syrup,
Choice of: Crisp Bacon, Smoked Ham, Sausage Links, or Canadian Bacon,
Served with Whipped Butter with Fresh Fruit Garnish
(maximum of 50 people)

MID WESTERN
2 - 2oz. Medallions of Beef Tenderloin,
Fluffy Scrambled Eggs, Lyonnaise Potatoes
with Fresh Fruit Garnish

PIGS IN A BLANKET
Three Sausage Links Wrapped in Buttermilk Pancakes,
Served with Syrup and Whipped Butter,
with Fresh Fruit Garnish

CROISSANT SANDWICH
Open Faced Croissant with Fluffy Scrambled Eggs, Topped with Cheese and
Canadian Bacon or Sausage Patty, with Fresh Fruit Garnish

SOUTH OF THE BORDER
Breakfast Burrito (Scrambled Eggs, Potatoes,
and Spicy Sausage), Topped with Salsa and
Monterey Jack Cheese, with Fresh Fruit Garnish

EGGS BENEDICT
Canadian Bacon, Hollandaise Sauce, Served with
Breakfast Potatoes with Fresh Fruit Garnish
(maximum or 75 people)

FRESH FRUIT BREAKFAST PLATE
Sliced Melon, Fresh Berries, Nut Bread or Muffin,
Cream Cheese, Whipped Butter, Assorted Jellies and Yogurt Sauce (for Dipping)

All Breakfasts Include: Orange Juice, Beverage, Chef's Baked Goods

DELUXE CONTINENTAL
Coffee, Tea, Decaf, Assorted Juices, Fresh Sliced Fruit,
Chef's Baked Goods, Bagels and Cream Cheese

FIGURE 13.3. *(Continued)*

BRUNCH BUFFETS

$35.00 Service Charge for Less than 50 People

BRUNCH BUFFET I
Fresh Sliced Fruit Platter
Assorted Juices
Pasta Salad
Marinated Vegetable Salad
Garden Green Salad
with Choice of Dressings

(Choice of Two)
Sauteed Sole Florentine
Garden Fresh Quiche
Beef Stroganoff
with Fresh Egg Pasta
Chicken Veronique
Seafood Newburg

Fluffy Scrambled Eggs
Crisp Bacon and Sausage Links
Breakfast Potatoes
Mini Croissants
Butter and Jams
Beverage Choices

BRUNCH BUFFET II
Assorted Juices
Fresh Sliced Fruit Platter
Assorted Cheeses
Two Seasonal Chilled Salads
Bagels with Smoked Salmon
and Cream Cheese
Chef's Omelette Station with
Assorted Condiments

(Choice of Three)
Garden Fresh Quiche
Beef Tips Chasseur
Chicken Veloute in Pastry Shell
Grilled Porkloin
Salmon Bernaise
Cashew Chicken

Roast Beef
(Carved to Order add $2.00 per person)

Fluffy Scrambled Eggs
Seasonal Vegetables
Crisp Bacon and Sausage Links
Breakfast Potatoes
Chef's Baked Goods
Beverage Choices

2-Hour Champagne Service

Our Catering Manager is ready to help you create that special theme brunch buffet:
South of the Border, French Bistro, All American Hero, and Swiss Alps . . .to name a few.
Make your program a memorable one with unlimited opportunities.

DOUBLETREE
HOTEL · KANSAS CITY

FIGURE 13.3. *(Continued)*

LUNCHEON BUFFETS

$35.00 Service Charge
for Less than 50 People

SALAD BUFFET
Soup du Jour, Assorted Crudite with Herbal Dip,
Tossed Salad with Choice of Dressings,
Bacon Bits, Croutons, Cheddar Cheese,
Toasted Almond Pineapple Chicken Salad,
Tuna Salad, Sliced Fruit with Domestic Cheese Tray,
Assorted Crackers and Bread Sticks, Mini Croissants,
Chocolate Mousse and Strawberries Romanoff

ITALIAN BUFFET
Tossed Salad with Choice of Dressings,
Bacon Bits, Croutons, Cheddar Cheese,
Marinated Tortellini Salad, Antipasto Tray,
Lasagne with Italian Sausage, Linguini with
Marinara and Alfredo Sauces, Chicken Parmesan,
Garlic Toast, Vegetable Medley
Spumoni Ice Cream and Canolli

MARKET PLACE DELI BUFFET
Tossed Salad with Choice of Dressings, Bacon Bits, Croutons,
Cheddar Cheese, Marinated Artichoke Salad, Pasta Salad, Cole Slaw.
Relish Tray, (Sliced Onion, Tomato, Dill Pickle Spears, Olives)
Choice of Four Meats: Ham, Turkey, Beef, Pastrami or Corned Beef
Cheddar and Swiss Cheeses, Assorted Breads and Condiments
Doubletree Chocolate Chip Cookies, Fruit Pies, Double Fudge Brownies
Soup du Jour - Add 1.00 per person

COUNTRY PICNIC BUFFET
Tossed Salad with Choice of Dressings, Bacon Bits,
Croutons, Cheddar Cheese, Southern Fried Chicken,
Country Fried Pork Chops, Mashed Potatoes and Gravy,
Farmers Style Green Beans, Crudite with Herbal Dip,
Biscuits with Honey and Whipped Butter,
Fruit Cobbler, Pecan Pie and Cinnamon Rolls

ORIENTAL BUFFET
Oriental Chicken Salad, Mandarin Fruit Salad,
Marinated Vegetable Salad, Egg Drop Soup,
Chinese Egg Rolls with Sweet and Sour, and
Hot Mustard Sauce, Beef with Broccoli and Oyster Sauce,
Sweet and Sour Tempura Pork, Fried Rice,
Stir Fried Vegetables, Chinese Almond and Fortune Cookies

LUNCHEON BUFFET
Tossed Salad with Choice of Dressings, Bacon Bits, Croutons, Cheddar Cheese,
Spinach Salad with Hot Bacon Dressing, Artichoke Salad, Tortellini Salad, Waldorf Salad
Choice of Two: Fried Chicken (KC Spiced), Top Sirloin with Mushroom Sauce,
Marinated Grilled Chicken Breast, Beef Stroganoff or Stuffed Sole with Lobster Sauce
Rice and Potato, Vegetable du Jour, Rolls and Butter
Doubletree Chocolate Chip Cookies, Cheesecake, Chocolate Mousse and Carrot Cake

SOUTH OF THE BORDER BUFFET
Build Your Own Taco: Shredded Lettuce,
and Cheeses, Diced Onions, Olives, Tomatoes,
amd Scallions, Tortilla Chips, Corn and
Flour Tortillas, Mexican Style Ground Beef,
Guacamole, Chicken Enchiladas, Spanish Rice,
Pinto Beans, Ice Cream with Kahlua,
Sopapillas in Cinnamon Sugar with Honey

KANSAS B-B-Q
Tossed Salad with Choice of Dressing,
Bacon Bits, Croutons, Cheddar Cheese, Hamburgers,
Hot Dogs, Bar-B-Que Chicken, Buns and
Condiments, Relish Platter, Potato Salad,
Cole Slaw, Sliced Fruit Tray, Doubletree
Chocolate Chip Cookies, Double Fudge Brownies
($35.00 grill fee)

DOUBLETREE
HOTEL · KANSAS CITY

FIGURE 13.3. *(Continued)*

LIGHT LUNCHEONS

LIGHT LUNCHEONS
(*Naturally Lower in Sodium and Cholesterol)

COBB SALAD*
Tossed Salad with Chicken Breast, Bleu Cheese Bits, Crumbled Bacon,
Tomato and Cucumber Slices, Olives, and Chopped Eggs,
Served with Choice of Two Dressings

SAMI'S THAI BEEF SALAD
Marinated Beef and Vegetables in a
Shallot Dressing, Served over Assorted Greens
with Appropriate Garnishes

MARINATED GRILLED CHICKEN BREAST*
Served over Pasta with Broccoli,
Tomato, Black Olives in a
Peppercorn and Parmesan Dressing

CHEF'S SALAD*
Crisp Salad Greens, Julienne of Turkey Breast and
Ham, Swiss and American Cheeses, Quartered Eggs, Tomatoes,
and Fresh Vegetable Garnish with Choice of Two Dressings

BOX LUNCH
Two Pieces of Fried Chicken and 1/2 Hoagie
Sandwich, Doubletree Chocolate Chip Cookie,
Fresh Whole Fruit and Potato Chips,
Accompanied by a Cold Soft Drink

ARHAM SANDWICH
Lavosh Bread Rolled with Ham,
Turkey, Cheddar, Swiss, and
Herbed Cream Cheese, Served with
Pasta Salad and Egg Garnish

INDIVIDUAL DELI PLATTER
Roast Beef, Smoked Ham, Sliced Turkey, Swiss and American Cheeses,
Potato Salad, Pasta Salad, Bermuda Onion and Tomato Garnish,
Served with Appropriate Condiments and Assorted Breads

CROISSANT SANDWICH
Large Croissant Filled with Your Choice of
Chicken Salad, Tuna Salad, Club Sandwich
or Vegetarian, or Choose any Two with Mini Croissants

BROILED SALMON*
Served with Your Choice of Two Sauces
Bearnaise or Chinese Mustard Glaze,
Stir Fry Vegetables and Grilled New Potatoes

GRILLED CHICKEN BREAST CAESAR SALAD*
Classic Salad Topped with Broiled Chicken Breast,
and Appropriate Garnishes

DESSERTS
Fruit Sorbet with Cookie, Brownie a la Mode,
Apple or Peach Cobbler, Cheesecake with Strawberry Sauce, Carrot Cake

All Light Luncheons Include: Rolls, Butter and Beverage

DOUBLETREE
HOTEL · KANSAS CITY

FIGURE 13.3. (Continued)

LUNCHEONS

STARTERS
Fresh Fruit Cup, Fresh Seasonal Greens
with Choice of Dressing,
Soup du Jour or Marinated Artichoke Salad

SPECIALTY STARTERS
Spinach Salad with Hot Bacon Dressing,
Butter Lettuce with Raspberry Vinaigrette,
Seafood Pasta Salad or Kansas City Steak Soup
(Priced Individually)

SOUTHERN FRIED CHICKEN BREAST
Southern Fried Chicken Breast with Georgia Cured Ham,
Whipped Potatoes and Country Gravy, Garden Vegetables

LONDON BROIL
Marinated Grilled Flank Steak,
Served Over French Bread Crouton,
Potato du Jour, and Garden Vegetables

STUFFED PORK CHOP CORDON BLEU
Stuffed with Ham and Swiss Cheese,
Served with Potato du Jour
and Garden Vegetables

MARINATED GRILLED CHICKEN BREAST
(Healthy Choice)
Marinated with Fresh Herbs and Olive Oil,
Served with Wild Rice and Garden Vegetables

CHICKEN PARMESAN
Boneless Breast of Chicken, Breaded and Lightly
Sauteed with Provolone Cheese and Marinara Sauce,
Served over Fresh Egg Pasta and Garden Vegetables

OPEN FACE STEAK SANDWICH
6oz. K.C. Strip on Sourdough Bread,
Served with Your Choice of Potato,
and Garden Vegetables

BEEF, CHICKEN OR PORK FAJITA
Served with Soft Flour Tortilla, Shredded Lettuce, Diced Tomato,
Sour Cream, Guacamole, Spanish Rice and Your Choice of Meat.
(Choice of Two - $1.25 Extra)

PRIME RIB SANDWICH
6oz. Prime Rib, Served on French Bread Crouton,
Potato du Jour, and Garden Vegetables

BOSTON BAKED COD
Lightly Breaded Cod Filet with
Potato du Jour and Garden Vegetables

SEAFOOD LINGUINI
Tender Linguini Noodles with Crabmeat and Shrimp Tossed with
Alfredo Sauce and Topped with Parmesan Cheese, Served with Garlic Toast

All Luncheons Include: Rolls, Butter and Beverage

DESSERT SELECTION

DOUBLETREE
HOTEL · KANSAS CITY

FIGURE 13.3. (*Continued*)

SPECIALTY DINNER BUFFETS

SPECIALTY DINNER BUFFETS
$35.00 Service Charge for Less than 50 People

STEAK FRY
Tossed Seasonal Greens - Choice of Dressings,
Crudite with Herbal Dip, Deviled Eggs, Sliced Watermelon,
Choice of Two: 12oz. KC Strip, 16oz. T-Bone Steak, 8oz. Tenderloin,
Marinated Chicken Breast, 10oz. Pork Chop or Marinated Tuna Steak,

Grilled Ears of Corn, Baked Potatoes, Ranch Beans,
Rolls and Butter, Beverage, Hot Fruit Cobbler a la Mode,
Pecan Pie, Fudge Brownies
($35.00 Grill Fee)

ITALIAN BUFFET
Antipasto Tray, Seasonal Greens with Italian Dressing, Tortellini Salad,
Baked Lasagna, Chicken Parmesan, Fettucini with 2 Sauces - Alfredo and Marinara,
Garlic Toast, Zucchini with Red Pepper, Beverage,
Cannolli, and Amaretto Cake

CHUCK WAGON BUFFET
Potato Salad, Cole Slaw, Relish and Crudite Tray, Sliced Watermelon,
Fried Chicken, Sliced Brisket, BBQ Spare Ribs,
Steak Fries, Corn on the Cob, Farmers Green Beans,
Rolls and Butter, Beverage,
Fruit Cobbler, Strawberry Shortcake, Pecan Pie
($35.00 Grill Fee)

DOUBLETREE
HOTEL · KANSAS CITY

FIGURE 13.3. *(Continued)*

DINNER BUFFETS

$35.00 Service Charge for Less than the Minimum Amounts

DINNER BUFFETS

BUFFET I

Seasonal Greens - Choice of Three Dressings,
Marinated Vegetable Salad, Tri-Color Cheese Tortellini Salad

CHOICE OF TWO:
Braised Tenderloin Beef Tips in Red Wine Sauce, Seafood Newburg,
Chicken Parmesan, Braised Pork Chops, Roast Sliced Sirloin Bordelaise,
Baked Cod with Fresh Herbs and Lemon Butter, Roast Baron of Beef
(with Carver - Add 2.00 per person)

CHOICE OF TWO:
Oven Roasted Potatoes, Wide Egg Noodles, Wild Rice,
Cappelini, Lemon Herb Rice, Anna Potatoes

Vegetable du Jour, Rolls and Butter, Beverage Choices

Cheesecake with Fruit Sauce, Chocolate Layer Cake, Strawberry Mousse
(minimum 50 people)

BUFFET II

Seasonal Greens - Choice of Three Dressings,
Spinach Salad with Hot Bacon Dressing, Marinated Artichoke Hearts with Hearts of Palm,
Relish and Crudite Tray with Herbal Dip, Fresh Sliced Fruit Tray

CHOICE OF THREE:
Stuffed Pork Loin with Apples and Almonds, Steak Dijon, Baked Salmon Bearnaise,
Stuffed Sole with Lobster Sauce, Sirloin Pepper Steak in Brandy Sauce,
Chicken Piccata, Chicken Breast Hunters Style, Roast Baron of Beef
(with Carver - Add 2.00 per person)

CHOICE OF TWO:
Pommes Berni, Potatoes Anna, Wild Rice, Herb and
Lemon Rice, Cappelini, Wide Egg Noodles

Vegetable du Jour, Rolls and Butter, Beverage Choices

Petit Fours, Pecan Pie, Mini Eclairs, Pound Cake with Raspberry Sauce and Whipped Cream
(minimum 50 people)

BUFFET III

Romaine, Spinach and Bibb Lettuce with Raspberry Vinaigrette Dressing,
Marinated Artichoke Hearts and Hearts of Palm, Fresh Fruit in Port Wine,
Seafood Salad - Shrimp, Scallops and Crab Vinaigrette, Sami's Thai Chicken Salad

CHOICE OF THREE:
Veal Oscar Mousseline, Sliced Stuffed Beef Tenderloin with Glace de Viande,
Ballantine of Chicken Breast with Morel Sauce, Roast Long Island Duckling with Lingonberry Sauce,
Shrimp and Scallop Kebobs Served over Angel Hair Alfredo,
Marinated Grilled Tuna Steak Beurre Orange, Whole Roast Entrecote Dijonaise, Baron of Beef
(with Carver - add 2.00 per person)

CHOICE OF TWO:
Pommes Berni, Potatoes Anna, Wild Rice, Lemon and Herb Rice, Au Gratin Potatoes, Cappelini

CHOICE OF TWO:
Asparagus with Hollandaise, Broccoli and Cauliflower with Cheese Sauce, Snow Peas
with Water Chestnuts and White Wine Stir Fry, Broiled Tomato with Herbs and Parmesan Cheese

Rolls and Butter, Beverage Choices

Creme Brulee, Cream Puff Swans, Chocolate Layer Torte
Strawberries Romanoff, Petit Fours
(minimum 50 people)

DOUBLETREE
HOTEL · KANSAS CITY

FIGURE 13.3. *(Continued)*

STARTERS

Spinach Salad with Hot Bacon Dressing
Fresh Seasonal Greens with Choice of Dressings
Soup du Jour (Tureen)
Spinach, Watercress and Romaine with Choice of Dressing
Caesar Style Salad (prepared tableside Add $1.00 per person)
Antipasto Salad

SPECIALTY STARTERS
Shrimp and Crab Claw Cocktail
Seafood Louie in Avocado
Lobster or Shrimp Bisque with Caviar and Sour Cream
Coquille St. Jacques
Smoked Salmon with Traditional Garnishes
Kansas City Steak Soup (House Specialty)
Marinated Artichoke Salad with Garlic Crouton
Bibb Lettuce, Toasted Pecans, Bleu Cheese Croutons with Raspberry Vinaigrette
Three Cheeses and Apples with Cracker Assortment
(Priced Individually)

DESSERTS
Chocolate Sundae, Pecan Pie, Brownie a la Mode,
Cheesecake with Fruit Sauce, Chocolate Torte, Carrot Cake,
Fruit Sorbet with Cookie, Creme Brulee, German Chocolate Cake

SPECIALTY DESSERTS
Bananas Foster, Strawberries Romanoff, Ginger Flan,
Poached Pear in Chocolate Cup, Cherries Jubliee,
Chocolate Cup with Fresh Berries, Cream Puff Swans
(Priced Individually)

FIGURE 13.3. (*Continued*)

DINNER

DINNER

ROCK CORNISH GAME HEN
Boneless, Served with Blended Wild Rice, Broiled Tomato

KANSAS CITY STRIP STEAK
10oz. or 14oz. Maitre d'Butter and Onion Straws

MEDALLIONS OF BEEF & CHICKEN
Sauteed with Shallots and Finished with Cream

TOURNEDOS OF BEEF
Sauteed Tenderloin Medallions of Beef Served
with Bearnaise and Topped with Fluted Mushroom Cap

VEAL OR CHICKEN OSCAR
Your Choice, with Crabmeat and
Asparagus Spears, Topped with Bearnaise

STUFFED SOLE WITH CRAB & SHRIMP
Topped with Lobster Sauce

VEAL MARSALA
Tender Veal Medallions Sauteed and
Served over Fresh Egg Pasta

GRILLED VEAL CHOP
Served with Glace de Viande,
Wild Mushroom and Proscuitto Ham

CHICKEN PICATTA
Two Breasts, Egg Dipped and Rolled in Parmesan Cheese, Sauteed with Capers
and Lemon Butter Wine Sauce, Served over Angel Hair Pasta

FILET OF BEEF DIJONAISE
8oz. Beef Tenderloin Broiled to Perfection
Served with Champagne Dijon Sauce

GRILLED SALMON
Buerre Blanc Sauce
Garnished with Diced Cucumbers

ROAST PRIME RIB OF BEEF
10oz. Cut, Seasoned and Roasted in Natural Juices
Served with au Jus and Horseradish Sauce

BREAST OF CHICKEN CHAMPAGNE
Topped with Champagne Sauce and Morels
or Burgundy Sauce and Fresh Herbs
with Proscuitto Ham

DOUBLETREE MIXED GRILL
Lamb Chop with Mint Juniper Sauce, Quarter Roast
Long Island Duckling with Port Glaze,
and 4oz. Medallion of Beef Burgundy

FILET MIGNON
Your Choice of 8oz. or 10oz. Served with Sauce Bearnaise
and Fluted Mushroom Cap

DOUBLETREE
HOTEL · KANSAS CITY

FIGURE 13.3. *(Continued)*

HORS D'OEUVRES

SPECIALTY PLATTERS

KILO OF BRIE EN CROUTE
Baked In a Savory Pastry with Almonds
Served with Assorted Crackers and Tart Apples

ISLAND FRUIT FONDUE
Pineapple Palm Tree Display with Seasonal Fresh
Sliced Fruits and Hot Fudge Fondue for Dipping

FRUIT, VEGETABLE AND CHEESE DISPLAY
A Selection of Seasonal Fresh Sliced Fruits, Vegetables and Cheeses
with Whole Fruit and Vegetable Montage, Displayed with Breads and Crackers

EAST SIDE DELI PLATTER
A Wide Selection of Deli Delights to Include:
Cold Cuts, Cheeses, Assorted Breads, Relishes,
Condiments Whole Kosher Dills
and Deviled Eggs

SEASONAL FRESH FRUIT PLATTER
Melons, Pineapples, and Berries,
Served with Choice of Dipping Sauces:
Honey Lime, or Sour Cream
and Brown Sugar

ASSORTED CRUDITE WITH HERBAL DIP
Selected Fresh Vegetables with Creamy Herb Dip

DOMESTIC CHEESE PLATTER
Finest Domestic Cheeses Displayed with
Grapes, Berries and Assorted Crackers

IMPORTED CHEESE PLATTER
Finest Imported Cheeses Displayed with
Grapes, Berries and Assorted Crackers

SMOKED SALMON WITH TRADITIONAL GARNISHES
To Include Capers, Red Onion, Boiled Eggs,
Cream Cheese, Mini Bagels and Assorted Crackers

DOUBLETREE
HOTEL · KANSAS CITY

FIGURE 13.3. (*Continued*)

CARVED TO PERFECTION

WHOLE ROAST BREAST OF TURKEY
Traditional or Hickory Smoked

GLAZED BONE-IN HAM

BAR-B-Q ROAST BEEF BRISKET

ROAST STEAMSHIP ROUND OF BEEF

WHOLE ROASTED PEPPERED TENDERLOIN OF BEEF

WHOLE ROAST ENTRECOTE DIJONNAISE (Striploin)

**WHOLE ROAST LEG OF LAMB WITH
GARLIC AND FRESH ROSEMARY**
All of the Above are Served with Rolls and Appropriate Condiments
$35.00 Carver Fee (2-hours)

LIGHT SNACKS

Mixed Nuts	French Onion Dip
Smoked Almonds	Ranch Style Dip
Potato Chips	Bleu Cheese Dip
Tortilla Chips	Salsa Dip
Butter Mints	Guacamole
Honey Roasted Peanuts	Chili Con Queso
	Herbal Dip

DOUBLETREE
HOTEL · KANSAS CITY

FIGURE 13.3. (*Continued*)

BEVERAGES

BEVERAGE MENU

We proudly display and pour the following as our Select and Premium Brands on both Hosted and Cash Bar functions

	SELECT	**PREMIUM**
Scotch	Grants	Cutty Sark
Bourbon	Jim Beam (White)	Weller's Reserve
Vodka	Smirnoff	Stolichnaya
Gin	Seagrams	Beefeaters
Rum	Bacardi (Silver)	Barcardi
Tequila	Jose Cuervo White	Jose Cuervo (Gold)
Wine	Sebastiani	Your Catering Manager will assist with wine selections from our Premium Wine List.
Champagne	Available upon request	
Cordials	Available upon request	

NOTE: In addition to the brands listed above, the Doubletree Hotel will be happy to quote pricing on any liquor, beer or wine your hospitality requires. Simply ask your Catering Sales Manager.

BOTTLE SALES ARE AVAILABLE FOR HOSPITALITY ROOMS ONLY.

HOST SPONSORED CONVENIENCE PLAN

Our completely stocked bar with Bartender charges included will offer unlimited consumption of beverages, based on a per person rate for the length of time that the bar is open. Your cost will be based upon the guaranteed attendance or the actual attendance, if higher. We offer our Select and Premium Brands - mixed drinks, beer, and wine.

PER PERSON	**SELECT**	**PREMIUM**
One Hour	7.95	8.95
Two Hours	13.00	15.00
Each Additional Hour	3.00	3.25

HOST SPONSORED CONSUMPTION PLAN

Our Bartender will offer your guests Select or Premium brand liquors. The bar will be stocked completely, including all mixes, bar fruits, and soft drinks. Charges are based upon measured quantities of liquor consumed at a 1¼oz. serving of liquor per drink.

SELECT	**PREMIUM**
3.25 Mixed	3.75 Mixed
2.75 Beer	2.75 Domestic Beer
3.25 Imported Beer	3.25 Imported Beer
3.25 Wine	Wine - (Select from our List)
3.00 Wine Coolers	3.00 Wine Coolers
Soft Drinks - Complimentary	Soft Drinks - Complimentary

DOUBLETREE
HOTEL · KANSAS CITY

FIGURE 13.3. *(Continued)*

WINE LIST

Our Catering Sales Manager has available a wide variety of Domestic and Imported Wines. Doubletree Hotels is proud to offer a selection of Sebastiani as our Select Wines.

CASH BAR

The Doubletree Hotel will have a Cashier sell drink tickets to your guests, who may exchange the tickets for beverages served by our Bartenders.

	SELECT	PREMIUM
Cocktails	3.50	4.00
Wine	3.50	4.00
Wine Coolers	3.50	4.00
Beer	3.00	3.00
Mineral Water	2.00	2.00
Imported Beer	3.25	3.25
Soft Drinks	1.75	1.75

LABOR CHARGES

A $15.00 per hour charge (with a minimum of 3 hours) will be charged for the bartender. Unless otherwise requested, the hotel will schedule one (1) bartender for every 100 people at a hosted or cash bar.

A $10.00 per hour charge (with a minimum of 3 hours) will be charged for a cashier on a cash bar. Unless otherwise requested, the hotel will schedule one cashier for every 200 people at a cash bar.

The hotel agrees to waive the cost of the bartender and cashier fees at the rate of one per each $450.00 in bar sales.

The Doubletree Hotel of Overland Park is the only licensed authority to sell and serve alcoholic beverages for consumption on the premises. Therefore, liquor is not permitted to be brought into the hotel.

All alcoholic beverages served under our licenses will require that beverages be dispensed by Hotel servers and bartenders.

In accordance with Kansas State Law, the Doubletree Hotel will request proper identification of any person of questionable age and refuse service if the person is under age or cannot produce proper ID. Service will also be refused to any person who, in the Hotel's judgement, appears to be intoxicated.

With the exception of cash bars, all prices are subject to a 10% Excise tax.

DOUBLETREE
HOTEL · KANSAS CITY

FIGURE 13.3. *(Continued)*

PRICE LIST

PRICE LIST

BETTER THAN COFFEE BREAKS
Johnson Country Fair 5.95
Country Store 5.75
Post Time 6.25
VIP Conference Setting 3.50
High Tea 7.50
Health Food Break 5.50
Hot Summer Day 4.50
Soda Fountain 5.95
Mom's Cookie Jar 5.75

REFRESHMENTS, ETCETERA
Coffee Service (Gallon) 27.00
Coffee/Tea/Decaf 1.95
Coffee/Tea/Decaf/Chef's Baked Goods 3.25
Coffee/Tea Decaf/Chef's Baked Goods/
    Assorted Juices 5.50
Coffee/Tea/Decaf/Assorted Soft Drinks 2.75
Assorted Soft Drinks (each) 1.75
Orange Juice 1.95
Fresh Sliced Fruits 1.95
Chef Baked Goods (dozen) 15.00
Cinnamon Rolls (dozen) 18.00
Croissants with Whipped Butter and Jam (each) 2.50
Assorted Fruit Muffins (each) 1.50
Biscuit and Patty Sausage Sandwich (each) 2.75
Hot Chocolate 1.75
Bottled Mineral Water (each) 1.95
Individual Bottled Juices 1.95
Grapefruit Juice 1.75
Tomato Juice 1.75
Lemonade 1.75
Iced Tea 1.75
Fresh Fruit Punch 1.75
Stuffed Croissant (each) 2.25
Birchmeusli 4.95
Granola Bars (each) 1.75
Doubletree Chocolate Chip Cookies (dozen) 12.00
Fudge Brownies (each) 1.75
Whole Fruit (each) 1.75
Popcorn 1.50
Hot Pretzels and Mustard (each) 2.00
Fruit and Cheese Platter 1.75
Vegetable and Dip Platter 1.50
Honey Roasted Peanuts 2.00
Mixed Nuts 2.50
Fruit Yogurt (each) 2.50
Assorted Hard Candy 1.50
Breadsticks 1.00
Fresh Pizza (Slice-2 Toppings) 3.00
Mini-Fruit Turnovers (each) 1.75

BREAKFAST
All American 8.25
Country Breakfast 8.50
Baked Omelette 10.50
Belgian Waffles 9.25
Mid-Western 14.25
Pigs In A Blanket 8.00
Croissant Sandwich 9.75
South of the Border 8.50
Eggs Benedict 12.25
Fresh Fruit Plate 9.75
Deluxe Continental Breakfast: Coffee/Tea
    Decaf/Assorted Juices/Sliced Fruit/Chef's
    Baked Goods/Bagels and Cream Cheese 6.95

BREAKFAST AND BRUNCH BUFFETS
Buffet I 11.50
Buffet II 12.50
Healthy Buffet III 11.00
Buffet IV 19.75
Omelette Station (per person) 3.95
Brunch I 23.50
Brunch II 28.50

LUNCHEON BUFFETS
Salad Lunch Buffet 14.25
Italian Buffet 16.95
Market Place Deli Buffet 13.25
Picnic Buffet 15.50
Oriental Buffet 16.75
Luncheon Buffet 16.25
South of the Border Buffet 14.95
Kansas BBQ 16.50

LIGHT LUNCHEONS
Cobb Salad 9.95
Sami's Thai Beef Salad 10.50
Marinated Chicken with Pasta 9.50
Chef's Salad 9.95
Box Lunch 9.50
Arham Sandwich 9.95
Individual Deli Platter 11.25
Croissant Sandwich 11.00
Broiled Salmon 16.75
Grilled Chicken Caesar 10.75

LUNCHEON
Southern Fried Chicken Breast 12.25
London Broil 13.50
Stuffed Pork Chop 13.25
Grilled Chicken Breast 11.75
Chicken Parmesan 12.00
Open Face Steak Sandwich 15.00
Fajitas 11.50
Prime Rib Sandwich 15.00
Boston Baked Cod 11.75
Seafood Linguini 14.25

Please Add 18% Service Charge and 6.5% Sales Tax to All Food and Beverage Items.

DOUBLETREE
HOTEL · KANSAS CITY

FIGURE 13.3. *(Continued)*

(SPECIALTY DESSERTS AND STARTERS PRICED INDIVIDUALLY)

DINNER BUFFETS

Dinner Buffet I	22.95
Dinner Buffet II	25.95
Dinner Buffet III	31.95
Steak Fry	28.00
Italian Buffet	21.95
Chuck Wagon	21.95

HORS D'OEUVRES AND HOSPITALITY

Mixed Nuts	16.00
Smoked Almonds	18.95
Potato Chips	7.50
Tortilla Chips	7.50
Butter Mints	9.50
Honey Roasted Peanuts	9.50
French Onion Dip	10.00
Ranch Style Dip	10.00
Bleu Cheese Dip	14.00
Salsa Dip	12.00
Guacamole	14.00
Chili Con Queso	14.00
Herbal Dip	12.00

DINNERS

Rock Cornish Game Hen	19.75
Kansas City Strip Steak	
10 oz.	24.50
14 oz.	28.50
Medallions of Beef and Chicken	21.75
Chicken Oscar	18.75
Veal Oscar	25.50
Tournedos of Beef	22.50
Stuffed Sole	22.50
Veal Marsala	23.75
Grilled Veal Chop	28.50
Chicken Picatta	18.25
Filet Dijon	23.50
Grilled Salmon	22.25
Roast Prime Rib of Beef au Jus	22.75
Chicken Champagne with Morels	18.25
Doubletree Mixed Grill	25.50
Filet Mignon - 8 oz.	23.50
10 oz.	26.75

SPECIALITY PLATTERS

Kilo of Brie En Croute	50.00
Fruit Fondue Tree (100 People)	275.00
Fruit, Vegetable, Cheese Display	
(Serves 75 People, per person)	4.00
East Side Deli Platter (per person)	7.25
Seasonal Fresh Fruit Platter	175.00
Assortment of Crudites and Herbal Dip	125.00
Domestic Cheese Platter	200.00
Imported Cheese Platter	250.00
Smoked Salmon	200.00

CARVED TO PERFECTION

Whole Roasted Turkey Breast	120.00
Glazed Bone-In Ham	195.00
Steamship Round of Beef	475.00
Entrecote Dijonnaise	175.00
Brisket of Beef	125.00
Whole Peppered Tenderloin	175.00
Leg of Lamb	150.00

CARVER FEE $35.00 for Two Hours

COLD SELECTIONS (Priced per 50 pieces)

Cold Shrimp on Ice	135.00
Crab Claws	135.00
Clams on the Half Shell	80.00
Oysters on the Half Shell	85.00
Marinated Mussels	75.00
Marinated Green Lip Mussels (in Season)	85.00
Finger Sandwiches	80.00
Mini Club Sandwiches	80.00
Arham Sandwiches	85.00
Smoked Salmon Mousse in Cucumber	80.00
Medallions of Lobster	200.00
Steak Tartar	90.00
Cream Cheese Endive or Artichoke Petal	75.00
Assorted Canapes	75.00

HOT SELECTIONS (Priced per 50 pieces)

Chicken Satees	75.00
Beef Satees	80.00
Chicken Drummettes	75.00
Chicken or Beef Kebobs	80.00
Petite Quiche Lorraine	70.00
Breaded Mushrooms	65.00
Crab Rangoon	85.00
Clams Casino	90.00
Oysters Rockefeller	90.00
Italian Stuffed Mushroom Caps	75.00
Seafood Stuffed Mushroom Caps	85.00
Spinakopita	70.00
Potstickers	70.00
Chinese Egg Rolls	70.00
Seafood Quiche	80.00
Breaded Cauliflower	70.00
Breaded Mozzarella	70.00
Meatballs with Three Sauces	65.00

ICE CARVINGS - $150.00 and up

Please Add 18% Service Charge and 6.5% Sales Tax to All Food and Beverage Items.

DOUBLETREE
HOTEL · KANSAS CITY

FIGURE 13.3. *(Continued)*

BANQUET POLICIES

Our menus feature a selection of our most popular items. These are merely suggestions. We would be delighted to arrange banquet menus to suit your particular requirements. We also offer well known regional, national and international dishes, as well as theme parties complete with appropriate decorations, entertainment and costumed service personnel. In order to assure you and your guests a well organized function, we encourage you to read the following policies and discuss any clarification desired with our Catering Sales Manager.

PRICES:	All menu prices are subject to change without prior notice.
	The quotation herein is subject to proportionate increases to meet increased cost of foods, beverages and other costs of operation existing at the time of performance of our undertaking by reason of increases in present commodity prices, labor cost, taxes or currency values. Patron expressly grants the right to the Hotel to raise the prices herein quoted or to make reasonable substitutions on the menu and agrees to pay such increased prices and to accept such substitutions.
MENU SELECTIONS:	Menu selections are requested a minumum of three (3) weeks prior to event.
FOOD:	All food items must be supplied and prepared by the Hotel. Menu selections, room requirements and all other arrangements must be received three (3) weeks prior to the function. Banquet service is based on a set number of guests per food server. Should additional or special service be required, we will be happy to do so at an additional charge. Food may not be removed from hotel at end of function.
GUARANTEES:	Food function attendance must be definitely specified by 3:00 p.m. two (2) working days prior to the event. This number will be considered the minimum guarantee, not subject to reduction, and charges will be made accordingly. The Hotel cannot be responsible for service to more than 5% over the guarantee. The guarantee is the minimum number of guests that will be charged for. A Service charge of $35 will be charged for meal functions with less than our minimum amount of guests in attendance.
	**Saturday, Sunday, and Monday guarantees must be received by 3:00 p.m. the preceding Thursday.
BEVERAGES:	The Doubletree Hotel, as a licensee, is responsible for the administration, sale, and service of alcoholic beverages — liquor, beer, and wine — in accordance with the Kansas Liquor Laws. It is our policy, therefore, that all liquor, beer and wine must be supplied by the Hotel.
ROOM AND RENTAL:	Function rooms are assigned according to the anticipated guaranteed number of guests. If there are fluctuations in the number of attendees, the Hotel reserves the right to reassign the room reserved. Changes in room arrangements within twenty-four (24) hours of the function may result in additional labor charges if the assigned room has already been set up. The Hotel reserves the right to charge a service fee for any extraordinary room requirements. An additional labor charge will be added for functions held on our decks. The Doubletree reserves the right to cancel any banquet or meeting sixty (60) days prior to the scheduled function.
OUTSIDE FOOD AND BEVERAGE:	No food and beverage of any kind will be permitted to be brought into any public hotel area by the Patron or any of the Patron's guests or invitees. All food, liquor, wine and beer must be supplied by the Doubletree Hotel.
BARTENDER:	An additional service charge of $25.00 will be assessed per bar, should beverage sales not exceed $200.00 per bar.
SIGNAGE:	No signs or displays are permitted in public areas without prior hotel approval, we will be happy to assist in printing directional or informational signs.

DOUBLETREE
HOTEL · KANSAS CITY

FIGURE 13.3.   (*Continued*)

CONTROL:	If patron chooses to utilize tickets , add decorations or flowers, specify room diagrams, etc., for a function, please inform catering manager 2 weeks before scheduled function.
MUSIC AND ENTERTAINMENT:	The Catering Department will be pleased to arrange music and/or entertainment for any patron's functions. Should patron choose to make the arrangements, a copy of the signed contract should be provided to the Catering Office in advance of the function.
	Should the volume from musical groups, entertainment or public address systems create disturbances, the Hotel reserves the right to request of the Patron and/or entertainers to lessen volume and, if necessary, to perform without amplification. It is advisable that all entertainment programs be reviewed with the Catering Office prior to contracting said entertainment.
SERVICE CHARGE:	All food and beverage prices are subject to 18% Hotel Service Charge and all applicable state and local taxes in accordance with Agency 92 Article 19 of the Kansas Retailer Sales Regulations.
AUDIO VISUAL:	All audio visual equipment is contracted from Hoover audio visual company at modest prices. Enclosed is a complete audio visual list as well as price list. Please check with the Catering Department for arrangements, availability and confirmation of costs.
SECURITY AND LIABILITY:	The Hotel cannot assume any responsibility for the damage or loss of any merchandise or articles left in the Hotel prior to, during, or following an event. In the instance that valuable items are to be left in any banquet area it is recommended that a security patrol be retained at the group's expense. The Doubletree Hotel reserves the right to inspect and control all private functions through the service of a private security company. The hourly fee of said security will be passed on to the group. Liability for damages to the premises will be charged accordingly.
BILLING:	Payment shall be made prior to the function unless credit has been established to the satisfaction of the Hotel. Once credit is approved, the balance of the account is due and payable thirty (30) days after the date of the function. A service charge of 1½% per month is added to any unpaid balance over thirty (30) days old. A Credit Application may be obtained through the Catering Department. Once your firm's application has been approved, all catering charges along with any Master Account charges may be direct billed. All requests for direct billing should be authorized by the Hotel's Accounting Office at least thirty (30) days prior to scheduled events. If deposit is required it becomes non-refundable thirty (30) days prior to the event.
GROUP SHIPMENTS:	Any freight or shipping charges incurred as a result of materials, i.e., literature, audio visual equipment, etc., being shipped to the Doubletree Hotel remain the sole responsibility of the Conference, Association or Group, etc. The Catering Sales Manager should be informed prior to shipping. Return of materials, equipment are not the responsibility of the hotel, however, arrangements can be made. Parcels may not be received more than two days prior to event.
CANCELLATION POLICY:	Should a meal function be cancelled less than sixty (60) days prior to your group's arrival, the Doubletree Hotel will require that client pay the estimated banquet room rental for reserving the room on a definite basis. Should a meal function be cancelled less than 7 days prior to function, Doubletree Hotel would require that client pay 50% of estimated revenue based on menu function arrangements.

CATERING MANAGER: _____ DATE: _____

ACCEPTED BY: _____ DATE: _____

FIGURE 13.3. *(Continued)*

or a veal cordon bleu. Quite often, convenience foods can extend a kitchen's skill level, but caution should be exercised in terms of quality and cost. Always check out a product—convenience or staff prepared—prior to committing its service to a client.

The abilities of the service staff also need to be considered in the planning of an event. The majority of banquets are served either buffet style or American style. This normally poses no great problem for most restaurants and hotels. Some banquets, however, particularly the more traditional, use Russian-style service. Specialized training and experience are necessary to serve a traditional banquet properly with this style of service. Perfection is a key criterion in banquet functions, both in preparation and service.

A case in point: I recently attended an elegant event at a luxury hotel noted for its cuisine and service. During the cocktail hour preceding the banquet, canapés were served by waiters decked out in tuxedos and white gloves. One guest inquired as to the makeup of these canapés which were beautifully arranged on a silver tray. "Hell, if I know," was the waiter's reply. While amusing at the time, I thought of all the hard work, skill, and years of training the person responsible had put into the making of those canapés. What a shame it had to be ruined by a waiter who was probably an on-call, unskilled, part-time, moonlighting, and obviously untrained employee. What a blow to the reputation of that prestigious hotel. Make sure the employees can measure up to the function and menu planned. If they can't, don't book it.

PRICING

Previous chapters covered the principles of costing recipes and meals as well as determining selling prices for those meals. Those principles apply to banquets as well. There are, however, four additional factors that need to be taken into consideration when discussing a banquet selling price: long-range pricing, tax, gratuities, and guarantees.

Long-Range Pricing

Many times banquets are planned and booked several months in advance. To quote a selling price based on today's costs for a function six months away could leave the operator with little or no profit. To circumvent this problem it is necessary to project what the costs will be when the function is held. Careful study by the person responsible for determining the selling price should be undertaken to ascertain how the commodity futures market is behaving. To estimate what the costs will be for the period when the function will take place requires some speculation. Once these estimated costs are determined, a selling price can be quoted to the client. Because we are dealing with estimates on what is likely to happen in the future, these figures will not always be accurate. They will, however, help the establishment to avoid a loss and will greatly increase the odds for a proper profit margin. Some hotels opt to avoid this problem by setting menus with the client but will not quote a price until 30 days prior to the event. Although this makes it easy for the hotel or catering company, it may jeopardize signing the client who must have registration materials printed months in advance. Remember who is the buyer and who is the seller.

Tax

When quoting a price for a banquet, tax is added to the estimated price so that the client knows exactly what the function is going to cost. The tax added will reflect the percentage applicable for the particular governing unit. A few fortunate areas have no sales tax. Others are taxed by the state or province, county or municipality in which they are located. Some are taxed by all of their governing units, some of their governing units, or just one. Still others may have a tourism or convention tax imposed on top of sales tax(es). Therefore taxes on a banquet could range from zero to several percent, depending on location. A word of caution regarding the amount to be taxed: A few states impose sales tax on labor if it is charged for separately. In this case, a gratuity might not be taxed, whereas a service charge could be. In other words, watch the semantics of the tax laws in your locale.

Gratuities

Gratuities, too, are always discussed as part of the banquet costs, again so that the client knows exactly what the function will cost including meal, tax, and tip. If additional banquet costs are to be incurred, they also should be discussed at this time. These include setup charges, bar charges, room charges, and audio-visual fees, among others. Gratuities, or tips, are normally added to the bill at the rate of 17 percent. Some luxury properties charge 20 percent, while other establishments may go as low as 10 percent.

Inclusive Pricing

Occasionally, a client will want a price quoted that is inclusive (that is, there is $20 to spend per person for everything). To figure a quote of this nature, add together the tax and gratuity percents and add 1 (100 percent) to this figure. Divide the client's desired spending amount by this number.

For example:

5%	sales tax	
+20%	gratuity	
=25%	total plus 100% = 1.25	$1.25\overline{)\$20} = \$16$

Therefore, if a bride and her mother come to you with a budget of $20 per person, you could quote a meal selling for $16. When the tax and gratuity are added, the total cost would come to the budgeted $20.

Guarantees

The guarantee has little to do with pricing other than being used to figure the total bill. However, since it is usually discussed with the client during the price discussions, it is included here. Guarantees normally work in one of three ways: over-under, over-only, and no-variance. In all methods, the client must at some point guarantee that a certain number of guests will attend the banquet. This time period may vary anywhere from one week to 24 hours prior to the event. The variance in time depends on the operation's purchasing policies and delivery availability.

In the *over-under method*, management determines a percentage by which it will allow the client to vary from the guarantee. Normally this is 5 percent. For companies with very liberal policies it could be as high as 10 percent. For example, if a client booked a banquet with a guarantee of 500 people and the hotel had a 5-percent over-under policy, the variance of people attending (and being paid for) could range from 475 to 525 ($500 \times 5\% = 25$). The 475 is the minimum that would be billed and the 525 is the maximum that would be produced. If only 450 people showed up, the client would be billed for 475.

In the *over-only method*, the guarantee is the minimum, with the overage coming from a predetermined percentage, again usually 5 percent but in some cases 10 percent. In the foregoing example, 500 would be the minimum billed the client, with the production maximum set at 525 (using the 5-percent figure).

The *no-variance method* is exactly as the name implies: there is no leeway. Five hundred are billed and five hundred are prepared. Regardless of which method is used, it is imperative that an operation protect itself against no-shows. Certain variable costs, particularly food and labor, are inherent in preparing for a banquet. If lower sales are recorded than anticipated, the result will be a loss.

MEETING LENGTH

Although the length of the banquet and possibly the subsequent meeting has little to do with planning the menu, it is quite impor-

Dinner Party
(A Four Act Dinner for Six)

ACT I: **Autographed Mushrooms**
A Signature Dish. Fresh mushroom caps filled with Parmesan, scallions and white wine. Baked and served warm.

ACT II: **Caesar Salad with Onion-Bagel Croutons**
The role of "Anchovies" will be played my "Lemon" in tonight's presentation of a classic salad.

ACT III: **Shrimp and Herb Saute**
It's love at first bite when shrimp meets tomatoes and herbs in this sizzling saute.

Angel Hair Pasta Flan
A heavenly performance by the delicate Angel Hair pasta, reminiscent of the great Fettucini Alfredo.

Green Beans with Garlic-Black Pepper Butter
Featuring vegetables fresh from a starring role at the Farmer's Market.

ACT IV: **Individual Warm Chocolate Truffle Cakes**
A steamy grand finale filled with dark chocolate passion.

FIGURE 13.4. An example of a banquet menu with a theater theme. (*Courtesy of Feasts of Fancy Catering Co., Diane Dougherty, President, Fairway, KS*)

tant to planning the function itself. Often banquets are scheduled one right after the other in the same room. In this case, it is necessary to know the length of time needed to serve the meal, hold the meeting, clean the room, and reset it for the next function. All too often, in order to gain the optimum income by booking as many banquets as possible, inadequate time is allowed between functions. This results in upset, highly stressed customers and does nothing to enhance the goodwill of the organization.

SHOW MENUS

Show menus are used in operations that serve lunch or dinner followed by a theater presentation or a Las Vegas–type revue. Some dinner theaters serve a buffet prior to the performance. For those operations, the principles offered in the chapter on buffets should be followed. Other establishments opt to provide waiter or waitress service with meals served prior to the show. For those, the principles given for banquet menus apply to show menus, with one exception, a choice of foods is given to the customer.

In developing show menus of this nature, two factors should be kept in mind. First, the menu should be limited, and, second, it should be quick to serve. Limited means no more than five or six entrees. Although the number is limited, the variety doesn't have to be. Picking one entree per category would give a nice variety while still maintaining the limit on the number of menu offerings. The accompanying items, for example, appetizers and desserts, should also be limited in number.

Speed is essential because all meals must be served and the dishes cleared prior to the entertainment. Therefore, it would be prudent to list only "fast food" items on the menu: in other words, items that can be prepared prior to service and simply dished up on request. Avoid short-order foods that need to be cooked to order or items that require a lot of handling.

Prices on show menus are always higher than what would be considered a normal selling price because the entertainment charge is included. Some operations charge one price regardless of the entree selected, while others have a separate price for each entree. Nevertheless, whichever method is used, the price of entertainment is included.

CONCLUSION

For a successful banquet to happen, the menu must be right. Plan it with foods that are popular with the group involved. Take into consideration the theme of the event. Make sure the client understands all costs and the guarantee. Don't overshoot the skills of your staff and don't overbook the room. If you follow these principles, the event is bound to be a success. It's just that simple.

QUESTIONS

1. Explain in your own words the six principles of banquet menu planning.
2. Using all skills learned in this chapter, write a banquet menu for your local high school football team, which has just won the state championship.
3. Assume you have a 5-percent sales tax on the price of a banquet, a 15-percent gratuity charge, and a 5-percent over-under policy. Explain to your client the cost per person of a banquet selling for $20, as well as the total cost of that banquet assuming a guarantee of 1,000 people. Include in your discussion an explanation of the over-under policy.
4. Develop a menu for the Bell Road Barn Players dinner theatre rendition of *South Pacific*.
5. List the skill levels needed by all the staff required to run a banquet.
6. Choose a local operation and describe its long-range pricing structure.

CHAPTER FOURTEEN

Buffets

OBJECTIVES   By the completion of this chapter, the reader should be able to:

- Describe the advantages that a buffet offers over a traditional menu.
- Describe how visual appeal takes the place of descriptive terminology.
- Explain the importance of line movement and table placement.
- Describe how to set up buffet tables to control costs.
- Describe the different types of buffets.

IMPORTANT TERMS

Visual appeal	Zoning
Supporting displays	Arranging to profit
Table placement	Buffet
Garnishment	

INTRODUCTION

No other type of menu planning lets a person show off artistic skills better than a buffet. They can turn an ordinary menu or occasion into a festive party. A buffet offers several advantages to restaurant and food service operations. First and foremost, food can be presented to the customer in dramatic fashion. On the one hand, buffets can be elaborate culinary art displays requiring hours of preparation by highly trained and experienced *garde mange* chefs. These displays are carefully balanced and correct down to the smallest detail. On the opposite end of the spectrum, attractive buffets can be prepared by persons who are unskilled in the art of *garde manger,* but who nonetheless have the ability to put on an enchanting display of foods. With basic cooking skills and following a few fundamental concepts, anyone with a slight degree of artistic ability can prepare an attractive buffet.

A second advantage of buffets is that they can result in tremendous labor savings in any operation. Consider the dining room, where fewer service personnel are needed due to the fact that the customers are essentially waiting on themselves except for, in some cases, beverage service. In the production area, there is no short-order cooking, only mass production of multiple units of several predetermined items, which will increase productivity considerably. Thus, in both the front and back of the house, tighter scheduling results in lower labor costs.

A third advantage of buffets is that with proper menu-planning techniques, food costs can be lower than with a conventional menu. In-season foods along with leftovers can be incorporated into the menu with little difficulty. Since the majority of buffets do not require a printed menu, the food service manager has wide-open choices as to what foods can be used on a daily basis.

The planning of a buffet menu presents an approach somewhat different from the one used to plan conventional menus. First and foremost is the fact that the menu is presented to the customer visually rather than in printed form. Instead of selecting which items to consume by reading, the patron selects the food by viewing the actual fare itself. Because of this, certain principles must be followed to ensure the saleability of the buffet and, most important, to ensure profitability.

VISUAL APPEAL

The visual appeal of any buffet serves the same purpose as descriptive terminology on the printed menu—to sell. If the products look good and the overall merchandising effect is artistic, the buffet will be welcomed by the customer. The old adage "It looks good, therefore, it will taste good" couldn't be more true. To properly merchandise a buffet, three elements are required: fresh food, attractive garnishing, and creative supporting display material.

FRESH FOOD

Nothing can destroy the effect of a buffet more quickly than food that does not appear fresh. Wilted or brownish lettuce in a salad bowl; dried sauce with a skin covering an entree item; and stale, dried-out bakery items are all miscues that have appeared on buffet lines. They detract from the saleability of the buffet. The cause of this stale look is twofold: too much product is being placed on the table and at an improper temperature.

The menu planner must decide not only what should be served, but also how much of each item to place on the table at any one time. Various foods deteriorate over different time periods. Oftentimes stale-looking food was fresh at the beginning of the meal period, but deteriorated after several hours of sitting on the table. Small-batch preparation and timely table placement will overcome this problem.

Temperature is another factor that needs to be taken into consideration in maintaining a fresh look. This is especially critical in operations where buffets are not an everyday occurrence and where temporary setups are used. Cold foods need to be well chilled, not only from an appearance standpoint, but also to avoid contamination. Never set foods that are intended to be chilled on a nonrefrigerated table. Merely setting them on a bed of ice will not get the job done either. They must be set in dishes that are immersed in ice to a level equal to the top of the food line; otherwise the food that is above the ice takes on the temperature of the room and begins its deterioration and contamination process.

Simply stated, hot foods must be kept hot; and cold foods, cold. The guidelines of cold foods below 40°F and hot foods above 140°F ensure that the food on the buffet will be safe and more satisfying to the customer as well.

Safety and appearance must not compromise service. Service personnel must keep a watchful eye on the availability of food. To have an entree run out is a disaster. Imagine 10 to 20 guests standing around, empty plates in hand, complaining about the service.

GARNISHMENT

Garnishing a plate to enhance its presentation is a principle that most restaurants follow. This same concept is also important in buffet presentation. The guideline for plate garnishment, where everything on the plate must be edible, holds true also in platter

FIGURE 14.1. Platter arrangement and edible visual display material make for an attractive display. (*Courtesy of the Greater Kansas City Chef's Association*)

FIGURE 14.1. (*Continued*)

presentation. In addition to garnishing platters, chafing dishes, and other various and assorted holding vessels, buffet garnishment also includes decorative pieces.

Whole hams, turkeys, and fish are often used to enhance a table. One or two of these pieces, properly placed and displayed,

FIGURE 14.1. (*Continued*)

add to the overall color and excitement of the buffet presentation. Dried pastas such as pennes, macaroni, and spaghetti are often used, as are fresh fruits and vegetables. Accompanying items such as sauces and relishes can also be cleverly used as a garnish. Cranberry relish in baskets carved out of oranges makes a colorful display surrounding a platter of cold turkey. Various types of greens such as romaine, leaf lettuce, spinach, and savory cole could be used to underline cold presentations.

SUPPORTING DISPLAY MATERIAL

Supporting display material is slightly different from garnishments in that it includes all *nonedible* display pieces used to enhance the buffet. First and foremost among supporting display material are ice carvings. Over the years these have become a traditional part of many buffets. Often used as centerpieces, they are one of the binding factors that tie the theme of the party and the buffet together. In addition to being used as display pieces, ice carvings can also become serving dishes, typically serving shrimp, crab claws, fresh fruit, or fresh vegetables from a bowl carved of ice.

Other nonedible display devices include flowers, ferns, greens, and leaves. These can be used to add color to the table. An important fact to remember is that these should *not* be used on the platters of food, nor should they touch the platters. Only edible food should be on the platters. All nonedible goods are for table color enhancement only.

A final aspect of supporting display material is height. A long, flat-surfaced, one-level table is boring. Give the buffet dimension

FIGURE 14.2. Examples of supporting display material. Top left, blown sugar. Right, tallow. Bottom left, pastillage. Bottom right, chocolate. (*Photographs courtesy of the Greater Kansas City Chef's Association*)

FIGURE 14.3. Fresh-looking food, supporting display material, various heights, and clever use of linens combine to make up a buffet table with great eye appeal. (*Photographed at the French Embassy, Washington, DC. Courtesy of Marriott Management Services*)

FIGURE 14.3. (*Continued*)

by building up some of the areas. By using wooden boxes or bulk milk cartons covered with linen, the table can take on the added dimension of height. High and low stainless steel or silver serving dishes can also be used for height variance. Remember to achieve a balanced look when using height. The linen used to cover the boxes should be the same as the linen used on the table. White is the traditional color because it gives a clean appearance and enhances the food. However, other colors can be used to tie in with the decor of the room. Make sure that the color selected does not detract from the food served.

FIGURE 14.3.   *(Continued)*

LINE MOVEMENT AND ZONING

The speed at which the line moves is critical to the success of any buffet. Nothing puts the damper on a gala event more quickly than having to stand in a slow-moving line. To avoid this problem, the buffet table or tables should be zoned. A zone is a section that serves 50 people. Each zone should be identical, containing the same selection and assortment as every other zone. Thus, if 200 guests were being served, there would be four zones. In extremely large buffets, zones can be set for 100 guests. For service of 1,000 people, setting up 10 large zones would be easier than setting up 20 smaller ones. Zoning is most predominant in banquet buffets, where a large number of patrons are arriving at about the same time. In restaurants where the guests are arriving over a longer period, the number of zones would be determined by the number of seats in the restaurant and the estimated grouping, in terms of number, of the arrivals.

FIGURE 14.4. Two examples of zoning arrangements on a large grand buffet. (*Photographs courtesy of the Greater Kansas City Chef's Association*)

FIGURE 14.4. (*Continued*)

TABLE SHAPES AND PLACEMENT

Buffets do not require a long, rectangular table. They can take on any shape, with size of the table determined by the number of zones necessary. When deciding where to place tables, the location of the kitchen should be taken into consideration in order to service the buffet adequately. Traffic patterns, as well as space, are crucial as diners should not bump into each other.

An L-shaped table works well when the placement is in the corner of a room. A circle or U-shape is desirable for the center of a

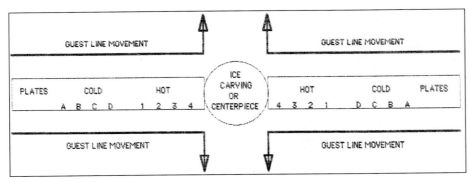

FIGURE 14.5.   A basic example of identical zoning for a multiple-line buffet.

room. When the table is to be placed along a wall, the familiar rectangle works best. Also consider combining table shapes for an interesting and varied look, for example, a long rectangular table with a circle in the middle. For large banquets, where multiple zones are used, consider spreading the tables throughout the room for maximum effectiveness as well as speed of service.

WRITING THE MENU

Several factors need to be taken into consideration when deciding what food items should be placed on a buffet table. First and foremost, of course, is profit. Other factors warranting consideration are customer demographics, the theme of the group or restaurant, and the general ambiance of the selected foods.

Profit

In considering profit on a buffet, the person responsible for planning the menu has a much more difficult task at hand than writing a standard printed table service menu. In a table service menu, the selling price is determined by a cost for which the portion, as well as the item, is predetermined. If all goes well the exact cost, as well as the exact profit, is known for each listing. With buffets, the portions and selections of foods are left up to each customer. How much of which items will they select? The only answer to this dilemma is to deal with it in generalities. In other words, the food cost and subsequent profit must be looked at in total rather than for each specific item. (See Chapter 3 for a discussion of salad bar costs—the same principle applies for buffets.)

Action to control costs can be taken, however, by the person responsible for buffet planning. Once the selling price is established, items can be selected in a cost range to adhere to that particular price. For example, look at chicken. A buffet in a low price range could have chicken and dumplings, while a moderate price range would indicate baked or fried chicken. A higher-priced buffet could call for chicken duxelles or Kiev (not necessarily because of food cost but rather because of labor cost). The same format can be followed for all menu items. Crab claws and shrimp would be eliminated from a low-cost buffet but included on a high-cost offering.

Another action that can be taken to control costs is plate size. The scientific axiom that "nature abhors a void" is definitely true here. Given an empty space on a plate, a customer will fill it. A large plate rapidly becomes filled on a buffet line because the customer is hungry when going through the selection process. This large plate may be filled to a point where the customer will not be able to consume it all. Thus waste occurs. Conversely, with a smaller plate, while the customer is finishing the first plate and returning for seconds, the digestion process is taking place. The customer becomes filled, and thus selects a lesser amount on the return trip.

Demographics

When writing a buffet menu, one of the key considerations should be the demographics of the customers involved. Age, income, education, sex, and ethnic origins all need to be taken into account when deciding not only what items are to be placed on the buffet, but also how much of each item. Teenagers, for example, eat more than do older adults, and quantity becomes a consideration. They also eat different foods; therefore menu selection must be thought out carefully. The guests' income, as well as their level of education and occupation, becomes important as higher-income, better-educated people tend to be risk takers and eat more trendy and unusual foods than do their counterparts. Men tend to eat more and enjoy heavier, fattier foods than do women. Ethnicity is important, as some ethnic groups like certain foods better than other groups. Give consideration to the fact that some religions, as well as ethnic groups, have banned particular foods.

Theme

In addition to demographics, another factor must be accounted for in planning buffets: the theme of the group or restaurant. When booking banquet buffets, the theme of the group must be taken into consideration by choosing menu items that reinforce that theme. In addition to the menu, supporting display material should also carry out the theme of that function. For example, if the group decided on a western theme, barbecued beef, ham, and chicken could be featured with the appropriate accompanying items. Ice carvings depicting cattle or horses along with straw, cowboy hats, and lassos could make up the supporting displays. In restaurants where buffets are an everyday occurrence, the theme and decor of the *establishment* should be reflected in the buffet items. If the restaurant is generic in nature, then the buffet is open to a wide assortment of menu choices. In either situation, however, it is wise to change items from time to time to keep the customer's curiosity aroused. In addition to periodically changing the menu, from time to time feature a theme party, for example, a Friday seafood buffet, a Valentine's Day buffet, or a regional bounty buffet. The ideas are endless.

Balance and Contrast

One final consideration on buffet menus. Make sure that the items selected complement each other as far as taste and flavor are concerned. Contrast should be exploited in the areas of texture, shape, and size, as well as in cooking methods and color. In addition to contrast, make sure that balance also is achieved. A well-planned buffet with many vivid, contrasting colors will whet the appetite of even the most discerning diner.

ALL YOU CAN EAT BUFFETS

All you can eat buffets should be merchandised to profit by the arrangement of items on the table, that is, the lower-cost items should be placed first with succeeding items placed in direct proportion to their cost. This should be done for each food category: salads, starches, vegetables, entrees, and desserts. The categories themselves should also be arranged according to cost. For example, on the hot food section, starches should be first, vegetables second, and entrees third. In the entree section, extenders come first, semi-solid entrees second, and solid entrees third. Roasts should be hand carved to control portions.

Color and texture distribution also need to be taken into account when arranging the table, but not to the exclusions of cost. Some clever manipulation and well-conceived planning are essential to properly achieve this goal.

HORS D'OEUVRE BUFFETS

A different style of buffet, the hors d'oeuvre buffet, is used primarily for cocktail parties and, in some cases, for appetizer service prior to a banquet. Consequently, the menu for an hors d'oeuvre buffet should be drawn up entirely of finger food, that is, food items that do not require utensils. Also, the buffet tables should be scattered throughout the room. In other words, several tables rather than one with a line effect should be used. This arrangement encourages people to move about and socialize rather than stand in line, filling a plate, and sitting down. Each table should be categorized differently. For example, one table could have fruit and cheeses, another canapés, one or more with hot hors d'oeuvre, still another could have seafood, and so on.

Another style of buffet service is called the heavy hors d'oeuvre buffet, which basically follows the same principles as the hors d'oeuvre buffet, the one exception being that, quite often, utensils are used. Hot stations such as pasta or stir fry are added; however, the portions are plated by an attendant and are usually small. Probably the best way to classify this style of buffet is as a cross-breed between the hors d'oeuvre buffet and the formal buffet.

FORMAL BUFFET

In more formal buffet presentations, one rule is eliminated: arrange foods to cost. In formal buffets, items are arranged to taste rather than cost. Also remember that arrangement always follows the normal category selection, that is, appetizers, salads, cold platters, hot foods, and desserts.

Another criterion of formal buffets is that they are more exacting and artistic. They tend to follow closely the standards and guidelines for culinary arts expositions and competitions as written by the American or Canadian Culinary Federation. Formal buffets feature more classical items and dishes than would be found in a regular buffet, as well as several cutting-edge items. A higher degree of art form is also found in formal buffets including such things as tallow carvings, salt sculptures, and pulled and blown sugar pieces. Formal buffets should be attempted only by chefs with several years of training and culinary expertise.

CONCLUSION

Buffets are an exciting alternative to regular menu service. Make sure they are visually appealing. Color contrasts, different heights, ice carvings, flowers, and unusual table arrangements all help to make a buffet a successful event. Proper food selection for the client with a variety of tastes, textures, and color will make it gastronomically appealing. Tie the foods, colors, and decorations together to match the theme of the event. All these criteria create a buffet that is an exciting and successful party. It's just that simple.

1. Explain what is meant by arranging to profit on a buffet.
2. Write a menu and do a diagram for an hors d'oeuvre buffet serving 300 guests for an American Medical Association meeting.
3. Discuss why buffets are essentially more profitable than a la carte menu service.
4. Explain the importance of visual appeal of buffets. Tell what you can do and should avoid in creating good visual appeal.
5. Give several examples of supporting display material on a buffet with an Oriental theme.
6. Discuss the factors that would make a buffet profitable, including how the cost of the buffet should be determined.

CHAPTER FIFTEEN

Cafeteria and Cycle Menus

OBJECTIVES   By the completion of this chapter, the reader should be able to:

- Explain how to use various times frames for cycle menus.
- Explain how cycle menus fit into different types of food service.
- Describe the difference between the various cafeteria designs.
- Explain the difference between the two categories of cafeterias.
- Explain the principles of writing cafeteria menus.
- Describe the concepts for food arrangement in a cafeteria line.

IMPORTANT TERMS

Straight-line cafeteria
Sawtooth
Institutional cafeteria
Cycle menu
Food merchandising

Bypass system
Free-flow cafeteria
Commercial cafeteria
Line diagram

INTRODUCTION

Cycle menus are used in many food service operations and present their own particular set of standards or rules. Commercial restaurants in almost all categories use them for their daily specials to augment the regular printed menu. The major user, however, of cycle menus is cafeterias, both in commercial businesses and in nonprofit food service operations. These include schools, colleges, hospitals, nursing homes, in-plant feeders, and so on. Here, cycle menus are used almost exclusively. Because cycle menus and cafeterias are so intertwined, they are discussed together in this chapter, starting with cycle menus.

LENGTH

Cycle menus are written for a specific period of time and are then repeated, intact, over and over until a new cycle is written. The length of time for which a cycle menu is written varies, depending on the nature of the operation and its clientele. For example, in a hospital food service, where the patient stay is short term, normally three to four days, the length of the cycle would be short. In this instance, a one- or two-week cycle would suffice for patient service. Since these people eat there year round, a longer cycle would be needed for the employee's cafeteria. Thus, a patient menu would be written for breakfast, lunch, and dinner for each day of the week for a one- or two-week period. At the end of this period, the cycle would then be repeated.

A menu for a college dorm, where the length of stay is substantially longer (a semester or academic year), would require a longer cycle. In this case, a cycle would be written for four or five weeks and then repeated. The four- or five-week cycle menu has a greater variety for the patrons than the two-week cycle. Quite often, after a four- or five-week cycle menu has been in use for a period of three months, the menu is discontinued and a new cycle is written. Often this is done four times a year corresponding with the four seasons. Not only is variety ensured, but seasonal goods such as fresh fruits and vegetables can be used as well as seasonal *themes*. On the other hand, commercial cafeterias, because they serve more transient customers, use a shorter cycle of two to three weeks.

RESTAURANT USE

In restaurants, cycle menus may be used in two ways: first, as an operational plan for daily specials that are sold on clip-ons or the chalkboard and, second, as a production list for items listed on the menu as *du jour* (of the day). In setting up a cycle for daily specials, several factors need to be considered: price, balance, and use of leftovers.

Price is important, as the customer perceives that an item listed as a daily special is a greater value than an item listed on the regular printed menu. Therefore, care should be exercised by the menu planner to choose carefully items that will reinforce this perception. Specials that have a lower ingredient cost than those listings appearing on the printed menu will achieve this goal. For example, a restaurant that serves luncheon entrees in the $4 to $5 range would probably have for those entrees an ingredient cost between $1.20 and $2. By developing a cyclical menu of daily specials that have an ingredient cost of a dollar or less, they could then sell the special for $3.50 or less. This would still maintain the restaurant's food cost standard and, at the same time, give the customer a greater perceived value.

As discussed in a previous chapter, the menu writer needs to strike a balance when putting menus together. This also holds true when writing cycle menus for daily specials, particularly when several specials are listed. Balance must exist among categories such as meat, poultry, seafood, and nonmeat entrees. Also, a good balance should occur among cooking methods—broiling, roasting, grilling, and sauteing—and among solid entrees, semi-solid entrees, and extenders, or casserole items. Color and texture balance also need to be taken into account with regard to plate presentation.

One of the primary reasons behind many daily specials is the use of leftovers. Therefore, the cycle menu should not be so tight as to preclude this important function. One of the methods used to incorporate leftovers into a cycle menu is to have a listing, either daily or periodically, known as Chef's Choice. This leaves the manager or chef free either to test market a new item or to utilize a leftover.

Frequently, many restaurants develop a one-week cycle for their specials and run it continuously without changing it. The purpose of this is so that their regular customers know in advance what will be served on a given day. Monday's listings are the same every Monday and so on throughout the week. Although this takes away the element of variety, it can develop a restaurant's reputation for certain products. Bender's Tavern in Kansas City has a waiting line on Wednesdays for ham hocks and beans. Several restaurants in your area probably follow this type of cyclical menu planning successfully.

Quite often a restaurant opts to inject variety on the printed menu by use of the French term *du jour,* rather than daily specials. Translated, *du jour* means "to day" or "of the day." Listings such as soups, vegetables, potatoes, and sometimes house specialties—for example, quiche—have *du jour* listed after them. Examples include soup *du jour,* vegetable *du jour,* or quiche *du jour.* In this case, it is wise to set up a cycle menu to encompass these items. In this way, purchasing and production can be adequately covered and the service personnel will know exactly what is to be served day by day. Without a cycle menu there is too much repetition. Pretty soon, the soup *du jour* is vegetable or French onion day after day. Sometimes employees become complacent in this area and tend to resist change. Suddenly the menu is in a rut.

NONPROFIT FOOD SERVICE

The term *not-for-profit food service* covers a broad spectrum of the hospitality industry. Once called institutional food service, this title covered only a small part of the business, that is, hospitals, nursing homes, and prisons. Left out were industrial in-plant feeding, corporate food service, school food service (primary grades), and college feeding. Another misnomer placed on this group was *captive-audience feeding.* Although some patrons of this group are indeed captive, many clients have a choice of either eating in the food service operation or going elsewhere for their meal or break. The makeup of cycle menus becomes extremely important in food service operations where the patrons (even though they may have the option to leave) are the same day after day. Although selection and popularity of items are to be carefully considered, in no other type or style of menu is nutrition and variety as important as it is in captive-audience cycle menus.

SELECTION AND POPULARITY

Selection and popularity go hand in hand. A rule of thumb here is that the fewer the selections offered in each category, the more popular they must be. Although additional selections pose additional problems for production, purchasing, and inventory, the benefit derived from patrons having the opportunity to make a choice far outweigh the problems. Another rule of thumb is that the larger the food service operation, the more choices should be made available within each category. Thus, a large corporate office building cafeteria could have several entree stations built around ethnic themes such as Italian, Pacific Rim, and Mexican, with several offerings at each station. In contrast, a small rural hospital with 100 beds may have only two entree choices or no choice at all. In this case, because of the limited selection, at least one item in each category should be popular or, if there is no selection on the menu, then all offerings must be popular with the clientele involved. If, for example, a nonselective menu of pan fried liver and onions, buttered Brussels sprouts, and Harvard beets were served, there would probably be few takers. Although this meal is fine nutritionwise, colorwise, texturewise, and otherwise, the items are all low on the popularity poll.

VARIETY

Due to the fact that people who eat in a food service operation may receive many, if not all, of their meals there, variety becomes an important factor. The single largest complaint heard in employee cafeterias, hospitals, dormitories, and schools is that the food is terrible. "Terrible" usually means boring, the same, lacking variety.

There is no reason whatsoever that a person should be bored. Variety can easily be achieved by avoiding repetition of items within the cycle and also by not repeating the cycle too often. As previously discussed in Chapter 5, to avoid monotony, offer a variety of food items within each category. Cooking methods, temperature (both hot and cold), consistency, color, and texture should all be taken into account when writing food service menus.

FIGURE 15.1.   One way of injecting variety into a cafeteria menu is to use various theme promotions. (*Courtesy of Marriott Management Services*)

MENU-PLANNING PROCEDURES

Planning a cycle menu is quite easy if you are organized. A menu-planning worksheet with the seven days of the week across the top and the three meals down the left side helps make the job effortless. Surrounding oneself with several good cookbooks and reference sheets helps spark the imagination. The following simple steps ensure that the process flows smoothly.

1. Plan your main dinner entrees by compiling a list and grouping them by category (meat, fish, fowl, meatless) and texture (solid, semisolid, casserole, sauce); decide on frequency of popular and less popular items.

2. List the entree on your menu-planning worksheet using popular items only.

3. Complete steps 1 and 2 for lunch and breakfast.

4. Add the second and third entrees. These entrees should complement the main entree and can be from the less popular list.

5. Plan the vegetables, starches, and soup for lunch and dinner.

6. Plan the salads. Salads should offer variety in type, color, and consistency.

7. Plan desserts with variety, as was done for the salad category.

8. List breads, condiments, and beverages.

9. List hot and cold cereals, breakfast fruits, and juices.

10. Review menu for color, frequency of items served, texture, and consistency. Make adjustments as necessary.

CAFETERIAS

Cafeterias can be placed into two categories: commercial-for-profit restaurants and not-for-profit, in-house operations. Commercial cafeterias have their strongest customer base across the southern part of the United States and are growing in popularity in the Midwest. Although there are a few independent operators, the majority of these operations is owned by large chains. Popular with senior citizens and, to some extent, families, they owe their success to a wide variety of freshly prepared food with an emphasis on nutritional offerings such as fruits, salads, and a selection of vegetables. Of course, the fresh baked breads, cakes, pies, and pastries don't hurt sales either. They give the customer something that is missing in the majority of quick service and theme restaurants, which is the opportunity to select a nutritionally well-balanced meal.

Not-for-profit, in-house cafeterias are a huge part of today's food service industry. They can be found almost anywhere: in schools, colleges, nursing homes, hospitals, manufacturing plants, office buildings, correctional facilities, and others. Although many of these facilities run their own operations, the majority are contracted out to firms who specialize in running this type of food service operation. Commonly thought of as captive audience feeding, nothing could be further from the truth. Except for a few instances (for example, correctional facilities, hospitals, or some nursing homes), the majority of customers in these places can exercise a choice to either eat in, bring a sack lunch, or leave the premises to eat out at a local restaurant. It is, therefore, a highly competitive business and the menu is of paramount importance in the success of the operation.

Menu writing for cafeterias follows most of the principles of printed menus that were previously discussed; however, a few peculiarities need to be addressed.

CAFETERIA STYLES

Cafeterias come in many different styles, but most follow four basic designs:

1. straight line
2. bypass line
3. sawtooth
4. free flow

The *straight line* is designed exactly as the name implies—a straight line. Of all the styles, it is the slowest-moving, as two things determine speed in a cafeteria line. First, the speed at which the cash is taken and, second, the fact that the line moves as fast as the slowest person. In this design the customer is reluctant to pass a slower-moving patron. The straight-line cafeteria is, however, the most common design found in commercial cafeterias because it takes up the least amount of square footage, which in turn allows for more seats in the dining room and thus additional sales. More important is the fact that the average customer feels most comfortable with this particular design. In the other three designs, customers are encouraged to pass other customers who are either slow in determining what to purchase or are waiting for service personnel to plate their order. Thus blockages in the line are avoided.

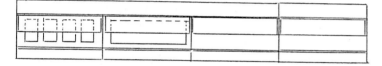

FIGURE 15.2.   Example of straight-line style.

The *bypass line* is a variation of the straight-line system, with the first section serving primarily salads and cold sandwiches, the second section serving hot foods, and the third section serving desserts and beverages. The second section is indented, thus making it easier for customers to jump the line if they do not wish to order hot foods. This system is particularly popular with those operations that offer grill service, since it allows the line to continue moving while other patrons are waiting for their grilled items to be prepared.

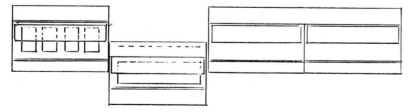

FIGURE 15.3.   Example of bypass line.

The *sawtooth* is also a variation of the straight-line system, with each section being set at a diagonal to the previous section. These separate sections each have their own category or combined categories of food. For example, one section could have soups and salads, another cold sandwiches, and still another hot foods; one section would have beverages and, still another, desserts. The number of sections in this layout would be determined by the number of categories offered. With this design, customers can go directly to the area or areas of their choosing.

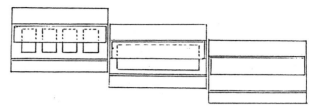

FIGURE 15.4. Example of sawtooth line.

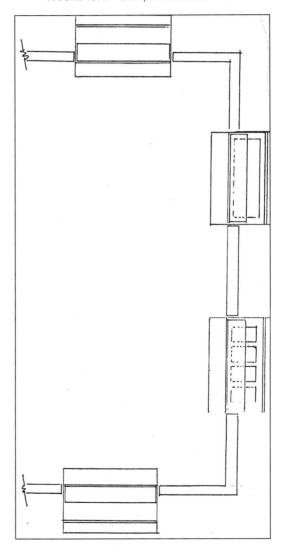

FIGURE 15.5. Example of free-flow system.

The *free-flow system* is designed so that patrons can go directly to the area or areas serving those items that they desire. Although there are many different layouts for the free-flow system, one of the most popular is the shopping center concept, which is shaped like a giant *U*. Another popular design is to have stations scattered around the service area. Each of these stations offers, individually, a different style of food such as pasta, stir fry, or grilled and steam table items. Quite often the hot food stations have an ethnic theme to them. In addition to these stations, there are usually a salad/soup bar, dessert section, and beverages. Free-flow systems are very common in employee cafeterias and other operations where there is repeat business. Due to the fact that they are confusing to the uninitiated, they have not had much success in commercial operations, where the straight-line design is the preferred system. Once the free-flow system is figured out by the customer, it offers quicker service with a minimum of waiting.

FIGURE 15.6. The shopping-center approach in a cafeteria layout enables the operator to set up several stations, thus injecting variety into the menu. Here an ethnic theme is used. (*Photographed at American University, Washington, DC. Courtesy of Marriott Management Services*)

FIGURE 15.6. (*Continued*)

FIGURE 15.6. (*Continued*)

DEMOGRAPHICS

In order to discuss cafeteria demographics, it is necessary to look at the two categories—nonprofit and for-profit. The demographics of nonprofit cafeterias are as diverse as the operations themselves. There is considerable difference between the menus for a college dormitory cafeteria and an in-plant cafeteria for General Motors. In order to develop a menu properly, the menu writer must first ascertain the needs of the group in that particular institution. Some contract feeders ignore this fact and send menus from the home office to the client cafeterias. These menus, generic in nature, cannot meet the specific needs of each institution and, consequently, result in dissatisfied patrons. As stated in an earlier chapter, customers' wants and needs must be carried out in menu selections.

The astute contract companies, as well as the firms that operate their own food services, leave the menu planning up to the unit manager. This works well in that the local manager is in tune with the client base and can fit menus to the demographic diversity of that particular group.

Commercial cafeterias, on the other hand, fit a rather tight demographic spectrum. Predominantly located in the South and Midwest, cafeterias are rather evenly split between downtown and suburban locations, which can be either free standing or located in shopping malls. Commercial cafeterias are popular with people over 40 years old. Since a large portion of this group constitutes senior citizens, the ideas of no tipping and selecting a few items from a wide choice are particularly inviting. Small portions with low prices charged for quality, nutritious food also enhance the cafeteria's image with this group.

Several cafeteria chains are attempting to change their demographic base. As one chain executive put it, "Every time we read the obituaries we find that we've lost some customers." One Midwest chain in particular has instituted an advertising campaign comparing their cafeterias to quick service chains in an effort to lure the younger set. In it they compare value, price, speed of service, and nutrition. This campaign has had success in that the chain's family business has increased dramatically.

CAFETERIA MENUS

When writing menus for cafeterias, several of the principles previously discussed need to be either modified or emphasized. The primary reason for this is that the customer is making the selection based on actually viewing the food rather than reading about it on a printed menu. Therefore, the merchandising of the cafeteria line takes the place of descriptive terminology on the written menu. Because of this, principles of variety in regard to color, texture, cooking methods, and food items become paramount, since the line must look appealing in order to sell.

When selecting menu listings, how they look is as important as how well they complement each other. Variety is the key. First, consider color. For example, to put green beans lyonnaise, peas and pearl onions, spinach with bacon bits, and buttered broccoli spears on the menu together would probably not be a good idea. Although these vegetables could very well be excellent complements to the entrees selected, they will not merchandise well, as they are all the same color. Even though some of them are garnished with a different color, the overall effect to the customer looking at the line is green. Items selected must complement the entree, as well as each other, and at the same time give a good spectrum of color. In this case, the spinach might be replaced with beets and the broccoli with carrots.

Variety in textures should also be sought. How boring the line would look if all the textures in each category were the same. Consider the salad section. There should be *variety* in texture. Include roughage (tossed garden salad), smooth gelatin salads, smooth and crunchy cole slaw, and contrasts in fruit such as fresh versus cooked or stewed. With imaginative selection in regard to texture, it is quite easy to work in color at the same time.

Various cooking methods also need to be considered. Variety in this area—simmered, braised, roasted, sauteed, fried, deep fried, and baked foods—should be included on the menu. Remember, customers are selecting food based on sight, not on a printed menu. Consider how the hot food line would look if all the entrees were deep fried. Imagine also what the color spectrum would be.

Food variety is the final principle to be considered for heightening the customer's dining interest. Each area on the cafeteria line should have the widest variety of foods possible. For example, the salad section would include fruits, vegetables, starches, dairy, and miscellaneous items such as gelatins. Entrees could include beef, veal, pork, lamb, poultry, variety meats, cheese, eggs, and meatless dishes as well as vegetable plates. All these groups may not be possible or even desirable. Maybe lamb is a slow seller; if so, eliminate it. Remember, regardless of size or demographics, variety must be built into the menu plan.

Not only must the principles of variety be considered, but production must be taken into account. Since the customer is choosing by sight, it is imperative that all foods on the line *look* fresh at all times. It is a known fact that some foods have excellent holding qualities while others deteriorate rapidly. Foods that withstand a longer time frame on the line can be produced in larger batches, while foods that lose color and quality quickly should be produced in smaller batches. In writing the menu, care must be exercised so that there is a proper mix of large-batch and small-batch cookery.

Another criterion is the plating of the final product. Ideally, this should be rapid, with one motion. More than one motion will slow the customer line movement, with several motions bringing it to a complete stop. Fast lines mean high profits. For example, fried chicken quartered is plated in one motion, from the steam table to the plate. If it's served with cream gravy, then it's two motions. Either way it's fast. On the other hand, a sandwich prepared from scratch requires several motions by the server, and the entire line stops while it is being constructed.

Most successful cafeteria chains prefer to emphasize foods cooked fresh from raw ingredients as opposed to using convenience foods. Indeed, some chains that introduced frozen entrees and premade salads stopped using this approach when customers complained and sales dropped. Some institutional cafeterias, on the other hand, are leaning more and more on convenience foods to keep labor costs down. Sometimes this is not as cost effective as it first appears. Could it be that convenience foods, not properly used, are one of the contributing factors to dissatisfaction with captive-audience feeding?

Once the menu is written, the job is not complete. The menu writer must next diagram the serving line, indicating where each and every menu item is to be located. Failure to do this could result in a haphazard arrangement if the person setting the line does not fully understand the proper location of each item. Diagramming the line ensures that all the work to incorporate color, texture, cooking methods, and variety into the menu will be properly executed.

FOOD ARRANGEMENT

The proper way to set up a cafeteria line is to follow the normal meal sequence. Start with appetizers, then salads and entrees. Entrees should be in the order of solids (roasts), semi-solids (Salisbury steaks, croquettes), and extenders (casseroles). After entrees come vegetables, starches, breads, desserts, and beverages. There could be two significant exceptions to this order. Many cafeterias do not serve appetizers. Why they don't is a mystery. Appetizers are excellent add-ons and many lend themselves to cafeteria service, for example, shrimp cocktail, fruit compotes, and relish plates. Another exception to this order is that some cafeterias opt to offer desserts twice: once at the start of the line and later in the natural order. The philosophy behind this is that a customer will purchase a dessert with a relatively empty tray at the start of the line. Conversely, with the dessert at the end of the line and a full tray, the customer may decide that enough has been spent and bypass dessert. Other customers, however, choose dessert at the end of the line to round out the meal. Other than these two exceptions, the order of foods normally follows the regular sequence.

Once the menu is written and the line sequence set, do not forget to merchandise the food. Garnishes should be indicated for items that require them. Make sure that garnishes are included as part of the overall menu plan so that they are not overlooked or ignored. One would think that, with all of the prior planning to ensure a colorful, fresh-looking line, garnishing would be unnecessary. This notion could not be farther from the truth. Again, in cafeterias more than any other type of operation, people eat with their eyes. Garnishing is imperative. A well-merchandised line sells, and sales is the name of the game.

CONCLUSION

Write the menu for the customer, taking demographics into account. Build the menu around this theme and take into account color, texture, cooking methods, and variety of available foods for a well-rounded menu. Specify exactly how the line is to be set and merchandised. Doing this properly results in a successful cafeteria operation. It's just that simple.

QUESTIONS

1. Discuss the various styles and shapes of cafeteria lines and explain the advantages and disadvantages of each.

2. Explain the difference between institutional and commercial cafeteria demographics.

3. What is the basic difference between an a la carte menu and a cafeteria menu?

4. Discuss menu cycles and tell what length of cycle should be used for which type of cafeteria. Give examples.

5. Diagram a buffet table and a cafeteria line using the same menu.

6. List the food service career opportunities that use cafeteria service and/or cycle menus. How many levels of employment are available?

CHAPTER SIXTEEN

The Menu as a Management Tool

OBJECTIVES By the completion of this chapter, the reader should be able to:

- Illustrate how profitability is tied to a menu.
- Explain how product mix can define an operation's problem areas.
- Describe how a menu interrelates with each department in a food service.

IMPORTANT TERMS

Standard costs
Inventory turnover
Portion control
Product mix

Quality control
Purchasing
Production

INTRODUCTION

As we stated at the start of the text, everything starts with the menu and, most important, profit starts with the menu as well. Exactly how the menu relates to profitability is sometimes a confusing issue. To clarify this, a logical walkthrough of a typical operation is taken. Starting with the menu itself, then moving on to purchasing, receiving, storage, production, and service—observe how the menu interrelates to each of these areas and also how in some cases it interrelates to established controls.

THE MENU

Before any discussion of profitability and its relationship to the menu, an understanding of the term *standard cost* is needed. A *standard cost* is an ideal cost. In other words, it is what a cost should be. Standard cost is determined by management and is used as a measurement against actual costs. Normally, a standard cost is stated in percent for measurement purposes. Only after standard cost percents have been determined can the menu selling prices be figured. As studied in the chapter on menu pricing, the selling price needs to cover all costs, not just food costs. How well an operation meets its objective in relation to standard costs is shown on the income statement. When variable and semi-variable costs, such as food and labor, are out of line, many things could have gone wrong to cause this to happen. The first logical step in tracing this problem is the menu.

Management in the hospitality industry is normally responsible for variable and semi-variable costs. Fixed costs (rent, insurance, utilities, etc.) are for the most part beyond management's control. The largest variable and semi-variable costs are food and labor. These are also called prime costs: those that are the primary responsibility for management to control. When these costs—food and labor—are high, a number of causative factors could be involved. In order for management to find the source of the problem and hence its solution, several details need to be investigated. The first logical step in tracing the problem is the menu. The composite food cost of the menu can be checked by either developing the product mix (Chapter 4) or completing menu scoring (Chapter 5). Menu engineering (Chapter 5), although it does not directly give a composite food cost, does make it fairly simple to figure. Total column H (total revenue) and column I (total food cost) and divide these totals (divide the total of column I by the total of column H). The result is composite food cost. Prior to embarking on one of these studies, make sure that all costs are accurate by reviewing the cost cards and updating them if necessary.

The composite food cost percentage derived from the product mix, menu engineering, or menu scoring, should then be compared with the standard food cost for the restaurant. If the composite varies from the standard, and this variance equals the difference between the standard and the actual on the income statement, then the problem of the high food cost lies in the menu pricing structure. For example, if a food cost of 35 percent has been decided on by management as its standard, and the income statement shows an actual food cost of 36 percent and a subsequent analysis also shows 36 percent, then the menu needs to be adjusted to lower the composite food cost to 35 percent.

FIGURE 16.1.   Product mix.

Item	No. Items Sold	Price	Sales	Food Cost %	Food Cost $
Prime Rib	350	$8.50	$2,975	38%	$1,130
Red Snapper	190	6.95	1,320	34%	449
Chicken Kiev	340	6.75	2,295	30%	689
K.C. Strip	225	8.50	1,913	42%	803
Rack of Lamb	40	7.95	318	40%	127
			$8,821		$3,198

$3,198/$8,821 = 36.3% food cost

The first inclination of most restaurant managers is to increase prices. Although this could certainly be a solution to the problem, it may not be the wisest choice. Care must be taken when increasing prices not to exceed the price-value relationship perceived by the customers.

Some of the other alternatives, as discussed in previous chapters, would be to eliminate high-cost–slow-selling items (dogs) and replace them with low-cost items that have high sales potential. Another consideration would be the evaluation of portions. However, as in the case of increasing prices, care must be exercised not to affect the price-value relationship by cutting portions to the extent of causing customer discontent.

While these are but a few of many alternatives available to bring menu pricing in line with the standard, the fact remains that no matter what happens operationally, food cost will always be out of line if the menu price does not relate to the standard cost. The restaurant's standard food cost and the composite food cost from the overall menu pricing structure must equal each other. For example, assume that a restaurant's standard food cost was 28 percent and the income statement showed 32 percent. The manager ran an analysis that showed a composite food cost of 32 percent. That manager could watch portion control, theft, cooking procedures, standardized recipes, and every other control 24 hours a day and not solve the problem. The only solution to this problem is to adjust the menu to obtain a 28 percent food cost. This is an extremely important concept to master. Many managers have unfortunately been terminated because they could not attain the company's standard food cost when, realistically, they had no shot at attaining it.

In looking at variances between the standard food cost and actual food cost, consider a different scenario. If the composite food cost percent and the standard food cost percent were equal and the actual had a variance, then the entire problem becomes operational and relates to other areas of the restaurant. For example, if the composite food cost were 35 percent, which met the standard of 35 percent, and the actual food cost in the income statement were 40 percent, then the issue is not related to the menu because the composite food cost and the standard food cost equal each other. The dilemma therefore is in failure to comply with one or more of the operational controls.

To investigate these potential problems, a walkthrough of the operation should be taken following a logical sequence of events. Too often, management panics when food cost goes out of line and goes helter-skelter through the operation looking for solutions. A logical sequence of events is first to review the menu. Everything starts with the menu. Since that has been completed, the next area to investigate is purchasing, then receiving, storage, production, plating, service, and cash-handling. In that order. Because the discussion here concerns the menu, all these areas are not discussed; the analysis here is limited to only those factors that apply to the menu.

PURCHASING

Three areas should be looked at in the relationship between the menu and purchasing. The first of these is the price fluctuation of goods purchased. The menu should be carefully scrutinized to see whether it contains an unusual number of listings that have ingredients with costs that change dramatically from season to season. Fresh produce is a prime example. Although menu items of this nature cannot be avoided, they should be kept to as low a level as possible. In an ideal world, the menu would contain only those items that have a stable price structure throughout the year, thus giving a constant cost-price ratio. Since this is impossible, a worst case scenario should be used when pricing those listings that have highly variable costs. In other words, when costing an item that has a high seasonal price fluctuation, use the highest projected purchase price.

The second area to be checked is the quality level of goods purchased, which should be compatible with the quality level that is stated on the menu. Using a different level of quality would be in violation of the truth in menu standard (Chapter 8). Furthermore, the quality level stated on the menu and subsequently purchased should be compatible in its selling price with the demographics of the customer (Chapter 1). For example, if the menu states USDA Prime steaks and this is what is purchased, is the customer willing to pay for this level of quality? Would more steaks be sold if the menu listing were changed to USDA Choice at a lower selling price? This would have to be ascertained for each individual restaurant, depending on the income level of its customers. The best way to analyze this is through menu engineering (Chapter 5). The point is that an overzealous menu writer can sometimes put the operation in a bind when purchasing costs and, subsequently, menu selling prices are not compatible with what the customer is willing to pay.

The third area to be investigated is inventory turnover. The menu should be selling a sufficient number of any particular item to warrant its being offered. Here we return to our discussion of dogs (Chapter 5). They should be removed from the menu in order to avoid purchasing unused goods that do nothing more than spoil, drive up the food cost, and tie up cash flow.

STORAGE

Closely related to the purchasing of goods is the storage of goods. Two issues need to be considered here: first, the aforementioned purchasing of unnecessary items that take up storage space; and, second, the storage of goods in the proper inventory level to conduct business. Because the first of these considerations has already been discussed, attention will be directed toward the second issue. To elaborate further on this subject, foods need to be divided into two categories: perishable and nonperishable. Perishable goods are those items that have a very short shelf life, such as fresh meats, fresh produce, dairy products, and bakery items. Perishables should be inventoried and ordered frequently, depending on the product. Most perishables are purchased daily or, at most, every three days. Nonperishables, on the other hand, have a longer shelf life. Staples such as canned goods, dehydrated items, flours, and mixes fall into this category. Nonperishables are normally ordered weekly.

When inventory levels go awry, two things can happen, both bad. One, the supply of goods is inadequate to meet consumer demand. As discussed in Chapter 7, one of the worst things that can happen in the restaurant business is to be out of a menu listing and have a disgruntled customer as a result. The second bad thing is to have an overabundance of goods in storage, thus tying up cash flow. To avoid both these scenarios, an accurate account of customers and their selections is necessary. This information can be readily obtained from either the product mix sheet or menu scoring.

PRODUCTION

The relationship between the menu and production controls lies primarily in two areas: quantity and quality. With quantity control, the prime consideration is producing only the amounts necessary to meet demand. To properly achieve this, the aforementioned methods (product mix and menu engineering) for determining the amount of goods to purchase can also be utilized to specify the number of each item on the menu to prepare for any given meal period. The primary objective of quantity control is to eliminate leftovers, which increase food cost. Although the goal of absolutely no leftovers is practically impossible to achieve, the closer the operation comes to achieving this, the closer its food cost will be to the standard. When confronted with a leftover problem, management oftentimes struggles with various options, trying to figure out a way to disguise the leftovers as saleable items. Often the selling price gets reduced, resulting in a higher food cost percentage. Worse yet is avoiding using the leftovers, which leaves the operator with a cost that will never be recovered. As stated by many wise restaurateurs, the best way to handle leftovers is not to have them in the first place.

Quality control in the kitchen is also an important aspect of controlling food cost. Starting with the menu, the customer perceives a certain item tasting the way the menu describes it (Chapter 5). This listing is, in turn, described that way because the standardized recipe indicates the outcome. The item cost (Chapter 3) is based on the amounts of those particular ingredients called for in the standardized recipe. The selling price (Chapter 4) is determined by the financial needs of the restaurant and is based on the recipe cost. All

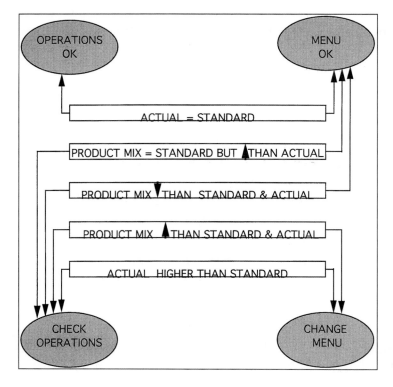

FIGURE 16.2. Actual vs. Product Mix vs. Standard.

this, as you have discovered, is an exacting science. When quality control is lacking and the standardized recipes are not followed, the whole scheme falls into disarray. The item could very well be "over-prepared," using more expensive ingredients or more of one particular ingredient, resulting in a higher cost than was originally intended. Worse yet, costs may be cut by eliminating or using low-quality ingredients, resulting in dissatisfied customers and, consequently, lost sales. For all these reasons, standardized recipes are a very important component of food cost controls.

PLATING

The final consideration for using the menu as a cost control device is the plating function. Here again, two things can go wrong: over-portioning or underportioning. On many menu listings, the portion is explicit, for example, a "12 oz. sirloin steak." Many times a portion is implied, such as a "heaping serving of spaghetti." To cut a portion below what the menu states or implies would be in violation of truth in menu (Chapter 8) and would result in an irate customer. On the other hand, to overportion would result in a cost for that item over and above the original intention. Portion control is an exacting science and must be followed without exception to please both the customer and the income statement.

The third scenario to consider when comparing the actual food cost with the standard food cost and the composite food cost occurs when the actual is higher than the standard and the composite is somewhere between both of them. In this case there are problems with both the menu and the controls. For example, if the actual food cost percent on the income statement was 40 percent, the composite showed a food cost of 38 percent, and the standard food cost was 35 percent, the conclusion could be drawn that 3 percent of the variance was in menu pricing and 2 percent was an operational problem. The reason for this is that, with the standard at 35 percent and the composite at 38 percent, there is a difference of 3 percent that must be adjusted through either menu changes, price increases, or both. The remaining 2 percent between the standard food cost of 35 percent and the actual of 40 percent would therefore be in the control systems of the restaurant. In other words, to correct this problem, both of the previously discussed solutions would have to be used.

CONCLUSION

Although many controls are available for use in a food service operation, only those that pertain to the menu have been illustrated here. The menu, in essence, ties the entire operation together, and without using it as a control, the manager loses one of the most effective tools available to keep food costs in line. The entire operation starts with the menu. Product description and portions help the customer decide what to order. This same menu tells the operator which items to purchase and how much, how to prepare items, and what size portions to serve. By planning and writing the menu properly and by following the plan set forth on the menu, two things will happen—both good. The restaurant will have satisfied customers and the operation will most likely be profitable. It's just that simple!

QUESTIONS

1. If you had a standard food cost of 38 percent, a product mix of 38 percent, and an actual food cost of 42 percent, tell what you would do to correct the problem.

2. If you had a standard cost of 38 percent, a product mix of 42 percent, and an actual food cost of 42 percent, tell what you would do to correct the problem.

3. Complete a product mix using the following data.

4. Complete a menu item by percent chart using the following data.

5. Assuming that you project a total of 600 covers sold, tell how many of each item you should prepare.

Entree	Number Sold	Sell Price	Food Cost %
Item I	20	$10.95	40%
Item II	100	8.75	30%
Item III	50	12.00	32%
Item IV	150	9.50	38%

6. List the possible controls on production and menu design that you could put in place to improve profitability. How would you get your employees to follow them?

Descriptive Wording for Menus

Abundance
Abundant
Accented
Accentuated
Accompanied
Accompaniment
Additional
Adorned
Adventure
Aflame
Al dente
Alternate
Alternative
Ambrosiac
Ambrosial
Ample
Appeal
Appealing
Appetite
Appetizing
Aroma
Aromatic
Arrangement
Array
Assorted
Assortment
Attractive
"Au jus naturel"
Authentic
Awesome
Baby
Baked
Barbecued
Basted
Batter dipped
Beautiful
Beautifully
Beginning
"Best"
Beverage

Big
Blackened
Blanched
Bland
Blend
Blooming
Boned
Boneless
Bonne bouche
Bordered
Bountiful
Bouquet
Braised
Brandied
Brilliant
Broiled
Buffet
Buttered
Butterflied
Candied
Capped
Carefully
Carved
Catch
Celebrated
Celestial
Charbroiled
Chilled
Choice
Chunks
Classic
Coals
Coated
Coddled
Combination
Colorful
Colossal
Complemented
Compote
Concoction

Cooked
Covered
Creamed
Creation
Creative
Crisp
Crisped
Crispness
Crisply
Crispy
Cuisine
Culinary
Dainty
Delicacy
Delicious
Deliciously
Delicate
Delicately
Deep fried
Deglazed
Delectable
Delight
Delightful
Deluxe
Diced
Dieter's
Dimension
Discriminating
Discriminatingly
Discriminative
Display
Distinctive
Distinguished
Divine
Dressed
Dusted
Elegantly
Enchanting
Enhanced
Enjoyment
Entire
Entrenched
Epicurean
Epicure's
Essence
Excellent
Exceptional
Exciting
Exotic
Extra-fine
Extra-flavor
Extra lean
Extraordinary
Extra thick
Extravaganza
Fabulous
Famous
Fancy
Fanfare
Favorite
Featuring

Festive
Fiery
Filled
Finale
Finely
Finest
Finished
Flaky
Flamed
Flaming
Flavor
Flavored
Flavorful
Florentine
Fluffy
Forte
Fragrant
Framed
Fresh
Freshly
Fried
Frosted
Frosty
Frothy
Frozen
Full flavored
Gaily
Garden
Garnished
Garniture
Gastronomy
Gems
Generous
Genuine
Gigantic
Glazed
Golden
Goodness
Gourmet
Graced
Gracious
Grade
Grand
Grandeur
Grated
Green
Greens
Grill
Grilled
Haute cuisine
Healthful
Healthy
Heartwarming
Hearty
Heavenly
Herbed
Hickory smoked
Highest
Highlighted
Hint
Home style

Honey cured
Honeyed
Hot
Iced
Ideal
Imagination
Impeccable
Imported
Impressive
Incredible
Individual
Inexplicable
Interlaced
Jardiniere
Jelled
Jellied
Juicy
Julienne
Jumbo
Kosher
Laced
Large
Lavish
Layered
Lean
Liberal
Light
Lightly
Liking
Live
Magnificent
Magnifico
Marinated
Marvelous
Matchless
Medallions
Medley
Melt away
Melted
Midwestern
Mild
Milk-fed
Minced
Miniature
Minted
Minute
Mixture
Moist
Morsels
Most
Mound
Mounds
Mouthwatering
Natural
Nectarous
Nested
New
"New-fashioned"
Notable
Nourishing
Novel

Numerous
Old-fashioned
Open-faced
Original
Oven baked
Overflowing
Palatable
Palate
Pan broiled
Parchment
Parsleyed
Particular
Perfect
Perfection
Permeating
Petite
Piping hot
Piquant
Plain
Pleasing
Plentiful
Plump
Poached
Popular
Potpourri
Preference
Premium
Prepared
Preserved
Prime
Properly aged
Pure
Quality
Quick
Radiant
Ragout
Rainbow
Rare
Refined
Refreshing
Regal
Renowned
Reputable
Rich
Ripened
Roast
Roasted
Robust
Sassy
Sauce
Sauteed
Savorous
Savory
Scented
Seasonal
Select
Selected
Selection
Sensational
Shredded
Silky

Simmered
Simple
Sizzled
Sizzling
Skewered
Skillfully
Sliced
Slow roasted
Small
Smooth
Smothered
Soft
Softened
Softly
Soothing
Sparkling
Special
Specially
Specialty
Spectrum
Spiced
Spicy
Spirited
Splendid
Spread
Spring
Sprinkled
Steamed
Steaming
Stewed
Stir fry
Strips
Stuffed
Succulent
Sugar cured
Sultry
Sumptuous
Super-fine
Superb
Superior
Supreme
Supremely
Surprising
Sweet
Sweetness
Sweltering
Tableside
Tangy
Tantalizing
Taste
Tasteful

Tasty
Tempting
Tender
Tenderized
Tenderly
Textured
Thick
Thin
Thrill
Throughout
Tidbit
Tiny
Toasted
Topped
Torrid
Totally
Touch
Tremendous
Trimmed
Tropical
Ultimate
Uncommon
Uncommonly
Undefinably
Unequalled
Unique
Unparalled
Unprecedented
Unsurpassable
Unsurpassed
Utmost
Variation
Variety
Vine ripened
Warm
Warmed
Warming
Warm weather
Wedges
Whipped
Whole
Wholesome
Winter
Wonderful
Wondrous
Wrapped
Young
Zest
Zesty
Zippy

Nutritional Labeling Laws

The following is a list of terms, established by the FDA, to be used when making nutrient claims. The description accompanying each term defines the criteria that a food must meet in order to use the term. As you will see, this is where Reference Amounts come into play. Under wording options, alternatives for some of the terms are also given. Remember: terms that are not defined by the FDA may not be used to characterize the level of nutrient content in a food.

Calories

Free	Less than 5 calories per Reference Amount.
Wording Options:	Free of Calories No Calories Zero Calories Without Calories Trivial Source of Calories
Low	40 calories or less per Reference Amount when Reference Amount is 30 grams or more, or more than 2 tablespoons.
	Food with Reference Amounts of 30 grams or less or 2 tablespoons or less, such as olives, croutons, grated cheese, can be called "low calorie" only if they contain 40 calories or less per 50 grams. This prevents a "low calorie" claim being based on a small amount of food.
	For main dish items and meals, 120 calories or less per 100 grams.
Wording Options:	Low in Calories Low Source of Calories Few Calories Contains a Small Amount of Calories
Reduced	Minimum 25 percent fewer calories per Reference Amount.
	For main dish items and meals, minimum of 25 percent fewer calories per 100 grams.
	This claim may not be made if the food to which comparison is being made meets the criteria for "low calorie."

Example: Reduced calorie blueberry coffee cake, with 25 percent fewer calories than a standard blueberry coffee cake recipe. Calorie content has been reduced from 200 to 150 calories per serving.

Wording Options:	Lower Calories Fewer Calories Calorie Reduced
Light/Lite	If food derives less than 50 percent of its calories from fat, 1/3 fewer calories or 50 percent less fat per Reference Amount. If food derives greater than 50 percent or more of its calories from fat, 50 percent less fat per Reference Amount.

Example: Our lite rice pudding has 100 calories per serving compared to a standard rice pudding recipe with 150 calories.

For main dish items and meals, meet the requirements for low calorie or low fat and identify nature of the claim.

Example: A lite chicken stir fry with brown rice, a low calorie meal. (See definition of low calorie meal.)

The words "light" and "lite" may be used for other descriptions, such as "Lite Bites" referring to smaller portion sizes. If so, explanation must appear with, or in close proximity to, the statement.

Alternative Usage:	Light in Color Light in Texture Lightly Flavored Light Bites (smaller portion sizes) Light Corn Syrup (statement of identity)

Fat

Free	Less than 0.5 grams of fat per Reference Amount and per serving.

For main dish items and meals, less than 0.5 grams of fat per serving size.

Consistent with FDA's labeling requirements for packaged foods, restaurateurs should be prepared to identify on request any ingredient that adds a trivial amount of fat to the food, main dish, or meal that is the subject of the claim.

Wording Options:	Free of Fat Nonfat No Fat Zero Fat Without Fat Trivial Source of Fat Negligible Source of Fat
Low	3 grams of fat or less per Reference Amount when Reference Amount is greater than 30 grams, or more than 2 tablespoons.

Foods with Reference Amounts of 30 grams or less or 2 tablespoons or less, such as olives, croutons, grated cheese, can be called "low fat" only if they contain 3 grams of fat or less per Reference Amount and per 50 grams. This prevents "low fat" claims from being based on a small amount of food.

For main dish items and meals, must contain 3 grams of fat or less per 100 grams and not more than 30 percent of calories from fat.

Wording Options:	Low in Fat Little Fat Low Source of Fat Contains a Small Amount of Fat
Reduced	Minimum of 25 percent less fat per Reference Amount.
	For main dish items and meals, minimum of 25 percent less fat per 100 grams.
	This claim may not be made if the food to which it is being compared meets the criteria for "low fat."
	Example: Reduced fat chocolate cake has 30 percent less fat than a standard chocolate cake recipe. Fat content has been reduced from 10 grams to 7 grams.
Wording Options:	Lower in Fat Lower Fat Less Fat Fat Reduced Reduced in Fat
Light/Lite	If food derives greater than 50 percent or more of its calories from fat, 50 percent less fat per Reference Amount. If the food derives less than 50 percent of its calories from fat, 50 percent less fat or 1/3 fewer calories per Reference Amount.
	Example: This lite bleu cheese dressing has 50 percent less fat than a standard bleu cheese dressing recipe. Fat has been reduced from 10 grams to 5 grams per serving.

Saturated Fat

Free	Less than 0.5 grams of saturated fat and less than 0.5 grams trans fatty acid per Reference Amount and per serving.
	For main dish items and meals, less than 0.5 grams of saturated fat and less than 0.5 grams trans fatty acid per serving.
	Consistent with FDA's labeling requirements for packaged foods, restaurateurs should be prepared to identify on request any ingredient that adds a trivial amount of saturated fat to the food, main dish, or meal that is the subject of the claim.
Wording Options:	No Saturated Fat Zero Saturated Fat Without Saturated Fat Free of Saturated Fat
Low	1 gram of saturated fat or less per Reference Amount and no more than 15 percent of calories from saturated fat.
	For main dish items and meals, must contain 1 gram of saturated fat or less per 100 grams and less than 10 percent of calories from saturated fat.
Wording Options:	Low in Saturated Fat Low Source of Saturated Fat A Little Saturated Fat Contains a Small Amount of Saturated Fat
Reduced	Minimum of 25 percent less saturated fat per Reference Amount.
	For main dish items and meals, minimum of 25 percent less saturated fat per 100 grams.
	This claim may not be made if the food to which it is being compared meets the definition of "low saturated fat."

Example: This Garden Omelet is lower in saturated fat than a standard vegetable omelet recipe. Saturated fat has been reduced 50 percent from 6 grams to 3 grams.

Wording Options: Less Saturated Fat
Lowered Saturated Fat
Reduced in Saturated Fat
Lowered in Saturated Fat

Cholesterol

Free

Less than 2 milligrams of cholesterol per Reference Amount and per serving and 2 grams or less of saturated fat per Reference Amount.

For main dish items and meals, contains less than 2 milligrams of cholesterol and 2 grams or less of saturated fat per serving.

If the total fat content of a food, main dish, or meal exceeds the following levels when making a cholesterol free claim, you must declare the total amount of fat next to the claim.
        Per Reference Amount
Food = more than 13 grams per serving
Main dish = more than 19.5 grams
Meal = more than 26 grams

Consistent with FDA's labeling requirements for packaged foods, restaurateurs should be prepared to identify on request any ingredients that add a trivial amount of cholesterol to the food, main dish, or meal that is the subject of the claim.

Example: Cholesterol free french fries. Contains _____ grams of fat per serving. (If potatoes are fried in a vegetable oil, they are still a fairly high fat food. If your particular finished product contains more than 13 grams of fat per Reference Amount, you must declare the fat content in grams.) This type of regulation guards against customers being misled into thinking "cholesterol free" is synonymous with low fat.

Wording Options: Zero Cholesterol
No Cholesterol
Free of Cholesterol
Without Cholesterol
Trivial Source of Cholesterol

Low

20 milligrams or less of cholesterol and 2 grams or less of saturated fat per Reference Amount. Must also contain 13 grams or less of total fat per Reference Amount.

Foods with Reference Amounts less than 30 grams or less than 2 tablespoons, such as croutons or grated cheese, can be called "low cholesterol" only if they meet the above criteria based on the Reference Amount and on a 50 gram basis. This prevents a "low cholesterol" claim from being based on the small amount of food.

For main dish items, must contain 20 milligrams of cholesterol or less and 2 grams of saturated fat or less per 100 grams and 19.5 grams or less of total fat per serving.

For meals, must contain 20 milligrams or less of cholesterol and 2 grams or less of saturated fat per 100 grams and 26 grams or less of total fat per serving.

When fat content exceeds the listed criteria, the total fat content in grams must be declared.

Example: Low cholesterol poundcake. This poundcake contains 15 grams of fat per serving. (If a recipe has replaced butter and eggs with vegetable oil, lowering cholesterol but maintaining a fat content higher than 13 grams, then the fat content declaration must be made.)

Wording Options:	Low in Cholesterol Little Cholesterol Contains a Small Amount of Cholesterol
Reduced	Minimum of 25 percent less cholesterol and 2 grams or less of saturated fat per Reference Amount and 13 grams or less of total fat per Reference Amount and per serving (and per 50 grams if the Reference Amount is 30 grams or less or 2 tablespoons or less).

For main dish items, minimum of 25 percent less cholesterol and 2 grams or less of saturated fat per 100 grams and 19.5 grams of total fat or less per serving.

For meals, minimum of 25 percent less cholesterol and 2 grams or less of saturated fat per 100 grams and 26 grams of total fat or less per serving.

When fat exceeds listed criteria, fat content in grams must be declared.

Example: This cholesterol reduced seafood Newburg has 30 percent less cholesterol than a standard seafood Newburg recipe. Cholesterol has been reduced from 80 mg to 55 mg per serving.

Wording Options:	Less Cholesterol Lower Cholesterol Reduced in Cholesterol Lower in Cholesterol

Sodium

Free	Less than 5 milligrams of sodium per Reference Amount and per serving.

For main dish items and meals, must contain less than 5 milligrams of sodium per serving.

Consistent with FDA's labeling requirements for packaged foods, restaurateurs should be prepared to identify on request any ingredients that add a trivial amount of sodium to the food, main dish, or meal that is subject of the claim.

Wording Options:	No Sodium Zero Sodium Without Sodium Free of Sodium Trivial Source of Sodium
Low	140 milligrams or less of sodium per Reference Amount when Reference Amount is 30 grams or more, or more than 2 tablespoons. When Reference Amount is 30 grams or less or 2 tablespoons or less, use same criteria based on Reference Amount and 50 grams.

For main dish items and meals, must contain 140 milligrams or less of sodium per 100 grams.

Very Low	35 milligrams or less of sodium, based on above criteria.
Wording Options:	Very Low in Sodium
Reduced	Minimum of 25 percent less sodium per Reference Amount.

For main dish items and meals, minimum of 25 percent less sodium per 100 grams.

This claim may not be made if the food to which it is compared meets the requirements for "low sodium."

Example: Made with a reduced sodium soy sauce—50 percent less sodium than regular soy sauce. Sodium content has been reduced from 700 mg to 350 mg per serving.

Wording Options:	Reduced in Sodium Less Sodium Lower Sodium Lower in Sodium
Light in Sodium/ *Lite in Sodium*	Minimum of 50 percent less sodium per Reference Amount. For main dish items and meals, must meet the criteria for low sodium.
Salt Free	Meet criteria for sodium free.
Unsalted *No Salt Added* *Without Added Salt*	These terms are allowed if: • there is no salt added during preparation • the food it resembles is normally prepared with salt If the food does not meet the criteria for a sodium free food, a declaration statement, "not a sodium free food" or "not for the control of sodium in the diet" appears near the claim.
Lightly Salted	Minimum of 50 percent less sodium added than is normally used in preparation. If a food does not meet the criteria for a "low sodium" food, a declaration statement, "not a low sodium food," must appear near the claim. Remember, salt and sodium are not the same and you cannot use these words interchangeably. Salt refers to sodium chloride, which is composed of 40 percent sodium. It is the sodium content of a food that is the basis for nutrient content claims.

Sugar

Free	Less than 0.5 grams of sugar per Reference Amount and per serving. For main dish items and meals, must have 0.5 grams or less of sugar per serving. If the food is not labeled "low calorie" or "reduced calorie," a declaration statement, "not a low calorie food" or "not a reduced calorie food," must appear near the claim. Consistent with FDA's labeling requirements for packaged foods, restaurateurs should be prepared to identify on request any ingredients that add a trivial amount of sugar to the food, main dish, or meal that is the subject of the claim.
Wording Options:	Free of Sugar Sugarless No Sugar Zero Sugar Without Sugar Trivial Source of Sugar
Low	Cannot be used as a claim.
Reduced	Minimum of 25 percent less sugar per Reference Amount. For main dish items and meals, minimum of 25 percent less sugar per 100 grams.

Example: Our reduced sugar lemonade has 25 percent less sugar than a standard lemonade recipe. Sugar content has been reduced from 8 to 6 grams per serving.

Wording Options:	Reduced in Sugar Less Sugar Lower Sugar Sugar Reduced Lower in Sugar
No Added Sugar *No Sugar Added* *Without Added* *Sugar*	These terms are allowed if: • no sugar or ingredient that contains added sugar, such as jam, jelly, concentrated fruit juice has been added during preparation • the food it resembles normally uses sugar in the preparation If the food does not meet the criteria for a low calorie or reduced calorie food, a declaration statement, "not a low calorie food" or "not a reduced calorie food," must appear near the claim.

Other Nutrient Content Claim Terms You Need to Know

Provides Contains Good Source	To use these terms, the food must contain 10 to 19 percent of the Daily Value per Reference Amount. These terms cannot be used to make a total carbohydrate claim.... If using these terms to describe a main dish or meal, identify the food component that is the subject of the claim. *Example:* The black-eyed peas in this meal provide fiber.
High Excellent Source of Rich In	To use these terms, the food must contain 20 percent or more of the Daily Value per Reference Amount.... If using these terms to describe a main dish or meal, identify the food component that is the subject of the claim. *Example:* The fruit compote in our breakfast special is an excellent source of vitamin C.
More Added Enriched Fortified	To use these terms, the food must contain at least 10 percent more of the Daily Value for protein, vitamins, minerals, fiber, or potassium per Reference Amount compared to the reference food. *Example:* These apple bran muffins contain 25 percent more fiber than our regular apple muffins. Fiber content of an apple muffin is 3 grams per serving: apple bran muffin is 4 grams per serving. If using these terms to describe a main dish or meal, use the above criteria based on 100 grams of product. "Fortified" and "enriched" cannot be used to describe single ingredient meat or poultry products.
Fiber	To make any fiber claim, the food must meet the criteria for either "good source" or "high." If the food is not "low fat," you must declare the fat content per serving.
Lean	To use this term for meat, poultry, seafood, and game, food must have less than 10 grams of fat, less than 4 grams of saturated fat, and less than 95 milligrams of cholesterol per Reference Amount and 100 grams. If using this term to describe a main dish or meal, use the above criteria based on 100 grams and serving size.

Extra Lean	To use this term for meat, poultry, seafood, and game, food must have less than 5 grams of fat, less than 2 grams of saturated fat, and less than 95 milligrams of cholesterol per Reference Amount and 100 grams.
	If using this term to describe a main dish or meal, use the above criteria based on 100 grams and serving size.
Fresh	When "fresh" is used in a manner that implies that the product is unprocessed, the food must be in its raw state and not have undergone freezing, thermal treatment, or any other form of preservation. Apart from this restriction, terms such as "fresh," "freshly prepared," and "freshly baked" should be used in a truthful and non-misleading manner. The use of these terms will be reviewed on a case-by-case basis.
Natural	There is no set definition or regulation governing the use of this word. Current FDA policy, however, treats a claim of "natural" as meaning that nothing artificial or synthetic has been included in the food that would not normally be expected to be in the food.
Healthy	To use this term, a food must be low fat; low in saturated fat; contain 480 milligrams or less of sodium per serving; and provide at least 10 percent of the Daily Value per Reference Amount for protein, fiber, iron, calcium, and vitamins A or C. Seafood or game meats must have 5 grams or less of fat and 2 grams or less of saturated fat per Reference Amount and 100 grams, and 95 milligrams or less of cholesterol per 100 grams. The sodium and other nutrient criteria are the same.
	Raw fruits or vegetables are exempted from the requirement that "healthy" foods provide at least 10 percent of the Daily Value per Reference Amount for the above-referenced nutrients.
	If using this term to describe meals or main dishes, they must be low fat, low in saturated fat, and have 600 milligrams or less of sodium and 90 milligrams or less of cholesterol per serving. A main dish must contain 10 percent of the Daily Value for 2 nutrients, and, for meals, 3 nutrients.

Courtesy of the National Restaurant Association, Washington, DC.

Foreign Wording for Menus

A La. (French) According to the style of.

A La Carte. (French) Signifies that each course is priced separately.

A La King. (French) A dish in a rich cream sauce containing mushrooms, pimentos, green peppers, and usually sherry.

A La Mode. (French) Usually refers to ice cream on top of pie, but may be other dishes served in a special way.

A La Provencale. (French) Prepared with garlic and olive oil.

A La Rousse. (French) In the Russian style.

Al Dente. (Italian) Term used to describe pasta or rice cooked until tender but not soft, firm enough to be felt between the teeth—literally, "to the tooth."

Agneau. (French) Lamb.

A L'Orange. (French) In an orange sauce.

Amandine. (French) Made with or garnished with almonds.

Anglaise. (French) In the English style.

Antipasto. (Italian) Assorted hors d'oeuvre served before the main course, literally, "before the pasta."

Aspic. (French) A clear, savory jelly made from meat or vegetable stock used to mold cold meat, fish, poultry, or vegetables, or to garnish same.

Au Beurre. (French) With, or cooked in butter.

Au Gratin. (French) Food covered with a sauce, sprinkled with crumbs or cheese, and baked or browned in oven or boiler.

Au Jus. (French) Literally, with juice; refers to meat dishes served with their natural juices.

Au Lait. (French) With milk.

Baba Au Rhum. (French) Cake that has been soaked in rum after it's been baked.

Baguette. (French) Long loaf of French bread.

Bearnaise Sauce. (French) A thick sauce made with shallots, tarragon, thyme, bay leaf, vinegar or wine, and egg yolks.

Bechamel. (French) A basic white sauce made with butter, flour, and milk.

Beignet. (French) A doughnut or light sweet or savory fritter.

Beurre. (French) Butter.

Biscotti. (Italian) Anise-flavored cookies.

Biscuit Tortoni. (Italian) Dessert made of egg whites and whipped cream, and topped with chopped almonds.

Bisque. (French) Thick cream soup or puree, usually of shellfish, bivalves, and crustaceans.

Blancmange. (French) A puddinglike dessert flavored with almonds or vanilla and shaped in a mold—literally, "white food."

Blanquette. (French) White, cream stew (ragout) based on lamb, chicken, or veal.

Boeuf. (French) Beef.

Boeuf Bourguignon. (French) Braised beef prepared in the style of Burgundy, with small glazed onions, mushrooms, and red wine.

Bordelaise. (French) Brown sauce made with wine and bone marrow.

Bouillabaise. (French) A Provence fish soup-stew dish cooked in either water or wine with garlic, parsley, oil, and tomatoes; the ingredients vary with the restaurant.

Boulangere. (French) A style of cooking potatoes beneath roasting meat.

Bourguignonne. (French) Pertaining to Burgundy wine-flavored sauces and a garnish of lardons, mushrooms, and pearl onions.

Brochette. (French) A skewer; anything cooked on a skewer may be called a "brochette."

Buche De Noel. (French) A special Christmas cake made to look like a yule log.

Cacciatora, Alla. (Italian) Prepared in the hunter's style, with mushrooms, herbs, shallots, tomatoes, wine, etc.

Cafe. (French) Coffee.

Cafe Cappuccino. (Italian) Coffee with whipped cream topping and cinnamon flavor.

Cafe Glace. (French) Cold coffee with whipped topping.

Calamari. (Italian) Squid.

Calzone. (Italian) Pastry crust with ham and cheese.

Canape. (French) A toasted slice of bread; can be topped with a variety of spreads and used as an appetizer.

Cannelloni. (Italian) Meat-stuffed rolls of pasta, baked.

Cannoli. (Italian) Custard-filled pastry in a tubular shape with candied fruits and rum flavoring, sometimes sprinkled with powdered sugar.

Capelli D'Angelo. (Italian) A very thin noodle—literally, "angel hair."

Caponata. (Italian) A mixture of eggplant, onions, and tomatoes.

Champignons. (French) Mushrooms.

Chanterelles. (French) A type of mushroom.

Chantilly Cream. (French) Vanilla whipped cream.

Chantilly Sauce. (French) Hollandaise sauce with whipped cream.

Chasseur. (French) Prepared and served in a tomato sauce with mushrooms, wine, etc.—literally, "hunter style."

Chateaubriand. (French) Thick slice of steak, classically grilled and served with a garnish of potatoes cut in strips and with a Bearnaise sauce.

Coquille. (French) Shell.

Coquilles St. Jacques. (French) Scallops in a shell.

Coulis. (French) Thick soup made with crayfish, lobster, prawns, and other crustaceans.

Coupe. (French) A shallow cup made of glass or silver, usually on a low stem, used for serving ices or fresh fruit salad.

Creole, A La. (French) Prepared with rice.

Croustade. (French) A dish made with flaky puff pastry shell or with bread that has been hollowed out.

Demitasse. (French) A small cup of coffee served after dinner.

Dijonnaise. (French) A sauce of egg yolks, Dijon mustard, salt, and pepper beaten with oil and lemon juice to the consistency of mayonnaise.

Du Jour. (French) Of the day.

Duxelles. (French) Mushrooms chopped and sauteed in butter and oil, mixed with onions, shallots, and a bit of wine and parsley, and sometimes breadcrumbs.

En Coquille. (French) Served in a shell, usually a rich, creamed seafood dish.

En Croute. (French) Baked in a pastry crust.

Entremets. (French) All side dishes. Also, the various sweet desserts served after the cheese course.

Escalopes. (French) Boneless slices of meat or fish, usually fried in butter.

Escargots. (French) Snails cooked in an aromatic garlic-butter-parsley mixture, usually served in their shells but sometimes in mushroom caps.

Fagioli. (Italian) Dried white beans.

Farci. (French) Literally, "stuffed."

Fettuccine. (Italian) Ribbonlike pasta, about 1/4" wide.

Fettuccine Al Burro. (Italian) Noodles with melted butter.

Fettuccine Alfredo. (Italian) Noodles tossed with butter, cream, and Parmesan cheese.

Filet De Boeuf En Croute. (French) Filet of beef in a pastry crust.

Filet Mignon. (French) Small choice cut of beef prepared by grilling or sauteeing.

Fines Herbes. (French) Fresh, finely chopped parsley, alone or in combination with chives, tarragon, chervil, and other herbs.

Flambe. (French) To flame; applies to foods that are doused in warm spirits and ignited just before serving.

Florentine, A La. (French) Foods cooked in this style, usually eggs, fish, or poultry, are put on spinach, covered with mornay sauce, and sprinkled with cheese.

Foie Gras. (French) The livers of specially fattened geese and ducks.

Fondue. (French) Literally, "melted," indicating roasted or melted cheese.

Fricassee. (French) Today, a method of preparing poultry, and sometimes veal, in a white sauce.

Frappe. (French) Iced drinks and desserts made from fruit juices and frozen to a mushy consistency. Literally, "iced."

Fromage. (French) Cheese.

Fruits De Mer. (French) Seafood served cold in salads or hot in special sauces. Literally, "fruits of the sea."

Fume. (French) Smoked.

Galantine. (French) Boned game, poultry, or meat, stuffed and re-shaped—steamed or poached, served hot or cold, sometimes in aspic.

Gateau. (French) Cake.

Gelato. (Italian) Ice cream.

Genoise. (French) A rich cake using eggs as its leavening agent.

Genovese, Alla. (Italian) With pine nuts, cheese, basil, garlic and other herbs.

Gnocchi. (Italian) Small (potato) dumplings.

Grissini. (Italian) Bread sticks.

Hollandaise. (French) Hot sauce of egg yolks, butter, lemon juice, and seasonings, served with vegetables and fish.

Homard Saute. (French) Chunks of lobster sauteed in butter with herbs added.

Hors D'Oeuvre. (French) Appetizers, hot or cold.

Insalata. (Italian) Salad.

Jardiniere, A La. (French) Garnished with fresh vegetables, served with roast, stewed or braised meat, and poultry; the vegetables may be broiled or glazed and are placed around the meat.

Julienne. (French) Meat or vegetables cut into thin strips.

Lasagna Verde Al Forno. (Italian) Spinach lasagna baked in a meat sauce.

Legumes. (French) Vegetables.

Linguine. (Italian) Narrow, flat noodles.

Lyonnaise. (French) Prepared with onions.

Maitre D'Hotel Beurre. (French) Seasoned butter with fresh parsley and lemon, served with grilled foods.

Manicotti. (Italian) Large pancake-like noodles that are stuffed and baked with a sauce.

Marinara. (Italian) Sauce made with tomatoes, olives, and garlic, and no meat.

Marzipan. (German; French) Sugar, almond, and egg-white paste candy shaped into various forms.

Medaillon. (French) Food cut into a round or oval shape.

Meuniere. (French) Method of preparing fish. Seasoned, floured fish fried in butter and served with lemon juice, parsley, and melted butter.

Milanese, Alla. (Italian) Coated with bread crumbs and cooked in butter.

Minestrone. (Italian) A thick vegetable soup with pasta.

Mornay Sauce. (French) A cream sauce with cheese added.

Mousse. (French) A light and airy dish made with cream and eggs and the addition of fish, chicken, fruits, or chocolate.

Mousseline. (French) Hot or cold molds or sauces, as well as certain desserts, that have been lightened and enriched with whipped cream.

Noir. (French) Black.

Noisettes. (French) In combination with other words, small round cuts of meat, vegetables, etc.

Normande. (French) With oyster juice—used with fillet of sole.

Oignons. (French) Onions.

Oreganato. (Italian) Baked with oregano.

Orzo. (Italian) Rice-shaped pasta.

Osso Buco. (Italian) Veal shank stewed in tomatoes and wine.

Palmier. (French) Pastry formed from many horizontal layers, then baked with powdered-sugar glaze.

Papillote, En. (French) Baked in buttered parchment, aluminum foil, or other paper to retain the food's juices.

Parmigiano, Alla. (Italian) Prepared with Parmesan cheese.

Parplit. (French) Light, sweet ice of various flavors.

Pasta Verde. (Italian) Spinach noodles.

Pastina. (Italian) Very small macaroni, usually used in soups.

Pate. (French) Dough pastry. Originally the term *pate* was applied only to a meat or fish dish enclosed in a pastry and baked; now it describes any dish of ground meat or fish baked in a mold that has been lined with strips of bacon.

Pate Maison. (French) A pate unique to a particular restaurant.

Patissier. (French) Pastry chef.

Pauplettes de Sole. (French) Slices of sole that are stuffed and rolled.

Penne. (Italian) Short, tubular pasta.

Pesto. (Italian) Paste or sauce made from fresh basil, garlic, cheese, and olive oil.

Petit. (French) Small.

Petite Marmite. (French) A strong consomme with beef, chicken, and vegetables.

Petits Fours. (French) Bite-sized iced or fondant-coated and decorated little cakes and confections.

Petits Pois. (French) Small green peas.

Piccante. (Italian) Highly seasoned.

Piece De Resistance. (French) Main dish.

Pizzaiola. (Italian) Sauce of tomato, garlic, and marjoram.

Plat Du Jour. (French) Specialty of the day.

Pois A La Francaise. (French) Peas cooked with lettuce leaves and onions.

Poisson. (French) Fish.

Potage. (French) Soup, usually thickened.

Pots De Creme. (French) Small individual pots of rich, mousse-like cream—vanilla, chocolate, coffee—served chilled, sometimes with whipped cream.

Printaniere. (French) Garnish of spring vegetables cut in small dice.

Profiteroles. (French) Small, round cream puffs filled with custard, ice cream or creme patissiere and glazed or sauced in chocolate.

Quenelles. (French) Dumplings made with either fish or meat.

Quiche. (French) Unsweetened custardlike tart or pie with various fillings.

Radicchio. (Italian) Red lettuce.

Ragout. (French) A dish made of meat, poultry, or fish that has been cut up and browned, with or without vegetables.

Ragu. (Italian) May mean a sauce or a meat stew with garlic, tomatoes, and herbs.

Ratatouille. (French) A dish of eggplant, zucchini, tomatoes, and onions stewed in olive oil with garlic, served hot or cold.

Ravioli. (Italian) Envelopes of pasta that are stuffed with either meat or cheese and eaten in soup or with a sauce.

Rigatoni. (Italian) Large macaroni-shaped pasta that is grooved.

Risotto. (French; Italian) Rice baked in a chicken stock.

Risotto Alla Milanese. (Italian) Risotto with saffron, Parmesan cheese, and ham added.

Robert Sauce. (French) Sauce of onion, white wine, and mustard; served with grilled pork dishes.

Rossini. (French) Garnished with truffles and foie gras.

Roulade. (French) A rolled piece of thin meat.

Rugola. (Italian) Field lettuce.

Sabayon. (French) Dessert served in glasses with whipped egg yolks, vanilla, sugar, sherry, and white wine.

Salade Nicoise. (French) Potatoes and string beans with an oil and vinegar dressing, trimmed with olives, capers, anchovies, and tomatoes.

Salsa Alla Milanese. (Italian) Sauce of ham and veal cooked in butter with fennel and wine.

Saltimbocca. (Italian) Slices of veal seasoned with sage and prosciutto and braised in white wine.

Sauce Soubise. (French) Cream sauce with onion puree added.

Sauerbraten. (German) Rich, dark pot roast with a sweet and sour gravy usually made with gingersnaps.

Scalloppine. (Italian) Thin slices of meat, most usually of veal.

Scalloppine Alla Florentina. (Italian) Thinly sliced veal on spinach with a white sauce.

Scampi. (Italian) Shrimp.

Schnitzel. (German) Cutlet, usually veal.

Schnitzel A La Holstein. (German) Cutlet topped with baked egg, often with anchovies, capers, smoked salmon, or mushrooms.

Souffle. (French) Dish made with pureed ingredients, egg yolks, and stiffly beaten egg whites; may be made with vegetables, fish, meat, fruit, nuts, etc., and served as an appetizer, a main dish, or a dessert.

Spaetzle; Spätzle. (German) Tiny dumplings of egg and four, noodlelike, pressed through a colander into boiling water or soup.

Spaghetti Al Burro. (Italian) Spaghetti with butter.

Spaghetti Alla Carbonara. (Italian) Spaghetti tossed with oil, eggs, bacon, and cheese.

Spumone. (Italian) Dessert of ice cream, candied fruits with whipped cream and nuts.

Steak Au Poivre. (French) Steak made with crushed peppercorns.

Steak Tartare. (French) Raw steak seasoned and served with a raw egg yolk on top and capers, chopped onions, and parsley on the side.

Terrine. (French) Meat, fish, or fowl chopped finely, baked in a dish called terrine, and served cold; often called pate in the United States.

Timbale. (French) Large or small case of pastry crust, deep-fried noodles, or julienned potatoes or a hollowed brioche. Also a jellied mold containing vegetables used to garnish meats.

Torte. (German) Extremely light, delicate cake baked in round layers and filled with whipped cream, fruit, chocolate, other icings, jams, jellies. (Includes sacher, linzer, dobos, and black forest cherry.) Also, a flan or tart with filling. In the United States, commonly cake in which the flour has been replaced by bread crumbs or cookie crumbs and finely ground nuts.

Tortellini. (Italian) Meat or cheese or other stuffed twisted pasta.

Tournedos. (French) A small slice of beef, round and thick, from the heart of the fillet of beef—sauteed or grilled.

Tournedos Rossini. (French) Tournedos sauteed in butter and arranged on toast, a slice of foie gras and truffles topping the meal, covered with a sauce overall.

Truffle. (French) A famous fungus that grows underground.

Veloute. (French) Smooth white sauce, made with veal or chicken stock, egg yolks, and cream.

Vermicelli. (Italian) Long, thin threads of pasta, finer than spaghetti.

Vichyssoise. (French) A cream soup of leeks, potatoes, and chicken broth, served cold.

Vinaigrette. (French) Mixture of oil and vinegar, seasoned with salt and pepper, and at times herbs.

Zabaglione. (Italian) A thick, frothy dessert composed of egg yolks, sugar, and Marsala wine, served hot or cold. Also, a sauce similarly composed for puddings, bombes, etc.

Zeppole. (Italian) A type of fritter.

Index